Total Liberation

Total Liberation

*The Power and Promise of Animal Rights
and the Radical Earth Movement*

David Naguib Pellow

UNIVERSITY OF MINNESOTA PRESS

MINNEAPOLIS • LONDON

Portions of the book will appear in David N. Pellow and Hollie Nyseth Brehm, "From the New Ecological Paradigm to Total Liberation: The Emergence of a Social Movement Frame," *The Sociological Quarterly* (forthcoming).

Published by the University of Minnesota Press
111 Third Avenue South, Suite 290
Minneapolis, MN 55401–2520
http://www.upress.umn.edu

Library of Congress Cataloging-in Publication Data

Pellow, David Naguib.
Total liberation : the power and promise of animal rights and the radical earth movement / David Naguib Pellow.
Includes bibliographical references and index.
ISBN 978-0-8166-8776-3 (hc : alk. paper)
ISBN 978-0-8166-8777-0 (pb : alk paper)
1. Animal rights. 2. Animal rights movement. 3. Environmentalism.
4. Radicalism. I. Title.
HV4708.P45 2014
179´.3—dc23
2013048789

Printed in the United States of America on acid-free paper

The University of Minnesota is an equal-opportunity educator and employer.

20 19 18 17 16 15 14   10 9 8 7 6 5 4 3 2 1

For
Allan and Hazel

Contents

Abbreviations

AEDPA	Antiterrorism and Effective Death Penalty Act
AEPA	Animal Enterprise Protection Act
AETA	Animal Enterprise Terrorism Act
AETA4	four activists charged under the AETA
AIM	American Indian Movement
ALEC	American Legislative Exchange Council
ALF	Animal Liberation Front
AMA	American Medical Association
ANC	African National Congress
APOC	Anarchist People of Color
AR	Animal Rights
ARC	Animal Rights Conference
ASPCA	American Society for the Prevention of Cruelty to Animals
BLA	Black Liberation Army
BLM	Bureau of Land Management
BPP	Black Panther Party
BWM	Because We Must
CALPIRG	California Public Interest Research Group
CFA	Cascadia Forest Alliance
CFD	Cascadia Forest Defenders

CLDC	Civil Liberties Defense Center
CMU	Communications Management Unit
COINTELPRO	Counter Intelligence Program
COW	Challenging Oppression Within
CSLC	Cold Snap Legal Collective
DGR	Deep Green Resistance
DWW	Dominant Western Worldview
EF!	Earth First!
EF!er	Earth First!er
EJ	environmental justice
EJP	Environmental Justice Paradigm
ELF	Earth Liberation Front (also the Environmental Life Force)
EWOK!	Earth Warriors are OK!
FBI	Federal Bureau of Investigation
FNB	Food Not Bombs
GARC	Grassroots Animal Rights Conference
GE	genetically engineered
GM	genetically modified
GMO	genetically modified organism
G8	Group of Eight nations
HLS	Huntingdon Life Sciences
HSLF	Humane Society Legislative Fund
HSUS	Humane Society of the United States
ICE	Immigration and Customs Enforcement
IDA	In Defense of Animals
IRA	Irish Republican Army
IWW	Industrial Workers of the World
JTTF	Joint Terrorism Task Force
LGBTQ	lesbian, gay, bisexual, transgender, queer
MFD	Mazama Forest Defenders
MNDOT	Minnesota Department of Transportation
MSU	Michigan State University

NAACP	National Association for the Advancement of Colored People
NAALPO	North American Animal Liberation Press Office
NAELFPO	North American Earth Liberation Front Press Office
NAFTA	North American Free Trade Agreement
NARN	Northwest Animal Rights Network
NEP	New Ecological Paradigm
NWLF	New World Liberation Front
NYPD	New York Police Department
PCRM	Physicians Committee for Responsible Medicine
PETA	People for the Ethical Treatment of Animals
POCLAD	Program on Corporations, Law, and Democracy
RC-ALB	Revolutionary Cells—Animal Liberation Brigade
RRR	Round River Rendezvous
RSPCA	Royal Society for the Prevention of Cruelty to Animals
SCSC	Scott and Carrie Support Committee
SDS	Students for a Democratic Society
SEI	socioecological inequality
SF8	San Francisco 8, former BPP activists
SHAC	Stop Huntingdon Animal Cruelty
SHAC7	Stop Huntingdon Animal Cruelty imprisoned activists
SLAPP	strategic lawsuits against public participation
SOAR	Student Organization for Animal Rights
SSCS	Sea Shepherd Conservation Society
TINA	"There is no alternative"
TWAC	Trans and Womyn's Action Camp
USAID	United States Agency for International Development
USEPA	United States Environmental Protection Agency
USPIRG	United States Public Interest Research Group
WAR	Win Animal Rights
WTO	World Trade Organization

Preface

I began this study in 2008 with the goal of understanding how radical environmental and animal liberation activists seek to effect change, particularly in the face of state and corporate repression. I conducted one hundred semi-structured interviews and extensive fieldwork at conferences, activist gatherings, meetings, and other related public events (which involved hundreds of additional informal conversations with activists) and performed exhaustive content analyses of thousands of pages of newsletters, magazines, journals, websites, and zines produced by activists. Overall, the three components—interviews, fieldwork, and document analysis—offer an opportunity to triangulate sources of evidence to provide a more complete presentation of the data.

I began by identifying key organizations, groups, and individuals within the radical environmental and animal rights movements, as acknowledged in both academic and activist literature (I frequently use "animal rights" and "animal liberation" interchangeably).[1] Importantly, I only considered groups "radical" if they sought to effect change at the root of perceived problems rather than reform the system. While mainstream groups seek reform and work within the current political and regulatory system, radical groups attempt to disrupt and transform the system more directly, though in practice some groups support a combination of extralegal and legal approaches to change (see p. 58 for a discussion of these labels and the continuum in which they fall). Some of the core groups I identified include Earth First!, Earth Liberation Front (ELF), Sea Shepherd Conservation Society, Animal Liberation Front (ALF), Stop Huntingdon Animal Cruelty (SHAC), and People for the Ethical Treatment of Animals (PETA), although many interviewees came from smaller local or regionally based groups and informal collectives that are less well known. Additionally, I interviewed a small sample of members of several mainstream animal rights and environmental organizations, a small sample of key members of historically relevant movements that have heavily influenced contemporary radical environmental and animal liberation activists (e.g., Black Panther Party, Black Liberation Army, and Puerto Rican Independence movements), as well as numerous activist attorneys working with environmental and animal rights groups and individuals.

I used respondent-driven and reputation sampling to locate interviewees. I chose to employ a semi-structured interview technique that allowed for standardized questions yet flexibility in answers and elaborations. Sixty-nine interviewees identified as men, and thirty-one identified as women, a reflection of the fact that many of these organizations are male-dominated. People whom my research team and I interviewed for this project came from Arizona, southern and northern California, Florida, Illinois, Minnesota, Maryland, Missouri, Montana, New York, Oregon, Tennessee, Texas, Utah, Washington, D.C., Washington State, and West Virginia.

In an effort to gain a deeper understanding of the movements and ensure I was interviewing a wide range of participants, my research team and I also attended several environmental and animal rights conferences, and major events in the United States, including the Their Lives Our Voices conference, the Let Live conference, the Earth First! Roadshow, the Trans and Womyn's Action Camp (TWAC), and the Earth First! Round River Rendezvous. I also attended many smaller gatherings, workshops, and events organized by activists in several cities. At each event I attended panel sessions and discussions, observed, and interviewed participants. Fieldwork at some events even necessitated camping in forests and digging latrines.

I also conducted content analyses of each organization's website, which included but was not limited to their organizational history, their mission, their activities and actions. Furthermore, I acquired and coded copies of movement newsletters, where available. I also collected and analyzed hard copies of all handouts given out at the events attended. I engaged in a process of open coding to discover key themes in the data. Once I identified themes, I focused the coding to allow patterns in the data to emerge.[2]

Following Rik Scarce, one of the preeminent scholars of radical environmental movements, at times I rely heavily on the *Earth First! Journal* "because it remains a crossroads vehicle for communication within the movement generally. In any given issue of the *Journal*, one is likely to read not only about Earth First! actions but those by the Animal Liberation Front (ALF), the Earth Liberation Front (ELF), the Sea Shepherds, and by grassroots environmental activists around the planet."[3] I would add that one is also likely to read about actions by Indigenous and people of color movements in the United States and around the globe fighting environmental racism and imperialism and for political prisoners from a range of social causes.

Academia as a Space of Liberation and Repression

Here I present a somewhat personal exploration of the ways that my research for this book provided me with a firsthand experience with state repression. I offer this material not to suggest that my case is particularly important, but rather as a way of being transparent about the way this project was shaped not only by my observations and interviews with earth and animal liberation activists but also by the operations of the state institutions that seek to contain them and occasionally those scholars studying them.

Angana Chatterji is a scholar-activist and colleague of mine who once encouraged me to think of sustainable knowledge as a necessary foundation for the development of sustainable communities. That is, knowledge must be produced not just for profit or personal gain, but also for the purposes of nurturing all members of society and the ecosystems upon which we depend. That requires building relationships and institutions that are committed to democracy and social and environmental justice. I have tried to keep that in mind every day since she spoke those words at an environmental justice conference at the University of Michigan in 2002. Linking Chatterji's point to the role of social movements, sociologists Ron Eyerman and Andrew Jamison write:

> A social movement is not one organization or one particular special interest group. It is more like a cognitive territory, a new conceptual space that is filled by a dynamic interaction between different groups and organizations. . . . It is precisely in the creation, articulation, formulation of new thoughts and ideas—new knowledge—that a social movement defines itself in society.[4]

In other words, social movements are not just driven and made possible by a passion for change, but by the development of ideas. The power of ideas is something scholars have long been aware of. More than a century before Eyerman and Jamison came along, Karl Marx and Friedrich Engels reminded us: "The ideas of the ruling class are, in every age, the ruling ideas: i.e., the class which is the dominant material force in society is at the same time its dominant intellectual force."[5] In other words, ideas matter in politics and society, and precisely because elites seek to control the contours and content of ideas in public circulation, social movements are some of the most important forces for the creation and application of new and transformative knowledge. While everyone produces knowledge and theory, it is the job of scholars to do this every day, in our teaching, research, and writing. Of particular importance are the roles of activist-scholars, because they are among the many groups of persons whose job it is to produce and communicate alternative and counterhegemonic knowledge in any society. Many activist-scholars work in solidarity with social change efforts inside and outside the academy. Not surprisingly then, both activist-scholars and social movements with which they may be linked frequently become targets of state repression.

The Davenport Grand Jury

On November 17, 2009, Scott DeMuth was sent to a county jail for contempt of court, since he refused to answer questions posed to him by a federal grand jury in Davenport, Iowa. The grand jury was interested in questioning him about his knowledge of an unsolved Animal Liberation Front (ALF) action in 2004 at the University of Iowa. At the time, DeMuth was a University of Minnesota graduate student whom I was advising. He was also a Dakota language student and a Twin Cities activist involved in ecoprisoner support and Indigenous decolonization politics. DeMuth took a stand against the grand jury and paid for it with a contempt charge and, two days later, a charge of conspiracy under the Animal Enterprise Terrorism Act (AETA). He was believed to have information on who might have committed the University of Iowa action, since he had been researching and interviewing animal and earth liberation movements for some time, dating back to his undergraduate days.[6] Soon after his release from jail, in 2010, the state issued another indictment against DeMuth, charging him with involvement in an ALF fur farm raid in Minnesota in 2006. DeMuth pleaded guilty to a lesser offense associated only with the 2006 case and was sentenced to five months in federal prison. His colleague Carrie Feldman spent four months in jail on contempt of court, since she also refused to talk to the grand jury about the University of Iowa case. She was released in March 2010.

In a motion to the judge seeking a revocation of Scott DeMuth's release from jail (related to the contempt charge), Assistant U.S. State's Attorney Clifford Cronk wrote: "Defendant's writings, literature, and conduct suggest that he is an anarchist and associated with the ALF movement. Therefore, he is a domestic terrorist." In other words, DeMuth's ideas and beliefs, his constitutionally protected political activities (such as volunteering with an ecopolitical prisoner support group in the Twin Cities), and his alleged affiliations were sufficient for the state to brand him a "terrorist." Several University of Minnesota graduate students launched a support group for DeMuth (and later other scholars under siege) called Scholars for Academic Justice, and many scholars from around the United States and internationally spoke out in support of DeMuth and signed a petition we posted on line. Scott DeMuth released a statement regarding his decision to adhere to strict research ethics, which forbade him from speaking to a grand jury:

> As part of my academic career, I have been involved in researching the animal rights and environmental movements and interviewing participants of those movements. The identity and contents of interviews are protected by confidentiality agreements, and I have an obligation to this confidentiality . . . because grand jury proceedings are held in secret, there is no real way to verify if I had only given my name or if I had given away the identity and contents of each interview I have done. Therefore, if for no other reason, I believed that my participation would violate the trust and confidentiality of those who I have interviewed. I went to Davenport . . . knowing that I could be jailed for contempt of court, and I was willing to deal with whatever legal consequences came with that decision.[7]

DeMuth's words reveal the inherent conflict between government coercion in such investigations and academic freedom. Unfortunately, the federal government did not stop with him. The FBI soon contacted me for information about DeMuth and about my own research on earth and animal liberation movements.

On the advice of lawyers and activists, I maintained my resolve not to speak to the authorities. I was also concerned that my own university might not offer me the kind of support I would need to withstand a grand jury investigation, should it come to that. The University of Minnesota has an inglorious history regarding academic freedom going back at least to 1917 when (during the anti-German hysteria of World War I) the Regents fired political science professor William Schaper for allegedly being "a rabid pro-German" who was unwilling "to aid the United States in the present war."[8]

Accordingly, I took new precautions. My research team began using non-university e-mail communications in order to conduct business related to my research project (which was ironic because it is university business). This was done specifically when we made any mention of research participants, interviews, or the sharing of transcriptions for coding and record keeping. We did so because we believed there was a reasonable probability that our communications were being monitored, and we sought to protect our research participants and their privacy, as well as the privacy of colleagues, coworkers, and student employees. I also decided to move the project's paper archives to an off-site location, on the advice of my attorney, who made it clear that the authorities could raid my university or home office at any time and remove materials for scrutiny and return them at their leisure (if at all).

Then on June 18, 2010, the Department of Justice asked the University of Minnesota's Human Research Protection Program for a copy of all human subjects materials related to my research project on environmental and animal rights activists. This included my interview questionnaire and rationale for conducting research on this topic and various university forms that would ensure the protection of my research participants. The university informed me that they would comply with the request and sent the information out promptly. The Department of Justice letter reads in part: "The information we are requesting includes, but is not limited to, the study file, the application for the research project, along with documentation to support the plan, and the names of the participants in the project." That last part about participants was worrisome, because while only I possessed that information, I had pledged to hold it in confidence (as required by my professional association's code of ethics). Since the University of Minnesota is a public institution, much of what is contained in the file is basically public information.

However, the university informed me that they would delete the names of students and employees working with me on the project, so that privacy would be preserved. As Scott DeMuth had been working on the project with me since earlier that year (2010), it appeared that this was a continuation of ongoing efforts to explore possible connections between him and any activists that we may or may not have interviewed for the study.

Rik Scarce's case is perhaps the most infamous with regard to scholars studying animal and earth liberation movements. He is a professor of sociology at Skidmore College and a noted expert on radical social movements. He is also the author of the classic book *Eco-Warriors*. Scarce spent five months in jail for contempt of court when he refused to testify to a grand jury in 1990 regarding an investigation of an unsolved break-in at an animal research and testing lab. He refused to testify on the grounds that his confidentiality agreements associated with academic research protected him and his research participants just as shield laws do for journalists. According to Scarce, up until the time his own case made headlines, the American Sociological Association had perhaps the most robust code of ethics of any academic association (which is not all that great, considering that as of this writing, the American Economics Association has no code of ethics regarding protection of research participants). For example, section 11.01(b) of the ASA Code of Ethics reads in part:

> Confidential information provided by research participants, students, employees, clients, or others is treated as such by sociologists even if there is no legal protection or privilege to do so. Sociologists have an obligation to protect confidential information and not allow information gained in confidence from being used in ways that would unfairly compromise research participants, students, employees, clients, or others.

This would seem to offer the strongest possible protection for scholars and their research participants in the event of a coercive move by authorities to seek the identities or other particulars of research informants. Unfortunately, according to Rik Scarce, soon after his case hit the news, the ASA (with the vote of its national membership) amended its code to add Section 11.02(a), which reads: "Sociologists inform themselves fully about all laws and rules which may limit or alter guarantees of confidentiality and, as appropriate, inform research participants, students, employees, clients or others of any limitations to this guarantee at the outset." This amendment had the clear effect of undoing the protections offered in the previous section of the code, and Scarce was understandably furious that this change substantially weakened the code as well as the protections sociologists can offer research participants.[9]

Independent of the mixed messages from my professional association—the ASA—I chose not to cooperate with federal authorities for a number of reasons. Aside from the clear historical documented evidence that the FBI has done its best to destroy nearly every freedom movement that I have ever researched, taught about, and supported, the real issues here are ensuring the protection of our study participants—particularly those who requested anonymity (a small percentage of my sample), ensuring our ability to do future research and grant participants the right to confidentiality, and standing up for the integrity and future of the social sciences. The names of interviewees who did not request anonymity are printed in this book, but to give their names and any other information to the authorities outside of the parameters of my research plans would be an ethical violation. If the authorities can force any scholar to give up their records and the names of research participants, many people would sensibly choose *not* to participate in future research studies, potentially threatening the intellectual foundation of entire fields of knowledge.

The United States has a long and troubling history of silencing and disciplining academics whose research and teaching emphasize the importance of collective efforts to effect radical social change. In recent years, professors studying various peoples' movements have been censored, demoted, fired, and jailed here in the United States.[10] This is an issue of academic freedom, and I believe other scholars and the public should support such people because of the importance of the kind of work these scholars do for rethinking our history and for reimagining what kind of futures we can create for ourselves.

Acknowledgments

Numerous people contributed to this book in innumerable ways, and I am forever grateful to them: Hollie Nyseth Brehm, my primary research assistant on this project and an extraordinary colleague and collaborator; Scott DeMuth, my research assistant, colleague, and partner in crime; Stephanie Burgess for transcribing countless interviews and conference recordings, and for helping me think through some of the most critical ideas and conundrums that vexed me during the process of researching this project; Katherine Gruebele and Sergey Berg for their tireless transcription and other key contributions; Miles Swammi, Ellen Schneeberger, Wahutu Siguru, and Dejan Selimovic for their critical research assistance; my wonderful colleagues (staff, faculty, and students) at the University of Minnesota's Department of Sociology, including Michael Goldman, Chris Uggen, Doug Hartmann, Liz Boyle, Cawo Abdi, Rachel Schurman, Teresa Gowan, Ron Aminzade, Lisa Sun-Hee Park, Josh Page, Mary Drew, Hilda Mork, Hollis Schnoonover, Kerrie Deef, and Ann Miller; Jane Rhodes, Lynn Hudson, Leslie Byster, Gus Speth, John Passacantando, Phil Radford, Jigar Shah, the Greenpeace USA Board of Directors and staff, Michelle Brown, Paul Gellert, Robert Emmett Jones, Damayanti Banerjee, Asafa Jalata and the University of Tennessee Department of Sociology, Joni Adamson, Bill Gleason, Patrick McCully and the International Rivers Board of Directors and staff, Ann Waltner and the faculty and staff of the University of Minnesota's Institute for Advanced Study (Efe Iyambe, Phyllis Messenger, Susannah Smith, Michael Gaudio, Yolanda Padilla, Nikhil Anand, Kathy Quick, Karen Kinoshita, Emily Tubman, Shaden Tageldin, Gary Kroll, Ray Schultz, Murat Altun,

Wenyi Guo, Mingyan Tang, Sharon Fischlowitz), Louis Mendoza, the University of Minnesota Institute for Diversity, Equity, and Advocacy (IDEA), Orrin Williams, Isabelle Anguelovski, Kevin Van Meter, Nancy Herther for being a world-class librarian, Autumn Cavender-Wilson, Bron Taylor, Yuichiro Onishi, Rik Scarce, Barbara Ann Nimis (for being an amazing attorney and good friend), and Will Potter (for support and guidance throughout); my colleagues at University of Minnesota Press: Jason Weidemann, for cultivating and supporting this project early on, and Richard Morrison and Doug Armato for their enthusiasm; Stu Sugarman, Luce Guillen-Givens, Carrie Feldman, Claude Marks, J. Tony Serra, Ricardo Jimenez, Garrett Fitzgerald, Robert Czernik, Jude Ortiz, Donny, Panagioti, John Bellamy Foster, Kari Norgaard, Odette Wilkins, Anthony Nocella and the Arissa Media Group Collective (Kim Socha, Rose Brewer, Waziyatawin, Drew Winters, Matthew Hernandez, Sarat Colling, and Travis Stearns), the *Earth First! Journal* Editorial Collective, Earth Warriors are OK! (EWOK!), Scholars for Academic Justice (Krissy Haltinner, Raphi Rechitsky, Meg Krausch, Andrea Strano), the Scott and Carrie Support Committee, the MARS Collective at the Minnehaha Free Space for providing me with a supportive community of anarchists who shared their knowledge and hopes for a better world; scott crow, Courtney Bell for being a sharp student who instantly got the link between radical ecological politics and the phenomenon of racial deviance, Jane Curran and Letta Wren Page (aka the Jargon Slayer) for their phenomenal work editing this project, Rod Ferguson, George Henderson, and Bruce Braun. Finally, I thank my parents for their instructive lessons on how to balance scholarship with commitment in hopes of both causing and avoiding trouble.

All Oppression Is Linked

Animal liberation is the ultimate freedom movement, the "final frontier."

—Robin Webb, British ALF Press Officer, in Steven Best and
Anthony Nocella II, *Terrorists or Freedom Fighters? Reflections on the
Liberation of Animals*

We should always be wary of talking of "the last remaining form of
discrimination."

—Peter Singer, *Animal Liberation: A New Ethics for Our Treatment of Animals*

A business card. How innocuous. But when it's the business card of an
FBI special agent, slipped nonchalantly into your mailbox at work—*my*
mailbox at work—it takes on a little extra heft. That morning in April
2010, I was pretty sure what the agent wanted to talk about, but a staff
member's note "Re: student" backed up my suspicions, as did the voice
mail that greeted me when I got to my office at the University of Minnesota, where I am a professor of sociology. The agent reiterated that he'd
like to interview me and asked that I return his call. Instead, I called
lawyers and activists. Two days later, I received a message on my home
phone: "I'd like to ask you a couple of questions about one of your students you are the advisor for at the U, Scott DeMuth. I'd like to ask you
a couple of questions about the research that you do and the research
that he does for you."

My research, since 2008, has included a focus on radical ecological
movements. Many movements begin with a grievance or a critique, but
what sustains them and pushes people out into the streets (or underground) is often a vision, a dream of something better. In other words,
movements are driven and sustained by ideas.[1] This book is about the
power of ideas and how movements for social change are some of the
most important intellectual forces in society. That perspective applies to

every other movement I have studied and researched, taught my students about, and supported or opposed. That list includes the movements for environmental justice, Indigenous sovereignty, women's rights, human rights, labor rights, racial justice, slavery abolition, and radical environmental and animal liberation.

In the pages that follow, I explore the origins and social significance of the earth and animal liberation movements and consider how they speak to and grapple with questions of social change, inequality, and repression. I do so by elaborating on what I call the "total liberation" framework and reveal how its adherents approach issues of hierarchy, state violence, and capitalism, and how they work to challenge the intertwined crises of ecosystem decline, nonhuman species exploitation and extinction, and human oppression. Those challenges range from articulations of visions of another world to verbal and written protests, and direct action targeting individuals, institutions, and ideas that perpetuate socioecological inequalities. Predictably, those actions have caught the attention of government and corporate leaders, resulting in a forceful response that has included surveillance, infiltration, wiretapping, harassment, entrapment, jail or prison time, and new legislation targeting these movements. I consider the implications of state and corporate repression for these movements and for the future of civil liberties and other freedom struggles—and what this all means for the uncomfortable, underlying truths that must be confronted to address inequality in all of its manifestations. Fortunately, my discomforting encounter with the FBI never went beyond their repeated requests for information and my refusal to speak with them. Other activists and scholars have not been so lucky.

Radical Movements and Radical Ideas

In July of 2001, Earth Liberation Front (ELF) activists nailed metal spikes into hundreds of trees in the Gifford Pinchot National Forest (in Washington State). They were protesting the U.S. Forest Service's decision to sell the trees to a timber company. Activists sent a communiqué to several media outlets that read, in part:

> This timber sale contains 99 acres of old growth and is home to at least 3 pairs of spotted owls, grizzly bear, lynx, wolf, goshawk, just to name a few of its many inhabitants. This is truly a beautiful area, unfortunately one of the last of its kind because of the system we all live under. We want to be

clear that *all oppression is linked, just as we are all linked*, and we believe in a diversity of tactics to stop earth rape and *end all domination.* Together we can destroy this *patriarchal* nightmare, which is currently in the form of techno-industrial global *capitalism.*[2]

The emergence of the Earth and Animal Liberation Fronts (ELF and ALF) in the United States in the 1980s and 1990s marked a new stage in the evolution of ecological politics in the country.[3] This moment was punctuated by a discourse of radical analysis and action rarely seen in environmental or animal rights movements previously. By the late 1990s and early 2000s, segments of these movements were converging around new ideas and tactics, producing a broader discourse that linked ecology, social justice, anti-oppression, and animal liberation, taking hold of and transforming groups like Earth First! (EF!), which had historically been hostile to such ideas.

As a sociologist concerned with social movements and personally involved in the environmental justice movement, I began taking notice. The first question I had was to what extent are radical environmental and animal liberation movements also struggles over social inequality? The movements that had begun as radical environmental and animal liberation movements now looked more like struggles over social justice; not only were they focused on defending nonhuman natures, but they were also confronting oppression within human communities (including racism, patriarchy, heterosexism, capitalism, state power, and empire). I also wondered how the work of these activists in particular and social movements more broadly reveal engagements with nonhuman natures— what I call the human/nonhuman nexus—and why that might matter. Finally, I sought to explore the implications of the "ecoterrorist" label that states, corporations, and media impose on activist groups. I saw radical environmental and animal liberation movements confronting various forms of power within and across the species divide, as well as the costs activists incurred as dominant institutions pushed back.

What sparked the development of this kind of movement? I offer three reasons: the increase in reports of threats to planetary sustainability and continued massive exploitation of nonhuman species through industrial agriculture, chemical testing, and entertainment; frustration with the elitism, racism, and tactical reformism of mainstream animal rights and environmental movements; and influences from other social justice movements, particularly movements of generations past that emerged from struggles among white working-class and people of color communities.

In responding to the varied local and global threats to nonhuman ecosystems and animal populations, earth and animal liberation activists "hear" a "call" or "interpellation" from nonhuman natures that pushes them to defend ecosystems and nonhuman animals.[4] Attention to the ways that movements articulate and invoke the human/nonhuman nexus allows us to extend the boundaries of social movement scholarship to explore the ways that ecological politics is redefined as an effort to create change that involves not just actions to defend nonhuman natures but a form of collaboration and participation by nonhuman actors as well. The varied ways that movement frames, ideas, values, goals, tactics, and actions result from interactions between human and nonhuman forces has been undertheorized in the sociological literature. The unstated assumption has been that social movement struggles are entirely human-led processes that occur because humans motivate other humans to adopt ideas and values and pursue goals and actions independent of other forces. But as scholarship from the fields of environmental sociology and political ecology reveals, there is nothing that humans do that is entirely isolated from influence and guidance from other species, ecosystems, and inanimate objects. The important role of nonhumans—ecosystems, animals, technologies, and so forth—in animating the activist imagination, in motivating action, and in producing interactions forces us to rethink what constitutes a social movement and how far its impacts can be felt. In many ways, earth and animal liberation activists challenge the traditional borders of "society" by constructing a polity or publics that are inclusive of nonhuman species and natures.

In the second shift I noted above, I have seen frustration among radical activists with mainstream ecological movements' orientation, values, and tactics. These generally include a lack of awareness of and commitment to anti-oppression politics, an embrace of state-centric and market-oriented "solutions," and a rejection of aggressive direct action tactics. Radical activists see these as insider strategies, and so they become more likely to challenge the racial, gender, sexual, and class privileges of ecological movements, and more willing to risk personal freedom in pursuit of social change.

As for mining the history of social movements in radicalizing contemporary efforts, important influences on radical earth and animal liberation movements include discourses around the politics of social justice. These influences have permeated other social movements, social change organizations, and academic disciplines on university campuses across the United States. Concepts such as intersectionality (the idea that oppression cannot be reduced to one fundamental type of inequality) and discourses that were critical of social privilege took hold in many of these spaces beginning in the 1990s and affected the language and practices of social movements in the United States, including environmental and animal rights causes.

The idea that we can no longer understand, analyze, or resist a single form of oppression in isolation from other forms materialized in feminist and antiracist movements and academic circles globally, and radical animal rights and environmental activists followed suit and moved away from a language of single issues. They became concerned with the rights and liberation of human and nonhuman species, ecosystems, and societies. These ideas were combined with tactics and language inspired by previous generations' liberation movements: the Diggers and Levellers of Britain, slavery abolitionists, the Luddites, anarchist movements, the Industrial Workers of the World (IWW), movements for civil rights, black power, Puerto Rican independence, the American Indian Movement, the Weather Underground, the AIDS Coalition to Unleash Power (ACT UP), and many others.

From Europe to Australia, Latin America, Canada, and the United States, radical earth and animal liberation movements gained visibility and notoriety. More direct and flagrant actions made headlines: significant property damage and economic damage to laboratories, slaughterhouses, power lines, elite housing developments, ski resorts, fur farms, and industrial agricultural and poultry facilities through arson, sabotage (also known as *ecotage*), animal rescue/liberation, and vandalism. Through these actions and the discourse that supports them, today's activists question what they view as the violence of capitalism, state power, multiple forms of oppression within human communities, speciesism (the belief that one species is superior to another), and ecological destruction. And while these movements often reflect different emphases, there is a prime convergence around the discourse of "total liberation" of ecosystems, nonhuman species, and humans.

The concept of total liberation stems from a determination to understand and combat all forms of inequality and oppression. I propose that it comprises four pillars: (1) an ethic of justice and anti-oppression inclusive of humans, nonhuman animals, and ecosystems; (2) anarchism; (3) anti-capitalism; and (4) an embrace of direct action tactics. This framework animates earth and animal liberation movements, and I explore it throughout this book.

The Nature of Inequality and Its Consequences

The problem of inequality is rightly an obsession for many sociologists. However, most of us think about, study, and teach the subject within a particular—and therefore limited—framework. This might include economic, political, institutional, racial, gender, sexual, spatial, and national inequalities, all of which are important for understanding how social systems work to the benefit of some groups and to the disadvantage of others. But by focusing primarily on *human* inequality, we miss a great deal with regard to how far and wide inequalities actually extend. Accordingly, one of this book's threads is a story of inequality, its many forms and far-reaching consequences, as well as unconventional efforts to challenge it. My research has always focused on the intersection of social inequalities and ecological politics, and my goal here is to expand our understanding of inequality by making sense of the often tense and violent relationships among humans, ecosystems, and nonhuman animal species. By doing so, we might achieve a better grasp of inequality's ramifications while also deepening our understanding of the nature of inequality itself.

So I suspect I should start at the beginning: what is inequality and why does it matter? At its most basic level, inequality means that if you are "on top" of, or higher on the social ladder than someone else, then you possess or have access to greater resources, wealth, and social privileges. But more importantly—and from the standpoint of ecological politics—your elevation above others also means that your *life* is of greater value than others living within that social system. You likely own or control and affect more of the planet and its constituent ecosystems than others, you likely own or control and affect more living beings (and therefore likely produce more death) than others, and you likely control and benefit from the ideational systems that give meaning and legitimacy to such dynamics.[5] Inequality is a means of ordering the human and nonhuman worlds for the relative benefit of some and to the detriment of others.

Life expectancy, morbidity, mortality, and well-being are highly correlated with key measures of human inequality.[6] In the case of environmental inequality and environmental racism, working-class people, people of color, women, immigrants, and Indigenous persons are more likely to face health risks as a result of environmental racism and inequality—the uneven exposure to environmental harm that social and institutional forces routinely perpetrate (practices that are rooted in multiple forms of social inequality and hierarchy).[7] Thus, social or human inequalities derive their existence through inequalities that also divide, rank, and exert control over nonhumans and ecosystems. Inequality is, above all, *unnatural* in the sense that it does not "just happen"—it requires a great deal of energy, labor, and institutional effort to produce and maintain unequal societies.[8] This point is crucial because there is also so much energy invested into making inequalities seem like a natural state of affairs. As ecofeminist Greta Gaard writes, "Appeals to nature have often been used to justify social norms, to the detriment of women, nature, queers, and persons of color."[9] Inequality is not just an imbalance of resources or power but is frequently experienced as unearned privileges made possible by domination and injustice. It is also routinely resisted by those who suffer its consequences.

Extending Environmental Inequality: Toward Socioecological Inequality

This is the foundation of what I call *socioecological inequality*; that is, the ways in which humans, nonhumans, and ecosystems intersect to produce hierarchies—privileges and disadvantages—within and across species and space that ultimately place each at great risk. Socioecological inequality (SEI), as a research approach, builds upon environmental inequality in a number of ways. While environmental inequality highlights the links between threats to humans and ecosystems with a primary emphasis on human well-being, the focus of SEI is on the hierarchical relationships among humans, ecosystems, and nonhuman animals that produce harms across each sphere. In this way, socioecological inequality underscores that humans, ecosystems, and nonhumans are intertwined in the production of inequality and violence and that relationships that might privilege humans in the short run may also place them in jeopardy in the long term. SEI also moves beyond the human/environment or culture/nature binary embedded in many environmental studies concepts such as the Environmental Justice Paradigm (EJP) and the New Ecological Paradigm (NEP). Instead, within the SEI, we see that humans, nonhumans, ecosystems, and even built environments are characterized by an enormous internal variation and diversity. Moreover, SEI builds on—while also departing from—the NEP, deep ecology, social ecology, ecofeminism, the EJP, and political economy in that it does not claim a primary source or origin of our ecological crises, such as racism, capitalism, classism, patriarchy, androcentrism, dominionism, or Western culture.[10] Rather, SEI argues that there are varied and multiple forms of inequality and hierarchy driving our socioecological crises, revealing the importance of intersectionality.

There are three primary vectors through which this relationship can be expressed, but it is important to keep in mind that they are, in fact, interchangeable:

humans exploiting ecosystems can produce harm to both nonhuman animals and humans, especially those dependent upon and/or living in or near those ecosystems. For example: (1) the construction and operation of hydroelectric dams inflict extensive damage on river systems, fish populations, and estuaries, while often threatening the livelihoods of human communities that rely on rivers for sustenance;[11] (2) industrial coal, gold, and coltan mining operations destroy rivers, threaten numerous nonhuman species, and are often accompanied by unhealthy and violent working conditions for human employees and threats to the stability of their communities.[12]

humans exploiting other humans can produce harm to both nonhuman animals and ecosystems. For example, an oil extraction or petrochemical facility located in a community of color or Indigenous community (a traditional environmental justice concern) that involves hazardous working conditions for human employees, the production and distribution of hazardous effluence within the surrounding community where humans and nonhumans reside, and the pollution of air, land, and water systems.[13]

humans exploiting nonhuman animals can produce harm to both humans and ecosystems. For example, industrial ranching and farming operations designed to harvest livestock or plant crops that displace or endanger Indigenous human settlements lead to deforestation and water source pollution,[14] while a slaughterhouse where human workers commonly experience high levels of occupational hazards in the killing of nonhumans for mass consumption also pollutes water tables and supports industrial ranching operations.[15]

Whether the example is a slaughterhouse, a petrochemical facility, industrial agriculture, a hydroelectric dam, or a mining operation, each reveals the ways in which humans exploit and produce harm among other humans, nonhuman animals, and ecosystems. While these forms of hierarchy and violence are uniquely experienced across species and space, they are inseparable and interrelated. They necessarily begin and end with human actors imagining and giving meaning to these behaviors. It is that cultural framework that makes socioecological inequalities possible and legitimate.

Radical environmental and animal rights movements are not the first people who come to mind when most of us think about the politics of social inequality and social justice. But this is a logical site for such a study precisely because many activists are developing new ways to imagine a society free of oppression and hierarchy. After all, these movements are posing one of the most fundamental questions one could contemplate: what does it mean to be human? Over the centuries and across many societies, the answer to that question has included the right to dominate all other species and ecosystems, no matter the consequences. The facts of speciesism and dominionism have been considered the birthright of Homo sapiens by many scholars, political and religious leaders, dominant institutions, and everyday people for most of modern history. In other words, to be human has often meant to embrace and benefit from hierarchy and the privilege of membership in a particular species. To be human has also meant to participate in various systems of hierarchy that rank and sort people by social categories (e.g., nationality, class, gender, sexuality, race, ability, and age) to distribute power and privilege unevenly. Earth and animal liberation activists are calling into question these ideas and practices because they see them as a threat to the future of all species, including our own.

What it means to be human is up for discussion, debate, and transformation. But radical social change is exceedingly difficult and fraught with its own challenges. So as earth and animal liberation movement activists confront various forms of hierarchy, they also frequently reproduce existing inequalities and sometimes produce new ones. Despite these and other shortcomings, for some people these movements represent hope for a better world in that they threaten those institutions deeply invested in inequality. They seek to confront social systems that produce and maintain hierarchies in an interconnected world of humans, nonhumans, and environments.

Not only does SEI help explain why the activists I study are so committed to their work, but, more critically, it also suggests why the rest of us might also be concerned: inequality is a form of domination and control over people, nonhumans, ecosystems, the planet, and life itself. *Rising* inequality means that most of us are losing control over our ability to influence our own destinies and protect the people and nonhuman relations we care about. Radical animal liberation and environmental activists may indeed be on the political fringe, but they offer crucial lessons for why the rest of us might pay closer attention to inequality in its multiple forms.

It is not just the *practice* of inequality that contributes to environmental and transspecies violence; it is the construction and persistence of *ideas* that maintain these inequalities. It is the interplay among the material structures, practices, and ideas associated with inequality that I find most productive to understanding our socioecological crises. More to the point, I find that the ideas that legitimate and support inequality are just as consequential, if not more so, as material inequality itself. Those ideas are ultimately what these social movements are combating. Conversely, the repression that states and corporations visit upon these movements is directed less at the physical mobilization of people and direct actions of activists than at the ideas and discourses they articulate and seek support for.

Social scientists study the material fact of inequality and the notion that inequality is a set of relations that is variously imposed, embraced, or contested. I concur with these approaches, but my emphases here include inequality as a material reality, a relational phenomenon, and an *idea* that is constructed and debated. That is, in addition to understanding inequality as a state of being unequal and as a set of relationships among unequal groups, I am also interested in exploring the cultural symbols and systems of meaning that produce, reinforce, and disrupt hierarchies. I hope to advance a more comprehensive and sociologically robust way of theorizing activism and politics through a perspective that reflects the Gramscian view that struggles over meaning are as much material conflicts as they are discursive.[16]

Returning to total liberation, it is clear from my research that the activists featured in this book believe there are multiple, interlocking, and reinforcing systems of inequality and domination that give rise to our socioecological crises, including statecraft, capitalism, speciesism, dominionism, patriarchy, heterosexism, racism, and classism. These activists maintain that ecological crises cannot be reduced to any one (or two) of these systems of domination; rather, they work together to contribute to the problem. I draw this conclusion based on my interviews with activists, my observations of movement gatherings, and analyses of thousands of pages of documents produced by radical earth and animal liberation activists. Total liberation sees inequality as a threat to life itself—for oppressed peoples, species, and ecosystems—and is organized around the struggle for life. These movements organize and mobilize in favor of symbols, metaphors, language, signs, representations, practices, and structures of equality and justice to do what social movements have always done: to imagine and create a better world. Only this world would be based on the idea that inequality and unfreedom in all their known manifestations should be eradicated.

In the pages ahead I offer a critical assessment of the total liberation framework, its origins, nuances, and applications. I come to three broad conclusions: earth and animal liberation movements are indeed struggles over social inequality within and across species, including a particular focus on human liberation; these movements rely on approaches that both challenge and reproduce longstanding forms of oppression; and the "terrorist" label imposed on these movements reveals not only repression against a politically radical "other" but also a momentary designation of these movements as politically *racial* others—people who are criminalized because their ideas and actions are at odds with white supremacy and human supremacy.[17] These movements are of sociological and political significance because they simultaneously confront and embrace systems of inequality that reflect the dominant social order.

The emergence of the total liberation framework is a response to socioecological inequalities, but to realize its promise, earth and animal liberation movements must confront hierarchy both outside and within their ranks. The struggle is necessarily human centered—led by humans and directed at other human beings, institutions, practices, and ideas such as social categories of difference and oppression, speciesism, dominionism, capitalism, the state, and imperialism. As the biologist Barry Commoner once wrote: "The earth is polluted neither because man is some kind of especially dirty animal nor because there are too many of us. The fault lies with human society—with the ways in which society has elected to win, distribute, and use the wealth that has been extracted by human labor from the planet's resources. Once the social origins of the crisis become clear, we can begin to design appropriate social actions to resolve it."[18] The ways in which nonhuman animal species and ecosystems are imagined and defined are necessarily authored by humans.[19] Therefore, ironically, much of the fight against oppressive social systems must take place *within* these movements themselves, as they grapple with the racism, patriarchy, heteronormativity, nativism, classism, and imperialism that have traditionally permeated and haunted environmental and animal rights causes. Hence one of the many spaces of contention occurs on terrain occupied by a particular kind of human, because these movements are largely white, middle class, and heterosexual.

These movements also reflect struggles over particular kinds of nonhuman natures—ones that are cast as vulnerable, in need of rescue, and exuding an innocence and purity found nowhere else. In that sense, nonhuman species and ecosystems become important symbols imbued with a power that mediates and gives meaning to an otherwise largely anthropocentric political force.

Repression and Its Consequences: Privileged Radicals and Racial Deviants

State and corporate repression directed at radical environmental and animal rights movements has been particularly harsh in recent years, prompting comparisons to histories of repression against other freedom movements, including the American Indian Movement, Black Panther Party, Black Liberation Army, and Puerto Rican Independence Movement. I argue that the discourse and legal apparatus that defines radical ecological movements as "ecoterrorism" works to place activists outside the realm of citizenship in order to successfully label them as threats to the nation and facilitate their neutralization. Hence, the repressive treatment of these activists might also be thought of as part of a state tradition of producing *racial deviants*—those whites who refuse to conform to cultural, political, and social disciplinary norms and are labeled as not-quite-white within the politico-legal discourse of "terrorism."[20] In other words, these are white people unwilling to adhere entirely to the norms of whiteness, and are therefore racialized as "probationary whites," even if momentarily.

Historically, probationary whites have included militant working-class and poor persons, feminists, gays and lesbians, prostitutes, Jews, Irish immigrants, criminals, alcoholics, anarchists, the chronically ill, and the mentally disabled, viewed as "atavistic throwbacks to a primitive moment in human prehistory, surviving ominously in the heart of the modern, imperial metropolis."[21] These "degenerate classes" also required policing and regulation since they were viewed as threats to the moral, economic, and political fabric of Victorian England during a time of great social upheavals. This process of racialization and regulation occurred in other places as well. For example, the United States' own immigration policies reveal the practice of policing and expelling many "degenerate" whites using laws originally devised to exclude Chinese and other Asian immigrants.[22] As historian Mai Ngai writes, "the first federal immigration laws established qualitative criteria for selective or individual exclusion that expressed normative definitions of social desirability—those not welcome included criminals, prostitutes, paupers, the diseased, and anarchists, as well as Chinese laborers."[23] According to the dictates of immigration law in decades past, these "aliens" could be summarily deported. Radical earth and animal liberation activists are under no illusion about the fact that they are mostly white movements, but their repressive treatment by state and corporate institutions can remind activists that racial privileges can be revoked, even if only temporarily. When white activists express solidarity with othered populations, should they expect to fare differently? Thus, earth and animal liberation activists are, in some ways, "getting what they asked for" when they cast their lot with oppressed humans and nonhumans. They are racial deviants and are punished as such.

These activists are also racial deviants because they refuse to conform to the expectations and benefits of *human* supremacy. That is, they reject a humanism rooted in speciesism and dominionism that are, for most of us, the unexamined and unearned privileges of membership in the human race. And just as the state has treated these activists as probationary whites, they have also made it clear that their very humanness is conditional. Threats of jail time means privileged activists risk facing some of the "subhuman" treatment that the majority working-class and people of color prison population faces everyday. These radicals then are *racial* deviants in two ways: as white activists who are labeled "terrorists" and as human activists who are antihumanist and antidominionist.

Several other concepts are helpful for exploring the character and consequences of repression directed at these movements, as well as activists' responses:

ecologies of repression (the ripple effects of repression that extend beyond the immediate targets to include bystanders, would-be future activists, and supporters and would-be supporters of other social change movements, as well as nonhuman natures);

cultures of repression (the discourses, ideas, language, and behaviors—both explicit and implicit—that publics practice wherein resistance movements and dissent are discounted, refused, disallowed, misrecognized, and devalued; this can also be a source of division within social movements, particularly between mainstream and radical wings);

repression as a science (repression as more than just a series of acts of brute force, but a series of practices rooted in a desire to *know* and to develop and deploy knowledge for the advancement of particular interests. This knowledge results from careful, empirical observation, experimentation, data gathering and analysis and follows the logic of Foucault's idea that knowledge of a population often leads to power and control over that group);

cultures of resistance (shared understandings, ideas, and knowledge that inform and support individual and collective practices of resistance; these practices are often motivated and aided by interpellation on the part of nonhuman animals and ecosystems).

Together these concepts expand existing scholarship on repression and resistance by viewing both phenomena as dynamic, adaptive, and involving multiple modes of expression that impact both people and nonhumans both inside and outside of social movement communities.[24]

These movements are ultimately aimed at human liberation, and that is what makes earth and animal liberation movements of interest to anyone outside of these activist communities and is what threatens dominant institutions. If, as these activists contend, violence against ecosystems and nonhuman animals is linked to and rooted in inequalities among human beings, then human liberation is the key to total liberation. Human liberation must involve emancipation from the long list of oppressions that exist in society, including the shackles of humanism itself, which constrains us to live in ways that are ecologically unsustainable, dominionist with respect to nonhuman natures, and socially unjust.

Theories of Socioecological Politics

The idea of total liberation must be placed in its proper context, so here I consider its relationship to some of the most important political and intellectual movements associated with ecological politics in recent history, many of which have already been referenced.

The New Ecological Paradigm (NEP) is a popular worldview in the United States that, since the 1960s, has embraced the call for ecological conservation in the face of concerns about species extinction, habitat loss, and rising global pollution levels. The NEP was a response to the Dominant Western Worldview (DWW), which placed human society's needs above those of all other species. The NEP sought to achieve a balance among these competing needs.[25] As groundbreaking as it was at the time of its emergence, the NEP is also restrictive in its critique of ecological crises and in its vision of a sustainable future because it stops short of confronting a host of hierarchical and anti-ecological systems that maintain inequalities within human society and across species, including class domination, racism, patriarchy, and speciesism. Moreover, the NEP advances little more than a reformist critique of state formation and capitalism.[26]

Pushing further the desire to address ecological crises, deep ecology rejects the anthropocentricism implicit and inherent in the NEP by arguing that humans are just one of many species on Earth and have no unique value above any other population. Deep ecology refuses the ideological orientation that the preservation of human society is our primary goal and promotes a biocentric politics: all species are interconnected and critically important to the web of life. The decentering of humans is this framework's most important and lasting contribution. However, deep ecology and the NEP share a fixation with the ecological impacts of human population growth, which tends to reveal a Western cultural bias in that the policy prescriptions that usually follow from this perspective place the blame for global ecological decline on non-Western nations and often specifically on the reproductive capacities and practices of non-Western women and families.[27]

These limitations of the NEP and deep ecology were a major reason for the emergence of ecofeminism, which addresses both ecological unsustainability and patriarchy. Ecofeminism or ecological feminism is an umbrella term that encapsulates a range of perspectives whose "basic premise is that the ideology which authorizes oppressions such as those based on race, class, gender, sexuality, physical abilities, and species is the same ideology which sanctions the oppression of nature."[28] Furthermore, ecofeminism "calls for an end to all oppressions, arguing that no attempt to liberate women (or any other oppressed group) will be successful without an equal attempt to liberate nature."[29] What makes ecofeminism a distinct body of ideas is its position that nonhuman nature and dominionism (that is, the domination of nonhuman nature) are *feminist* concerns.[30]

Ecofeminism is an extraordinarily diverse body of theory and politics, making generalizations about it difficult (if not impossible).[31] Its various origins include the antimilitarist and peace movements, the women's health movement, the labor movement, and the feminist rebellion within environmental and animal liberation movements and the academy.[32] While dominated by white women, ecofeminism has, from the start, embraced antiracism,[33] albeit often through problematic approaches that sometimes impose ecofeminism on women of color environmental activists and romanticize Indigenous women's lives.[34] Some scholars view ecofeminism as the leading edge of the third wave of feminist theory and politics because it questions the logic of domination that its proponents believe undergirds all forms of oppression rooted in dualistic thought, thus offering a framework that might conceivably unite people across numerous social and cultural divides.[35] While ecofeminists have not consistently incorporated nonhuman animals into their analyses,[36] many *have* inspired scholars and activists to expand the scope of the logic of domination across species.

Murray Bookchin was the most prominent scholar associated with the concept of social ecology. According to Bookchin, hierarchy within human societies predates and is at the root of the human domination and control of nature.[37] Thus social ecology calls for the eradication of hierarchy in order to produce ecologically sustainable societies. Bookchin's social ecology is strongly anticapitalist and anarchist,[38] but he was clear in rejecting what he viewed as the irrationality of the personal, individualist, and spiritual brand of anarcho-primitivism associated with many early Earth First!ers and deep ecologists. He insisted that all environmental problems are social problems and must be confronted collectively.

Ecofeminist scholars have challenged social ecology for being less attentive to gender, race, and other forms of social difference that are frequently not respected in the kinds of small communal groups Bookchin envisions as ecologically sustainable social formations.[39] Moreover, Bookchin's writings are, for some critics, problematic in their overall masculinist orientation.[40] Other feminist scholars take Bookchin to task for his anarchist politics. He appeared to set up the only choice for society as either pro-state or no state, ignoring the fact that states have made it possible for many women to participate in public life and labor markets.[41] Furthermore, Bookchin's commitment to the supremacy of Western philosophical rationality does not sit well with some critics. Val Plumwood writes that "these critics of oppositional and colonizing forms of reason have not sought to reject reason as such, but rather to reject its traditional Western 'rationalist' construction as inferiorizing, opposing, and controlling other areas of human and nonhuman life (usually those counted as 'nature')."[42]

Political economic perspectives embodied in the work of sociologists such as O'Connor, Faber, Foster, and Schnaiberg and Gould focus on the devastating effects of capitalism on socioecological dynamics.[43] These studies reveal a Marxist viewpoint in that when struggles over the means of production tend to favor the capitalist classes, they also produce greater ecological damage and mass social suffering. Relatedly, some social scientists have produced studies demonstrating that general measures of social and political inequality are correlated with and contribute to greater levels of ecological harm.[44] For example, James Boyce finds that the level of egalitarianism in a society may be one of the strongest predictors of the general degree of environmental harm in that society. That is, societies exhibiting higher levels of economic and political inequality are characterized by higher overall ecological harm, and the reverse is true for societies with greater egalitarian structures.[45] This body of research is of great importance for linking inequality to ecological harm. Even so, much of it is focused on economic or political measures of inequality that fall short of capturing the complex ways in which inequality also functions across race, gender, sexuality, and species.

Finally, the Environmental Justice Paradigm is a perspective that builds on many of the above conceptual orientations in that it focuses on entire human populations suffering directly from ecological harm. The EJP directs its attention to the urgent conditions that people of color, Indigenous populations, women, immigrants, the working classes, and the poor confront in the form of degraded environmental conditions and threats to public health. In that regard, the EJP refuses deep ecology's strict biocentric emphasis on ecosystems and the New Ecological Paradigm's blind spot for social justice as it advances an effort to redefine environmental issues as human rights and civil rights issues. As Dorceta Taylor and other scholars have amply documented, the NEP emerged from a movement dominated by "primarily White, middle-class activists who work in predominantly White, male-dominated, environmental organizations."[46] The environmental justice (EJ) movement and the EJP largely developed in response to that limited demographic slice of the social fabric, featuring organizations led and supported primarily by working-class people, women of color, Indigenous persons, and immigrants.

In the eyes of deep ecologists, the EJP is arguably anthropocentric because it places a strong priority on the health of human beings, particularly those who are politically vulnerable. For their part, some ecofeminists rightly view the EJP as paying insufficient attention to gender dynamics, since its priorities exist largely at the nexus of the politics of race and class. The EJP is also limited in that it combines elements of protest and demands for change with an underlying embrace of dominant political and economic institutions. In other words, this movement generally aims to push the state and corporations to embrace some degree of EJ practice, while accepting the fundamental legitimacy and existence of those institutions.[47] Even so, the most unique and productive aspect of the EJP is that it recognizes critical relationships between human inequality and environmental policy and encourages dominant institutions to begin addressing these issues.

The NEP, deep ecology, ecofeminism, social ecology, political economic perspectives, and the EJP are among the most pivotal intellectual and political forces emanating from the twentieth-century and early twenty-first-century (socio)ecology movements. They have emerged in the context of intensified industrialization, urbanization, and globalization in post–World War II United States. Building on this body of sociological research and ideas, the total liberation approach broadens and challenges the boundaries and assumptions of these traditions to encompass a wider intersection of concerns linking social justice and ecological politics. Above all, it is a response to the problem of socioecological inequality.

Total Liberation

The total liberation frame combines important elements from other intellectual and political paradigms to chart a new course for social movements challenging socioecological inequalities. As noted above, the total liberation frame comprises four components: (1) an ethic of justice and anti-oppression inclusive of humans, nonhuman animals, and ecosystems;

(2) anarchism; (3) anticapitalism; and (4) an embrace of direct action tactics. This new frame is marked by ideas, discourses, and practices focused on intrahuman community dynamics and relationships among human and nonhuman species and ecosystems. The narrative that emerges from this study of earth and animal liberation movements is a framework that sees the exploitation of ecosystems and nonhuman animals as necessarily linked to the inequalities within human society, and that recognizes there can be no liberation of one without the other. I explore the problems, limitations, and possibilities of the total liberation framework throughout the following chapters and conclude that these data and this emergent movement framework suggest a number of new directions in ecological politics that are relevant to scholars working in the fields of environmental studies, environmental justice studies, social movements, critical animal studies, and ethnic and gender studies.

Most other prominent scholarly and social movements that focus on ecological politics have stopped short of linking systems of oppression and inequality across species and have generally only called for moderate reform of political and economic institutions. Thus, the total liberation frame challenges (among other paradigms and frameworks) the Environmental Justice Paradigm to embrace anti-oppression politics across multiple categories of difference (not just race, class, and occasionally gender and sexuality), including species and nonhuman natures. Through its anarchist and anticapitalist orientation, total liberation challenges the EJP's reformist embrace of state and market-based strategies for addressing socioecological inequality. And in its support for direct action of all kinds (both legally sanctioned and illegal), the total liberation frame unsettles the EJP's generally reformist approach to tactical choices.

The total liberation frame also speaks to key issues in ethnic and gender studies because it invokes and expands on the concept of *intersectionality*. Critical legal theorist Kimberlé Crenshaw's concept of intersectionality reminds us that various forms of inequality—such as race, class, ability, gender, and sexuality—interrelate and work together to produce advantages and disadvantages for individuals and groups.[48] Race, class, ability, gender, and sexuality are also what feminist theorist Anne McClintock calls "articulated categories"—that is, we define each of these categories through the others.[49] While scholars have done an admirable job of pursuing this line of theorizing among and across the above categories, there remains little work on how we might expand this concept.[50] For example, categories such as nonhuman animal, land, and nonhuman nature or eco-systems are virtually absent from this literature and might be useful for deepening our analysis of intersectionality. We can then consider what happens when we extend this concept to include nonhuman catego-ries, particularly when we think about them as "articulated categories." For example, if we define race, class, ability, gender, and sexuality through each other, do we not also define these categories by drawing on images and popular understandings of nature, land, and nonhuman animal spe-cies? Decades of research reveal that we tend to *naturalize* those categories and the social difference associated with them by implicitly or explicitly linking them to biological and nonhuman processes and actors.[51]

The total liberation frame suggests that if intersectionality begins and ends with humans, then that concept is unnecessarily restrictive. Total lib-eration activists contend that one cannot fully grasp the foundations of racism, classism, ableism, heterosexism, and patriarchy without also under-standing speciesism and dominionism because they are all ideologies and practices rooted in hierarchy and the creation of oppositional superior and inferior subjects. The total liberation frame links oppression and privileges across species, ecosystems, and human populations, suggesting a theory and path toward justice and freedom—something missing in traditional models of intersectionality. Thus, the concept of total libera-tion reveals both the complexity of various systems of hierarchy while also suggesting points of intervention, transformative change, solidarity, and coalition building across group boundaries. Total liberation is, above all, a *cultural* force because its greatest power lies in the strength and audacity of its vision. And while it may never gain widespread appeal, it is sociologically significant because the ideas embodied in this concept constitute a threat to the core of socioecological inequalities.

As an environmental justice scholar, I have often asked myself why I became interested in these largely white, middle-class, and relatively privileged radical movements. There are two reasons: first, I was drawn to the radical tactical and direct action work these activists practiced since that pushed the envelope well beyond what I had seen in the EJ movement in the United States. On that note, some people have argued that people of color do not enjoy the privileges and protections to be able to take similar actions, but that claim is challenged by the rich histories of slave insurrections, immigrant rights movements, farm worker move-ments, the Black Power movement, Asian American movement, Chicana/o movement, gender justice movements, and the everyday work of other civil rights and human rights activists who, by simply engaging in public nonviolent protests, place their freedom and lives in jeopardy. The second reason I became attracted to these movements was that after I began studying them, I realized that some—certainly not all or even most—of these activists were articulating a serious critique of hierarchy and oppression in all forms. Despite its many shortcomings (see the conclusion), that combination of radical analysis and action was remarkable.

I am careful not to romanticize these movements. My position is this: I am presenting data and analysis that underscore why these movements are sociologically significant and of possible interest to anyone concerned with ecological politics. I am also critical of these movements for their many shortcomings but make those critiques from a position of solidarity. That has always been my position on the environmental justice movement, and in that regard, this study is no different.

Never Apologize for Your Rage

Radical Origins and Organizing

No one in his right mind can honestly state that the popular environmental movement using state-sanctioned tactics has been successful. It is very obvious something more is needed.

—Earth Liberation Front statement in Leslie James Pickering,
The Earth Liberation Front: 1997–2002

Social movements do not form spontaneously. Accordingly, in this chapter I investigate what energizes earth and animal liberation movements, how these activists became radicalized, and how the total liberation framework has taken hold in these evolving movements.

I begin with the stories of several activists to provide a sense of how some individuals move toward activism outside the mainstream. I then consider the wider social and historical forces and contexts that have pushed entire *groups* of people into radical activism, creating movements for transformative change. I then probe the conflicts and tensions between radicals and mainstream groups and discourses, concluding with some thoughts about what actually constitutes "radical" politics. I offer no definitive answers, hoping only to provide some clarity and suggest new questions.

Radical Lives

Radical environmental and animal rights activists can be found in every corner of the United States and around the world as well.[1] Many activists I interviewed indicated that they developed a strong sense of fairness and justice in their early years and that general orientation to the world translated into their earth and animal liberation work. Others took a while longer to develop their political views and gained a new consciousness through exposure to radical ideas during early adulthood; they were transformed from passive consumers to active producers of knowledge and participants in collective political projects. Key influences in these activists' awakenings include their parents, friends, music, books, teachers, professors, travel abroad, and past social movements, but for some, their turn toward more radical approaches to change grew out of work in more conservative, mainstream groups. They saw the depths of the problems facing nonhuman natures and concluded those problems required more transformative approaches to change.

Gina Lynn is a nationally known animal liberation activist who served jail time for refusing to speak to a grand jury about Animal Liberation Front (ALF) actions on the West Coast. I met Lynn in 2009 when she was giving a public presentation on the fourth anniversary of what radical animal liberation activists call the Green Scare—the beginning of a new era of heightened state repression directed at the movement. She has participated in illegal animal rescues, including the release of two hundred chickens from an egg farm, and had worked as an animal liberation activist "24/7 for fifteen years" before she was called to a federal courthouse to testify about an alleged arson attributed to the ALF.

Lynn told me how she came to the realization that nonhumans should be defended from those who might harm them:

> I always loved animals as a kid. My mom loves to tell the story of . . . what we really consider my first "action." I was . . . about four or five years old and we went down to the pier. And there were people that were fishing off the pier. And I'd never seen a dead animal before. I had never seen *anyone* dead before, and I saw these men just pulling fish out of the water and chopping them up right there on the pier. And I was absolutely horrified, and I do remember just being disgusted, and I couldn't believe what I was seeing. And I, literally, all the way down to the end of the pier and all the way back, I went up to every single fisherman and said: "How would you like it if somebody took you out of your home and away from your family? How would you like being chopped up?" . . . [M]y sister, who was in a stroller . . . never said much. She was absolutely quiet the whole time. And then she finally looks and she goes, "Gina, why don't you shut up?" So I guess one could say that's how I got started.[2]

Lynn also remembers reading "A Mother's Tale" by James Agee. Lynn recalled that this story "was a big influence" and said she is astonished that so "many animal rights people are familiar with it." She continued:

It's the story of a mother cow, as told to her baby cow, about the trip to slaughter . . . the story's been passed down through generations of cows. You know, that's the way the story is written. And so the mother cow is telling her baby cow, "This is what it's like. You get shoved onto a truck." And, I mean, all the brutal details, knowing that her baby cow is going to maybe make this trip. And it just tore my heart out. But I think I was eleven when I read that. I read it in school, actually, and it absolutely tore my heart out. I cried for days. And then I totally remember going to a restaurant with my family, and I ordered a hamburger. And they put it in front of me, and I was like, "That's that baby cow." And, like, that was it. I didn't eat meat anymore. So I would say, that was, like, one of the biggest influences on me.[3]

Years later, Lynn would stage two hunger strikes while in jail for refusing to cooperate with grand juries seeking indictments against ALF activists. Her story is a good example of an activist who is devoted exclusively to animal liberation activism and is willing to resist the state's efforts to contain that movement.

Kim Marks is someone who typifies the ways in which, for many activists, animal liberation and earth liberation come together. When I asked about her background, Marks began her story by describing her forest defense work in the Pacific Northwest. She told me that she "had an animal rights background" and was an avid backpacker with a love of old-growth forests. She moved to Oregon in 1994 and witnessed first-hand the massive clear cuts the federal government enabled private timber corporations to undertake. She joined a group of activists working on salmon protection and strengthening the Endangered Species Act, and she was dismayed when "the Clinton administration . . . just opened up logging" to private companies. That was a turning point for her, cementing her view that seeking change *through* public institutions was a fool's errand:

That was definitely a moment where I was like, "Whoa. Putting your hopes in the government is just not going to work." . . . [H]onestly, all we had in our tool bag was direct action to save our forests. And so, that's what we did night and day for about a year and a half. We worked at the Warner Creek road blockades for months, at the time, the longest standing road blockade in the U.S. And it just kept going from there. The direct action movement was strong, and we were aiming for a fight.[4]

Marks continued by recalling how she built on her animal rights experience to embrace a multi-issue approach to social change:

> I did some animal rights stuff in high school. Honestly, my middle school teacher was the one that got me interested in animal rights. She educated me about cosmetic testing on animals. And we started an animal rights group in high school. . . . [T]he problem for me was, you know, I saw what Dian Fossey [the famous primatologist who studied and advocated for endangered gorillas] was doing as animal rights, and forest protection as animal rights. And the animal rights groups I was working with couldn't make the link between the destruction of the animals' home in the forest being about animals *and* forests. . . . And so, that was my jump. That was where I kind of left a lot of the vertical organizing around animal rights behind. I felt very disappointed. The folks that worked so hard on stopping cruelty to animals don't understand where the loss of their entire habitat would rank in their campaign. And the animal rights groups deemed it as a separate issue. And, you know, I just think that . . . the single-issue activism isn't what's gonna win.[5]

In addition to blending environmental and animal liberation politics and insisting that effective activism must be multi-issue, Marks shared Lynn's lack of faith in government as a trusted guardian.

Enna's (a pseudonym) lifework builds nicely on Lynn's and Marks's in the sense that she is an animal rights activist with a strong anarchist orientation who extends her politics into the realm of social justice for LGBTQ (lesbian, gay, bisexual, transgender, queer) populations. She has been a vegetarian since age fourteen and a vegan since seventeen (a co-worker gave her a leaflet with "images of cows and chickens in dairy and factory farm settings," and Enna immediately decided to "stop participating in any form of animal suffering or as much as I could control within my own life"). She began volunteering for an animal rights group, doing tabling and public outreach at festivals and schools, and attending demonstrations around issues like fur, vivisection, and factory farming.

Enna took her analysis and actions a step further as she began entertaining "more radical thoughts in my mind, just making the connections between different forms of oppression, and knowing that big business and big corporations were not only contributing to animal suffering, but then also the people working in those conditions were also suffering and not being treated fairly. I just started to do more research and look at all forms of oppression and how they're linked together."[6] Through her animal rights work she met a number of other activists who were "making the connections to other social justice concerns," and she soon began working for a group called the Seattle Lesbian Avengers:

> There's different chapters of the Lesbian Avengers, and this group was mostly antipatriarchy, queer, vegan, mostly women, but we had honorary people who weren't born women or who weren't queers because they thought they were behind our politics so they definitely belonged within our group. We made connections of how corporate global domination affects the earth, animals, and women, and the major action they took part in was the 1999 WTO protest.[7]

Chris Irwin is a life-long environmental activist who, early on, drew direct connections between harms being visited upon ecosystems and threats to human health in his town:

> When I was sixteen, I lived in the Kanawha Valley in West Virginia, which is the headquarters of many chemical companies like DuPont and Union Carbide. The river caught on fire once and everybody had somebody dying of cancer in their family. I couldn't get beer when I was sixteen, but I could get morphine-based painkillers because there was just so much cancer in the area. It rained one time and ate the paint off our car when it was parked beneath the Union Carbide facility. I actually went to Nitro High School. And you could tell what part of town you were in from the chemical stench of the day.[8]

Irwin felt beaten down by the pollution, the illness in his family and community, watching his stepfather suffer from cancer. One day he "reached a point where I just didn't really want to live anymore," but it led to a dramatic turn:

> I was staring at the canopy of the forest and realized that if life was that bad, and I didn't really care about life or death, I could maybe give my life to something. I noticed I really liked the trees and the forest and decided, "Well, I might as well give my life to that." And that alleviated a lot of my misery and pain right then. And it's pretty much been the path I've been on ever since.[9]

Irwin soon started an Earth First! chapter in east Tennessee. They built a formidable coalition of activists who forced numerous companies to change their practices while also organizing for racial justice throughout the South. His work fits comfortably at the intersections of radical environmentalism, environmental justice, antitoxics, and antiracism.

Storm (his activist name) is a veteran radical environmentalist who was transformed by his experience as a Peace Corps volunteer in West Africa. There he connected environmental injustices to global economic and colonial politics:

> Well, while I was there . . . I basically, you know, started seeing firsthand, you know, neocolonialism and corporate globalization and plantation economics. I was seeing raw timber and diamonds and coal and oil . . . , hoards of chickens and goats, and tropical fruit, pineapples and all this stuff being shipped out of the country . . . all this crap, and then all the black people are starving, you know? And I'm like, "Wait. This is really screwed up." And then, of course, I'm seeing the internal bullshit that the Peace Corps is basically a way of maintaining an American presence in a so-called nonaligned third world country. And, I'm just seeing all the crap for what it is, you know? I'm actually seeing the little man behind the curtain.[10]

Underground music and popular culture also play an important role in shaping many animal and earth liberation activists' worldviews. There are many punk and hardcore music bands that support these movements, and their political message is frequently cited as an influence. Josh Harper's story is typical of this radicalization. He remembered, "I had been involved with the hardcore music scene, the punk rock music scene, and really started reading about issues of vegetarianism and veganism and animal rights. And then [reading about] more direct action stuff and about the Animal Liberation Front, the Earth Liberation Front, that it really started to make sense to me. And it was really something I wanted to be involved with."[11]

Finally, Tre Arrow is a good example of how it sometimes takes years for the multiple issues associated with animal, earth, and human liberation to become linked in activists' minds. Arrow is a nationally known activist who was once labeled the United States' "most wanted ecoterrorist." His story exemplifies the ways in which many activists came to embrace total liberation:

So this progression happened over an amount of time—it didn't happen all at once, but the more and more information that I gathered and the more involved that I became, then the more passionate I became about having as little impact on the planet as possible and contributing to as little suffering, as little detriment to all living beings. And so all that stuff just kind of ties in together when it comes to animal rights issues and human rights issues and environmental justice and environmental protection. At one point I had an automobile—my dad bought me this truck when I was in college. . . . And Exxon Valdez happened, and I was living in Florida, and Chevron was trying to drill off the coast of Florida, and we were opposing that, and I was finding out all these things that were going on with Shell in the Niger Delta,[12] so I was trying to find some oil company that I could feel happy about supporting and patronizing, and I couldn't. So I said if there's no way of doing this consciously then I just need to get rid of this truck. So I sold it and since then I've been committed to living without an automobile. And the same thing happened with my diet: I went from dead animals, then vegetarian, then vegan, then all organic, and then raw vegan. So my progression and my involvement in direct action was just a natural progression in what I felt was an important component to doing everything I possibly could to get in the way and stop that which I was determining was desecrating and oppressing and destroying that which was sacred.[13]

Arrow also credits the mainstream advocacy group USPIRG with being an early influence on his ideas; the group mobilized young people to campaign for sustainable industrial practices during his time in Florida.[14]

Radical environmental and animal liberation activists have rich and varied biographies, but there are certain themes that reflect the ways many transformed into advocates for social change using methods that most Americans might find extremist. They read books, listened to underground music, traveled abroad, and were exposed to what they viewed as the violent consumption of nonhuman animals and industrial practices that harmed ecosystems and human health. They found others who shared their views and pushed their thinking, people who gave them the confidence to speak out and act and who inspired them to extend their analysis of ecological politics beyond single-issue approaches. As the individual activists felt a pull toward direct and impactful action, broader political-economic and socioecological forces pushed the emergence of radical *collective* action.

External Drivers of Radicalism

The Anthropocene

There is increasing evidence of widespread, human-driven harm to ecosystems and nonhuman species. According to leading scientists, damage to ecosystems over the last fifty years has been more severe than during any other time in human history. The health of coral reefs, fisheries, oceans, forests, and river systems declined precipitously, while climate disruption indicators, species extinction, and air and water pollution rose dramatically. At the same time, there has been an enormous increase in factory farming and industrial animal production, consumption, and experimentation that results in the slaughter of billions of nonhuman animals each year. This activity has created and accelerated negative impacts on ecosystems and nonhuman species.[15]

Scientists have termed the age we live in the "Anthropocene" as a way to conceptualize this geological epoch in which humans are the primary driver of rapid changes across the globe's ecosystems. The moniker underscores "that a potentially fatal ecological rift has arisen between human beings and the earth, emanating from the conflicts and contradictions of the modern capitalist society."[16]

The threats to ecosystems and nonhuman animals produce an interpellation (a call) that beckons earth and animal liberation activists to take action individually and collectively. They feel compelled to halt or reverse environmental harms and defend endangered species, forests, and animals in slaughterhouses. This is to say, inanimate and nonhuman actors spur activists. Threatened wildernesses and genetically engineered chickens exert agency and impact the imaginations, motivations, and actions of activists—an aspect of social movement scholarship that remains undeveloped. In fact, if nonhumans are active participants in social movements, our definition of a "social movement" must be revised dramatically. Political theorist Jane Bennett notes that this kind of ecological politics significantly expands the boundaries of the polity as well—to include both humans and the more than human world.[17]

Moving beyond a strict ecological view of the problem toward a socioecological frame, we must also consider the human costs of the Anthropocene. Large numbers of people die each year as a result of exposure to pollution and accidents in hazardous workplaces and in communities across the United States. As sociologist Daniel Faber puts it, "American capitalism is killing hundreds of thousands of U.S. citizens and causing hundreds of billions (if not trillions) of dollars in damage to property, human health, the community, and the environment every year—all in the pursuit of higher profits."[18] Social movement responses to this grim reality vary widely, from the actions of mainstream, reformist organizations, such as the Sierra Club, Environmental Defense, and the Humane Society of the United States, to those of radical organizations and movements. This book focuses on radical movements that reject structured, bureaucratic approaches to target what they believe to be the roots of the problem.

The rise of neoliberalism has functioned in the United States to reduce regulation to enable record profit making and minimal protections for workers, citizens, consumers, and nonhumans. These policies have led to major reductions in workers' wages, a massive spike in the number of people of color in the prison system, the intensification of ecological crises, higher levels of hazardous chemical production and disposal globally, and a marked rise in sweatshops and occupational safety risks for the U.S. labor force.[19] And the public, within the United States and around the world, is experiencing an environmentally driven cancer epidemic that is likely to get much worse.[20]

Despite all this, the environmental regulations in the United States are among the most stringent in the world. They are just not strong enough or enforced enough, and they are being systematically weakened and removed by pro-business, anti-regulatory organizations and institutions—what Faber calls the "polluter-industrial complex."[21] These are the corporations, politicians, media outlets, think tanks, foundations, and other organizations that deny the existence of climate change in particular and environmental crises in general. They proclaim that social inequality is a good thing since it demonstrates "equality of opportunity," and they work to convince others that low-wage, non-unionized, dangerous, temporary, dead-end jobs for a desperate population are the most we can hope for.

Taken together, we can see that radical movements have emerged, in part, because of a perceived urgency of the problems. Because, according to total liberation activist-scholars Steven Best and Anthony Nocella:

> "Reasonableness" and "moderation" seem to be entirely unreasonable and immoderate, as "extreme" and "radical" actions appear simply as necessary and appropriate. After decades of environmental struggles in the west, we

are nevertheless losing ground in the battle to preserve species, ecosystems, wilderness, and human communities. Politics as usual just won't cut it anymore.[22]

Mainstream Groups

Disappointment and alienation have also led many who tried mainstream approaches to environmentalism and animal rights to turn to a more radical path. The tensions between radical and mainstream environmental and animal rights movements are legion and considered in greater depth by other authors,[23] so I offer an overview of the politics that separate these factions and a consideration of cases that illustrate the depths of the issues—particularly the divide over questions pertaining to total liberation.

First, there is the question of what kind of activism makes a difference. For many of us, the figure of environmentalists and animal rights (AR) activists in our cultural imaginary is of ragtag, motley groups of unshaven, unhygienic, vegan, long-haired misfits yelling through bullhorns. While this image can be reinforced by observing activists in cities from Portland to Miami, the reality is that most of these movements' resources are actually controlled by highly educated white-collar professionals who routinely rub elbows with government and industry elites. Since the 1970s, the professionalization of the mainstream AR and environmental movements has meant that activists sought to create modest change within the framework of dominant institutions. They "played by the rules," working within steeply hierarchical organizations that increasingly resembled the corporations they sought to reform, raising millions of dollars and renouncing more radical approaches and activists.[24] These mainstream groups generally refuse to link environmental and AR issues to social justice politics, limiting the scope of their vision and political possibilities.[25] One might find this to be rational if such an approach were effective.[26]

Landmark legislation such as the Animal Welfare Act and the Clean Air Act, along with numerous state and municipal laws, suggests mainstream movements have seen more than a modicum of success. Unfortunately, these gains are far outweighed by the continued plundering of ecosystems through rainforest and critical habitat destruction, climate disruption, and the consumption and decimation of nonhuman species nationally and globally.[27] As one of my colleagues asked rhetorically, "How much failure can we take?"

Speaking about mainstream approaches to environmental change through compromise with the U.S. Forest Service, Earth First! cofounder Howie Wolkie once stated: "We played the game, we played the rules. We were moderate, reasonable, and professional. We had data, statistics, and maps. And we got fucked. That's when I started thinking, 'Something's missing here. Something isn't working.'"[28] Soon after, Wolkie helped launch Earth First! The Earth Liberation Front (ELF) concurs and takes the point a step further to embrace underground illegal direct action:

> The ELF does not engage in more traditional tactics simply because they have been proven not to work. . . . The . . . mainstream environmental movement . . . has failed in its attempts to bring about the needed protection to stop the destruction of life on this planet. . . . There is also a certain intelligence and logic to the idea that with one night's work, a few individuals can accomplish what years of legal battles and millions of dollars most likely did not.[29]

Animal liberation activist-scholar Steven Best weighed in on this issue from the perspective of the AR movement's track record:

> One has to confront the startling facts that ever more animals die each year in slaughterhouses, vivisection labs, and animal "shelters," while the fur industry has made a huge comeback. Similarly, after three decades of activity, the animal advocacy movement remains overwhelmingly a white, middle-class movement that has gained few supporters in communities of color or among other social justice movements. So if we are counting the number of casualties in this war of liberation, to single out one criterion, our side is hardly winning.[30]

Radical activists contend that confrontation and illegal direct action are far more effective than reformist, insider tactics. Whether it is home demonstrations, blockades, boycotts, property destruction, or arson, the actions of radical movements have resulted in businesses and laboratories shutting down, investors and businesses divesting from large companies, and delays to or the cessation of objectionable practices (see chapter 4).

Radical activists believe strongly that their mainstream counterparts are increasingly ineffectual and irrelevant. They argue that mainstream groups decry aggressive tactics while preferring to negotiate with the state and corporations to address animal and ecosystem exploitation but fail to challenge the systems of power that produce those problems. The evidence of the limits of the reformist orientation is often in full view, as announcements of endorsements and partnerships between mainstream groups and corporations and individuals whom radical activists hold beneath contempt make the news.

Radical activists accuse mainstream groups of "sleeping with the enemy." When Peter Singer wrote *Animal Liberation* in the 1970s, his book became the movement's landmark text, and he is considered the father of animal rights advocacy. At the time of the book's first printing, Singer took a number of animal advocacy groups to task, pointing out that the American Society for the Prevention of Cruelty to Animals (ASPCA), the American Humane Association, and the Animal Welfare Institute were "actively collaborating with those responsible for cruelty," such as rodeos and animal research laboratories, and by doing so, the groups "lent an air of respectability to practices that ought to be condemned outright."[31] However, Singer himself became a "collaborator" with similar institutions years later. In 2006, he sent a letter to John Mackey, the CEO of the Whole Foods grocery chain. The letter was written on behalf of Singer's organization—Animal Rights International—and seventeen other animal advocacy groups expressing "appreciation and support" for "the pioneering initiative being taken by Whole Foods Market in setting Farm Animal Compassionate Standards."[32] Few if any animal liberationists (that is, radical or abolitionist activists) would endorse the concept of "compassionate standards" that give moral weight to any kind of slaughter and sale of nonhumans for mass consumption. Moreover, while mainstream animal welfarists may view Whole Foods' "compassionate standards" as laudatory, that same corporation's anti-union stance went unmentioned. The letter killed the possibility of even a conversation—let alone an alliance—between AR groups and labor advocates.[33]

Other animal-focused groups have lost credibility in collusion, too, at least insofar as radicals see it. The Humane Society Legislative Fund is the legal arm of the Humane Society of the United States—the nation's largest animal advocacy organization. HSUS has a $100 million budget, millions of members, and offices throughout the world. Together, the HSUS and the HSLF are, according to many radical AR activists, the poster children for what is wrong with the mainstream movement. I personally received a mailing from the HSLF requesting donations and featuring the following language: "Intentional cruelty is a warning sign. People who mistreat, abuse, or torture animals are five times more likely to engage in other violent behavior. They also are more likely to batter their partner." Those claims are consistent with other activists' views that there are strong links between violence against nonhumans and humans. However, as the organization's letter continued, it endorsed a state-centric solution to animal abuse: "Our government and law enforcement agencies do not . . . track violent crimes committed against our defenseless animal friends. . . . We need the FBI to take animal cruelty and abuse seriously, and not just for our animal friends. The links between animal abuse and human violence are clear and undeniable."[34]

The HSLF/HSUS, then, view violence in strict criminological terms. They embrace a "tough on crime," authoritarian, and pro-state surveillance perspective that many radical groups reject outright. They support a carceral solution (and a security state) that systematically and disproportionately imprisons working-class people of color and women.[35] Another opportunity to build coalitions with social justice groups is squelched by language like this.

And it's not just talk. The notoriously nativist and racist sheriff Joe Arpaio and social conservative commentator Paul Harvey publicly joined with mainstream groups including the HSUS, the Arizona Humane Society, Farm Sanctuary, and the Animal Defense League of Arizona in 2007. Together they made Arizona the first state to ban veal crates and pig gestation crates (so small that the animals are unable to turn around) previously used in industrial agricultural operations. Activists were proud of their victory, but joining forces with men like Arpaio and Harvey earned the groups the enmity of not only radical activists but also many people of color and immigrant communities.[36]

Many mainstream environmental groups commit similar offenses, accepting funds from and creating partnerships with some of the globe's worst polluters. For example:

> The Sierra Club partnered with the Clorox Company to endorse a line of "green products" in exchange for a percentage of the sales. In Traverse

City, Michigan, the Sierra Club chapter saw its entire board of directors resign in protest. Monica Evans, former chair, stated, "We just were stunned when we found out. We just couldn't be part of an organization that jumped into bed with one of the most negative environmentally impacting companies in America."[37]

In 2008, Environmental Defense partnered with Walmart on a project to reduce waste from shopping bags.[38] Of the many objections raised against this partnership was the fact that Walmart is widely condemned for forcing down employee wages, union busting, and putting small companies (even whole towns) out of business. It is also alleged to be a frequent perpetrator of gender discrimination.[39] For any environmental organization to collaborate with this corporation would reflect a blatant insensitivity to basic social issues.

In 2008, Conservation International partnered with Newmont Mining Corporation on Walmart's Sustainable Value Network for Jewelry, which aims to ensure that gold sold in its stores is produced in socially and environmentally responsible ways.[40] Newmont, however, is one of the world's largest gold-mining companies and has spawned spirited resistance at many of its operations because of ecological and public health concerns associated with leaking cyanide, mercury, cadmium, and arsenic in its mine tailings.[41]

In an exposé about such turncoat environmental groups, journalist Johann Hari writes: "They simply need to be shunned. They are not part of the environmental movement: they are polluter-funded leeches sucking on the flesh of environmentalism, leaving it weaker and depleted."[42]

Another longstanding complaint by radical activists is the lack of diversity within mainstream groups. "Yep. We're too white." That was the headline of a newsletter sent to Sierra Club members in July 2009 after U.S. Environmental Protection Agency administrator Lisa Jackson (the first African American EPA administrator and a member of the Obama administration) gently criticized the environmental movement for its inattention to racial diversity.[43] Predictably, the Sierra Club's approach amounted to lip service: "The Sierra Club not only agrees with her, we're also doing something about it with diversity programs ranging from our Environmental Justice and Community Partnerships program to Building Bridges to the Outdoors for inner-city youth." In other words, the Sierra Club thinks it needs to reach out and convince people of color to be a part of its programs rather than rethinking the way the organization has defined its mission, the problem, and the solution in the first place. Stances like these understandably alienate many radical activists, whose very identities seem to shut them out of mainstream groups.

The U.S. environmental and animal rights movements are as white as any Republican Party gathering. As one activist attending the 2008 Animal Rights Conference in Washington, D.C., put it, all he saw were "rooms full of well-educated white people." He went on, "it is shockingly clear that our movement is painfully monochromatic and socioeconomically limited in scope."[44]

Mainstream groups have crassly squandered opportunities to diversify their ranks, rethink and reframe their narrow goals, and connect their work to issues people of color and social justice activists cherish time and again, sparking an almost inevitable radicalism. From messages and campaigns that compare nonhuman animal exploitation to the enslavement of African Americans to efforts to characterize dog breeders as equivalent to the Ku Klux Klan, many animal advocacy organizations and activists display the stunning ignorance, insensitivity, and ugliness of white privilege.

Environmentalists have demonstrated equal cluelessness. Dana Alston was a revered environmental justice leader who never shied away from speaking out about the racism of mainstream environmental organizations. Alston once publicly pointed out the National Wildlife Federation's hypocrisy: "They have Waste Management, Inc. on their board of directors which engages in supreme environmental racism. They will dump some of the most hazardous materials known in people of color's communities."[45] For many environmental justice activists, that kind of collusion and coziness is unacceptable. It makes mainstream environmental groups complicit in environmental racism.

But perhaps nothing irks radical AR and environmental activists more than outright betrayal by mainstream groups. Compromise in political negotiations and the public condemnation of radical groups (so as to curry favor with the state and corporations) are prime examples. Jay Hair, the president of the National Wildlife Federation, once denounced Earth First! as a terrorist organization, declaring that he saw "no fundamental difference between destroying a river and destroying a bulldozer."[46] Likewise, Greenpeace International suggested in a letter to the president of Iceland that the Sea Shepherd Conservation Society was behaving like a terrorist group when activists Rod Coronado and David Howitt sank two Icelandic ships used for illegal whaling operations.[47]

Predictably, the Humane Society of the United States has performed this role in the animal advocacy movement. With open hostility, the aforementioned animal liberationist Steven Best writes: "The Humane Society of the United States (HSUS) . . . [has] unctuously adopted the murderous voice of the corporate-state apparatus and denounced direct action as violent, terrorist, and antithetical to the values of the animal advocacy movement. The lethal virus of McCarthyism has infected our own movement."[48]

Despite the rancor, there *is* some good will between mainstream and radical groups, at least at the philosophical level. One of the main points of agreement is that the more aggressive wings of the movements serve as a "radical flank" that allows mainstream organizations to demand more and push harder with institutional targets.[49] Many activists can point to campaigns and policy changes where this "good cop–bad cop" dynamic may have played a critical role in successful outcomes.[50] Writing the foreword to Rik Scarce's book *Eco-Warriors*, David Brower of the Sierra Club called on all wings of the environmental movement to work together because none has a monopoly on the most effective approach— the more people working together, the more powerful the movement might become.[51] Ecofeminist and AR activist-scholar pattrice jones offers a similar sentiment regarding animal advocacy movements: "There's simply no evidence to support the idea that either ALF actions or welfare reforms in any way inhibit the long-term struggle for animal liberation.[52]

Drawing Inspiration

While dramatic political-economic and socioecological changes—along with reformist responses—have had clear and direct effects on the development of these movements, radical formations also gain inspiration, energy, cultural legitimacy, and strategic and tactical knowledge from other social justice movements.

For example, the website of the Earth Liberation Front (ELF) invokes the Luddites, the abolitionists, the suffragettes, and the Boston Tea Party movements: "The tactic [of economic sabotage] has a rich and plentiful history in movements around the globe and makes sense from a purely logical standpoint. If an item or piece of property is threatening life for the sake of profit, shouldn't it be destroyed?"[53] Specifically, the

ELF recalls: "The Luddites fought back using tactics very similar to those performed by the ELF today. Some factories were forced to shut down and others agreed to stop running the industrialized machines due to the Luddite activity and threat." The website also points to other social struggles, including those led by slaves: "There are numerous accounts of slaves sabotaging the property of their 'masters' and engaging in various tactics to disrupt the flow of commerce in the slave system." Finally, the ELF contends that "the suffragette movement, particularly in England, used sabotage in addition to other tactics to successfully gain rights for women."[54]

Jake Conroy is an animal liberation activist who worked on a campaign targeting Huntingdon Life Sciences (HLS)—one of the largest chemical testing companies in the world. HLS tests chemicals on thousands of animals and has been the subject of numerous animal welfare investigations and a multiyear campaign to shut the company down. Stop Huntingdon Animal Cruelty (SHAC) was an organization that drew on many tactics to highlight HLS's practices and cripple the corporation. In "secondary targeting," activists would pressure companies doing business with HLS to cancel their contracts, and in "tertiary targeting," activists would do the same with firms that did business with other firms that did business with HLS (you might call it "Three Degrees of HLS"). This effort was quite successful, and major corporations providing services for HLS withdrew. And those tactics? Secondary and tertiary targeting were borrowed directly from the anti-apartheid movement, which forced many companies to stop doing business with the racist South African regime in the 1980s. Movements for black liberation have heavily influenced earth and animal liberation activists like Conroy. He told me that the black liberation struggle is "for me . . . the most inspirational movement" because it

> encapsulates everything you need to know about how to run a campaign or a movement or a protest . . . that whole "every tool in the toolbox" thing. From the littlest welfarist [reformist] type of action to the most extreme, you know? . . . Everything from the NAACP stuff to the most radical Black Liberation Army stuff . . . [and] the Black Panther Party for Self Defense. . . . And obviously, the civil rights movement isn't over. We haven't really solved all those problems. But the amount of change that they made in such a small time with the means they had is . . . remarkable.[55]

This is a generative way of linking contemporary radicals' cause—and the state repression directed at them—to historical movements that now enjoy considerable legitimacy. A speaker on a panel at a recent national Animal Rights Conference (ARC) session, "Applying Direct Action," offered the following words of encouragement:

> Never apologize for your rage. Being a part of this movement . . . you're going to be called "fanatical wackos," "kooks," "terrorists" . . . [and] "extremists." Never apologize for that because looking back over history, the finest people have always been called those names, whether we're talking about the abolitionists fighting against slavery or people fighting for women's suffrage or the civil rights movement. The finest people have always been called those names. So you're in good company.[56]

Activists in both earth and animal liberation movements consciously draw inspiration from environmental and social justice movements around the world, both past and present. The environmental justice movement in the United States revealed the disproportionate concentration of pollution, chemical toxins, and other industrial hazards in communities of color, Indigenous communities, and working-class white communities. Environmental justice (EJ) activists from these communities had been fighting against environmental injustices for decades before Earth First! (EF!) and the ELF appeared. In turn, one early influence on these radical white earth and animal liberation activists was MOVE—a black revolutionary group founded in Philadelphia in 1972 by John Africa. MOVE was organized around a commitment to improve public health, challenge the state and capitalism, and fight the racism, homelessness, police brutality, and industrial pollution they produce. Clearly an example of an early EJ organization, MOVE's mission statement reads:

> MOVE's work is revolution . . . a revolution to stop man's system from imposing on life, to stop industry from poisoning the air, water, and soil and to put an end to the enslavement of all life. Our work is to show people how rotten and enslaving this system is and that the system is the cause of homelessness, unemployment, drug addiction, alcoholism, racism, domestic abuse, AIDS, crime, war, all the problems of the world. We are working to demonstrate that people not only can fight this system, they must

fight the system if they ever want to free themselves from endless suffering and oppression.[57]

Many MOVE members were vegetarians and staunch animal rights activists:

> Maintaining the hundreds of pounds of food we keep stocked is a big job, too. We have seeds for the birds, nuts for the squirrels, raw meat for the dogs and cats, and fruits and vegetables for the people. We love all life. It is tremendously upsetting for us to see someone mistreat an animal and we will take immediate action to stop anyone from beating a dog, throwing stones at birds, or causing similar impositions on innocent life.[58]

Eventually, MOVE was the target of an infamous police repression campaign, including the bombing of members' homes and the imprisonment of several members on questionable charges. Many of these activists are still behind bars and widely considered political prisoners today, including by the earth and animal liberation communities.

The EJ movement today is considerably more reformist than MOVE was, and is perhaps less of a model for earth and animal liberation movements with regard to its tactical approach and its orientation toward the state and capital. Even so, the EJ movement's integration of social justice with environmentalism continues to influence white radical environmental and animal rights movements.

This dynamic underscores the critical power of transmitting and sharing knowledge and ideas from one generation or movement to the next. It would be difficult to overstate the importance of movement activists and historians, organic intellectuals, and educational institutions in facilitating that knowledge transmission. This is precisely why states seek to repress the histories and ideas associated with many social movements.[59]

Animal Rights and Beyond

Edward Carpenter (1844–1929) and Henry Salt (1851–1939), both English, were early activists who observed connections among various forms of oppression. Carpenter was a labor activist, pacificist, and poet who supported LGBTQ rights, women's rights, and vegetarianism, while opposing vivisection and the air pollution already visible in urban areas. Salt was a socialist, pacifist, naturalist, vegetarian, and public proponent of prison reform and animal rights. He founded the Humanitarian League, an organization to ban hunting.

Elitism was evident in the animal protection movement of the nineteenth and twentieth centuries (as it would be in the environmentalist circles). Early efforts featured a blend of animal advocacy, child welfare, and Christian temperance. Urbanization and industrialization had removed animals other than pets from the daily lives of most people, so a certain sentimental attachment to nonhumans had arisen, but cruelty was still a problem. The social class dimensions were on clear display in these groups, as they relied on wealthy donors and took the view, as Leonard Eaton (president of the American Humane Association in 1888) put it, "the more reasonable and intelligent portion of the community" regarded nonhumans as "having rights that humans are bound to respect."[60] Eaton thought his views would be obvious to those of his own class and education but must be taught to everyone else.

He was not alone. The American Humane Association was a direct offshoot of the British organization, and along with the Royal Society for the Prevention of Cruelty to Animals in Britain (RSPCA) and the American Society for the Prevention of Cruelty to Animals (SPCA), it emphasized exhorting working-class people to practice kindness to nonhumans. In fact, the RSPCA became a favorite charity of the British upper classes, gaining an endorsement and funding from Queen Victoria as well. Ultimately, the reformist goals of these organizations focused on moral uplift and improvement of humankind—primarily aimed at children and the working classes.

The humane movement also reflected changing gender relations as urbanization and industrialization took hold and the boundaries between the private and public spheres and the spaces for middle-class men and women became more pronounced. As is the case today, middle-class women formed the largest contingent of supporters and volunteers for the animal protection movement—while men served as the formal leaders—and signaled the linkage among popular conceptions of caring and kindness, gender, and animal protection.[61] Women were expected to exhibit the stronger "feminine" emotions that "naturally" predisposed them to kindness toward nonhuman animals.

Despite this, the connections between the early humane movement and other social causes are of critical importance to understanding the roots of total liberation struggles today. Many might mistakenly assume that contemporary animal rights activists are singularly focused, leading to the assumption that AR activists care more deeply about nonhumans than humans. There may be such activists, but I have found that many people in the AR community are deeply involved in and committed to other social movements.[62] Peter Singer, a philosopher and inspirational figure for the modern animal rights movement, even declares: "Historically . . . the leaders of the animal welfare movement have cared far more about human beings than have other humans who care nothing for animals."[63] He points to the extensive overlaps among early movements for animal protection with the movements for women's rights and slavery abolition. There was also a great deal of overlap with child protection and labor rights movements.

There are numerous examples to support this claim. William Wilberforce and Fowell Buxton, two of the most prominent leaders in the antislavery movement in Britain, were cofounders of the RSPCA. The Bands of Mercy was a branch of the RSPCA and an organization of clubs intended to promote kindness among children. Founded in the 1870s by antislavery activist Catherine Smithies, this organization urged children to support animal welfare.[64] Many early U.S. feminist leaders such as Susan B. Anthony, Lucy Stone, and Elizabeth Cady Stanton had strong ties to the vegetarian movement and joined antislavery publisher Horace Greeley in promoting women's rights and vegetarianism. With regard to the rights of children, it is telling that Henry Bergh, a leader and founder of animal welfare societies in the United States, also worked to support children's protection legislation.[65] Similarly, in Britain, Lord Shaftesbury was a founder of the National Society for the Prevention of Cruelty to Children (started by the RSPCA) and authored legislation to stop the widespread use of child labor in that country.[66] None of these individuals' biographies necessarily signals that these movements were highly integrated or collaborative beyond specific cases, but they do suggest significant philosophical links laying the groundwork for such possibilities in later movements.

In the 1950s, the animal welfare movement witnessed an expansion as the Animal Welfare Institute, the Friends of Animals, and the Humane Society of the United States (HSUS) were founded (the latter as a breakaway group from the American Humane Association). Activists focused largely on problems associated with pets, including abuse and cruelty, animal shelter conditions, and "overpopulation" and abandonment of companion animals. They believed abuse was the result of individual behavior (bad people, not bad institutions or bad societal practices), and they lacked a consensus around opposition to vivisection (it was generally seen as necessary for the advancement of science and as a benefit to human health and development).

By the 1960s and 1970s, all began to change. Activists and animal welfare organizations began to argue that institutions—particularly corporations—and a deeper national culture of animal exploitation were largely responsible for animal abuse and that nonhumans had "rights" that should be respected. Groups that supported these ideas included Cleveland Amory's Fund for Animals, Friends of Animals, the International Society for Animal Rights, and the American Fund for Alternatives to Animal Research. *Animal Liberation* became a bible for many activists, who soon began using the term *speciesism*—the notion that one species is superior to another—a form of inequality they compared to racism or sexism.

Animal *welfare* was redefined as animal *rights*, with activists drawing inspiration and language from the civil rights, Black Power, gay rights, and feminist movements. Unfortunately, these invocations belied a simplistic worldview and troublesome ignorance of how various forms of dominance might be linked. For example, Singer wrote: "This book is about the tyranny of human over nonhuman animals. This tyranny has caused and today is still causing an amount of pain and suffering that can only be compared with that which resulted from the centuries of tyranny by white humans over black humans."[67] Regrettably, this is the kind of blanket equivalence of oppressions that is unhelpful for thinking about how power functions across populations and for building coalitions. Moreover, Singer was a reformist who believed that humans could use animals for the benefit of society so long as we worked to reduce their pain and suffering. Radical activists later supplanted this utilitarian approach and chose philosopher Tom Regan's *The Case for Animal Rights* over Singer's more moderate orientation. Regan's book offered a robust rationale for a rights-based path toward the abolition of nonhuman animal abuse.[68]

The animal rights movement was still quite diverse in terms of the approaches activists and organizations pursued. James Jasper and Dorothy Nelkin divide the movement into three groups: *welfarists*, *pragmatists*, and *fundamentalists*. The *welfarists* are groups like the ASPCA and the HSUS (and activists like Singer), who accept most human uses of nonhuman animals but work to minimize pain and suffering. These organizations are the most well funded and visible, but also the least controversial and most compromising. They work toward their goals through public education campaigns and lobbying for protective legislation.

The *pragmatists* also approve of humans using animals, but only when the benefits outweigh nonhuman pain and suffering (assuming, alarmingly, that this is calculable). Henry Spira is a good example of the pragmatist mold. In the 1980s, he was a prominent opponent of ingredient and product testing on animals at corporations like Revlon. He sought to change practices through legal action, negotiation, and public protest.

The *fundamentalists*—people I would call liberationists or abolitionists—believe that humans should never use nonhumans for their own interests or pleasures, regardless of any alleged benefit. The single best exemplar of this orientation may be the Animal Liberation Front (ALF), which uses education, arson, animal rescue/liberation, vandalism, harassment, and property destruction to achieve its goals. Other abolitionist groups include SHAC, Win Animal Rights, the Animal Rights Militia, the Justice Department, and many others.

One fundamentalist group deserves particular mention: People for the Ethical Treatment of Animals (PETA) is one of the most recognized names in the animal rights movement. It is an exemplar of the movement's successes and its many problems. PETA made headlines soon after its founding in the early 1980s when it highlighted the suffering and abuse of animals in research laboratories. PETA is credited with organizing a series of hearings on Capitol Hill that led to the passage of the 1985 Animal Welfare Act and the 1986 U.S. Public Health Service guidelines that strengthened regulation of animal research facilities receiving federal funding. The organization's discourse and tactics have been controversial. They have compared the consumption of animals with the Nazi Holocaust, likened the confinement of farm animals to human slavery, and frequently featured naked women in their public messages. Like many other animal rights groups in the 1980s and today, PETA's single-issue focus makes it difficult to imagine—let alone pursue—coalition building with social justice movements. The organization's inability and unwillingness to understand why many people of color, Jews, and feminists (among others) are offended by its campaigns reflects the more general and longstanding problems of whiteness, heteronormativity, patriarchy, and unexamined privilege that are hallmarks of much of the animal rights movement. At the same time, PETA is a "bridge" organization in that it exhibits characteristics of pragmatist/mainstream and abolition-ist/radical perspectives. It is even known for controversial collaborations with the ALF.

Environmentalism

Most of what passed for environmentalism in nineteenth-century United States was a mixture of spiritual attachment to an imagined, feminine, nonhuman "nature" imbued with class, racial, and gendered characteristics such that only wealthy white heterosexual male elites were viewed as the true stewards of ecosystems. The working classes, immigrants, and women were cast as unable to grasp the importance of or appreciate the countryside and "getting back to nature."[69] This was a time when the dualist view positioned human culture as the opposite of "nature." Philosopher and activist Henry David Thoreau was a notable exception, deeply immersed in ecological thinking and action and engaged in anti-slavery and antigovernment work through his support for John Brown, the Underground Railroad, and civil disobedience.

Environmental historians have argued that we might consider those social reformers who advocated on behalf of immigrants working in sweatshops and living in urban slums in the United States during the late nineteenth and early twentieth centuries as early environmental justice leaders. This group included Jane Addams of Hull House and her col-leagues Florence Kelley and Alice Hamilton. Most of their energy was focused on advocating for working class and politically marginalized peoples who lived and worked in hazardous environments. These women consciously linked the working environment with the broader environ-ment and insisted that in order to improve public health in these Euro-pean immigrant communities, the state, landlords, and employers had to act to reduce hazards associated with long working hours, minimal wages, lead poisoning, and garbage dumps.[70] The mainstream environmental movement (then and today) chose to largely ignore these concerns. That decision crippled the movement's capacity for significant change and greatly diminished its relevance. The same could be said for much of the early *radical* environmental movement, though that would soon change.

Emerging Radical Movements

The same year that Peter Singer's *Animal Liberation* was published (1975), Edward Abbey's soon-to-be classic novel *The Monkey Wrench Gang* told the story of a small group of rambunctious, radical eco-activists. They held mainstream environmental groups in contempt and, in neo-Luddite fashion, boldly practiced ecotage (property destruction) to defend ecosystems. They dreamed of blowing up Arizona's Glen Canyon Dam— later the actual site of the first Earth First! (EF!) action in March 1981: the unfurling of a large banner with a "crack" painted on it over the dam. Howie Wolkie, Mike Roselle, Dave Foreman, Bart Koehler, and Ron Kezar all converged at Glen Canyon, having been inspired by Abbey to found EF! a year before. Fiction, by making the impossible a possibility even between the covers of a book, helped move activists to imagine and work for a different future.

The Glen Canyon Dam was an important site in the U.S. environmental movement's history, not just because of the 1981 action. It was actually built as the result of a compromise made by mainstream national environmental groups like the Sierra Club in exchange for the cancellation of a dam-building plan at Dinosaur National Monument in Utah and Colorado in the early 1960s. The founders of Earth First! and the emerging radical environmental movement would never forget or forgive that betrayal. They quickly adopted the slogan "No Compromise in Defense of Mother Earth" as a reminder of how politics as usual rarely yields satisfying results for ecosystem protection efforts.

Known as the group that "cracked" Glen Canyon Dam, EF! graduated to tree spiking (placing spikes inside trees slated for harvesting to discourage timber companies from cutting them), tree sitting, and creating road blockades to challenge the destruction of forests across the western United States. Tree sitting alone is believed to have cost the timber industry millions of dollars in losses, as a single activist camping out in a tree could delay a company's work for weeks and months as they battled environmentalists on the ground and in court.[71]

EF! began publishing a rough-hewn newsletter, which eventually became the *Earth First! Journal* and enjoyed a national and international readership. EF! also developed a proposal called the Earth First! Wilderness Preserve System, which would make vast swaths of the western United States almost entirely off-limits to human beings. The proposal's preamble expressed the essence of biocentrism: "the central idea of Earth First! is that humans have no divine right to subdue the Earth, that we are merely one of several millions forms of life on this planet. We reject even the notion of benevolent stewardship as that implies dominance.

Instead, we believe, as did Aldo Leopold, that we should be plain citizens of the land community."[72]

Lest one think that Earth First! was focused only on *opposing* anti-ecological practices, it is critical to remember that activists in this group also pushed the idea of restoration and "rewilding" forests and ecosystems in order to rehabilitate areas damaged by human activity. They proposed this work be done by unemployed timber industry employees.[73] I find this idea fascinating. While EF! has been rightly criticized by some scholars for its dualistic thinking (seeming to separate humans from an otherwise pure and unfettered "nature"),[74] this proposal saw humans as an integral component in both the threats and the solutions to ecological sustainability. Moreover, Earth First!'s biocentric ethic is an example of an integrated worldview that comes closer to articulating what some scholars call "socionatures"—the ways in which human and nonhuman natures are deeply entwined, inseparable, mutually impactful.[75]

But EF! was rarely consistent and often reproduced the nature/culture divide. It was a site of pitched battles over its sexism and patriarchy, considered a hostile climate for women and feminists in its early days (perhaps unsurprising given that the movement's founders were all men who expressed a desire to live in a state of "primitive" and "tribal" bliss— a clichéd understanding of hierarchical, patriarchal gender relations as natural). One scholar studying Earth First! found the group completely overwhelmed by sexism and male domination, whether in forest campaigns, tree sits, or the everyday work settings inside and outside the movement's offices.[76] Women left the movement in droves, and similar racial dynamics have kept EF! almost lily white to this day.

The late 1980s and early 1990s ushered in a slow, but significant, change in the discourse around social difference and social justice within EF! Feminist and pro-labor EF! leader Judi Bari, along with Darryl Cherney, Mike Roselle, Karen Coulter, Pam Davis, and others, publicly rejected the anti-labor, patriotic, misanthropic, racist, and patriarchal biases of some of the movement's founders. They challenged the earlier "rednecks for wilderness" image celebrated within EF! and declared that an environmentalism without a critique of human oppressions was not revolutionary at all.[77] Veteran EF!er Karen Coulter told me she "was fairly instrumental and present when the split happened between the 'Formanistas' and more of the anarchist contingent." She describes herself as an anarchist and recalled that, "by that point, the majority of us were anarchists in sympathy," while the "Formanistas, or Dave Foreman types," were in the minority. She recalled a critical moment at one of EF!'s annual Round River Rendezvous gatherings. The divide between the besieged Formanistas and the growing number of EF!ers who embraced anarchism and social justice boiled over: the Formanistas were promoting the U.S. flag as a symbol the movement should revere. Nancy Foreman (Dave Foreman's wife) had a U.S. flag prominently displayed at a media table. Coulter says:

And we [the anarchist contingent] resented that because we thought the flag represented genocide. . . . And they [the Formanistas] were very nationalistic. And they revered Ed Abbey, who was a misogynist and a racist and . . . very anti-immigrant and so forth. So we were reacting against all of that.

In response, the anarchist/social justice wing burned a U.S. flag. They hung the "tattered, burned flag up on a juniper tree . . . and put a big . . . placard under it that stated why we rejected the flag as our symbol." Nancy Foreman tore it down. "And that was the beginning of the war." Coulter continued, recalling that legendary EF! activist Judi Bari took the exchange a step further:

So Judi Bari and [another] woman . . . went over to her [Nancy's] table, and they knew how to fold the flag ceremoniously. I mean, into the tricorner, the way flags are supposed to be treated if you respect them. So Judi played taps on her violin while the two of us did that, and left her flag folded up neatly with a note, [stating], "If we can't have our flag, you can't have your flag." And then, all hell kind of broke loose, and there was a big consensus meeting, which I was very much a part of. And the split formed . . . and was very definitive. And so we moved away from some of the macho posturing, which had fueled a lot of the women leaving in droves earlier. . . . So we moved away from a lot of the racism and misogyny that was associated with Ed Abbey and things like that. It was a very purposeful split.[78]

This social justice message spread throughout the ranks. "Second-generation" EF!ers like Mike Jakubal were beginning to articulate a worldview that was anticapitalist and anarchist, moving beyond the movement's fixation with "wilderness" preservation. It was an effort to redefine and challenge what "radical" environmentalism was and could be. At the same time, many EF! activists were moving away from property destruction (ecotage) and monkey wrenching toward an embrace of nonviolent direct action—"basically a lot of civil disobedience."[79] Even Bari was said to have denounced tree spiking, creating a major controversy among the old guard but opening up a space in which coalitional politics with labor and other movements could take root.[80] Soon after, EF! co-founder Mike Roselle founded what became one of the most effective offshoots of Earth First!—the Ruckus Society (founded in 1995), a nonviolent civil disobedience and direct action training organization that has been behind some of the most public global justice mobilizations in recent years and has collaborated with labor and social justice groups around the United States. These changes in EF! and in radical environmentalism formed part of the context for other important transformations.

Paul Watson is most famous for being the leader and founder of the Sea Shepherd Conservation Society (SSCS), a group that has recently enjoyed fame from its television series, *Whale Wars*. The SSCS was born a year before Earth First!, when Watson was pushed out of Greenpeace for his confrontational tactics with seal hunters.[81] Watson then received a grant from Cleveland Armory's Fund for Animals and funding from Britain's Royal Society for the Prevention of Cruelty to Animals to start SSCS. So it was AR groups who helped make the SSCS possible, even as it broke away from the world's largest and most visible environmental movement organization—Greenpeace.

While environmental groups like Greenpeace and Earth First! emphasize "wilderness" protection and restoration, the Sea Shepherds focus on specific endangered species such as seals, whales, and sharks.[82] They have harassed and rammed whaling ships, interfered with seal hunts, cut drift nets, and been labeled "eco-terrorists" by the FBI and numerous governments.[83] Members of SSCS were animal rights activists and largely delinked their activism from the wider ecological forces affecting the species they sought to defend, an unfortunate blind spot found across most of the AR movement.

Interestingly, Watson, SSCS's founder, has some social justice credentials, having lent support to the Black Power and Red Power movements, serving as a medical aide at the 1973 American Indian Movement (AIM) uprising at Wounded Knee. Since that time, however, he has generally focused on single-issue AR and environmental politics, even arguing for reductions in immigration to the United States because of his view that human "overpopulation" is harming ecosystems and wilderness habitat.[84] But because of its work in various ocean habitats on issues that many Americans see as "environmental" as much as "animal protection" oriented (particularly since Greenpeace is most well known for its work on whale protection and is one of the most recognized environmental organizations on the planet), the Sea Shepherds as a group serve as a conceptual "bridge" between animal rights and environmentalism. And despite its tactics being aimed at forcing various governments to simply obey existing endangered species protection laws (a reformist strategy), its daring and militant actions have also inspired a new generation of AR and environmental activists willing to up the tactical ante. Many of those newer activists would mobilize under the banners of the Earth Liberation Front (ELF) and the Animal Liberation Front (ALF).

The ALF, ELF, and Beyond

In March 1979, the ALF broke into an animal research laboratory at New York University Medical Center, removing a cat, two dogs, and two guinea pigs in its first publicized action in North America. This would be the first of many direct actions carried out by anonymous ALF cells. The movement gathered steam, and its actions are carefully planned and are rarely solved by the law enforcement community. The ALF has been labeled a "terrorist" group since at least 1986, when California's attorney general applied that term to it.[85] Like Stop Huntingdon Animal Cruelty (SHAC), the ALF in the United States was a British import (begun there in 1976), reflecting the growth of transnational AR movement networks and prompting even more attention from concerned governments and corporations. These groups represented a stark departure from animal welfarist politics in their willingness to use property destruction and illegal tactics to challenge animal exploitation.

A 1984 ALF action at the University of Pennsylvania Medical School was a pivotal moment in the evolution of the radical AR movement. In addition to destroying equipment used in controversial research on baboons to study the effects of severe head trauma, the activists found and removed hours of videotapes from the laboratory. PETA came into possession of those videos and produced a short film, *Unnecessary Fuss*, depicting the researchers as heartless and cruel overseers of violent experiments on innocent primates. The film proved both an effective message conveyance and recruiting tool.

ALF has been successful at avoiding the authorities largely because it is an underground movement with no national leaders, and it operates through autonomous, independent cells. As Best and Nocella explain:

> This decentered structure defies government infiltration and capture, and thereby thwarts the kind of success the FBI had in its illegal surveillance, penetration, and disruption of the Students for a Democratic Society, the Black Panthers, the American Indian Movement, the Committee in Solidarity with the People of El Salvador, and numerous other groups.[86]

A number of activists and scholars have argued that the very structure of the ALF lends itself to "overcoming hierarchy, patriarchy" and "has some key affinities with anarchism and radical feminism."[87] That may be wishful thinking, but the ALF does widely publicize guidelines for would-be activists, specifying that any group of vegetarians or vegans who carry out actions according to these guidelines can claim membership:

1. To liberate animals from places of abuse (i.e., laboratories, factory farms, fur farms, etc.) and place them in good homes where they may live out their natural lives, free from suffering.
2. To inflict economic damage to those who profit from the misery and exploitation of animals.
3. To reveal the horror and atrocities committed against animals behind locked doors, by performing non-violent direct actions and liberations.
4. To take all necessary precautions against harming any animal, both human and non-human.
5. To analyze the ramifications of any proposed action and never apply generalizations (e.g., all "blank" are evil) when specific information is available.[88]

The group's rhetorical appeal to fairness and justice helps underscore the link between animal liberation and human liberation. As one particularly memorable ALF communiqué declared:

> If we are trespassing, so were the soldiers who broke down the gates at Hitler's death camps; if we are thieves, so were the members of the Underground Railroad who freed the slaves of the South; and if we are vandals,

so were those who destroyed forever the gas chambers of Buchenwald and Auschwitz.[89]

While the exact origins of the Earth Liberation Front are disputed, what is clear is that a brand of radical environmental politics that far exceeded Earth First!'s boundaries was emergent in both the United Kingdom and the United States even before EF! developed. While SHAC and ALF were British imports to the United States, EF! migrated in the opposite direction in 1991. The following year, at a British EF! gathering in Brighton, a group of activists decided that in order to maintain EF!'s legitimacy and the strength of the larger movement, EF! should concentrate on mass demonstrations and civil disobedience, while another group—the ELF—would engage in illegal ecotage tactics.[90] The name was chosen to affiliate the environmentalist effort with its inspiration, the ALF.

The ELF first appeared in the United States in 1996. On Columbus Day, activists glued shut the locks at a Chevron gas station in Eugene, Oregon, and spray-painted "504 YEARS OF GENOCIDE" and "ELF" on the walls. The "504 years" tag references the colonization of the present-day United States, starting with Columbus's voyage in 1492. For several days after this first action, activists targeted McDonald's restaurants, gluing their locks shut to support the case of the "McLibel Two." The two British environmental activists had been sued for libel, in an event that shocked the legal community, after distributing leaflets claiming that McDonald's exploits its workers, supports the torture and murder of nonhuman animals, facilitates economic imperialism in the global South that results in human poverty and starvation, and harms ecosystems in various parts of the world. The action by the British activists and their ELF supporters in the United States signaled the emergence of the total liberation framework, while the lawsuit McDonald's brought against them became a model of corporate repression against social movements in the years to follow.[91]

An ELF communiqué made public over the Internet in early 1997 summed up much of what that group stood for:

Beltane 1997.[92] Welcome to the struggle of all species to be free. We are the burning rage of this dying planet. . . . ELF works to speed up the collapse of industry, to scare the rich, and to undermine the foundations of the

state. We embrace social and deep ecology as a practical resistance movement. We have to show the enemy that we are serious about defending
what is sacred. Together we have teeth and claws to match our dreams. Our
greatest weapons are imagination and the ability to strike when least
expected. Since 1992 a series of earth nights and Halloween smashes has
mushroomed around the world. 1000's of bulldozers, powerlines, computer
systems, buildings and valuable equipment have been composted. . . . We
take inspiration from Luddites, Levellers, Diggers, the Autonome squatter
movement, the ALF, the Zapatistas, and the little people—those mischie-
vous elves of lore. Authorities can't see us because they don't believe in elves.
We are practically invisible. We have no command structure, no spokespersons, no office, just many small groups working separately, seeking vulnerable targets and practicing our craft. . . . [L]et's dance as we make ruins of
the corporate money system.[93]

This message reflects the four pillars of the total liberation framework
discussed in the introduction: an ethic of justice and anti-oppression
linking all beings, anarchism, anticapitalism, and direct action.

While the ELF may have begun its work in the United States in 1996,
another radical ELF—the Environmental Life Force—was active many
years earlier, having formed in 1977. In August of that year, the Environmental Life Force targeted the Publishers' Paper Company in Oregon
City, a company that grew trees for pulp and used herbicides believed to
be a threat to salmon and other aquatic life. Local residents shared those
concerns and had protested earlier by chaining themselves to company
property. When they refused to leave, the company allegedly sprayed
them with the herbicide Tordon from a helicopter.[94] The ELF placed a
pipe bomb at the paper company headquarters. No one was hurt in the
incident, which was accompanied by a demand that the company provide medical monitoring and life-long health care for the local protesters.

John Hanna, the founder of the Environmental Life Force, explained
his personal and political rationale for starting a radical environmental
group:

The excessive and inappropriate use of toxic pesticides being applied to our
food and land was alarming. Cancer, birth defects, immune system failures,
and other diseases were increasing. . . . After my girlfriend became ill from
pesticide exposure in a cannery where she worked and I was sprayed by

Parathion, I responded with a direct and purposeful counter attack. It was a matter of self-defense and retaliation.[95]

Hanna believed that few options were available to people of good conscience and that "most people had become complacent," so "the need to launch a radical environmental movement seemed necessary."[96]

Hanna served time in federal prison for his actions, and although the "original ELF" (as he calls it) is no longer in existence, it left its mark. Today's ELF (Earth Liberation Front) is of a different generation but takes much of its inspiration from movements of earlier eras that advocated aggressive direct action. Leslie James Pickering served as a spokesperson for the North American Earth Liberation Front Press Office for several years and stated bluntly, "The ELF has a broad major goal: to stop the destruction and murder of life on the planet."[97] Modeled directly from the ALF guidelines, ELF lays out its own guidelines for activists who wish to undertake actions in its name:

1. To cause as much economic damage as possible to a given entity that is *profiting off the destruction of the natural environment and life* for selfish greed and profit.
2. To educate the public on the *atrocities committed against the environment and life.*
3. To take all necessary *precautions against harming life.*[98]

The ELF had deliberately distanced itself from many activists in the first generation of Earth First!ers who were unwilling or unable to articulate links between environmentalism and social justice. On this point, one ELF activist, Tara the Sea Elf, wrote in the *Earth First! Journal*:

ELF dumped the American baggage that had followed Earth First! to Britain, especially the macho, male-oriented "eco-warrior image," which was in American pioneering culture. ELF also disavowed the reactionary, apolitical rantings about population controls and immigration that some Earth First!ers in the U.S. were voicing. . . . ELF is not a "radical environmental group" . . . it is an ecological resistance movement that embraces eco-feminism, animal, earth, and human liberation. . . . [T]argets should be not only the vivisection labs, but also the very foundation of capitalism: the sources of profit.[99]

This message appeared during the first year of the Earth Liberation Front's activities in the United States, at the same time as Earth First! was demonstrating an embrace of social justice.

Earth and Animal Liberation Convergences

There have been numerous intersections, collaborations, and discursive convergences between radical environmental and animal liberation movements. Reports of joint ELF/ALF actions are frequent. At a 2002 congressional hearing, James F. Jarboe, the domestic terrorism section chief of the FBI's Counterterrorism Division, stated: "In 1993, the ELF was listed for the first time along with the ALF in a communiqué declaring solidarity in actions between the two groups."[100] In November 1997, the ALF and the ELF undertook a joint action involving arson at a Bureau of Land Management (BLM) horse corral near Burns, Oregon. Before burning the facility to the ground, the activists released more than five hundred wild horses and burros into the wild. The joint public statement read, in part:

> The Bureau of Land Management (BLM) claims they are removing non-native species from public lands (aren't white Europeans also non-native) but then they turn around and subsidize the cattle industry and place thousands of non-native domestic cattle on these same lands. . . . [This action was taken] to help halt the BLM's illegal and immoral business of rounding up wild horses from public lands and funneling them to slaughter. This hypocrisy and genocide against the horse nation will not go unchallenged!– Animal Liberation Front, Earth Liberation Front.[101]

While the decentralized structure of both groups means that any activist can claim to represent the ALF or the ELF, or both, the BLM action followed the guidelines of both groups.

There is much more evidence of convergence and collaboration between these movements. In many editions of radical animal liberation publications "eco-defense" political prisoners are listed alongside animal liberation prisoners to garner support (letter writing and advocacy) and call attention to state oppression. These publications also feature interviews with and articles by earth liberation activists who regularly draw links between the issues driving each movement.[102] Similarly, every issue of the *Earth First! Journal* published over the last several years has seen articles calling for the defense of critical endangered species habitats, updates on animal liberation campaigns, and listings of animal liberation prisoners.[103] Rod Coronado embodied these intersections in a rare but powerful way: he has been active in the Sea Shepherd Conservation Society, Earth First!, and the ALF.

The history of animal rights and environmentalist interactions is broader than one might expect. In the 1980s, AR advocates used environmental laws to delay the construction of animal research laboratories in northern California by arguing that the environmental impact statements they produced were incomplete—they did not take into account potential negative consequences on wildlife. The Animal League Defense Fund was able to stop California's mountain lion hunt by claiming that it failed to consider larger ecological concerns like habitat loss and wildfires.[104] The AR movement also borrowed heavily from the environmentalist penchant for public protest and sensationalist media tactics (most often associated with Greenpeace's banner drops against corporate and government targets, ships, buildings, and bridges), as well as direct mailing in order to build memberships and raise millions of dollars from supporters.[105]

I find that the ALF's rhetoric became much more open to social justice politics after ELF and Earth First! adopted that orientation. To be clear, with very few exceptions, these movements remain entirely white. Despite the efforts of those on the fringe to embrace and articulate a total liberation framework, they must constantly be checked and held accountable for the privileged categories of people who comprise their "membership" and their adherents.

Further, when I use the terms *radical* and *mainstream,* I want to avoid setting up a binary. I understand the environmental and animal rights movements as fluid groupings of tributaries, including radical, progressive, and mainstream activists (mirroring Jasper and Nelkin's welfarist, pragmatic, and fundamentalist elements). The same activist, group, and movement will often embrace elements of all three. But generally speaking: radicals seek to replace the existing political and economic system with something entirely different; progressives work within the system, but they demand changes within that system and employ nonviolent direct action and (sometimes) illegal tactical approaches; and mainstream groups work entirely within the current system.

For example, in the environmental movement, radicals would include EF! and the ELF; progressive groups would include Greenpeace and

Friends of the Earth; and mainstream groups include the Sierra Club and the Natural Resources Defense Council. In the animal rights/liberation movement, radicals would include the ALF, the Animal Rights Militia, and the Justice Department; progressives would include PETA and the Sea Shepherd Conservation Society; and mainstream groups would include the ASPCA and the Humane Society of the United States.

In truth, the lines between radical, progressive, and mainstream are often blurred. When pushed, many radicals will support "good" legislation and are willing to pressure the state and corporations to introduce policies that address some of their concerns. Many mainstream activists also understand the motivations of radicals and share many of their goals. Groups like PETA and the SSCS have frequently voiced support for radical ecological philosophies and radical groups and tactics, while groups I would label mainstream have often been called "extremist" by voices in government and industry.

Norm Phelps, a well-known author and welfarist AR activist, stated at a recent University of Minnesota conference, "Animal rights is the most radical social justice movement in history." This is a popular view among his peers, but it worries me: many of these mainstream activists view racism, patriarchy, and other forms of oppression within human communities as concerns of the past, casualties of successful social movements, so now the animal liberation effort is, as British AR activist Ronnie Webb called it, the "final frontier" and the "ultimate" freedom struggle.

Other activists are a bit more nuanced and reflective. One Earth First!er told me: "In biology, the radical of a seed is the germinating part of a seed. And . . . in Latin, it means 'root.' So I think for me, a radical analysis is to look at the root of a problem. . . . [But] I think what's really defining as a radical is an insistence of real change."[106] His view was echoed by many activists I interviewed, while others turned the definition on its head. Kim McCoy, an internationally renowned AR activist with the SSCS, stated:

What's really radical is the rate at which animals—marine animals in this case—are being wiped off the face of the planet. So, you know, what's radical is that people are standing by and allowing whales to be murdered in a whale sanctuary, in direct contravention to a number of established international laws. What's radical is that a hundred million sharks are being killed every year. What's radical is that 325,000 or more baby seals are being clubbed to death and sometimes skinned alive in Canada, and that that's a government-subsidized industry. So those are the things that are truly radical, and what Sea Shepherd does—try and defend the creatures against that onslaught—certainly pales in comparison.[107]

For McCoy, the actions of activists are not extreme; the *problems* they seek to address are. Ben Rosenfeld, a longtime attorney for EF!, built on McCoy's perspective, stating:

> You know, you could define Earth First! as fairly conservative. Conservation is conservative. Trying to preserve life on earth is conservative. You know, radical is logging to infinity, and polluting the terrain in which we live to the point where we actually affect climate on a global scale—that's radical. Earth First! is conservative compared to that.[108]

There is also an interesting temporal dimension to defining radicalism, as Chris Irwin—an environmentalist working on issues ranging from recycling to mountain top removal in Appalachia—reminded me: "Well, what's interesting is what was 'radical' way back when is mainstream now."[109] He recounted how he was considered a "fruit loop" in the late 1980s for starting a neighborhood recycling program.

Even within radical earth and animal liberation movements, the dominant frame has long been what I call the "(non)human natures first" orientation. The rights of "nature" and "animals" are not linked to human rights, social justice, or oppression within human communities (see chapter 2). This perspective is slowly being challenged but serves as an enduring example of how radical movements can perpetuate inequalities. The total liberation frame is a relatively recent development and does not represent the majority activist view, but it signals a productive effort among activists to articulate linkages among systems of power for the possibility of transformative social change. When all oppression is linked, total liberation becomes thinkable—a future possibility to fulfill the idea of "liberty and justice for all."

CHAPTER 2

Justice for the Earth and All Its Animals

If you had to choose one word to characterize the nature of human society as it is currently arranged worldwide, there is no better word than "injustice."

—Daniel Dorling, *Injustice: Why Social Inequality Persists*

In chapter 1, I explored how radical animal liberation and environmental justice movements are fueled. The activists respond to a call for action and are often disillusioned with what they see as ineffective, overly compromising politics associated with mainstream organizations. Radical activists also draw on a long history of social movements and the politics of social justice, as well as grassroots organizing and ideas that took hold within academic disciplines.

The total liberation frame is composed of an ethic of justice and antioppression for people, nonhuman animals, and ecosystems; anarchism; anticapitalism; and an embrace of direct action tactics. Essentially: direct action for justice in a world not bound by the rules of government or market. Total liberation is not necessarily the dominant frame in the movements I consider here, but it is one of the primary frames and suggests a number of new directions relevant to scholars working in the fields of environmental and environmental justice studies, ethnic studies, critical animal studies, and social movement theory. The focus of this chapter is the first dimension of total liberation.

"(Nonhuman) Nature First" Narratives

Even in the radical wings, elitist, patriarchal, racist, and homophobic elements are strong in animal rights and environmental movements. In writings, speeches, and actions, activists reproduce inequalities and social hierarchies (often unwittingly). The total liberation framework is, in part, a response to this reality.

Many groups have limited themselves through what I call the "(non-human) nature first" narrative. Within this narrative, the goal for activists is to "save" wilderness, the environment, and nonhuman animals from exploitation and extinction. Activists focus only on issues narrowly related to ecosystems and nonhumans since humans can more easily advocate for themselves, while nonhuman species and nonhuman nature cannot (for a number of years, a popular animal liberation blog was titled "voiceofthevoiceless"). Concerns for social justice—that is, justice for humans—are an impediment in this approach, particularly because the poor and people of color are (implicitly and sometimes explicitly) viewed as part of the problem since such a small percentage of those populations are vegan or active in these ecological movements. This worldview necessarily makes it difficult to imagine or produce alliances with social justice movements.

At the 1987 Round River Rendezvous (an annual gathering of environmentalists), Earth First! (EF!) founder Dave Foreman and fellow EF! activist and author Edward Abbey described the peoples of Latin America and the Caribbean as backward and primitive. Abbey went on to publish his favorite essay, "Immigration and Liberal Taboos," in his 1988 book, *One Life at a Time, Please*. This man who inspired so many to activism alienated many when he wrote in that essay that "it might be wise for us as American citizens to consider calling a halt to the mass influx of even more millions of hungry, ignorant, unskilled and culturally-morally-genetically impoverished people."[1] As Earth First!ers denounced that portion of Abbey and Foreman's legacy, the damage had been done, and many knew these men were far from alone in their nativist and racists views. Perhaps most controversially, the focus of most of these discussions is on the reproductive capacity of women of color, immigrants in the United States, and women of the global South. These "others" are seen as drivers of overpopulation. One EF!er's comment assured me the issue was still part of the group's rhetoric:

> The other real hot-button issue is breeding in our circle. I don't know if you met "Jason" at the rendezvous, but he refers to babies as "earth stomping shit machines." Now I wouldn't necessarily walk into a maternity ward

and start throwing that around, but I understand that perspective very well. Because a lot of it really comes down to consumption.[2]

As my research assistant, Hollie Nyseth Brehm (who coauthored chapter 4 in this book), and I drove to the 2009 EF! Round River Rendezvous, we picked up two hitchhikers. They were Chicana activists, and when we mentioned that we were scholars doing research on EF! and social justice issues, one mentioned, "I have a friend who decided not to go to the 'Rondy' this year because she has a child and was told that EF! activists don't like 'breeders.'"[3] The other activist told us she knew another woman who had gone to a "Rondy" "back in the day and had a bad experience in terms of other activists' views of children and population growth." Both women expressed hope that things were changing.

These discourses pervade much of the environmental movement, and in other writings Lisa Park and I call this phenomenon "nativist environmentalism," because it is a perspective that comfortably embraces both anti-immigration and ecological politics.[4] Population control theories mesh nicely with some radical environmentalists' misanthropic fantasies of human population die-offs. On rare occasions, people of color and others who are the focus of such visions are witness to such bigotry. Veteran EF! activist Storm recounted an incident from 1995, when EF! invited members of the Black Panther Party to the Rendezvous. As Panthers and EF!ers gathered around a campfire, several EF! activists "who are really into the whole human extinction trip coined this little song about [the] Ebola [virus] because Ebola had broke out in Africa and it really was looking like something that could wipe out the human race." According to Storm, the persons singing the song were "drunk . . . all white . . . and started singing . . . 'Ebola's our salvation.'" The African Americans present "immediately walked away" in disgust. With dismay, Storm recalled, "I was standing off into the distance watching all this and I realized . . . people don't realize how insensitive that is. Right now this Ebola thing is only killing poor black people."[5]

Another incident occurred in Miami in 2006, when Storm lived in a "collective commune house" with "a bunch of activists . . . and radical queer folk and artists and musicians." One of the persons in the house was "a rather fiery, young, urban, black woman who was involved with APOC, which is Anarchist People of Color." Storm was telling a story about a person "who had been trying to infiltrate our circles and who was probably some kind of undercover" agent:

> And the term that I used to describe this undercover was, I said, "Yeah, we think he was probably a spook." . . . And then she said, you know, "Are you aware that's a racial slur?" And I says, "Oh yeah, yeah. I'm really sorry. I just wanted—this is what I was referring to." And she said, "I know what you were referring to." And then she said, "You eco-people have to monitor your language." So I think this is where—often, too often, whenever Earth First! opens its mouth, it ends up with one foot or the other in it.[6]

Storm is a rarity in that he is a white activist who is open to receiving criticism, even when it is blunt. Jade (a pseudonym)—a former EF! activist and woman of color involved in many Bay Area social and environmental justice groups—stated: "I have nothing to do anymore with Earth First! It was one of the most racist settings I've ever known."[7] In that sense, environmental movements are no different from the larger society in which they are anchored, and that is troubling on many levels.

Unintentional racism is no less harmful than blatant racism in the animal rights (AR) movement, either. At a recent national Animal Rights Conference (ARC), a speaker on a panel titled "Engaging Ethnic Minorities" boldly told the audience about his approach to cross-cultural cooperation:

> And you also get drunk with them. . . . Latin people love to dance. They love to party. Go dance and party with them. Get to know each other on a basic, basic level. I mean, it's really silly to say, but no, it's really true . . . it really takes a lot of bonding on a more personal level to be able to change and work with a community.[8]

Most likely, this person genuinely wants to work toward animal liberation and believes his organization is offering good, sociable advice—instead, they offer a classic liberal racist approach to working with people of color populations. The stereotype of Latinos dancing and drinking heavily is offensive and would likely be met with revulsion by this target population. Rather than endearing any Latino activist, that viewpoint could result in the wholesale rejection of whatever it is the AR activist hopes to achieve within a given community.

In another example, troubling AR rhetoric is notably evident in the 1988 film *Black Harvest*, though one might not notice it at first. The movie tells of the annual pilot whale slaughter in the Faroe Islands (near Denmark) and of the local people who seek to preserve this centuries-old tradition. The annual "harvest" dates back several centuries to when the Faroe Islanders first sought an abundant protein source. Every year, young men from the island still wade into the shallow waters of the bay to kill hundreds of whales, haul them to shore, butcher them, and distribute the flesh to the community for consumption. The film features the stories of wildlife conservationists and activists who are members of the Sea Shepherd Conservation Society (SSCS), who work to save the whales from extinction. For years, AR activists and conservationists, including SSCS, have tried to put an end to this practice on the grounds that it is cruel and unnecessary since, in the present era, the Faroe Islanders have multiple sources of protein.

The Faroe harvest is still a hot-button issue. In the spring of 2009 (nearly twenty years after the release of *Black Harvest*), I received an email from a colleague. It had been circulating among activists in the AR and environmentalist communities for a number of years:

> The Red Sea in Denmark: APPALLING, SHOCKING and UNBELEIV-ABLE!!! Why is the European Union so quiet about this? Where is Green Peace [*sic*], who make so much noise in other countries. . . . This happens only in uncivilized Denmark. DENMARK: WHAT A SHAME, A SAD SCENE. THIS MAIL HAS TO BE CIRCULATED. THERE IS NO WORSE BEAST THAN MAN!!!! While it may seem incredible, even today this custom continues . . . in the Faroe Islands, (Denmark). A country supposedly "civilized" and an EU country at that. For many people this attack to life is unknown—a custom to "show" entering adulthood. It is absolutely atrocious. No one does anything to prevent this barbarism being committed against . . . an intelligent dolphin that is placid and approaches humans out of friendliness. Make this atrocity known and hopefully stopped.[9]

The photos accompanying this message are disturbing: villagers look on as others slaughter pilot whales, turning the seawater a gruesome red. But as I separated the images from the message, I became troubled by its content as well, particularly from the perspective of activists who wish to build movements for both animal liberation and social justice. It dawned on me that this message insulted the people of the Faroe Islands by assuming they were a vile and cruel population, avoiding questions of sustenance and historical practices. It implied that Europeans must be civilized (presumably other regions of the globe are not and need not be) and, ironically, seemed to suggest that these *particular* creatures should be spared slaughter because they are apparently more intelligent and friendlier than other species. When I stopped to think about it, the depths of insensitivity, racism, and even speciesism in this message are astounding. They present little hope for building common cause between AR and social justice movements.

The single-issue (nonhuman) nature first orientation reflects a serious absence of attention to social and environmental justice concerns and is a primary reason for the rise of the total liberation framework, which articulates a more transformative challenge: the oppression of humans, nonhumans, and ecosystems are linked and must be thrown off simultaneously.

"I think it's totally possible to be against the corporations that engage in unnecessary animal cruelty, and also fight against the way that the police are unrestrained in the black community," Claude Marks told me. "That isn't an inherent contradiction. But it takes some initiative to both arrive at that understanding and to do something about it."[10] Beginning in the late 1990s, there was increasing evidence of a convergence between radical earth and animal liberation activists around a call for justice and anti-oppression politics focused on people, nonhuman animals, *and* ecosystems.[11] They sought to acknowledge the harms that humans regularly perpetrate against ecosystems and nonhuman animals as reflective of and linked to systems of oppression *within* human society, and this thesis was influenced by a number of intellectual and political forces including the New Ecological Paradigm, deep ecology, ecofeminism, social ecology, and environmental justice.

Earth and animal liberation activists drew on these ideas and theories in their public speeches, in discussions and presentations at gatherings and conferences, in their writings and publications, in their actions, and in their interviews with me and my research team. For some activists, an ethic of justice was linked to a language of "rights"; for others, the language of "liberation" was more appropriate. Despite differences in terminology, activists using the total liberation frame came to agree that ecosystems, nonhuman animals, and people should be free of oppression and injustice.

There are infinite ways to define justice, but if radical movements aim to confront the roots of a problem, it would follow that justice might be described as the elimination or prevention of conditions that produce injustice. As the Earth Liberation Front (ELF) declared, "The only way to stop the symptoms of the problem is to identify the main root cause and directly work to abolish it."[12] This is a critical starting point for these movements.

Beyond Single-Issue Politics

Anti-Oppression and Justice for Ecosystems

Every activist I spoke with believed the earth and its constituent ecosystems have value in and of themselves. In a letter to the *EF! Journal*, an activist wrote: "we must break though the brainwashing to see the world as it truly is—deeply complex and beautiful, interwoven and interdependent—and to see our place in it."[13] Another issue of the journal quoted the late naturalist Mardy Murie, who once asked: "Having finished all the requisites of our proud, materialistic civilization, our neon-lit society, does nature, which is the basis for our existence, have the right to live on? Do we have enough reverence for life to concede to wilderness this right?"[14]

Craig Rosebraugh, a former spokesperson for the North American Earth Liberation Front Press Office (NAELFPO), submitted the following as part of his testimony to the U.S. Congress at a hearing on radical environmental movements:

> The National Forests in the United States contain far more than just trees. In fact, more than 3,000 species of fish and wildlife, in addition to 10,000 plant species, have their habitat within the National Forests. This includes at least 230 endangered plant and animal species. All of these life forms co-exist symbiotically to naturally create the rich and healthy ecosystems needed for life to exist on this planet.[15]

And Storm came to realize that defending the earth and securing justice for ecosystems require decentering human society. He explained, "I mean, we come at it from an ecocentric perspective, which says that humans aren't any more important than anything else, and we're not."[16] While this language strongly resembles deep ecology, within radical environmental circles it also brings an urgency and call for direct action generally absent from traditional writings on deep ecology (see chapter 4). Direct action suggests certain entities are responsible for ecological harm and can be forced to cease such practices, if held accountable. The ELF website's Frequently Asked Questions (FAQ) says: "The ELF realizes that the destruction of life is not a mere random occurrence but a deliberate act of violence performed by those entities concerned with nothing more than pursuing extreme economic gain at any cost."[17]

Nik Hensey has been active in both animal and earth liberation movements for years, having worked with EF!, Viva!USA, and the SSCS. His view on deep ecology is a fitting segue:

> I consider myself a deep ecologist. . . . I think that the environment, the planet, you know, nature has an inherent value apart from the financial value that's placed on it. Just in the same way that an animal has a life and value independent of how much his or her skin is worth or how much milk she can produce. Taking that approach . . . you would have to have a . . . philosophy of trying to achieve complete liberation or freedom or cessation of exploitation.[18]

Anti-Oppression and Justice for Nonhumans

Ecosystems are interdependent webs of existence. Accordingly, for many activists, justice for ecosystems includes or extends to a focus on justice for nonhuman animals. Similar to the way that activists value ecosystems in their own right, nonhuman animals are seen as worth more than the value of their meat, skin, or labor. Activists told me they felt a special need to focus on animals as they are "voiceless" in our formal political system.

Paul Shapiro, founder of Compassion Over Killing and vice president of Farm Animal Protection at the Humane Society of the United States said: "In the animal protection movement, we have a situation where animals are not capable of organizing on behalf of themselves. They're completely reliant on us to voluntarily give up the power that we have over them for altruistic reasons."[19] Similarly, Norm Phelps—an AR activist and author—explained:

> The issue was moral parity for nonhuman sentient beings. Animals are the most helpless of the helpless, and they are completely defenseless against organized, systemitized, technologized human predation. They love, live, and fear death, seek joy and dread suffering as much as we do. Their lives

and their suffering matter as much as ours, and yet every custom and every institution in our society are lined up against them. It is an outrage.[20]

Phelps's outrage was mirrored in the words of many other interviewees who think the fact that most Americans eat cows and pigs while keeping dogs and cats as pets is hypocritical and unjust. One activist recalled his attempt to explain this problem to a friend:

> I said, "What would you do if there was a trap on your property or on the boundaries of your property . . . and you found out that your cat got trapped in a leg hold trap?" He said, "I would immediately free it." I said, "Well, what if the trap . . . was set legally on public property?" He said, "Well, I would still free it." . . . And I said, "To me, every cat is your cat. Every dog is your dog. Every mink is your mink. They have every right to live on this planet."[21]

Lauren Ornelas is one of the few people of color with a national reputation in the AR movement. She directs the Food Empowerment Project, an organization that highlights issues of justice and oppression that connect farm animals to farm workers, consumers, and ecosystems.[22] She told me what drives many activists like her is the simple fact that "people want to try and stop suffering. . . . It's about fighting an injustice. And all these injustices don't even have to take place."[23] Peter Young, an ALF activist who spent time in federal prison for releasing thousands of animals from fur farms, stated: "people that abuse animals, they're bullies. And I just very much hate bullies. I feel like it's just the duty of anybody to intervene in an injustice when they know it's happening all around them."[24]

I asked activists what they thought was driving the exploitation, consumption, and destruction of nonhuman life. Many said the root of the problem is a deep cultural phenomenon: speciesism, or "an attitude of bias in favor of the interests of members of one's own species and against those of other species."[25] Veda Stram, a veteran AR activist, author, and atheist who works for the Christian AR group AllCreatures.org, told a story:

> I had a really big insight a couple years ago about [how] deep speciesism is. As I was driving down the road one day and there was a dead raccoon on the side of the road. And I thought, "Oh, isn't that too bad." And, "Oh, if

we didn't have roads." And, "Why can't they build little fences?" And, "These poor wild animals." But I didn't do anything. If there was a human being lying dead on the side of the road, I would have stopped. . . . [I] would have squealed on the brakes immediately . . . that's how embedded speciesism is . . . how deep it is.[26]

Shapiro explained that speciesism is difficult to acknowledge and challenge:

You have a real problem in the fact that most people not only believe in human supremacy, but they are unwilling to diverge from a status quo that leaves us with quite a lot of privilege. . . . [P]ower seldom yields anything without a demand. And it's very infrequent when groups in power voluntarily give up the power they have over those who are more vulnerable.[27]

Josh Harper, an animal liberation activist who spent time in federal prison for his role in the Stop Huntingdon Animal Cruelty (SHAC) campaign, expressed how overwhelming speciesism can be:

I mean, you reach this point when you're an animal rights activist where you are such a statistically insignificant part of the population. You know, where everywhere you go, people are wrapped in the skins of creatures that you consider your equals. And you walk in the store, and it's a fucking atrocity exhibit everywhere you turn. You reach this point where you feel like no one cares. You know? No one cares . . . because there has never been a human holocaust in history that can compare to the number of animal lives taken in one year. I mean, there's nothing. I mean, we kill more animals every year—every single year—than humans have ever walked on this planet. If you were to chain up and kill every person who ever lived—every human who ever lived!—you would not equal the number of animals killed for food. In one, single, year.[28]

Katie (a pseudonym), a lawyer and former ALF activist, found some good in the issue: it pushes people to rethink what it means to be human: "I think . . . we have to stop looking at ourselves as humans and these other creatures as 'animals.' We're animals."[29] Katie expresses what some scholars have called biocentrism or a posthumanist politics—one that questions the dominionist understanding of humans as the rightfully dominant species on earth.[30] Celebrated earth and animal liberation activist Rod Coronado has said:

> Animal liberation and Earth defense to me is not the end product of any philosophical progression. . . . It is simply what I believe to be an obligation as a member of the most destructive species on earth. . . . It is my attempt to rekindle the most ancient of relations . . . where [humans] sat within the circle of all life rather than apart from and above it.[31]

For activists who embrace total liberation, that "circle of life" must include a demand for justice and freedom for humans as well.

Anti-Oppression and Justice for Humans

Environmental and animal rights movements have rightly been accused of prioritizing the protection of nonhuman animals and ecosystems over the needs of human beings, particularly communities of color, working-class populations, immigrants, and Indigenous peoples. While elitism and exclusion are certainly intertwined within the histories of the environmental and animal rights movements,[32] members of the radical wings of each movement have recently begun to grapple with issues like whiteness, racism, patriarchy, social class inequalities, homophobia, nativism, and social privilege. In other words, these activists are integrating a serious social justice critique into their politics—a core element of the total liberation frame. As ecofeminist and AR activist-scholar pattrice jones explains: "We don't live in a vacuum. Racism occurs in the same world that animal exploitation occurs."[33]

As noted in chapter 1, within some AR and environmental movement circles, the commitment to human liberation has a long history. Consider John Hanna, the founder of the Environmental Life Force. He described why his group opposed the production and application of pesticides by agricultural industries: "All people, all ethnicities and classes were being victimized by having their food poisoned with pesticides. We wanted to put an end to ecocide and supported everyone's right to a poison free diet."[34]

In March 1977, Hanna's group shot a BB gun at the windows of California senator Dianne Feinstein's vacation home to protest the government's unwillingness to provide decent medical care at San Francisco city and county jails. They were responding to the death of Larry Davis, an

African American man who passed away in jail from medical neglect for his diabetes. The group sent a message to local media explaining their rationale. Hanna remembers:

> Larry Davis's death was fully avoidable and underscored ongoing government abuse of the underprivileged and minority classes. It's the same official disdain that allows powerful chemical companies to despoil the land and poison farm workers and consumers. Larry Davis, like all of earth's creatures, deserved protection. A simple medical screening program at the San Francisco county jails would have saved Larry Davis from dying. . . . Eventually, a medical screening program was implemented. It would be rewarding to know if the ELF action actually helped.[35]

The Environmental Life Force's commitment to linking justice for ecosystems with justice for humans offered an early model for total liberation.

Numerous activists noted that making the links between the exploitation of ecosystems or nonhuman animals and humans depended upon recognizing the role of privilege—especially their own—as humans and as members of largely white, middle-class social movements. Kim McCoy, an animal rights and environmental activist with the SSCS, said when she looks around at activist meetings, most of the attendees "don't need to worry about their basic needs. They don't need to worry about whether they're going to get kicked out of the country, where they're going to sleep at night, where their food is coming from."[36] This privilege, left unexamined, can leave a movement unable to attract a diverse range of supporters and insensitive to oppression within its own ranks.

Hensey, mentioned earlier, was critical of how this privilege plays out in interactions with working-class people and communities of color when white AR activists attempt to share their views on animal liberation. He recalled a time when he and other activists protested animal exploitation at a circus where many immigrants and people of color were the audience members. He recalled embarrassment: "a bunch of just, like, white people rolling up in their cars and . . . passing out fliers and telling people not to go to the circus . . . something didn't sit right with me." Going further, Hensey said:

> On a strategic level, I mean, our literature's [only] in English, which is insane. I think it's kind of patriarchal. I think it's kind of ethnocentric to go

into another community, and I think, unfortunately, that's by and large for years what the animal rights movement did, you know, tell people what they should and shouldn't do, rather than trying to build bridges.[37]

Beyond individual campaigns, some fear tunnel vision as a threat to the whole movement. EF! activist Storm remembers early resistance to the call to embrace social justice politics:

> There was a lot of people who were basically indulging in their white, upper-middle class, primarily male privilege who really didn't want to confront these issues. It was too much for them. And they were resistant to change. And I as an Earth First!er [felt] that we need to be dealing with wilderness and biodiversity issues while at the same time confronting oppression within our circles simultaneously, or we will fail at both simultaneously.[38]

Many EF!ers got that message and embrace it. Others still struggle.

The Boston Animal Defense League consciously builds ties with a range of other movements to promote total liberation. This includes groups like Food Not Bombs and the Boston Anarchist Black Cross. In a statement that appeared in one activist publication, they write:

> The Boston Animal Defense League subscribes to the idea of total liberation and collective organization. All forms of oppression must be uprooted, from the exploitation of the Earth to the destruction of human and nonhuman animals. We have to get to the root of our exploitation if we are to combat it effectively. For this reason, we constantly traverse movements that are often seen as separate struggles, including ecofeminism, deep ecology and workers rights, and reject sexism, racism, homophobia and capitalism in the spirit of mutual aid. We are all in this movement together, in One Struggle, One Fight![39]

Many activists are learning from past and current tensions with Indigenous communities and people of color arising from offensive and insensitive campaigns, tactics, language, and behavior. They have decided one of the most important approaches to movement building should be developing anti-oppression and antiracist principles and practices within their ranks.[40] EF! created an official EF! Anti-Oppression Policy, published in 2007. It reads, in part:

The *Earth First! Journal* editorial collective recognizes that the institutional, economic, political, social and cultural dynamics of hierarchy, power and privilege that define mainstream society also permeate the radical environmental movement. These dynamics are expressed in various interlocking systems of oppression (e.g., racism, sexism, classism, heterosexism, ageism, ableism, speciesism, etc.), which prevent equal access to resources and safety, disrupt healthy communities and movement building, and severely— sometimes irreparably—harm our allies, our friends, our loved ones and ourselves. Over the years, the *Journal* has featured a growing number of articles addressing the need to challenge these systems of oppression. This is a reflection of the editorial collective's understanding that implicit in our desire to stop the domination and exploitation of the Earth is a need to create communities that are free of oppressive social relations. We understand that failing to address oppressive behavior not only weakens our movement by alienating and further victimizing our friends and allies, it also calls into question our commitment to a better world and our qualification as a radical movement. For these reasons, the *Earth First! Journal* editorial collective has drafted this policy of active opposition to oppressive behavior of all kinds within the editorial collective, the *Journal* community and the pages of the *Journal* itself.[41]

While EF!'s anti-oppression policy has a detailed rationale, it is short on specifics. The Cascadia Forest Alliance (CFA)—a group of radical environmental activists in the Pacific Northwest region—is more detailed in its policy, including a four-stage process for resolving disputes: "initial warning," "intervention," "commitments and ejection," and "follow up." In order to prevent "campaign hopping," the CFA policy states "someone who has been asked to leave the group because of oppressive behavior will be identified to other campaigns, as well as the activist community at large." The "follow up" stage involves activists ensuring that the survivor of the oppressive behavior is receiving any support or services they need.[42]

The anti-oppression policies of the *EF! Journal* and the CFA are groundbreaking, but do they have "teeth"? In other words, what are the consequences? Have CFA-type "ejection" protocols been enforced? To some extent, yes. For example, the conscious split between the "Formanistas" (activists in EF! founder Dave Foreman's ideological camp) and the anarchists/feminists in EF! represented the application of consequences for violations even before EF! formalized its policy. The Formanistas created a group and publication called *Wild Earth*, while the social justice wing of the movement retained the name EF! and took over the journal. In 2003, a group called the Cascadia Forest Defenders (CFD) announced that it was withdrawing its support from the Fall Creek tree village protest camp near Eugene, Oregon. An *EF! Journal* article explained:

> At the heart of the issue is the fact that Fall Creek base camp participants have allowed and will continue to allow people who have a recent history of sexual violence to participate in the campaign. After a meeting was held to discuss these concerns, Fall Creek refused to adopt an anti-oppression policy and requested to separate from CFD.[43]

The animal rights movement offers another example. At a recent Grassroots Animal Rights Conference (GARC), a male activist sexually assaulted a female activist. The female reported the incident and—following the GARC's sexual assault policy—fellow (male) activists confronted and expelled the attacker. When the offender attempted to reenter the conference the following day, he was expelled again. The GARC publicized the incident—including a photograph and the name of the perpetrator— to warn other women in the movement and reiterate its zero tolerance stance regarding sexual assault (inside and outside the movement). Writing about this incident, pattrice jones stated:

> When sexual assault occurs within activist movements—which it too often does—both the survivor and the movement are hurt. . . . The activists involved in this project see the exploitation of women, the Earth and animals as different elements of the same crime. That violation is at the root of all forms of violence. Only when we undo it can we liberate the Earth, animals and ourselves.[44]

The GARC is an above-ground group with open meetings, but I have also seen consequences for oppressive behavior and language in the underground animal liberation movement. In another example of intramovement discipline, the North American Animal Liberation Press Office (NAALPO) issued a press release titled "In Defense of Total Liberation" that castigated a group of animal liberation activists for racist language. The Chinese Business Association of Toronto had received a letter from a group calling itself Animal Liberation Canada/USA concerning a recent ban on the sale of shark fins, considered a delicacy by many restaurant goers. NAALPO stated that the "'communiqué' was shamefully shot through with slurs, crude generalizations and racially charged rhetoric directed towards Toronto's Chinese community and Chinese communities worldwide." NAALPO described the message as "blatant and disturbingly racist" and, in response, detailed the work of Chinese animal liberationists who are "fighting for their non-human brothers and sisters everyday [including] liberations and open rescues [that] have occurred in broad daylight." The NAALPO message then declared:

> In the strongest possible terms, we as animal liberationists denounce any ideology, communiqué or action that seeks to simplify animal or human oppression when it is an undeniable fact that part of the social group being blamed for such atrocities is itself opposed to the very practice. For example, not all Chinese people are responsible for shark finning, in the very same way that not all Americans are responsible for the wars in Iraq and Afghanistan.[45]

The press release continued by articulating the total liberation view that multiple forms of oppression are linked:

> Racism and racial generalizations perpetuate speciesism, and vice versa, due to the fact that such stereotypes and classifications have been closely intertwined throughout history and have been used to degrade one group or another. People are compared to "undesirable" non-human animals and associated with their perceived behaviors e.g. the Jewish Holocaust and rat references, with similar slurs also prevalent in the U.S. during WWII towards Japanese people. . . . As liberationists, we must embrace the fight and struggle for liberation of all oppressed beings on the planet. Since our struggles are interconnected, the liberation of one cannot be achieved without the liberation of the other. We would only continue to perpetuate a hierarchical ordering of beings if we fought to eradicate speciesism but not racism, sexism but not classism, heterosexism not speciesism, so on and so forth. We have one common goal: to liberate ourselves and others from the systemic injustices of modernity.[46]

In May 2013, the *EF! Journal* even repudiated Deep Green Resistance (DGR) movement leaders Lierre Keith and others when it was discovered that they had made or supported statements that were degrading to transgender people. DGR and its literary founder Derrick Jensen have enjoyed notoriety for supporting armed resistance and the dismantling of industrial civilization to achieve ecological sustainability. Unfortunately, they have always suffered from a lack of analysis of intersecting oppressions, and this episode confirmed what many people had already suspected. Aric McBay, the primary author of the book *Deep Green Resistance*, publicly severed ties with DGR: "I left the organization at the beginning of 2012 after a trans inclusive policy was cancelled by Derrick Jensen and Lierre Keith . . . transphobia–like racism and sexism and classism and homophobia—is a poison that those in power use to destroy movements and ruin lives."[47]

Buttressing official and unofficial anti-oppression policies, I frequently heard the discourse of anti-oppression in casual conversations, at workshops, on panels, and in activist literature. At the EF! Round River Rendezvous, I found a trove of literature including a pamphlet entitled "What Is White Supremacy?"[48] and many more newsletters and zines on the subjects of Indigenous solidarity, genocide, feminism, anarchy, the prison industrial complex, and pro-immigration politics. The workshops scheduled included sessions on anti-oppression and queer and Native solidarity.

The Trans and Womyn's Action Camp (TWAC) is another EF!-sponsored annual gathering and is designed to be a safe space for LGBTQ activists who have a growing voice and presence in radical ecology movements. My colleague and research assistant Hollie Nyseth Brehm spent several days at the TWAC in 2009 and offered the following account in her field notes:

> There are about twenty people at the Oppression workshop. We begin by defining oppression. The facilitator asks the audience for suggestions, and people throw out ideas like domination, something that someone/thing benefits from, discrimination, systems. Someone else points out the intersections of oppression, and the facilitator says that all oppression is intersected. She then shares her definition of oppression, which is: privilege + power + prejudice = oppression.[49]

While the TWAC is evidence of an acknowledgment of the many ways that women, queer folk, and transgender persons can more effectively participate in these movements, people of color have also organized within radical environmentalist ranks. In a "report back" from the 2008 EF! Rendezvous, a group calling itself the People of Color Caucus wrote "We See Color and It Fucking Matters." The report includes a list of grievances, beginning with "Earth First! is a predominantly white movement" and including "unchecked white privilege," "rampant cultural appropriation/fetishizing Indigenous cultures," and "tokenization." These are all problems for which the environmental movement and EF! are notorious. What is striking here is that there are *enough* people of color to have a caucus and that the *EF! Journal*'s editorial staff allowed or encouraged them to write this open letter.

The People of Color Caucus offered numerous suggestions for moving EF! forward, including continuing to hold anti-oppression and anti-racist workshops at the annual gatherings and insisting on a "more open conversation and analysis of our movement's culture." They urged readers and fellow activists "to realize that we cannot build a strong and powerful movement to oppose environmental destruction without incorporating a deep understanding of the links between ecocide and all other forms of oppression."[50]

Solidarity Work and Alliance Politics

One prominent way that activists grapple with privilege and social justice politics is to work in solidarity or declare solidarity with communities on the front lines of environmental racism, assaults on Indigenous sovereignty, homophobia, and patriarchy. Still, while there are numerous examples of white middle-class heterosexual activists working together with other communities on various goals, too many of those cases have ended with charges of homophobia, racism, patriarchy, insensitivity, elitism, and blindness to privilege and hierarchy. Many activists are working to repair some of the damage while building real bridges, but it is never easy.

During the 2009 EF! Roadshow in Minneapolis, EF! activists reminded the audience that they have collaborated with the Indigenous Environmental Network and the Common Ground Collective—two organizations with strong credibility for their work on environmental and social justice in communities of color facing a range of assaults from states and corporations.[51] The EF! activists stated that challenging racism and patriarchy are core values of the movement, and that this includes acting in solidarity with Indigenous peoples to protect their lands and with environmental justice organizations in communities of color to challenge gentrifiers and evictions.

During the EF! Roadshow, there was a workshop on challenging social privilege and being allies across various communities. The organizers of the Roadshow asked those in attendance: "How does the movement privilege white, male, middle class, able bodied youth?" Answers were varied: "the focus on climbing and other physically strenuous actions"; "the financial means to protest during work hours"; "valorization of direct action, which privileges able bodied people"; "the idea that U.S. radicals are the only ones who are really radical"; and "society views young white males as the natural leaders and agents of change and views others as objects."

One attendee pointed to EF!'s slogan, "No Compromise in Defense of Mother Earth," as a marker of privilege: some communities do not have the luxury of *not* compromising. He stated: "Maybe EF! should acknowledge that some communities have a stake, they have something to lose. Maybe instead it should be 'we compromise in those situations where compromise is absolutely necessary.'"

After tackling that question, the facilitators then asked how the movement can challenge these privileges. Several responded that EF! could "work *with* people not *for* them" and "think carefully and critically about how to become an ally to other communities." Other responses included statements like "thinking more deeply about how we define 'radical' and to recognize that for indigenous peoples, for example, just surviving genocide is radical" and "work on restoring ecosystems in urban and suburban areas." Kayla (a pseudonym), an activist at the Roadshow, had recently taken a class on building alliances between settlers and Indigenous peoples in the United States. She said, "I believe decolonization must be at the center of any ecodefense movement."

Tommy (a pseudonym)—an EF! activist traveling with the Roadshow—passed around a handout entitled "What is an ally?" According to the document, "a member of a dominant group who rejects the dominant ideology and takes action against oppression out of a belief that eliminating oppression benefits everyone."[52] When asked about solidarity, EF! activist Panagioti told me and Brehm of the group's involvement in the struggle to defend the Umoja Village in Miami, Florida's Liberty City neighborhood. African American residents there faced widespread evictions due to poverty and the lack of affordable housing. In a land reclamation campaign, EF! activists helped local residents and community leaders build outdoor latrines and taught resistors other kinds of tasks (and tactics) that EF! typically employs in the woods. Panagioti recalled:

> We worked pretty closely with Max [Rameau] and the Take Back the Land folks, and did a lot of the work helping build the initial infrastructure for the Umoja Village. And they're still doing work. You know, they're occupying foreclosed homes now, and . . . it's got to a new level. It's the same squatting movement that's been around for decades. But trying to highlight the economic crisis and, you know, its parallels. And also looking at the environmental implications of the housing crisis.[53]

Panagioti continued, "it would be fair to say that during the aftermath of Hurricane Katrina . . . a lot of Earth First!ers went down and worked on . . . solidarity and housing issues in New Orleans." He also told us about immigrant rights work that EF!ers do in Latin America and with the No More Deaths solidarity campaign on the U.S.–Mexico border in Tucson.[54]

Many other EF!ers have spoken out or written essays about social justice solidarity work in the *EF! Journal*. Chris Irwin wrote an article about his group's efforts at combating the Ku Klux Klan's presence in East Tennessee:

> Katúah Earth First! has been active in anti-racist activities since our inception. We marched with Black Panther Lorenzo Irving at one of the first marches against the 200 African-American church and home burnings several years ago. I think it's a sign of success that in the Moonshine capital of the South . . . Earth First! has more credibility and grassroots support than the KKK.[55]

Irwin later told me:

> We shut down the Ku Klux Klan's organizing efforts in east Tennessee. They had, I think, seventeen rallies, and every single place we confronted them, they never came back again. We hi-jacked their media and completely shut down that effort, which was really good. [We] changed a lot of peoples' perspectives. . . . [W]e shut down the Klan not because we wanted

black people to like us, but because they were a threat to the environmental community and everybody.[56]

In the late 1990s, the state of Minnesota sought to reroute State Highway 55 through an area that Indigenous peoples declared was of critical spiritual importance. EF!, members of the American Indian Movement (AIM), and many other local activists came together to block the project. Under cover of night, the ELF, in solidarity with the activists and Indigenous groups, sabotaged several construction vehicles at the site. The ELF's communiqué afterward read, in part:

> 4 machines had wires and hoses cut, dirt and sand poured into gas tanks, oil tubes and exhaust pipes, engine parts smashed, removed and destroyed, which has happened several times before and gone unreported. This site is only a quarter-mile from Coldwater Springs, a sacred site to the Dakota people, and the last source of fresh spring water in the twin cities. . . . The road is not nearly done and neither are we.[57]

While anti-racism is often the first topic of conversation among activists working on solidarity issues, the politics of sexuality is playing an increasing role in efforts to embrace anti-oppression. Heterosexual earth and animal liberation activists have begun to acknowledge and welcome the involvement of LGBTQ activists. pattrice jones is an animal liberation activist, ecofeminist, and author who is well known for running an animal sanctuary and for directing a center at the University of Michigan that focused on anti-oppression education and social justice movements.[58] jones is a tireless advocate for LGBTQ communities and linking those politics to the animal liberation movement's goals. Greta Gaard is an activist-scholar, the cofounder of the Minnesota Green Party, and a founder of the ecofeminist tradition in the United States. Like pattrice jones, Gaard has led the effort to extend ecofeminist and animal liberation politics to be fully inclusive of LGBTQ communities and queer politics. In the radical environmental movement, the anti-oppression policies of the *Earth First! Journal*, the Cascadia Forest Alliance, and other groups explicitly demand respect and safe space for LGBTQ folks, and there are regular features and essays in the *EF! Journal* on the need for challenging heteronormativity, homophobia, and transphobia, such as the following statement:

Waves of queer and transgender Earth defenders—each wave bigger than the last . . . have been joining forest campaigns, mass protests and other resistance efforts. They are laying their bodies on the line right next to yours and mine. There is always some asshole around who manages to corner them when they are alone with the express purpose of making them feel unwanted. No, homophobe: It is you who does not belong on our side of the barricades with that attitude.[59]

And, of course, with the TWAC described above, LGBTQ environmental activists come together annually, creating a growing voice and presence in radical ecological movements.

Other sites and spaces of solidarity work abound, particularly as it concerns oppressed communities outside the United States. On December 31, 1999, an ELF communiqué stated:

The ELF takes credit for a strike . . . at Michigan State University. . . . The offices were doused with gasoline and set afire. This was done in response to the work being done to force developing nations in Asia, Latin America, and Africa to switch from natural crop plants to genetically engineered sweet potatoes, corn, bananas and pineapples. Monsanto and USAID are major funders of the research and promotional work being done through Michigan State University. According to the local newspapers the fire cost some $400,000 in damage. Cremate Monsanto, Long live the ELF! On to the next GE target![60]

The politics of solidarity are tricky and problematic, to say the least. One scholar studying EF! argues that most of the articles on Indigenous peoples in the *EF! Journal* were actually updates on other movements' campaigns, suggesting that EF! uses Native issues to advance their own agenda rather than actually working alongside in those struggles.[61] The same study contends that EF! activists frequently seek a token acceptance of their goals or campaigns in Native country, but if the answer is "no" they simply ignore Indigenous peoples and move forward with their campaigns.[62]

At an EF! gathering I attended, I witnessed an example of this kind dynamic: at a morning circle, Shane (a pseudonym) announced that Crow Creek Nation representatives had concerns about EF!ers camping in the area and impacting the local ecology. He urged everyone to be mindful.

On a walk with Shane and others later, Kathy (a pseudonym) stated that she thought the group should have gotten the Crow Creek Nation's permission to be on their land, and I was surprised to hear Shane rebut her point by stating that the U.S. Forest Service (USFS) was actually the group in charge of this space. I found it interesting that the state's authority is used here by a group that often rejects that authority. Kathy did not accept this response. She is an active member of Unsettling Minnesota—an alliance of people who identify as white "settlers" and Indigenous people in the Twin Cities. Even so, the gathering went on.[63]

Radical groups may invoke or claim solidarity with various oppressed peoples, but doing so without invitation can reflect and reinforce white privilege, human supremacy, arrogance, and colonial approaches to movement politics.[64] It is high time for privileged folks to name these oppressions and act to challenge them, but they must do so respectfully. What makes solidarity politics even murkier is that no community with which one might seek solidarity is uniformly oppressed, monolithic, or homogenous; and there are always multiple and conflicting views on any given issue. Moreover, there are often oppressive and privileged elements *within* such communities (there might be members who are pro-empire, homophobic, or patriarchal, for example). If it is these members who have extended invitations to "outsiders," those practices may be deemed oppressive by other members of such communities.[65]

Connecting the Dots:
Ecosystems, Nonhumans, and Humans

The total liberation narrative that emerges from the data I gathered contends that the domination of nonhuman nature is necessarily linked to the domination of human beings, that there can be no liberation of one without the other. This narrative seeks to counter the "(nonhuman) nature first" traditions of these movements that are critiqued as racist, nativist, and heteropatriarchal. The total liberation narrative draws on ecofeminist theory, from biocentrism/deep ecology, from environmental justice theory, and from the concept of intersectionality (the idea that various forms of inequality—such as race, class, ability, gender, and sexuality—work together to produce advantages and disadvantages). Earth and animal liberation activists articulate a theory of intersectionality that expands that traditional concept beyond humans to include nonhuman species and ecosystems. They contend that the unequal relationship between human societies and ecosystems is reinforced and reflected in social inequalities among people. These ideas are not necessarily new, of course. Karl Marx recognized and decried the ways in which human labor and the earth are integrated and exploited by the same system of appropriation. In a famous passage, Marx wrote:

> All progress in capitalist agriculture is a progress in the art, not only of robbing the workers, but of robbing the soil; all progress in increasing this fertility of the soil for a given time is a progress toward ruining the more long-lasting sources of that fertility. . . . Capitalist production, therefore, only develops the techniques and the degree of combination of the social process of production by simultaneously undermining the original sources of all wealth—the soil and the worker.[66]

Regarding the inescapable fact that humans are but one species in a larger ecological chain of being, Marx wrote:

> Man *lives* from nature, i.e., nature is his *body*, and he must maintain a continuing dialogue with it if he is not to die. To say that man's physical and mental life is linked to nature simply means that nature is linked to itself, for man is a part of nature.[67]

This passage reflects Marx's refusal to separate humans from nature, something that many contemporary scholars still struggle with (as the "nature/culture" divide remains with us in many quarters of the academy).[68] Sociologist John Bellamy Foster writes that Marx moved beyond this conundrum early on, with the concept of *metabolism*, which he describes as "constituting the complex, interdependent process linking human society to nature."[69] Today political theorists like David Schlosberg argue that ecological movements, too, must extend their concepts of justice beyond distributional concerns among humans to include nonhuman nature.[70] A growing number of scholars concur: if social movements desire stronger democratization, then, as Carl Boggs puts it, "we will need a more inclusive view of politics, a deeper understanding of democracy, extending the conventional public realm to include the economy, social life, and ecosystems, as well as politics."[71] And anarchist and animal liberation scholar Bob Torres builds on the work of social ecologist Murray Bookchin when he writes: "Only by reorganizing society along radically anti-hierarchical lines, might we live *in* nature rather than *above* nature."[72]

The contention that hierarchy, oppression, and injustice across species and ecosystems are inseparable is at the core of the total liberation framework. A press release by NAALPO summed this up: "Animal liberation can never be fully realized within a global capitalist system spiraling out of control, and thus must be part and parcel of a larger struggle against class domination and hierarchies of all kinds."[73]

Several activists told me it was "natural" to recognize the need for justice for *all* living creatures. "Animal, nonhuman, and human issues are profoundly connected,"[74] said one, while another echoed, "I think there's just a natural progression, it seems, toward ending exploitation in all its forms."[75]

Many earth liberation activists drew direct connections between the harm visited upon ecosystems and other beings. Heather, a preteen activist, wrote in the *EF! Journal*: "Trees—they are special in a way. If we didn't have them, nothing would be here. . . . If we don't have trees, then there would be no animals. If there were no animals, then there would be no us."[76] More dramatically, EF! co-founder Foreman wrote:

> When a chainsaw slices into the heartwood of a 2,000-year-old redwood, it's slicing into my guts. When a bulldozer rips into a verdant hillside, it's ripping into my side. When a smelter poisons the atmosphere, it's poisoning me. When a California condor is imprisoned in the Los Angeles Zoo, I am behind bars as well. I am the land, the land is me.[77]

As ecofeminist and animal liberationist pattrice jones writes: "Everything is connected to everything else. That means that the old anarchist slogan—'no one is free while others are oppressed'—is literally true."[78] A focus on the interconnectedness of justice for ecosystems, animals, and humans stems from the belief that socioecological inequalities have similar root causes. Leslie James Pickering is a former spokesperson for the North American Earth Liberation Press Office who views all forms of oppression as linked, the root cause of the ecological crisis: "If it were not for the capitalism, racism, sexism, imperialism that the system perpetrates upon the world and each one of us, then there would be no clear cuts, no vivisection, no Persian Gulf War, no Nike corporation."[79]

Hensey, whom we met earlier, declared:

The same argument that allows people to objectify animals was the same argument that allowed people to objectify people of color, or treat women as nothing more than property. It's really the same, faulty, arbitrary lines that differentiate and allow people to exploit and abuse another person. And clearly people that have little regard for animals often have little regard for human animals as well.[80]

Much of the literature my research team and I saw at activist gatherings reinforced these perspectives. For example, one zine we found at two movement functions stated, "The same values that perpetuate sexist violence and eco-cide also perpetuate genocide, racist violence, classist violence, destruction of the earth, and the tearing apart of indigenous peoples and cultures."[81] The CFA's *Disorientation Manual* states:

> This battle isn't only for the earth. It's important to recognize that we must challenge the very mindset that allows the belief that it is an acceptable practice to exploit the earth for profit. It is this same mindset that empowers the domination and hierarchy so prevalent in our society. Our struggle isn't only for the earth but also to destroy the latent sexism, racism, classism, homophobia, trans phobia, and other isms and phobias that play into the dominant paradigm. The people who exploit the environment are the same people who help facilitate the exploitation of women, animals, workers, and the like. It is one struggle and one fight for the earth, human rights, and animal rights.[82]

This brings us back to the way in which the total liberation framework extends intersectionality into the nonhuman realm. On this point, pattrice jones told me about teaching a class at a major U.S. university—a multidisciplinary course on "the theory and practice of social change" with an emphasis on "weaving race, class, sex all the way through." But she soon discovered something was missing:

> I couldn't explain whiteness without sexism. I could not explain racism without patriarchy. I simply could not. It turned out I couldn't explain patriarchy without explaining pastoralism. And I'm teaching this course and I'm saying, "race, sex, class, sexual orientation, it's all linked. You can't separate them!" And animals aren't there! Like, how is that? But that's how it was. Like, somehow the [classic feminist slogan] "personal is political" does not

extend to that one choice? And then, suddenly, when I'm doing this dissertation work, [I realize] all this time, I've been leaving this out of my analysis. Speciesism is part of the matrix.[83]

Many activists drew parallels between the hazards facing human workers in factory farms and meatpacking plants and the plight of nonhuman animals and nearby residents in these same locations. For example, Rena (a pseudonym) is a woman who works with an animal liberation group on the West Coast. She made connections among people, nonhuman animals, and ecosystems in the following statement:

> If you are buying these products from a slaughterhouse, it's not just that you're harming animals, you're harming the people that work there. It's . . . these high accident rates, and they don't have any kind of worker protection, and they get paid lousy. But since a lot of them are illegal immigrants, then they're gonna get taken advantage of. And then the chicken producers and the pig producers and a lot of the ones that have a lot of waste are down South where there's less environmental laws. So they're, not only are they treating the workers poorly, but they're polluting where they live, too. . . . It's everyone that lives around these places that are just so environmentally destructive.[84]

Rena's words return to the work of Karl Marx and Upton Sinclair: the exploitation of working-class human labor and nonhuman natures are tightly bound. Further, as noncitizens, undocumented immigrants are often placed outside the boundaries of full humanity, perhaps uncomfortably close to those social spaces and places to which nonhuman animals are relegated.

Because We Must (BWM) is a collective of activists who refuse to restrict themselves to a single movement label. The group's slogan is "Animal, Earth, Human," and its logo invokes all three. BWM embodies the goals and discourse of total liberation, "founded on the idea that all forms of oppression and, in turn, the struggles against them, are intimately connected," and that "the white supremacist, patriarchal, capitalist culture that dominates the planet" must be confronted.[85] In her first posting on BWM's website, Rylee stated, "I believe in total liberation. I want to better connect ideas of human, animal, and earth liberation to create a more unified radical movement."[86] Jeff's first posting on BWM's site connected total liberation to solidarity actions concerning immigrant rights. He grew up in Southern California, "home to the racist vigilante group known as the minutemen," but also home to a vibrant punk music scene. He and his friends "felt that it was our duty to counter the actions of the minutemen," so they provided food to workers at day labor sites and attended city council meetings in support of day laborers and to counter the minutemen voices at those events. Jeff states: "Before I was on the streets fighting for animal liberation, I was on the streets fighting for human liberation and the rights of working migrant people. . . . I put in the same effort in fighting for the rights of the people, that I do to fight to give animals the rights they deserve . . . to keep the forests standing as they should be."[87]

Pushing the boundaries of intersectionality through a total liberation framework leads many activists to conclude the borders separating various social movements should be challenged as well.[88] If the issues are linked, the activists should be linked. On this point, Jeff "Free" Luers, a celebrated activist who spent nine years in federal prison for an (ELF) arson, told us, "Well, I don't really differentiate between movements. I think that all of our struggles are interconnected, and there are certainly different facets of struggle, but the bottom line is that we're all struggling against the same monster."[89] And Josh Harper, mentioned earlier, concurred: "I really think of the animal rights movement and the human rights movement and the environmental movement as being one thing."[90]

Unresolved Tensions, Unfinished Business

Within the radical environmental community, even though activists are wrestling with ecological and social justice politics, such efforts are always fraught with tension and, frequently, disappointment. While many activists embrace the concept of total liberation, many others do not. With respect to social justice politics, some activists with strong progressive political views think some of their colleagues have gone too far by trying to create and enforce a "politically correct" culture. They think social justice and anti-oppression politics have dominated the movement and displaced the "more important" goal of achieving ecological sustainability.

Ben Rosenfeld has been an EF! legal advocate for many of the movement's most celebrated activists, including Judi Bari and Darryl Cherney. He also serves on the Board of Directors of the Civil Liberties Defense Center (directed by activist attorney Lauren Regan). He explained that, while he supports efforts to challenge offensive and culturally insensitive language within the movement, he believes there is an "extreme political correctness and word policing that has gripped the movement or at least the people who are kind of running it, which has alienated a lot of the older folks in the movement."[91] In his view, the effort to create a safe space has alienated many people of color. He even wrote an article in the *EF! Journal* expressing his dismay on this topic.[92] Chris Irwin agreed with Rosenfeld but saw a different group suffering from anti-oppression policies. He wrote the following in the *EF! Journal*:

> I am struck that while one marginal social group is singled out for protection and space in the [EF!] journal, another larger group has been largely driven out of our movement. Yes, I'm talking about rednecks. It was in the late 80's and 90's that I saw the systematic driving away of rednecks from EF! circles by largely young white middle class "anarchists." Basically the white middle class drove out the poor working country class. . . . We have fractured along class lines with devastating results.[93]

This class divide Irwin decries is tightly integrated with a generational divide. Seego (a pseudonym), a longtime EF! activist and poet, stated:

> I went to my first RRR [EF! Round River Rendezvous] when I was sixteen years old, after reading Edward Abbey's *Desert Solitaire*. I fell in love with the desert. That was 1992 at the RRR in Durango, Colorado. Then, at that RRR, half of the people there were under thirty years old. There were none of these squatter kids you see here today. I'm dismayed with the lack of understanding of deep ecology—they are moving away from that. Most of the new EF!ers don't even know what it is! Biocentrism is the result of deep ecology thinking, and both are critical as foundations of the movement. Additionally, it is important to realize that someone can't be biocentric without being anarchistic because hierarchy is inherent in the government.[94]

I heard similar things from the "over thirty" cohort in conversations about the politics of gender and sexuality in the movement, too. Colt (a pseudonym) is a veteran EF! activist who feels there is now an overemphasis on recognizing people's differences in identity and life experiences:

> Some of the transgender orientation right now is just kind of confusing and distracting to me. Like, when I went to the Trans and Womyn's Action

Camp, I was happy that . . . [they] had created a safe space for people. And I like any action camp teaching activist skills as a space where they don't feel like it's too critical or too harsh or whatever. But at the same time, there were certain people in the group who would insist every time we would sit down and talk together, everybody going through and telling us what their preferred personal pronoun was. And that got really old. . . . So that's been kind of sticky with me. Sometimes I think it's too much emphasis.[95]

Similarly, Dara (a pseudonym) worried that the focus on oppression sometimes becomes overpowering: "The problem is that all these discussions about oppression take over instead of being a part of a larger framework around campaigns."[96]

Overall, these difficulties reveal that social justice issues remain contentious topics of discussion and consideration within radical ecological movements, with some activists embracing them while others are hesitant or resistant. Contentious issues of social privilege and difference will haunt environmental groups into the future. In the animal liberation community, there is a list of unresolved tensions at least as long and deep as those within the environmental community, particularly as it concerns whiteness and racism. The list includes a recent PETA action outside the Westminster Kennel Club convention that involved AR activists wearing Ku Klux Klan robes, handing out flyers protesting what they described as the dog breeders' efforts to create a "master race" of canines. PETA also produced an infamous exhibit that drew parallels between slavery and the lynching of African Americans and the treatment and exploitation of nonhumans, alongside its "Holocaust on a Plate" campaign, which claimed parallels between nonhuman exploitation and the Nazi Holocaust. Each of these actions was meant to connect speciesism and nonhuman exploitation to more familiar examples of human exploitation but largely failed to build alliances with people of color, Jews, and others for a number of reasons. First, in a speciesist world, any suggestion that human exploitation of nonhuman animals bears a resemblance to human exploitation of other humans requires a great deal of work—more than sloganeering and flyers can do. So if AR activists wish to make these connections clear, they must be prepared to delve into history, philosophy, and the politics of trans- and intraspecies hierarchies.

Second, the problem with comparing the exploitation of people of color to the suffering of nonhuman animals is that people of color have struggled for centuries—and *continue* to struggle—to resist such violent practices, so when asked if they support the notion that humans and nonhuman animals should have the same rights, they might justifiably bristle. Not only have people of color historically been (mis)treated like animals, but they have yet to enjoy full membership in this and other societies. In fact, people of color have, ironically, been struggling to maintain boundaries between humans and nonhumans because our dignity and survival have depended on it (despite the inherent speciesism of that stance), while privileged and largely unaware white AR activists wish to dismantle these borders.[97]

Finally, many leaders and activists in communities of color view AR work on privilege and inclusiveness as disingenuous because they seem to appropriate (some people have used the term "pimp") social justice movements for the cause of animal rights without respecting or working in solidarity with those movements. Specifically, when AR activists claim animal exploitation has strong parallels with chattel slavery, they must understand that people of color can view such statements as arrogant declarations that white AR activists know their history better than they do and that the activists are using their stories for their own ends, rather than in a genuine effort to build and support racial justice movements. In using tales of, say, "what happened to African slaves in the New World," the implicit message is that the worst manifestations of racism are in the past. On the issue of "pimping" or the appropriation of people of color's struggles, consider the following statement from Lauren Ornelas, mentioned above, at the annual Animal Rights Conference:

> Although many of us have chosen animal rights to be our passion and our main focus, I think it's important for us to recognize that oppression is oppression no matter what form it takes, whether it be chocolate from the Ivory Coast, or Coca Cola privatizing water in India, or killing union workers in Colombia, or the 17-year old farm worker who died in the fields last summer in California picking grapes. Some groups in this movement have started to use the words and images of Cesar Chavez because he was a vegan, but I do hope that they take to heart the many aspects of Cesar Chavez's work and not just use his image.[98]

Throughout this chapter, I have shown how many radical environmental and animal rights movement activists have articulated and supported the total liberation framework, particularly in its first tenet. They remain, however, in the minority, because the mainline voices continue to support the "(nonhuman) nature first" approach. This produces division, allowing for alienation and tension among environmental, animal rights, social justice, and environmental justice movements. They also face internal divisions, as old and new guard activists find themselves at odds; people of color, LGBTQ, and those of differing socioeconomic classes struggle to be heard and respected; and histories are appropriated and repurposed in ways that seem tone-deaf. The total liberation framework holds dear a commitment to shared oppression and shared liberation, but in practice, true solidarity can be hard to come by.

CHAPTER 3

Anarchism and Anticapitalism

Liberation from Government and Market

The state . . . is the most flagrant negation, the most cynical and complete negation of humanity.

—Mikhail Bakunin, "The Immorality of the State"

The second and third dimensions of the total liberation frame are anarchism and anticapitalism. In my view, there are few strict boundaries between anarchism and anticapitalism: both are directed largely at the capitalist state, the range of institutional and cultural forces that constitute it, and monopoly power itself. But for the purposes of organizing this chapter, I have chosen to write about them largely separately and in sequence.

Drawing on wide-ranging sources of evidence and interview data, I consider the history and evolution of these ideas in the development of radical environmental and animal liberation movements. Here I build on the work of a number of scholars around the fusions and tensions between anarchist and anticapitalist politics and visions of social and ecological justice.[1]

Anarchism

Ron S. is an anarchist and Earth First!er. He's been active in EF!– Indigenous solidarity actions, roadblock actions, and antibiotech actions (including participation in crop sabotage at farms with genetically modified plants), and he has been charged by the federal government with "conspiracy to riot in furtherance of terrorism" during the Republican National Convention in 2008.[2] Ron S. was twelve years old when he discovered an anarchist zine called *Wind Chill Factor*, "and that was the first thing that got me into anarchism." He moved from suburban Chicago to

West Virginia to live with his father, and music fueled his budding politics: "I was attracted to the political stuff in punk rock."[3]

Likewise, Panagioti, the *EF! Journal* Editorial Collective member mentioned in the previous chapter, told me, "There's been a pretty strong anarchistic sentiment throughout all Earth First! organizing. Certainly the past twelve years I've been involved I think that's been reflected. And I think it's evolved."[4] Anarchist politics have seen a major upsurge in both the radical environmental and animal liberation movements, part of the broader growing support of anarchism among the radical left.[5] Sociologist Rik Scarce (the professor you met in the introduction) points out that anarchism has been an element of EF! politics since the beginning, but it grew in influence and substance in the 1990s as younger activists were "centering social justice in their understanding of the problems and solutions the movement should be focusing on." The new EF! generation decided "the entire social system must change before there can be an assurance of permanent wilderness protection."[6]

Social movement perspectives that reject virtually any form of hierarchy tend to be compatible with anarchist politics—a theory and practice of society and governance that is anti-authoritarian, spatially decentralized, and premised on the traditions of mutual assistance and cooperation within groups that enjoy relative autonomy and freedom while practicing consensus-based decision making.[7] Anarchists are not only critical of, but also generally opposed to, the development of states, seen as inherently corrupt and predisposed to exercising what Max Weber called a monopoly on the legitimate use of physical force, or violence.[8] Many earth and animal liberation movement activists view the state monopoly on violence as extending to social control over vulnerable populations—both human and nonhuman—and ecosystems. That state domination over living beings, in turn, reinforces patriarchy, racism, class inequality, ableism, ageism, heteronormativity, and speciesism.

Moreover, activists oppose the state's insistence on the right to extract ecological wealth (or "natural resources") for nation building, revenue generation, job creation, or any other purpose. It appears that increased state-sponsored repression of these movements has strengthened the long-standing presence of anarchist thought within the groups (see chapters 5 and 6).

The type of anarchism most interviewees expressed to me was not stereotypical—the public protests often dismissed as youthful rebellion, outfitted with black clothing, red bandanas, and passionate shouts. These anarchists oppose the state, but primarily because they reject authoritarian rule, repression, and the primacy of property rights over the needs of all living beings. Instead, they prioritize democratic decision making and cooperation, mutual aid and assistance, and community building among ordinary people.

Property

The links between anarchist politics and anticapitalist politics are hard to untangle. In the United States, they go at least as far back as the signing of the Constitution.[9] EF! veteran activist and author Karen Coulter, mentioned earlier in this book, writes in *The Rule of Property* that the "founding fathers" enshrined private property rights and put them at the core of government: "the Constitution was designed as an economic document based on the concept that the private rights of property are the primary concern of government, morally and legally beyond the reach of the property-less majority."[10] This consecration of private property also enshrined hierarchy. Coulter writes that "private property was generally acknowledged as the source of social inequality. Nonetheless, economic inequality was considered both inevitable and necessary to protect the wealth of the ruling elite and perpetuate their political control."[11] As one of the Federalist framers of the U.S. Constitution, Gouverneur Morris, put it so eloquently and bluntly: "The severe law of property is, that in any well settled country, a few must soon possess all, and the majority, the great majority, nothing."[12]

Nineteenth-century French politician and philosopher Pierre-Joseph Proudhon famously equated property with theft. While this idea has been misconstrued by many nonchalant critics of anarchism and socialism as an extremist effort to outlaw material possession, Proudhon actually defined the issue as the "sum of its abuses: competition, isolation of interests, monopoly, privilege, accumulation of capital, exclusive enjoyment, subordination of functions, individual production, the right of profit or increase, the exploitation of man by man."[13] Today one might casually argue that whatever one person owns is rightfully theirs, but to do so ignores the force of governments in shaping ownership, for example, by determining who can own land and how much of it. The seventeenth-century enclosure of the English commons literally fenced off lands that were previously public, transforming those lands into private property for the exclusive use of the wealthy (and spurring the Diggers and Level-lers movements' comparisons of enclosure to slavery). This model was exported to the North American colonies, where countless laws dictated who could own land based on citizenship, nationality, wealth, gender, and race. Over time, socialist, communist, anarchist, feminist, immigrant rights, and civil rights movements would challenge these and other "enclosures" around the world.

Citizenship

Philosophers, historians, sociologists, and critical legal scholars have gone to great lengths to detail how the state (using the law) has historically defined U.S. citizenship in racist, classist, heterosexist, patriarchal, ageist, political, and speciesist ways. Your full access to the benefits of citizen-ship are curtailed if you are a woman, LGBTQ, young, poor, nonwhite or a person of color, a socialist/communist/anarchist, differently abled, an immigrant, or a nonhuman.

Feminist theorists like Carole Pateman, Iris Marion Young, and Susan Okin have traced the exclusion of women from Anglo-American concepts of citizenship to the writings of John Locke, Jean-Jacques Rousseau, and other Enlightenment philosophers who shaped U.S. political thought. They conclude that the model of the "universal citizen" defined in these writings is in fact male. In *The Sexual Contract*, Pateman argues that, in the liberal tradition, the public and the private spheres are constructed in opposition: the public sphere is the realm of citizenship and rights, where men dominate; the private sphere is the realm of sexuality and feeling, the realm of women. Thus citizenship has been defined in opposition to womanhood.[14]

Citizenship and immigration law are, indeed, heavily gendered along male/female lines, and immigration policy is shaped through and through by ideas about sexuality. Until 1990, U.S. immigration law prevented gays and lesbians from entering the United States.[15] Immigration laws barred LGBTQ immigrants from entering the nation, including them in a group of people known as "mental defectives" and "sex perverts."[16] Under *current* laws, gay and lesbian Americans in relationships with foreign nationals have no legal recourse to bring their partners into the United States, though heterosexuals enjoy those rights. Immigration control policies are, there-fore, a key site for the production and reproduction of heteronormativity: dominant sexual categories, identities, and norms in the United States.[17]

Charles Mills's book *The Racial Contract* contends that racial domination is at the core of the state's function, and in *The Racial State*, David Theo Goldberg extends this line of thought, focusing on the state's role in creating racial categories and enforcing racial exclusion or oppression.[18] In Goldberg's account, the constitution is mutual: racial classification and exclusion are a central raison d'être of the modern state, and the state takes a leading role in producing the meaning and implications of race. Enlightenment philosophers relegated non-Europeans to a "State of Nature" wherein they were viewed as largely incapable of modern self-government and developmentally stuck in a stage of collective childhood. So for Goldberg, opposing racism necessitates opposing state formation: the two emerged together in modern history. Goldberg does not explicitly argue for anarchism, but his deep historical and philosophical treatment of state formation suggests this path. All of this is critical to understanding growing support for anarchism by activists in communities of color and Indigenous communities (groups like Anarchist People of Color [APOC]) and why anarchism is perfectly compatible with—and even stems from—antiracism (in addition to its more obvious links to anti-authoritarianism and antihierarchical politics).[19]

Immanuel Kant wrote boldly: "The only qualification required by a citizen (apart, of course, from being an adult male) is that he must be his own master . . . and must have some property . . . to support himself."[20] He added a footnote: "The domestic servant, the shop assistant, the laborer, or even the barber are merely laborers, not artists or members of the state, and are thus unqualified to be citizens."[21] He may have been extraordinarily blunt about it, but these *were* commonly held views. Further, certain political affiliations and ideological leanings excluded some from the realm of citizenship, particularly immigrants with unpopular political views in the United States,[22] and religious beliefs have often been used for this purpose.[23]

Returning to the list of ways one can be denied legitimate, full citizenship, critical animal studies scholars and ecofeminist theorists remind us that humanness is an unearned privileged status used by the state to legally exclude other species from consideration as sentient beings with the rights of membership in the broader ecological community.[24] I should be clear: nonhumanity is an important qualifier not only because it excludes nonhuman animals from having rights, but also because it has been extended, in the past and present, to some humans seen as "not fully human." That has included, among others, those who are or have been incarcerated, various immigrant groups, racialized populations, differently abled people, LGBTQ persons, and the poor.

This modern notion posits that humans are separate and above other-than-human natures not as a result of a God-given force, but because of inherently superior human qualities—the essence of the Enlightenment.[25] Arguments for treating nonhumans as "persons" or community members fall on deaf ears. State systems are designed as inherently speciesist, naturist, and dominionist—all terms that critical animal studies scholars use to denote human dominance over nonhuman species and spaces. The most important point to be made here—and generally ecofeminists are the most visible advocates of this position—is that all of the above categories of difference are interrelated and produced in and through each other. One cannot understand the history of how race, class, gender, sexuality, and so on have been defined and deployed without also paying close attention to how these *human* categories were produced in relation to the nonhuman. As seen in the previous chapter, ecofeminist and total liberation theory links ecological politics to social categories of difference, calling for "an end to all oppressions, arguing that no attempt to liberate women (or any other oppressed group) will be successful without an equal attempt to liberate nature."[26] Anarchism returns us to freedom and justice for all.

Ecologist and philosopher Mick Smith argues for a radical ecology that opposes what he calls ecological sovereignty, or "human dominion over the natural world."[27] But Smith goes further and contends that "if we keep the political principle of sovereignty intact, then we automatically and continually give shelter to the notion of ecological sovereignty, and all talk of changed ecological relations is ultimately hollow."[28] Hence, in his view, radical ecology must ultimately be opposed to state sovereignty.[29] Smith spells out the implications:

> Radical ecological politics is *anarchic*. . . . It rejects the inversion of reality that defines politics as membership of a political citizenry always beholden to sovereign constitutional principles, emphasizing instead the creative mutualistic potential of politics. . . . In place of the political paradigm of (human) citizenship, it suggests a constitutive ecological politics of subtle involvements and relations between more-than-just-human beings, the denizens who together compose the world.[30]

Endorsing anarchism as a logical political path for activists concerned with freedom and justice beyond the boundaries of humanity, activist-scholar Bob Torres writes: "Out of all of the political traditions of the Left, social anarchism presents the most fertile ground for planting the seeds for a politics of equality, including an equality that recognizes species membership."[31] Smith and Torres concur with the work of others who insist on expanding the polity beyond the human and viewing it as an ecosystem itself (return to chapter 1 for more here).[32]

In sum, anarchist theory and politics—in the way I articulate them here—can be not only antistate, anti-authoritarian, and antihierarchical, but also antiracist, anti-speciesist/dominionist, antisexist, and antihomophobic. If modern state formation is necessarily authoritarian, monopolistic, racist, speciesist/dominionist, and heteropatriarchal, anarchism is, in opposition, *supportive* of values and practices that enable freedom and egalitarianism for all beings—human, nonhuman, and ecosystemic.

Antistatism, Anti-Authoritarianism

The vast majority of interviewees stated explicitly that they harbored "an inherent distrust of government." Chris Irwin of EF! said he believes his anarchism derives from traditional U.S. political philosophy:

> I believe that which governs best, governs least. I have an inherent distrust of government and corporations. And, you know, historically, that used to be called "being an American." But now it apparently makes me an anarchist, and if so, all right, I'll raise the black flag.[33] I mean, reading Jefferson and Franklin and the rest, it seems like, that they, too, would have been anarchists and dragged away by the PATRIOT Act if they were around today.[34]

Irwin's perspective is both radical and subversive: his anarchism echoes a traditional American value of limited government. His anticorporate politics are also arguably reflective of early populist discourses around the proper role of business in a democracy.[35]

Antistatist politics fit comfortably into radical ecological movement discourses because so much of the history of mainstream environmental movements has involved a reliance on the state to prevent harm to ecosystems. That hope has been met by repeated betrayal and disappointment. The Earth Liberation Front (ELF) website states:

At this point in time there exists the immediate need for individuals to step outside of societal law and work to directly stop the destruction of life, by any means necessary. . . . The ELF understands that this legal structure is part of the same system of government and now Westernized world domination that is causing the death of all life. It can never be trusted and ultimately needs to be abolished.[36]

Animal liberation activists point to the ways governments, through universities and state agencies, routinely experiment upon and slaughter nonhumans, feeding anarchist sentiment among this movement's participants. Many AR activists are highly critical of academia for the enormous level of animal experimentation conducted in the name of science and medicine. Universities—particularly public institutions—lie at the intersection of the state and capitalist institutions, doing publicly funded research that ultimately is geared toward profit-oriented enterprises in medicine, agriculture, the military, and other sectors. The state is involved in regulating (and therefore legitimating) animal experimentation via the Animal Welfare Act.

Concerning a campaign to pressure faculty experimenting on animals in the University of California system, NAALPO wrote:

After coordinated campaigns against . . . primate vivisection at University of California hell-holes, we now find those who profit from animal suffering in desperate straits . . . we are witnessing the final throes of an industry built and maintained on the suffering of the innocent. . . . For the perverts like [researchers] Jentsch, Ringach, Edythe London and Lynn Fairbanks at UCLA . . . there awaits a special place in hell.[37]

Josh Harper, imprisoned for participation in the Stop Huntingdon Animal Cruelty (SHAC) campaign, said, "none of us admire the United States government. . . . [and] I'm probably not going to hang out with anyone who admires the U.S. government."[38] When state funding and support lends credence to research these activists so passionately oppose, anarchism would seem to follow.

In the biographical sketch he gave me, legendary radical movement attorney Stu Sugarman writes that he started out his life as "a pissed off little kid, breaking his New York elementary school's record for discipline before the end of first grade." Sugarman has defended many high profile environmental and animal liberation activists whom the U.S. Department of Justice has labeled "domestic terrorists," and he is the author of the "Ask an EF! Lawyer" column in the *EF! Journal*. When I spoke with Sugarman, he implied that using the legal system to pursue individuals and institutions responsible for harming ecosystems is counterproductive:

> My friend Craig Rosebraugh [formerly of the North American ELF Press Office] says, "Well, you're using evil to counteract evil," because the criminal justice system is certainly evil. And that's a hard thing to do, to get your head around . . . we don't want that. We don't want stronger criminal justice laws . . . because they aren't about justice; they're about keeping certain subsets down.[39]

Perhaps the most hopeful message I heard from activists about why they practice anarchism is because they actually tried the mainstream path to politics and were inspired to demand much more than that limited path allows. One animal liberationist who worked for consumer advocate Ralph Nader's organization put it this way:

> I had been working on a campaign within the system . . . almost fifteen, sixteen years, and no matter what you asked for, they always took it away. And the reason I gave up on electoral politics and went to SHAC is that it's always the lowest common denominator in that if you ask for a piece of bread, and a piece of bread is really reasonable, they're only going to give you half a piece of bread, or they're going to give you a crumb. But if you say, we're taking over the whole fucking bread factory and this is ours, then they can't do anything about it. Because we're going to defend this because we believe it's right, because you guys are starving everybody to death. It's a bad analogy, but you understand what I'm saying.[40]

In fact, it may be quite an appropriate analogy. In 2001, Argentinian workers enacted actual factory takeovers and occupations during a national crisis. A popular movement arose amid harsh fiscal austerity and state unilateralism: people founded popular education institutions, printing presses, and employee-run businesses in what many activists called horizontalism—antihierarchical, democratic decision making.[41] Imagined possibilities became reality.

Anarchism, Community, Democracy

Former Black Panther Kwamé Touré (né Stokeley Carmichael) once told a group of students at the University of Tennessee, Knoxville (including me): "It's very easy for a movement to organize *against* something. It's much harder to figure out and tell the world what you're actually *for*." That is, even if you rally around opposing something, your movement gains strength in advocating for something else—a replacement for that which you find so odious. So, while many anarchists may be *against* authoritarianism and state governance, they are also in favor of decentralized and consensus-based decision making, egalitarianism, building community, and face-to-face relationships.

The type of anarchism practiced among the movements included in this book is often manifested in efforts devoted to building community through mutual aid and democratic decision making. This is certainly not a new political project. John Curl's *For All the People* details the ways in which, in both precolonial and colonial America, whether among Indigenous peoples or the Pilgrims who later settled their lands, "cooperation, not competition resounded as the dominant chord across the continent."[42] In his classic *Democracy in America*, Alexis de Tocqueville wrote admiringly of the mutual aid associations that characterized so much of life in the United States.[43] Over the centuries, these organizations were created by citizens, not governments, to provide housing, food, fire protection, electricity access, credit, insurance, death benefits, education, and decent jobs.

In the 1960s, according to sociologist Wini Breines, social movements of the New Left like Students for a Democratic Society (SDS) and the Free Speech Movement built on the history of cooperatives and focused it on "prefiguring"—"being the change you want to see." As Francesca Polletta describes it: "The label *prefigurative* has remained popular as a way to describe movement groups whose internal structure is characterized by a minimal division of labor, decentralized authority, and an egalitarian ethos and whose decision-making is direct and consensus oriented."[44]

I have had doubts about the virtues of this style of antihierarchical organizing, but I have come to appreciate the symbolic, cultural, political, and material power of prefigurative politics, even in the most intimate spheres of local level community work. After all, do any of us actually expect nation-states to embrace anti-authoritarian, antihierarchical democratic values and practices? Both history and anarchist theory suggest that only once communities move beyond state institutions and structures can they pursue a deeper form of democracy. Political theorist Carl Boggs writes, "any future retrieval of politics will have to be built on foundations that extend far beyond the parameters of existing state institutions since these have already been profoundly weakened as agencies within the public sphere."[45]

There are many eloquent activist answers to the simple question "Why anarchism?" EF! activist Chris Irwin, introduced earlier in this book, has written about and helped lionize a prominent early architect of anarchist theory and cooperative practice:

> Peter Kropotkin, he was a biologist and he went to the steppes of Russia to do a taxonomic inventory. . . . This was during the period where the Social Darwinists were taking competition between the species . . . and trying to transport that into a social theory to justify having eight-year-olds work in coal mines. And what Peter Kropotkin did was he went . . . and he says, "Yeah, I see an element of competition, but I see far, far more cooperation." He asked, "Well, why isn't cooperation more the rule among humans?" because it's definitely more the rule. And he wrote a book called *Mutual Aid* that was exhaustive—he listed all the species and examples of cooperation.[46]

The aforementioned pattrice jones, who ran the Eastern Shore animal sanctuary in Maryland for a number of years, sat with me in a coffee shop, where she explained her own embrace of anarchism: "Well, it's no secret . . . I'm not a fan of state solutions." She describes herself as an "anarcha-feminist," writing in a popular anthology about the ALF:

> Anarcha-feminists believe that liberation movements and organizations must be non-hierarchical and unselfish in order to overturn an oppressive social order that is based on private property and an algebra of hierarchical dualisms (e.g., men over women, people over animals, culture over nature, etc.). The ALF is non-hierarchical and unselfish. No one runs the ALF, and no one who is truly ALF tries to take credit for it. . . . Anarcha-feminists believe, as one manifesto put it, that "the world obviously cannot survive many more decades of rule by gangs of armed males calling themselves

governments." Thus, anarcha-feminists seek to destabilize and replace, rather than join and reform, governments. . . . Actions are aimed at undoing, rather than revising, power over animals.[47]

And scott crow, a community organizer, writer, strategist, and speaker, advocates the philosophy and practices of anarchism for social, environmental, and economic justice. His decades of political activities (with groups as varied as Anti-Racist Action, Greenpeace, and the Association of Community Organizations for Reform Now, or ACORN) earned him the FBI label "domestic terrorist." crow cofounded the Common Ground Collective, the largest U.S. anarchist organization since the peak of the International Workers of the World in the 1920s and 1930s, to provide basic services for survivors of Hurricane Katrina in the Gulf Coast in 2005. He proudly told me:

> We created a horizontal organization that defied the state and did our work in spite of the state . . . not only did we feed people and give them aid and hygiene kits and things like that, but we also stopped housing from being bulldozed, we cut the locks on schools when they said schools couldn't be opened, and we cleaned the schools out because the students and the teachers wanted that to happen. And we didn't do a one size fits all like the Red Cross would do—we asked the communities, every community we went into, we asked multiple people, the street sex workers, the gangsters, the church leaders, everybody, we talked to them: "What can we do to help your neighborhood, to help your community, to help you?"[48]

Such a horizontal organizational structure, focused on democratic decision making and shared power, is common in many of the movements and groups to which these activists belong. The Cascadia Forest Alliance (CFA) makes all its major decisions through consensus-based processes—a sort of "parliamentary procedure for anarchists":

> CFA itself is run nonhierarchically where decisions are made at consensus run meetings . . . we have no leaders and everyone participates in decision making. . . . So, what is this thing called consensus? Well, the basic idea is that it is a way to make decisions in a group where all voices have a say. An anarchistic model designed to empower every individual in the group. A basic outline of the process is:

1) Problem stated (What are we talking about?);
2) Question clarified (What needs to be decided?);
3) Discussion (What are all views?);
4) Proposal made (What action will the group take?);
5) Discussion (Speak to the proposal, clarify questions, good points, concerns);
6) Modify proposal by amendments or withdraw;
7) Test for consensus: A) Restate proposal, B) Call for concerns, C) Call for objections within consensus, reservations, stand asides, or blocks, D) Attempt to incorporate objections or blockers, E) If unable, decisions blocked. Come up with an alternative, F) If no alternative can be reached then consensus -1, -2, etc. can be made, G) Consensus reached. Show verbal, visual agreement;
8) Decision implemented, assign tasks.[49]

"Blocks" occur when someone feels strongly that a decision would be detrimental to the group and are done only occasionally. When someone "stands aside," this means they are not enthusiastic about a decision but can live with it.[50]

In their rejection of hierarchy and authoritarianism, anarchists signal that they wish to exercise collective power and deeper forms of democracy. Irwin says we treat democracy so casually it's "like chewing gum"— it's overlooked, discarded, literally walked upon:

> When you really look at the society and culture we're in . . . most American families [aren't even] democracies. It was hierarchies from the dog up to the father at the top. . . . So really, most Americans have very little experience working together in egalitarian relationships. And I think that's a real unstable model.[51]

Since anarchism is focused on egalitarian, collective forms of governance and living, it might logically lend itself to anti-oppression and anticapitalist politics. A number of activists made this link explicit, including a West Coast group called the Mazama Forest Defenders (MFD). The MFD describes itself as "committed to preserving and maintaining the integrity of remaining native and old growth forests in the Klamath-Siskiyou bioregion" through direct action focused on challenging "taxpayer subsidized logging practices of federal agencies and industrial logging corporations."

Reflecting the intersection of anarchist organizing and anti-oppression principles, the MFD "is a non-hierarchical, consensus-based organization working to eradicate racism, sexism, classism, homophobia, and all other forms of oppression."[52]

While some activists argue that mutual aid and cooperation are natural and come easy, the reality is that hierarchy and politics play such strong roles in society (Irwin pointed out that students do not vote on their homework, and workers rarely get to choose their own tasks) that actually practicing democracy takes a lot of energy and focus. It often produces failures. crow recalls ups and downs in Common Ground right after Hurricane Katrina hit the Gulf Coast. During its first few months, Common Ground had five thousand volunteers "on the ground doing work at any given time" holding meetings, delivering services, and "it was a fucking train wreck." Hastily setting up a brand new organization to respond to one of the biggest disasters in U.S. history was bound to be chaotic, but insisting it would be run based on anarchist principles added more complexity to the task. crow said, "I'm not going to lie to you. There was always tendencies to have a hierarchy [versus] to be flat in organizing, and there was always tension . . . the bigger we got, the more confusing it got, because we'd have to reinvent ourselves over and over again."[53]

A number of scholars have noted the upswing in anarchism's popularity among grassroots activists in recent years.[54] crow views anarchism's growth across social movements with both hope and caution:

> I think anarchism's influence across grassroots movements has been really valuable and like with what happened with SHAC, the fact that we're sort of decentralized is great on one hand because no one leader has emerged, no one movement has emerged, and all of these various entities can get support from each other. But the bad thing is that there's no accountability and some disconnection across the geography.[55]

Anarchism, Action, and Repression

A rejection of hierarchy that constitutes the foundation of anarchism is important for the structure and functioning of earth and animal liberation movements. One activist involved in a SHAC group in the southwest United States fondly recalled the way their campaign against Huntingdon Life Sciences and its business partners was structured:

It was a beautiful anarchist campaign, it was so decentralized and it was so much about information sharing, and there was a spectrum and diversity of tactics—nobody was going to tell you could or could not do this. And it was an evolution in the fact that it was targeting decision makers not to do something a little nicer, but to fucking stop what they were doing . . . and that to maintain business as usual was gonna cost them money.[56]

Anarchist politics organically lends itself to illegal direct action tactics, since activists do not recognize the legitimacy of the state, and state-sanctioned protest has its obvious limits. Before a U.S. congressional subcommittee in 2002, Craig Rosebraugh said there is a "striking amount of evidence" that, throughout U.S. history, significant social change has occurred only when activists "strayed beyond the state sanctioned" means of protest. He pointed to the Underground Railroad, slave revolts, the Suffragettes, and labor strikes and riots as examples in which people willfully broke the law but got results. Rosebraugh also mentioned another particularly instructive case of illegal direct action:

Perhaps the most obvious, yet often overlooked, historical example of this notion supporting the importance of illegal activity as a tool for positive, lasting change, came just prior to our war for independence. Our educational systems in the United States glorify the Boston Tea Party while simultaneously failing to recognize and admit that the dumping of tea was perhaps one of the most famous early examples of politically motivated property destruction.[57]

Related historical atrocities aside (the Boston Tea Party also involved the tarring and feathering—that is, the public torture—of at least one person), Rosebraugh presented this testimony to Congress under pressure from a subcommittee on "eco-terrorism." The force of state repression was right in front of him as Rosebraugh spoke.

Anarchist sentiment has been strengthened in recent years because of state-sponsored repression against more radical wings of environmental and animal liberation networks. These measures generally include surveillance, infiltration, intimidation, and imprisonment—a range of practices that have become known as the Green Scare (for more on this, see chapter 5). In 2005, a prominent federal government official named the radical earth and animal liberation movements the number one domestic "terrorist" threat in the United States.[58] Since then, legislation such as the 2006 Animal Enterprise Terrorism Act declared that it is a crime of terrorism to harm the profits of an industry whose products are primarily based on the use of animals. "Harming profits" can include boycotting, picketing, and any other form of constitutionally protected protest that leads to a decline in revenue for industries like furriers, circuses, animal research testing laboratories, and farms.

In the view of many anarchists, governments exercise monopoly power to repress virtually all freedom struggles. Earth and animal liberationists are often able to link their experiences to those of other social movements. As one activist wrote in the *NAALPO Newsletter*:

> For 250 years in this country, the government and their enforcers have consistently fought against people working for liberation: Indigenous resistance, land reformers, slave revolts, abolitionists, labor organizers & workers, free-speech advocates, women and civil rights workers, anti-war and anti-globalization protesters, and recently, animal rights and environmental activists. Your relationship with the police is at heart adversarial. While there may be cops with hearts of gold, the job of all police is to arrest and prosecute you.[59]

Another activist involved in supporting many social movements since the 1960s explained to me that state repression follows logically when social movements arise to challenge governments, no matter what the ideological predisposition of the party in power might be:

> The reality in the world is, if you look at the loss of human life, Republican and Democratic parties are responsible for more mass death than anything else on the planet. And the planet itself is threatened by their interests. So it's not surprising that, to protect their own interests, they create an infrastructure that supports what they do and opposes anybody who disagrees.[60]

Lauren Regan, a lawyer, is the founder and executive director of the Civil Liberties Defense Center (CLDC) in Eugene, Oregon, and has served as counsel for many of the nation's highest profile political prisoners. The "CLDC educates, supports, and defends grassroots activists."[61] Regan suggests earth and animal rights movements are being targeted not because they are committing crimes, but because of the more serious *political* threat they represent:

> It's not about keeping the public safe. It is clearly about targeting and putting the kibosh to an entire movement[;] . . . it was ideology that constituted this domestic security threat. . . . It was about an ideology that confronted and challenged the mainstream government and that they were afraid of. And radical activists, many of whom do have some affiliation with anarchism as a philosophy, were scary. These activists were challenging and questioning the way we live altogether. You know, humans on the planet even.[62]

In a nation founded by those willing to overthrow their government, movements inclined to undermine and circumvent the state have become a credible threat in the United States. And increased state-sponsored repression has strengthened the longstanding presence of anarchist thought within radical environmental and animal rights movements.

New Directions for the Anarchist Movement

Anarchism has the potential to easily mesh with myriad anti-oppression politics, including movements for racial, gender, LGBTQ, age, and ability justice. Most activists I spoke with understood and expressed this relationship, including those from movements outside my focus here. Ashanti Alston was a member of the Black Panther Party and the Black Liberation Army during the 1960s and 1970s, and for that he spent more than a decade in federal prison. He was widely regarded as a political prisoner and became a committed anarchist. Now Alston is a prominent member of APOC, as well as an author, educator, and prison abolition activist who has built bridges across the largely white animal and earth liberation activist networks, the anarchist movement, and the antiprison movement. Of all the existing social change frameworks, he says anarchism holds the most promise because

> even with the white anarchist community, I really feel like of all the groups, the anarchist mindset is still open to understanding all the different oppressions, that they're not stuck on that "it's just the system out there and you have to change the system." . . . Already, anarchists will deal with movements that silence queers, folks of color, even on an age level—ageism,

ableism. And when we start talking about how we have centered everything around us as human beings [speciesism], I think that's great shit.[63]

I was struck by how many eras and generations of freedom struggles Alston has incorporated into his life and work. But ultimately, he spoke most powerfully and eloquently of the anarchist spirit that promotes community building as a form of resistance, a way of reigniting the soul of democracy:

> I think of temporary autonomous zones and stuff like that in the black community, you . . . have people who wanted to take back their neighborhood, people who wanted to create community gardens. . . . [W]e need to see that as resistance. . . . You need to stop this empire from shutting down every instance of freedom and free living that we are trying to express. I like this anarchist cartoon that said for anarchists, we're not looking to overthrow the system, we're looking to pull ourselves together and create a new life so that we can see the system fading into the background. . . . [I]t means that we have to begin to take back our lives, we have to begin a time of democracy . . . we have to create new concepts of citizenship that are real, but beyond any of the institutions that are set up here.[64]

By linking concerns with hierarchy among people, nonhumans, and ecosystems to a distrust of states and the power they wield, anarchism is a core component of the total liberation frame. The refusal of state legitimacy stems from the observation that activists make of the state's direct involvement in the destruction of ecosystems, nonhuman animal populations, and its role in producing violence, inequality, and injustice within human society. Anarchism also serves as a basis for broadening the idea of the "public" to include both humans and nonhumans because state institutions generally exclude all but humans from the polity.[65] This antipathy for state institutions and monopoly power is complemented by anarchism's presentation of alternatives for thinking, living, governing, and decision making—a cultural project in which coercion is minimized and mutuality and cooperation are supported and practiced.

Anticapitalism

"EARTH NOT FOR SALE—ELF. Earth Liberation Front." This message was left on a property sale sign jammed into a bulldozer at a construction site on Long Island, New York, on November 24, 2000. Anarchist theory and movements committed to anti-oppression and justice for vulnerable populations are generally anticapitalist. If capitalism is an inherently hierarchical system of production and social relations predicated on the exploitation of human and nonhuman labor and ecosystems,[66] then the earth and animal liberation movements logically have many reasons to oppose it.

In recent years, a number of scholars have recuperated the sophisticated ecological thread within Karl Marx's early writings. For example, John Bellamy Foster writes that, for Marx, the domination of the earth occurred as people and institutions monopolized land and power over both nonhuman nature and the vast majority of human beings. This alienation of the earth and its control by a wealthy minority were key components of the system of private property in both feudalism and capitalism.[67] Sociologist Bob Torres echoes Marx and Foster when he points out that, although the exploitation of nonhuman animals certainly exists (and existed) outside of and prior to capitalism, "the structure and nature of contemporary capital has deepened, extended, and worsened our domination over animals and the natural world."[68]

The concept of the *metabolic* or *ecological rift* is meant to capture the environmental harm and disruptions of ecosystem processes produced by humans in general and capitalism in particular.[69] This rift has dire consequences for socioecological inequalities. It is, as Foster, Clark, and York write,

> the product of a social rift: the domination of human being by human being. The driving force is a society based on class, inequality, and acquisition without end. . . . No solution to the world's ecological problem can be arrived at that does not take the surmounting of capitalism, as an imperialist world system, as its object.[70]

What scholars call the "first contradiction" of capitalism comes from Marx: the "absolute general law of capitalist accumulation,"[71] or the inherent tendency toward overproduction. This results in vast inequalities, with great wealth at one end of the social spectrum and misery and poverty at the other. The "second contradiction" of capitalism, or the "absolute general law of environmental degradation," as James O'Connor put it, occurs as wealth is amassed among a minority, which is made possible by ecosystem depletion, habitat destruction, pollution, and injury to the local and broader socioecological terrain.[72] In other words, capitalism self-destructively deteriorates the conditions required for its existence. Historian Carolyn Merchant locates capitalism's second contradiction in the violence of production toward social and biological reproduction: the ability to reproduce all forms of life is threatened and curtailed by pollution and ecological degradation that are byproducts of that system.[73]

In a related dynamic framework, the treadmill of production theory contends that capitalist economies cycle. As economic "development" intensifies, so does the degree of ecological degradation. Within this model, the capitalist state underwrites private accumulation while also addressing the social upheavals associated with that system (falling wages, rising inequalities, structural unemployment, and environmental harm). The logic of such a system dictates that ever greater investments toward economic growth will usher in solutions to the socioecological crises the system caused in the first place. Accordingly, investors, the state, consumers, and working-class populations intensify their commitment to economic growth in order to generate goods for sale on the market, income for workers, and legitimacy for nation-states.[74] These actions create a self-destructive cycle of tortured logic wherein the solution to ecological degradation is to deepen society's investment in a system that is inherently ecologically detrimental.

Accordingly, the efficacy of any social movement (such as the labor movement and environmental movement) that focuses on only one of capitalism's "absolute general laws" will be limited.[75] Moreover, such movements generally fail to delve deeply into either contradiction and rarely connect them. Social movements willing to link and deepen their approaches to capitalism's contradictions may be more effective at articulating the causes and effects of this system's power to produce socioecological injury. No less a challenge, the treadmill of production reminds us, is that in order to devise methods of building alternatives to capitalism, social movements must also understand why people and institutions are so heavily invested in capitalism.

The dominant message is that there is no alternative to the current system, but ideas and practices that some have called "postcapitalist politics" have long been in evidence.[76] Many earlier Marxist scholars produced a portrait of a unified capitalist control of a universal, interchangeable form of abstract labor, but ironically, capitalism actually produces the conditions that give rise to increased social heterogeneity, in terms of greater diversity along the lines of skill, age, class, race, gender, and sexuality.[77] This happens in at least two ways: first through the recruitment and hiring of progressively lower-skilled, cheaper labor to replace higher-skilled, more costly labor; and second, by sparking rural to urban migrations and increased social densities among city dwellers, workers, and their families. Industrial capitalism, then, encourages the production and growth of nonheteronormative, racially, ethnically, and economically diverse populations in cities and towns around the globe.[78] These diverse social formations are also disciplined by capital and the state, and the attendant social inequalities are part and parcel of "free market" systems. Accordingly, activists seeking total liberation simultaneously embrace that heterogeneity and reject the system that produces and controls it.

Core Movement Perspectives

Capitalism and social movements organizing against it reveal the frictions, harm, and hopes that come from the recognition of the inseparability of humans from nonhuman natures and inanimate objects. They are the raw materials that fuel capitalism; without them, capitalism would cease. Earth and animal liberation movements are collectives of humans who decry the violent effects of human practices and policies on ecosystems and nonhuman animals and feel "called" or interpellated to protect and defend them.[79] Additionally, nonhuman inanimate objects play complicated roles in this drama: activists must alternately use these objects to aid in their direct action efforts (think of cars, roads, gasoline, matches, dwelling spaces, etc.) and are called to destroy such objects (buildings, bulldozers, laboratories, slaughter houses, restaurants, furriers, power lines, dams, etc.) to prevent further harm against living beings. Total liberation is a framework that is founded on the imagined, seen, felt, and often romantic and sometimes discomfiting intersections of the human and nonhuman worlds.

As many interviewees pointed out, capitalism requires continuous feedstocks of ecological materials, nonhuman animals, human workers, and consumers.[80] This treadmill of production also demands social compliance and thrives on the intensification of social hierarchies and militarism.[81]

Many activists indicated that they believed capitalism (and its related and supporting systems, such as science) is the root of most environmental and social injustices. For example, a plenary speaker at the national Animal Rights Conference spoke about shift that took place under the Renaissance and Enlightenment in Europe: in what has generally been viewed as a time of great progress for science and rationality over church hegemony, "this was not good news for animals." The new epoch of capitalism brought with it a "much more ferocious exploitation" of nonhumans "for scientific experimentation, as well as for entertainment, clothing, products, and, of course, for food." Within an emergent materialist age, nonhumans "were reduced to mere resources and commodities in the clutches of a surging industrialism."[82]

Similarly, an activist who describes himself as "an environmentalist [and] an animal liberationist," since he does not see these movements as separate, stated, "animal liberation and earth liberation are a direct challenge to the status quo. . . . [T]he capitalist system . . . treats not only workers but the environment and animals as, essentially, commodities to be exploited. Our entire culture is based on exploitation."[83]

At the 2009 Trans and Womyn's Action Camp (TWAC), Kay (a pseudonym) told activists that corporations are "essentially immoral" and are based on competition and aggression, a hierarchy "that bleeds into society," "a bottom-line mentality," and the exploitation of nature and labor. Through quantification, commoditization, linearity, and homogenization, corporations dehumanize.[84] Similarly, an activist writing in the *EF! Journal* declared:

> Capitalism forces people to sell themselves into wage slavery where everything is for sale; your time, your energy, your life. Where you know the price of everything but the value of nothing. We can no longer sit on the fence. It is not a matter of free trade or fair trade or a friendlier form of our oppression. Ourselves and our world are not for sale. . . . So let's act up.[85]

Raphi is a Ukrainian American immigrant who came to the United States when he was nine years old. As a teenager he became active in housing and animal rights causes, and soon he added earth liberation, animal liberation, and immigrant rights activism to his busy schedule. He told me "corporations profit off . . . of these oppressions, whether it be the exploitation of immigrants or the murder of animals in labs." He went on to say that keeping wages down and choosing animal testing over more expensive options were just two of the ways the companies maximize profit.[86] Former ELF political prisoner Jeff Luers made similar links:

> It becomes really obvious that industrial capitalism is wreaking havoc on our environment. From the toxins that are being put into the water in New Orleans that people are getting cancer from, the smog that's being breathed in Los Angeles, to people who are living in forested areas, seeing entire swaths of forests clear-cut . . . I would definitely say that capitalism is the main, driving force behind all social inequality and environmental degradation. The main premise of the theory of capitalism is a mathematical impossibility. The idea is to have infinite growth, and infinite profits, and you simply cannot do that with finite resources.[87]

This general anticapitalist perspective is often focused on a single corporation or industry sector that gains infamy for its troubling practices. Activists regularly protest large, household-name firms like ExxonMobil, Walmart, Monsanto, BP, KFC, McDonald's, and Georgia Pacific for acts viewed as harmful to people, nonhumans, and ecosystems. For example, Home Depot has been the target of an environmentalist campaign to eliminate the sale of old-growth forest products:

> Home Depot is the largest retailer of old-growth forest products in the world. On the shelves of over 700 stores you can find products ripped out of the heart of every major threatened forest on the planet. . . . The continued sale of products derived from these forests must stop in order to turn the tide of mass destruction.[88]

For nearly two decades, Huntingdon Life Sciences (HLS) has been the focal point of animal liberation protests in the United Kingdom, in the United States, and around the globe. SHAC has mobilized for years around HLS:

> Huntingdon Life Sciences (HLS) are the largest contract testing laboratory in Europe. They have about 70,000 animals on site, including rabbits, cats, hamsters, dogs, guinea-pigs, birds and monkeys. These animals are destined to suffer and die in cruel, useless experiments. HLS will test anything for anybody. They carry out experiments which involve poisoning animals

with household products, pesticides, drugs, herbicides, food colourings and additives, sweeteners and genetically modified organisms. Every three minutes an animal dies inside Huntingdon totaling 500 innocent lives every single day.[89]

McDonald's is another favorite target of both earth and animal liberation activists. In the early morning hours of Friday, December 7, 2000, a group claiming to be a joint collaboration of ALF and ELF activists smashed windows and spray-painted "anti meat slogans against environmental destruction" at the McDonald's corporate offices on Long Island, New York. An article reporting this action appeared the *ELF Resistance Journal*:

> The McDonald's corporation has been globally targeted by organizations for years due to its environmental destruction, animal slaughter, poor working conditions, and unhealthy food. Furthermore, McDonald's represents the core idea of American capitalism, which places profit, power, and greed ahead of life.[90]

While radicals target specific companies, whole industries are also the subject of much discussion among these activist communities because of the collective damage they are believed to wreak. Like many animal liberation activist groups, NAALPO makes a direct link between the pharmaceutical industry and mass nonhuman death:

> Big Pharma, one of the largest supporters and beneficiaries of nonhuman animal research, uses its significant influence—an influence derived from deep pockets and even deeper incestuous relationships with legislators, government regulators, peer-reviewed medical journals, publicly funded institutions, and doctors—to sustain the lie that it would be impossible to innovate and market new prescription drugs without vivisection. . . . To ensure the uninterrupted flow of their immense profits, they need vivisection to accelerate the drug approval process, to give consumers the illusion of safety, and to shield themselves from tort liability.[91]

Many activists share the belief that states and corporations are frequently too closely aligned—a perspective that is a hallmark of anticapitalist and anarchist politics.[92] Again, NAALPO writes:

The crisis in the natural world reflects a crisis in the social world, whereby corporate elites and their servants in government have centralized power, monopolized wealth, destroyed democratic institutions, and unleashed a brutal and violent war against dissent. Corporate destruction of nature is enabled by asymmetrical and hierarchical social relations, whereby capitalist powers commandeer the political, legal, and military system to perpetuate and defend their exploitation of the social and natural worlds.[93]

John Hanna, founder of the original ELF group, shares this belief that corporations and governments are too cozy. He cited the Monsanto Corporation, pointing out that the company's executives had "gone back and forth" between the government and corporate worlds, "public welfare and a sustainable biodiversity be damned."[94] Hanna's example raises a topic about which many people have an abiding concern: food systems and corporate control over agriculture. Industrial agriculture has been a significant battleground: environmentalists and animal liberation activists versus the biotechnology industry.[95] In particular, the emergence of genetically engineered (GE) and genetically modified (GM) foods has engendered controversy because many (and public health officials, particularly outside of the United States) are concerned about the risk of unknown and uncontrolled impacts of these "Franken-foods" on health, ecosystems, and wildlife. From Europe to the United States, activists have destroyed GE/GM laboratories and crops, sometimes in open acts of defiance, but often under cover of night (see chapter 4). Rosebraugh, with the North American Earth Liberation Front Press Office (NAELFPO), defends the actions:

Explain to me how else and for what other reasons is our food being genetically modified. Realize that you have never tasted, never really tasted what an orange, an apple, a peach, pear, carrot, or squash actually is like. In fact you have never drank pure water or actually eaten any of these natural foods. All that is available to us are replicas, poisoned forms which once existed as healthy nutritious food. . . . The only way a true positive societal revolution will be reached is to attack the heart of the beast. The idea. The ideology. Capitalism.[96]

Extending this common environmentalist critique, many animal liberation activists decry the "advances" of the genetic and genomic revolutions as practices that include "creating," patenting, and colonizing life forms for profit:

> It is important to frame the struggle for animal liberation as part of the global struggle against capitalism—for today animal slavery is driven by capitalist growth and profit imperatives which themselves must be eliminated. . . . These [problems] range from capitalist commodification, profit, and growth imperatives to its mechanistic-instrumental worldview and the system of private property that extends from land and animals to DNA itself (in the current regime of biopiracy and the postmodern gene rush to create and patent new forms of life).[97]

This NAALPO excerpt goes on to call for alliances across movements to stop the genetic engineering of crops and animals.

Anti-imperialism

A small but growing number of activists extend their anarchist and anticapitalist politics to explicitly embrace anti-imperialism–a fight against how states and capital work together to colonize bodies, space, place, ideas, cultures, and life itself. In the U.S. context this specifically refers to the ways the state and capital are implicated in the country's violent origins and history: conquest, genocide, slavery, and the subjugation of Native peoples, people of color, immigrants, women, LGBTQ populations, working-class peoples, nonhuman animals, and ecosystems. The mainstream environmental and animal rights movements are infamously blind to the role of empire in shaping both the domination of nonhuman nature and those very movements' rather myopic and problematic strategies for addressing socioecological crises.

Aforementioned EF! activist Judi Bari is a rarity in this regard. At an EF! gathering where some activists claimed they could be both patriotic Americans and radical environmentalists, she reminded attendees how radical radicalism is: "If we're going to try and pretend that we can continue to espouse such revolutionary concepts and still fly the flag . . . we're dooming ourselves. . . . I think we need to realize how revolutionary what we're saying really is."[98]

Rod Coronado, mentioned elsewhere in this book, made these connections from the beginning. Coronado, a Native American (Pascua Yaqui) activist and veteran of many animal and earth liberation movements, was one of movements' most celebrated political prisoners. While behind bars, he spoke and wrote using a total liberation perspective imbued with anti-imperialism. In the 1990s (from prison), he wrote:

> Until the U.S. government recognizes native sovereignty and suspends exploitative attitudes, teachings, and behavior against the First Americans, we will rise up against the modern Custers of U.S. society. The American flag represents the government of the occupying forces that have invaded North America. 220 years of colonization later and we are still fighting.[99]

In a piece for the radical publication *No Compromise*, an animal liberation journal, Coronadó stated defiantly: "I'm proud to be an enemy of the United States . . . A regime that routinely allows not only the torture of animals in its licensed and regulated laboratories, but people in its military concentration camps as well."[100]

Anti-imperialist essays have also appeared in the *EF! Journal* and other publications supporting total liberation.[101] For example, in a call to action against the Group of Eight nations (G8)[102] meeting held in June of 2004, EF! activists wrote:

> We should utilize the occasion of the G8 summit to collectively take aim at the notion of wealth itself. . . . It has always been accumulated through the limitless extraction and control of the Earth's resources: water, air, forests, oceans, diversity of life forms and culture, as well as the labor of people and animals. For wealth to be maintained, this extraction must spread like a cancer, always searching for new colonies. . . . The pursuit of wealth generates Empire. . . . A call has been made for Global Days of Action against Empire during the June G8 Summit in Georgia. In support of that mobilization, we call for strategic emphasis to be placed on the ecological costs of empire.[103]

While the existence of anti-imperialist politics among radical environmentalists is becoming well established, what may astonish many people is the growing anti-imperialist discourse among radical animal liberation activists. For example, in the fall of 2011, a group of animal liberationists freed more than a thousand mink from a fur ranch in Gifford, Washington. The group provided media with video of the mink running free, with an accompanying communiqué that read, in part:

We chose to do this not because we believe that humans wearing fur is inherently wrong. Rather we think that the callous disrespect with which the fur industry treats the animals is despicable. The fact that it has become an "industry" for the vanity and fashion of the rich is what we hate. In the Pacific NW the fur industry represents more than just animal abuse and speciesism. Trapping, killing, and skinning fur bearing mammals for profit was one of the first steps of westward expansion and manifest destiny in this area. It was one of the first parts of the colonial process that decimated many Native people and cultures.[104]

Postcapitalism and the End of Civilization

Ultimately, activists who embrace total liberation argue that the underlying sources of the challenges facing them necessitate a multi-issue approach toward a just and sustainable future without capitalism. As a press officer with NAALPO writes, "An effective struggle for animal liberation, then, means tackling issues such as poverty, class, political corruption, and ultimately the inequalities created by transnational corporations and globalization."[105] An indispensible element of this vision is the effort to end corporate personhood—the controversial legal status that affords corporations some of the same political rights as humans in the United States.[106]

Karen Coulter is spearheading the movement against corporate personhood, having long since worked on acid rain, ozone depletion, climate change, nuclear power, peace, old-growth forest defense, and Indigenous sovereignty campaigns around the United States and internationally.[107] For her, the work of the Program on Corporations, Law, and Democracy (POCLAD)—a group she cofounded—is critical for ushering in an era of true democracy and postcapitalism. She sees POCLAD as a "strategic, affinity group of people from all over the country . . . a bunch of activists with decades of experience." The group's main activity is producing and sharing knowledge through "research and writing about history of the rise of corporate power in the U.S., and activist struggles and lessons that can be learned from that for current activism."[108] During a discussion at TWAC, Coulter said people must look to alternatives to corporate dependency, including community building, self-sufficiency, mutual aid, economic alternatives, and democratic decision making, many of which are core anarchist principles and practices as well.[109]

April (a pseudonym) was at that TWAC gathering, and she spoke to my research team some weeks later. She has been an activist involved in a community effort to stop Interstate 69, also known as the "NAFTA Superhighway" because it will connect the U.S.–Mexico border with the U.S.–Canada border in order to facilitate and support the North American Free Trade Agreement (NAFTA). "I'm not going to pretend to know the answer to [creating a just and sustainable society], but I've got some ideas. We would need a major cultural shift, to end capitalism (particularly free market capitalism), fundamentally change structures of governance and to develop a whole lot more compassion."[110]

For some activists, capitalism is actually a secondary symptom of the advent of settled agriculture, pastoralism, and civilization itself. As April articulated:

> Large-scale agriculture is the root cause of many of the other root causes. Agriculture led to . . . anthropocentrism . . . sedentary living, population explosions, and eventually cities. After this came industrialization, destructive technology, and capitalism. Capitalism reinforced anthropocentrism by relying heavily on constant growth (i.e., exploitation of resources), favoring competition over cooperation . . . and concentrating wealth and power among the few.[111]

This representation may sound simplistic (and perhaps extreme), but it is becoming a more common understanding among radical ecologists, particularly those movement veterans from the "anarcho-primitivist" camp and those younger activists who are familiar with the writings of Derrick Jensen and John Zerzan.[112]

I once attended a public screening and discussion of the film *END-CIV*, which is an introduction to anticivilization and anarcho-primitivist politics. The film features Jensen and is built around his work, which argues (as April explained) that agriculture and civilization are at the root of ecological crises. To create meaningful social change, Jensen believes, we must embrace militant direct action and the use of force. In the film, I found it fascinating that Jensen and his colleagues critique not only civilization but the very idea of "being civilized." Because of the associated massive socioecological violence that has accompanied civilization, they embrace "primitivism." Problematically, the film rehashed the noble ecological Indian narrative—the exhortation that we can all learn from our Indigenous brothers and sisters who are "closer to nature"—without critiquing that narrative's simplistic, racist overtones.[113]

After the film screening and discussion, some of the organizers announced a meeting in a month to organize an "underground" movement to build on the message of the event. I went. It was one of the most fascinating and comical events I attended during this research project.[114] The first odd thing was that the "underground" meeting was publicly announced and openly advertised, even though the organizers of the film screening and the people in the film all cautioned that the only effective resistance movement would be an *underground* one. The event took place at a local progressive bookstore in the basement of a building in Minneapolis—the only thing "underground" about this meeting was its location.

Two well-known local media activists facilitated the event with another activist volunteering as the featured speaker. There were maybe twenty people (mostly white, wearing a range of conservative to tattered, torn clothing) seated in a circle. The guest speaker began by stating that her beliefs in education and truth telling as effective mechanisms for social change had been challenged by Jensen's writings: "This is particularly difficult for me since I am an educator. But Derrick's writings and the film *END-CIV* made it clear . . . that we are not going to change the world through moral suasion. . . . We need action." A bookstore volunteer repeatedly raised his cane and hand to offer comments like "I hope you all know what a total collapse of industrial civilization would mean: no running water, no electricity, no e-mail, no phone," until someone finally interrupted him with an exasperated "We get it."

At some other point, an apparently well-known character in the community from socialist circles entered the conversation using such terms as *the ruling class, the workers,* and *the vanguard.* However, he made it known quickly that "I'm just not comfortable with this conversation, and I don't think I can support this. But I've been involved in radical movements for years. I've been targeted by the FBI—just Google my name and you'll see it for yourself. But I have to leave since I cannot be a party to this." And off he went.

Other folks (white males, actually) repeatedly brought up a point that I thought was appropriate: how were existing power dynamics and inequalities to be handled in the event of an industrial collapse? One asked rhetorically: "Don't we need to simultaneously address power dynamics of racism, classism, patriarchy, homophobia, etc., while dismantling industrial civilization so that when we rebuild society we don't repeat those same mistakes and reinforce those hierarchies?" One of the men argued that Jensen "really doesn't deal with these issues in his writings." The featured speaker dismissed these questions, even as others wiggled their fingers in support. It was a telling moment: a short time later, Jensen's Deep Green Resistance (DGR) group would be publicly taken to task for its refusal to address questions about transphobia and oppression (see chapter 2).[115]

The speaker went on: if we stopped industrial civilization now, ecological health would automatically and immediately improve. Oppression would be irrelevant. She and another speaker gave a quick history lesson on militaries from Rome to the present and asserted we could bring the U.S. military to its knees by cutting off its petroleum supply. When one participant pointed out that millions of people would have to mobilize to achieve this goal, the speaker responded:

> There are so many points of vulnerability in this system that it takes very little to push it to its tipping point. That's the beauty of computer networks and our dependence on them, and the beauty of the interstate highway system: there are many bottlenecks that you can exploit quite easily and cause a lot of damage. [Near my house] there's a coal-fired power plant that puts a lot of mercury into the water we depend on. If anyone wants to take that down, that would be a great target.

At that moment, a sincere-looking woman interjected, "And what would happen to our 401k retirement plans?" Frustrated, the speaker replied, "None of that will matter after the collapse, because everything will be different."

The night ended on a staggering note when the featured speaker asked for a show of hands of "people who are committed to the collapse of industrial civilization." Nearly everyone raised their hands, with the exception of a woman who asked timidly, "In a nonviolent way?" One organizer asked the questioner to "define violence," and she gave no reply. The event wrapped up with no firm commitments to join the anticivilization movement. It seemed to me that the marginalization of the anticivilizational/primitivist perspective within radical ecological movement circles is largely of its own making.

Frame Transformation and the Human/Nonhuman Nexus

The total liberation frame's support for anticapitalist politics is a direct challenge to and transformation of other ecological movement frames. Those tend to critique capitalist institutions but ultimately accept their legitimacy and encourage collaboration with companies whose leaders claim "green," "socially responsible," or "humane" practices.[116]

The anticapitalist pillar within the total liberation frame also explicitly links the fate of human and nonhuman populations and ecosystems, detailing the ways in which all species have a shared experience of abuse. The abolition of capitalism, then, is a common interest. Since the sanctity of private property is considered, in this framework, a core component of the capitalist state and private property itself comprises a class of inanimate objects that can participate in the destruction of life, it is fair game in taking down the system. As ELF spokesperson Leslie James Pickering wrote, "If you have bought into the propaganda telling us that destroying a piece of private property is wrong—*regardless of the oppression and injustice that that property perpetuates*—then you have essentially subscribed to the belief that property is more valuable than life."[117]

Not only does Pickering indict capitalism and the state, but he also condemns the work private property does to facilitate injustices, revealing the view that nonhuman objects and technology exercise agency in contributing to socioecological crises. Building on Pickering's claim, a NAALPO activist speaks to the power of inanimate objects and nonhumans to animate human direct action and be part of the movement for total liberation:

> All animals are simply disenfranchised nations in search of the one thing that every sentient being demands: FREEDOM! They are not property. They are not objects. And they are not commodities. The earth and its inhabitants do not belong to humans, under any circumstance. So when inanimate objects—like buildings and machines—are destroyed during an animal liberation, the property-destruction issue is justified because an animal's inherent right to be free trumps economic damage, and *buildings that exist to torture living beings deserve to be eradicated forever!*[118]

The roles of nonhumans, as seen by radical activists, are varied and complex, ranging from participation in and support of violence to participation in their own liberation.

Activists articulating the total liberation frame do not view capitalism simply as an economic system; it is a system that depends on humans and nonhumans to serve as raw materials, workers, and consumers, producing linked oppressions and collective experiences. Thus, the total liberation frame is a transformation of other ecological movement frames in that it readily declares an anticapitalist perspective that aims to pay equal attention to all manifestations of oppression.

Radical environmental and animal liberation movements demonstrate strong opposition to the routine violence, suffering, and exploitation that states and capitalist institutions mete out to ecosystems, nonhumans, and humans. They also voice disdain for the inequalities that states and capitalism produce and thrive upon. They reject any system of commerce and governance that creates hierarchies and requires the appropriation of life and labor in order to sustain itself. They produce ideas and visions of a future society marked by an absence of capitalist, statist, and imperialist practices and ideologies. And they understand that radical social change requires going beyond analysis and proclamations to the final component of the total liberation frame: direct action.

CHAPTER 4

Direct Action

Confrontation, Sabotage, and Property Destruction

I don't know of any social justice movement that has leafleted its way to liberation.

—Stop Huntingdon Animal Cruelty activist, author interview

If someone had his hands around your throat, strangling you, would you gather petition signatures to politely ask him to stop? Would you go limp as a symbolic gesture of your non-cooperation? Hopefully, you would defend yourself by any means necessary.

—Leslie James Pickering, *The Earth Liberation Front: 1997–2002*

The final component of the total liberation frame suggests actions and practices aimed at bringing about justice for ecosystems, nonhuman animals, and humans (ideally, within an anarchist, noncapitalist society). Though just one part of radical movements, direct action has taken up nearly all of public discussion about radical politics. Here, we explore how activists practice direct action in a manner that meshes with the rest of the total liberation frame—anti-oppression and justice for all beings, anarchism, and anticapitalism. We also consider how these movements' direct actions illuminate the human/nonhuman nexus, expanding our ideas of what constitutes a social movement.

Defining and Debating Direct Action

Direct action is a core part of earth and animal liberation movements' tactical and philosophical repertoire, a defining feature of their cultures of resistance—those shared understandings, ideas, and knowledge that inform and support individual and collective practices of dissent. Direct action can mean mobilizing ideas, knowledge, symbols, and bodies to prevent or support a particular practice or policy (for example, protestors chaining themselves to a tree to keep it from being felled); personal confrontation and property damage (say, a protest outside a CEO's home or the hacking of a company's website); and solidarity with other movements and oppressed peoples (expressing support and allying with other causes). These actions are variously directed at the goals of securing justice for ecosystems, nonhuman animals, and humans through anarchist, anticapitalist organizing.

Direct action is frequently discussed among activists and fills many of the pages of movement websites, journals, newsletters, and zines. Every activist we interviewed supported the idea of taking action to free and defend nonhuman animals and ecosystems from captivity, harm, and destruction at the hands of governments and corporations. They all felt, as one animal liberationist who served prison time for mink liberations on fur farms put it, a "duty to intervene in an injustice when they know it's happening all around them."[1] In that sense, as explained in earlier chapters, activists "hear" a "call" or "interpellation" from nonhuman natures[2] that pushes them to action. Remember, too, that the activists help push the bounds of what we consider a "polity" by including nonhuman animals, ecosystems, and even inanimate objects within the realm of radical politics. They are the tools of destruction and defense, the objects of abuse and veneration, the living beings with whom activists identify, and the very environment in which we live together.

Radical movement activists are, in their actions, cultural workers: they develop ideas, knowledge, theories, visions, symbols, and meaning systems that support communities of resistance, imagining and working for a truly different future.[3] Direct action, then, can be seen as a wide range of practices that include and extend beyond materialist forms of politics.

Writing in the *Earth First! Journal*, one activist collective stated:

> We have no desire to merely turn the world upside down, but wish to create a human and nonhuman community of equals with no ruling elite. . . . We do believe in direct action, action that will bring power into our hands and not that of authority. For us, direct action is a practice based on people's struggles to overcome their own subordination. Direct action is a way for people to get in touch with their own power and capacities, to take back the power of naming themselves and their lives . . . only in action is freedom.[4]

Another activist collective writes: "Direct action—action that either symbolically or directly shifts power relations—is an essential transformative tool. . . . Direct action, if only for a moment, seizes leadership and thus injects into the public sphere a competing discourse—a strand of a new reality that has the ability to ripple outward."[5] For activists, it is not simply about confronting authorities: it is about transforming power relations to ensure that future practices and policies will arise from a different worldview than the current dominant paradigm.

That process often begins with an oppositional approach to politics: "You can't ask the government to be nicer, the police to be more polite, fast food chains to cut less rainforests, a patriarch to be less sexist or construction companies to build fewer roads. We have to stop them! Earth First! begins with a realization and progresses into action."[6]

While direct action is just one tool, other tactics are often considered insufficient to produce the desired radical change. On this point, one activist wrote: "There has yet to be any serious struggle that has ever been won by letters and mere words alone. From the right of women to vote, an end to child labor, civil rights, to the struggle for all species rights—what gains have been made have involved concerted action on behalf of many diverse people including public education, direct action, and the art of sabotage."[7] These words are echoed by a person who served time for arson against corporate targets:

> I think that if we're going to create real change, meaningful change that isn't just bullshit reform . . . we really need to recognize that it's going to take a combined effort of lobbying, lawsuits, civil disobedience, and illegal direct action, to create the social pressure we need to create change from our government.[8]

This reflects the "use every tool in the toolbox" sentiment we heard from many activists: by emphasizing that direct action is not the only path but is a valid one, they seek to prevent further alienation and division between radical and mainstream ecological movements. They encourage both sides to support (or at least not condemn) a wide range of tactics toward common goals.

Jake Conroy was one of the SHAC7, a group of activists convicted and imprisoned for activities related to the SHAC campaign directed at Huntingdon Life Sciences (HLS) corporation. Conroy has worked on campaigns for justice for people living with HIV/AIDS and anti–death penalty campaigns. Between his mother's stories of protesting the Viet Nam War, his reading about the Rev. Dr. Martin Luther King Jr. and the civil rights movement, his work on these social justice issues, and his involvement with "the hardcore music scene, the punk rock music scene," he became politically conscious. Conroy "really started reading about issues of vegetarianism and veganism and animal rights. And then more direct action stuff and about the Animal Liberation Front, the Earth Liberation Front . . . it was really something I wanted to be involved with."[9] His explanation for why animal liberationists began taking direct—and often illegal—action is a common refrain among interviewees: "I think there probably was a lot of people that were getting frustrated with the idea of just normal, sign-holding protests and felt like they wanted to do something more. And so they went and did it."[10] Many activists also believe direct action is necessary because working within the state and capitalist system will never achieve total liberation, if those institutions are at some level responsible for the oppression in the first place. At an animal rights conference panel, one activist compared "insider" or reformist approaches to social change to playing chess in a game where

> my chess pieces have the standard moves. But all of his [the opponent's] pieces can do whatever the hell they want. You're never going to win that game of chess playing by his rules in his house. That isn't to say that . . . direct action is the end-all, but I think if you believe in animal liberation or earth liberation or the end of the exploitation of humans, you're never going to get it by working fully within the system.[11]

Most of the organizations and networks included in this study are self-described "radicals" who operate "aboveground": they have a public presence and many of their participants and supporters can be contacted relatively easily. The ELF and ALF, however, are *underground* direct action movements. By intention and design, their participants are unknown to the public unless apprehended by law enforcement. As explored in chapter 1, the ELF was modeled after the ALF, and both groups commit sabotage against individuals and institutions believed to be profiting from violence toward nonhuman animals and ecosystems. Recall that the groups have nearly identical guidelines that exhort activists to defend and liberate ecosystems and nonhuman animals; inflict maximum economic damage on those persons and entities committing harm to nonhumans; reveal the extent and details of the abuse perpetrated by their targets through public education; and take all necessary precautions to avoid harming any animals, human or nonhuman.[12] Their actions are often publicized through the North American Animal Liberation Press Office (NAALPO) (and in the past, by the North American Earth Liberation Front Press Office).

Whether aboveground or underground, these activists, networks, and movements share a commitment to some form of direct action as they believe it is critical to social change. And while much of that direct action involves mobilizing bodies, it also involves mobilizing ideas. Radical ecological and AR activists must challenge assumptions and articulate new visions of the way the world could be. One collective stresses the need for imagination: "All successful direct actions ultimately challenge assumptions, [which] is the act of taking on the framework of myths, lies, loyalties and flawed logic that normalize injustice." This collective believes that one goal of direct actions is to encourage people to pursue "the most important act . . . in an era defined by systematic propaganda—to question!"[13]

Activists support and undertake direct action because they see it as effective and necessary, considering the urgency of the threat and the entrenched power structures of society.

Sabotage and Property Destruction

In his classic book, *Green Rage*, former EF! activist and EF! journal editor Christopher Manes (aka "Miss Anne Thropy") wrote:

> The practice of damaging property to prevent ecological damage is unanimously condemned by government agencies, industry, and the mainstream environmental organizations. It has become a litmus test of sorts, separating the radical from the mainstream . . . the socially acceptable defense of nature from the intolerable.[14]

Edward Abbey's novel *The Monkey Wrench Gang* was a major inspiration for the founding of EF!, which celebrated, but did not officially practice, monkey wrenching. Monkey wrenching is

> ecotage, ecodefense, billboard bandits, desurveying, road reclamation, tree spiking, even fire . . . a step beyond civil disobedience. It is nonviolent,

aimed only at inanimate objects. It is one of the last steps in defense of the wild, a deliberate action taken by an Earth defender when almost all other measures have failed.[15]

As EF! veteran Dennis Davey told us, "The early Earth First! neither condemned nor condoned monkey wrenching. [But] it was part of the culture."[16]

While monkey wrenching or other forms of property destruction are among the most controversial actions these movements practice, many activists proudly support it. Emma Murphy-Ellis (aka "Pitch" or "Usnea") is a longtime forest defense activist with the CFA and EF! She went to jail for several months in 2002 after the ultimately successful forest defense blockade at Eagle Creek in Oregon. Some years later, she stirred a range of emotions with an essay circulated around activist networks:

> I state without fear—but with the hope of rallying our collective courage— that I support radical actions . . . like industrial sabotage, monkey wrench- ing machinery and strategic arson. The Earth's situation is dire. If other methods are not enough, we must not allow concerns about property rights to stop us from protecting the land, sea, and air . . . the Earth needs our effective action using all the methods of resistance at our disposal.[17]

Murphy-Ellis speaks to the central question of property rights versus the protection of nonhuman ecosystems. It is at the core of this movement's anticapitalist/anarchist focus. Most activists told us they support sabo- tage only with careful consideration and analysis. In fact, they frequently debate the strengths and limitations of specific forms of direct action. At a national conference, an activist who had served prison time for his role in a fur farm action rationally discussed the merits of arson in ani- mal liberation: "The first ALF arson action in 1987 was at UC Davis, in the Animal Diagnostic Building. That cost them $4 million. Since then, we've seen 106 arsons by ALF. Arson can be very effective. It's fire, it gets the job done. It's fast and requires minimal people."[18]

Kim McCoy of the Sea Shepherd Conservation Society (SSCS) spoke to the issue of property destruction, and her view that this path is per- fectly compatible with a compassionate perspective on animal liberation: "we are a movement of compassion," and for that reason they have a "very strict policy of nonviolence." Over more than three decades, the

Sea Shepherds have, according to McCoy, "never harmed a single person." She continued: "I'm all for extremely aggressive, direct action. I don't have a problem with property destruction . . . and I don't view that as violence. I think that in order to commit an act of violence, you must commit that act against a living, sentient being."[19] Most of our informants agreed that property destruction is nonviolent direct action, but some questioned its effectiveness.

Unresolved Conflicts

Direct action is a topic of frequent debate in radical circles. It is never simply assumed to be a uniformly positive practice. For example, tree spiking is extremely controversial within ecological movements: many say it endangers timber workers who could be injured either while cutting down a tree or at a sawmill when the spiked tree is run through machinery. Even before Earth First! activist Judi Bari infamously and unilaterally declared that the group would renounce all tree spiking (without consulting EF! activists, apparently, but in an effort to build solidarity with timber workers), spiking was spurring infighting.[20] In a July 2001 action, the ELF spiked hundreds of trees up for sale in the Gifford Pinchot National Forest. Part of the post-action communiqué read:

> The forest service was notified of this action BEFORE this year's logging season so we could take all precautions to assure worker safety. We must ask why they never made this public. We were trying to let them cancel this sale quietly. However, as bosses jeopardize worker's lives every day we realized we needed to make this public.[21]

The ELF apparently hoped to stop the tree sale and harvest and protect workers because, according to the ELF, the Forest Service could have, but had not, made it public knowledge that the trees had been sabotaged.

Mainstream environmental and animal welfare organizations have publicly and frequently distanced themselves from their radical counterparts, particularly when the question of property destruction is raised. Radical movements do not take kindly to these denunciations, suggesting that mainstream groups follow that timeless rule of thumb: if you don't have anything nice to say, don't say anything at all.[22] Even the founder of the "original" ELF group in the United States has referred to today's radicals as destructive and lacking in maturity of focus and strategy.[23]

The radical environmental movement's primary publication, the *Earth First! Journal*, was not always openly supportive of the large-scale arson attacks of the ELF, and when they did express support they lost membership. In one incident, celebrated tree sitter Julia Butterfly Hill left EF! after the *Journal* gave positive coverage to the ELF arson at the Vail, Colorado, ski resort. Karen Coulter, profiled earlier, has long since ceased her involvement in property destruction: "in and of itself, it's not effective. You have to build a mass movement around it."[24]

Jake is an activist with the group Because We Must (BWM) and critiqued the mainstream perspective on sabotage online:

> It is necessary to move forward from the dichotomy of violence vs. non-violence. Proponents of non-violence reinforce statist oppression and sanctity of corporate livelihood by limiting the means of protest and valuing the "lives" of windows, cop cars, ATMs, etc. over the lives of their fellow protesters and over the lives that might be destroyed by the consequences of inaction.[25]

Like others, he feels he cannot disavow any tactic to challenge capitalism and state institutions' protection of nonhuman objects and technologies for the benefit of a minority of powerful humans.

Direct Action and Anarchism

Rod Coronado, with his usual eloquence (see chapter 3) and roots in anti-imperialist work, says:

> We have no obligation to any government. We have every obligation to protect the earth that gives us life and our future generations. Adherence to laws that sanction the destruction of our one home planet are crimes unprecedented in human history and demand active refusal and resistance.[26]

But anarchist politics is not just about an antistatist orientation to social change; it is about developing anti-authoritarian and antihierarchical modes of decision making and community building. One earth liberation activist exhorted fellow movement activists to respect this principle during protest campaigns:

> Within campaigns, there are numerous ways to plug in. It is important that we place no hierarchy on *any* roles. This will benefit those filling all roles

equally. No matter if the roles are media, legal, research or action, support and appreciation needs to be equal. Taking these precautions will help everyone feel validated—especially within the decision making process of actions.[27]

Pickering also considers the connection between anarchist or antihierarchical politics and direct action within the ELF and ALF, describing the structure of these movements as "autonomous, loose-knit, nonhierarchical," and noting that the form is consciously designed. First, it is a security culture adaptation intended to evade state repression. As Pickering writes, this mode of organization "protects them from capture. There is no leader. There's nobody they [authorities] can pin down." And second, the nonhierarchical structure is intended to be "a model of a solution to the sort of oppressive aspects of hierarchy which we are living under in this society."[28]

While the ALF and ELF may be thwarting law enforcement through their direct actions in autonomous secretive cells, "leaderless resistance" is also important because it is *prefigurative*—that is, it is a conscious effort to practice the kind of social change they would like to see blossom across society in the future. Instead of waiting for, hoping, and demanding that states, corporations, and other dominant institutions practice democracy, consensus-based decision making, and community building, these activists are going ahead and doing it within their own circles through direct action.[29] That is perhaps the most immediate and tangible result of anarchist politics in earth and animal liberation movements.

Direct Action, Anti-Oppression, and Solidarity

As discussed in chapter 2, radical earth and animal liberation activists also make conceptual links between harms visited upon ecosystems and animals and those injustices facing human beings. This component of the total liberation frame is one of its most sociologically generative aspects: all oppression is linked.

Low-income African American residents in the greater Detroit town of Highland Park, Michigan, faced steep water bills and a government bureaucracy that forced them to pay or face a water shutoff in 2003. In what EF! saw as a hypocritical move, in July of that year, the state gave Ice Mountain (a subsidiary of the Nestlé Corporation) a $10 million tax break to pump spring water *out* of western Michigan, while Highland Park and Detroit residents had their homes seized to pay "water debts" of up to $17,000 (local activists report these are some of the poorest cities in the United States, but they have astronomical water service rates of up to $800/month). Massasauga EF! unfurled a banner from the roof of an area municipal building that read "Stop the Cut-Offs—Water for Life." The activists declared "water is a human and natural right that should not be denied to anyone." The next day, Massasauga EF! and other local activist groups led a home demonstration protest at the governor's residence, demanding that she shut down an Ice Mountain water-bottling plant *and* all water shutoffs in Highland Park and Detroit.[30] The activists were explicitly drawing the connection between the privatization of water as a capitalist "enclosure of the commons" (see chapter 3) and a violation of the basic right to life and livelihood for all beings.

Katuah EF! is a group of activists, including Chris Irwin, from East Tennessee who also work to draw links between various forms of oppression. In the 1990s, as Irwin related in chapter 2, they successfully pushed the Ku Klux Klan to leave the area and cease open recruitment. He said: "That was a material antiracist action. And my friends like Perry Red and others that were involved in the . . . predominantly African American groups [also protesting], they knew that if they needed walkie-talkies, [help paying] fines, to grow a soup kitchen, bodies, that they could contact us."[31] The Katuah EF! antiracist work and collaboration hold extra significance as a white environmental group working with people of color in the southern United States.

Underground ELF direct actions have also reflected efforts to link justice for people, ecosystems, and nonhumans. A March 2001 ELF communiqué described an illegal action at an Old Navy Outlet Center on Long Island, New York. Windows and a neon sign were smashed:

> This action served as a protest to Old Navy's owners, the Fisher family's involvement in the clear-cutting of old-growth forest in the Pacific Northwest. . . . Old Navy, Gap, Banana Republic care not for the species that call these forests home, care not for the animals that comprise their leather products, and care not for their garment workers underpaid, exploited and enslaved in overseas sweatshops. . . . We will not stop.[32]

Banana Republic and Old Navy are subsidiaries of the Gap and have long been the subject of media reports and public concerns that some of their workers are underage (as young as ten years old), underpaid, abused, and forced to labor in unsafe, sweatshop conditions in Saipan and elsewhere. Further, as the ELF insinuates above, many believe the Mendocino Redwood Company (which is financed by the Fisher family, members of which founded and own Gap, Inc.) uses toxic herbicides to clear cut redwood forests.[33]

Less than a month later, an ELF group attempted to burn down a Nike store in Albertville, Minnesota, protesting the corporation's treatment of workers and nonhumans (Nike has faced condemnation for its global manufacturing practices since the 1970s):[34]

> All ELF actions are nonviolent towards humans and animals. But if a building exists which perpetrates, and sponsors violence towards people or animals (such as a Nike Outlet, or a Gap Outlet, etc.), then by God, it's got to be burned to the ground! The ELF wholeheartedly condones the use of violence towards inanimate objects to prevent oppression, violence, and most of all to protect freedom. Direct action is a wonderful tool to embrace on the road to liberation.[35]

The ELF communiqué was signed with the name of Nike's famed chairman and CEO, Phil Knight. In response, Nike took out advertisements in major media outlets describing ELF's action as "terrorism" and urging "activists to express their concerns through constructive dialogue and meaningful action." Presumably, Nike hoped for less flammable dialogue and action.

Other evidence of radical activists making the connection between direct action and anti-oppression politics abounds. The EF! Roadshow travels the United States to build support for campaigns and to recruit activists to join the movement. At a stop in Minneapolis, one workshop focused on anti-oppression and direct action. When the organizers asked participants to define direct action, the responses included everything from occupying forests and nuclear sites to participating in immigrant justice rallies and anti-foreclosure squatting to a U.K. action called "Reclaim the Streets," in which demonstrators jackhammered holes into paved roads while their peers scattered seeds into the newly opened earth. The list included traditional EF! concerns around forest defense and anti-nuclear and anti-incinerator campaigns, but the majority linked "environmental" concerns with human rights and social justice issues. We saw this pattern repeated multiple times at the annual Round River Rendezvous and in the pages of the *EF! Journal*.[36]

The Native Solidarity workshop at the EF! Roadshow event included a discussion of the links between environmentalism and imperialism/colonialism: "Resistance against colonization *is* ecodefense," said one participant, who went on, "in terms of privilege and colonization, you can't be neutral. Inaction is action in favor of colonization."[37]

Direct Action around the Politics of Gender and Sexuality

In the summer of 2003, a forest defense action and tree sit began in the Willamette National Forest near Eugene, Oregon. The U.S. Forest Service was attempting to sell what activists described as an ancient forest to two private logging firms in the Straw Devil Timber Sale. Since just 5 percent of native forests were left standing in Oregon at the time, the case was seen as urgent. Uniquely, it was also an "all womyn action," led by a group calling itself the Ecofeminist Front, which sought to highlight the links between the domination of ecosystems and women when they wrote:

> The womyn's action is dedicated to building a community that is intolerant of all forms of oppression. We are working to create a space of mutual learning and growth—a space where we can conquer not only the demons of capitalism, patriarchy and indifference that surround us but also the demons of oppression, self-loathing and fear that reside within us. The womyn's free state is a safe space where womyn can come and gain skills and perspective. . . . It is our belief that the oppression of womyn and the destruction of the Earth come from the same unsustainable need to dominate and control. The same people who wish to take away our autonomy also wish to take away the last of the wild beauty on Earth. As womyn, we cannot achieve liberation while the Earth is still in chains. We need oxygen, clean water and the forest to survive. We need to be able to walk around alone at night; we need our homes to be free of violence; we need a life where rape, assault and oppressive attitudes are not the norm.[38]

This article in the *EF! Journal* was accompanied by a dramatic photo: five female activists wearing bandanas and carrying crossbows in front of a massive tree in the forest.

Since at least the early 1990s, gender politics has been a major theme in earth liberation movements. Activists have approached the issues of patriarchy and sexual violence creatively, offering workshops focused on anti-oppression principles and integrating egalitarian principles into their campaigns and actions. Following the Ecofeminist Front's lead, activists launched an EF! working group called Challenging Oppression Within (COW). Soon after, the first Trans and Womyn's Action Camp (TWAC) was held (in 2007), offering workshops on tree climbing, road blockades, and do-it-yourself gynecology. The report back from that first TWAC stated, "TWAC was a step in the right direction for the Earth First! movement, which has been criticized for its lack of trans and feminist politics."[39] Just after the 2009 TWAC, we spoke with two male EF! veterans about the movement's gender politics. One of them, Doug, told us, "This actually was originally a problem with tree sits because of the close quarters that people live in up in the tree, and the problem of oppression." Another male EF! veteran, Dennis, agreed and recalled: "There were issues related to our society in general when some men don't know how to treat women. We did have sexual assaults on tree sits, so that was a real concern."[40]

At the 2009 TWAC, expanded workshops were specifically designed for direct action training and skill building among "transgendered, intersexed, gender-queer, androgynous- or womyn-identified folk [to] share skills in an empowering environment."[41] This event was followed by the EF! Rendezvous and Cascadia Summer—a much longer series of trainings and actions focused on defending Oregon's Elliot State Forest from timber harvesting.

In 2011, the TWAC upped the ante: they led an action to underscore their view that gender and sexual oppression are inseparable from human dominion over the forests. Participants occupied the Oregon Department of Forestry office in Molalla in solidarity with another ongoing defense action in the Elliot State Forest. The report by those involved was colorful, dramatic, and full of flair and humor:

> Lady and trans folk, with support from our allies, occupied the office in pink fishnets, underwear, and so much sass and glitter. Three folks locked down while the queerest takeover swallowed the hallways and main front desk. . . . People draped themselves around poles in front of the office, sissy-bounded, and temporarily stopped a logging truck, causing a road closure. Chants included "Beavers and Divas are our natural allies" and "We're a bunch of queer fucks, we don't want your clear cuts." Three arrests

followed suit (the arrestees are now dubbed the Rebel Bitchez) and the office remained shut down for the rest of the day.[42]

Gender and sexuality are issues that can variously unite and divide radical movements. The animal liberation movement has seen its own internal debates about this. Renowned ecofeminist scholar and activist Marti Kheel critiqued the routine and uncritical support of a militant approach to animal liberation. She viewed these practices as patriarchal, masculinist, and often destructive, reminding readers that early animal rights movement leaders focused their efforts on education and an ethic of care and compassion, and she advocated open animal rescues as one way of achieving that orientation in the present context.[43] Joshua Harper, a SHAC7 defendant and longtime animal liberationist, offered his thoughts on the macho image of his movement:

> People tend to think of direct action as being aggressive, and people tend to think of aggression as being a male trait. I know that a lot of my rhetoric early on, I mean—actually, if you look at some of the things I was saying in '99, 2000, 2001, I might as well have been George Bush talking about the war on terrorism. You know, "And if you're not with us, you're a coward." You know, I mean, there's definitely a lot of that very macho rhetoric. And in SHAC . . . there were times when that was very strong.[44]

The politics of gender and sexuality continue to provide opportunities for earth and animal liberation activists to challenge and reproduce social structures through their use of language, symbols, and action.

Indigeneity, Culture, and the Sacred

Rod Coronado

While much of the discourse of radical animal rights/liberation movements has embraced total liberation, that movement has yet to more fully integrate anti-oppression and solidarity principles into its direct action to the extent that we have seen in the earth liberation movement. One towering exception has been Rod Coronado, who is without a doubt one of the most eloquent theorists and spokespersons for total liberation. No other activist has been as visible and active across these movements, and none could articulate the links between earth and animal liberation and Indigenous peoples' struggles so powerfully.

In March 1995, Coronado pled guilty to aiding and abetting an ALF arson that caused over $100,000 in damage at Michigan State University.[45] The action targeted and destroyed thirty-two years of research documents that, in Coronado's words, were "intended to benefit the fur farm industry."[46] The ALF claimed responsibility for the raid, the seventh in a series of direct actions targeting fur farms and universities engaged in taxpayer-supported research jointly funded by the fur trade. It was known as "Operation Bite Back." Along with liberating animals, the actions deliberately targeted the fur industry's research and knowledge base. According to Coronado, the research that the arson at Michigan State University halted involved "experiments where mink and otters are force-fed toxins and other contaminants until they convulse and bleed to death."[47]

Coronado also pled guilty to theft of government property. He stole—and publicized stealing, under the name "the Crazy Horse Retribution Society"—a journal belonging to a Seventh Cavalry officer killed at the battle of Little Bighorn (near Crow Agency, Montana) in 1876. Coronado wrote that he was appalled to see a monument glorifying General George Custer and the Seventh Cavalry at the Little Bighorn Battlefield National Monument, where, in "Custer's Last Stand," Chief Gall and Crazy Horse (Tasunke Witko) defeated the cavalry. In his view, the soldiers

> were an illegal occupational force trespassing in clear violation of the Fort Laramie treaty of 1868 to attack peaceful encampments of noncombatants in the heart of the Lakota Nation. The theft of the Cavalryman's journal is a reminder of indigenous discontent with the treatment of our heritage and culture by the US Government.[48]

Coronado was sentenced to 57 months in prison for the journal theft and another 57 for the Michigan arson, for a total of 114 months. He lamented state repression in a statement:

> Like most indigenous people, I am unable to match the limitless resources of the US government in their efforts to incarcerate me, nor am I able to adequately defend myself amidst laws that criminalize the preservation of our sacred earth mother. . . . At a time when ecological and cultural destruction is common place and within the perimeter of the law, it sometimes

becomes necessary to adhere to the highest laws of nature and morality rather than stand mute witness to the destruction of our land and people.

Continuing, Coronado invoked nonhumans as part of his community:

> Over the last ten years I have placed myself between the hunter and the hunted, the vivisector and the victim, the furrier and the fur bearer, and the whaler and the whale. These are my people, my constituency. It is them that I owe my life. I have chosen to continue the time honored tradition of resistance to the invading forces that are ravaging our homes and people.[49]

Today, Coronado is out of prison, a living legend in the earth and animal liberation movements.

The Four Oaks/Minnehaha Free State Campaign

Coronado has, arguably, inspired other important efforts to build collaborations between radical ecological movements and Indigenous peoples, such as in the Four Oaks/Minnehaha Free State campaign, which used both discourse and direct action to link oppression and justice across species. In EF!'s first U.S. urban land occupation, a campaign was directed at the state of Minnesota's plans to reroute a highway through an area that activists claimed was ecologically sensitive and sacred to Native Americans. Specifically, Native leaders declared four oak trees at the site were used (historically) for Indigenous people's gatherings and that nearby Cold Water Spring was a sacred ancient water source. Both lay directly in the path of the proposed highway route. A number of EF! and American Indian Movement (AIM) activists came together to found the Minnehaha Free State, a land occupation that delayed the highway project for nearly two years.

Since the 1980s, radical ecology and Indigenous rights movements have used blockades to secure concessions from states and industry, including reducing the scope of operations or halting them altogether. The *EF! Direct Action Manual* (an out-of-print but widely circulated underground publication) justifies roadblocks:

> Since roads pave the way for logging, mining, grazing, development and utter destruction of the wild, natural places, they must be stopped, seized or ripped. Creating a people's road occupation is an effective way of protecting

a given area. The occupation or blockade enables activists to consistently monitor the area while creating a climate of strong resistance to the proposed annihilation of it. . . . Some would say that the road is now an autonomous zone, liberated from the government by the people. The blockade can attract a diverse group of people, and a progressive community of resistance can form in what has been identified as a Free State.[50]

In the two years that the urban blockade halted the State Highway 55 rerouting in the Twin Cities, EF! allied with Indigenous groups. Sharon Day, founding executive director of the Indigenous Peoples' Task Force in Minnesota (an HIV education, and service organization), told us she is "full-blood Ojibwe . . . from the Martin Clan," and she was born and raised in Minnesota. The clan system, a tribal governance practice used since the pre-Contact period, requires, Day says, members "to protect the people . . . and contribute . . . [f]irst to your family, the clan, the tribe, and then ultimately . . . humanity. So that was the way we were raised."[51] And that is how she came to work with the AIM and, ultimately, the Four Oaks/Minnehaha Free State action. She and other Indigenous leaders built and participated in a sweat lodge at the site of the occupation:

> That night when we went in the sweat lodge, we could hear this other singing, you know. It was a full moon. So there were these, this coven of [witches]—I had heard about them for years. In fact, some of the women I knew from my LGBT life, you know, they had talked about having ceremonies down by the river. And I never knew where that was. Well, here they were, like right over here, having their ceremony. We're in the sweat lodge, and we had the drums, and they had drums. We'd sing, and they'd sing, you know.[52]

For the Indigenous peoples and the white activists who identified as witches, the site of the occupation was sacred for different reasons. For the Indigenous peoples, the claim was rooted in their actual history on that physical site; for the witches it was a more contemporary connection to a place they viewed as imbued with special power. It made sense to Day: "This was . . . a sacred site. So it made sense to me, then, these witches would be having their ceremony there because . . . we all have a metaphysical relationship to the land. [So] when you go to a place . . . like the spring—that's a sacred place—you can feel that. So I guess it would be sort of like . . . if you were Catholic and going to the Vatican. Or if you were Muslim and . . . going to Mecca. You know, you would feel that."[53]

The unusual, but strong-willed, group of Wiccans involved describe themselves as witches and practitioners of centuries-old European spiritual traditions. Paul Eaves told us about how the witches got involved in the Minnehaha Free State. Talking to one of the Native leaders of the campaign, he said: "We're witches, we want to start doing ceremony here."[54] Though Day seems accepting of the witches, not all Native leaders were thrilled at the idea of white Wiccan practitioners claiming kinship with Indigenous lands, but they allowed it. Eaves's group held a ritual:

> We wanted to get direction from the land [as a] sacred space . . . and listen . . . to what the land had to say . . . about what we as humans could do to work with the land, to protect it. So we did that, and after that we did drum and dancing amidst the four oaks, and what we'd do is we raise energy, so essentially we wanted to raise energy to send this energy out to basically protect the land."[55]

Eaves's story reveals collaborations and frictions with Indigenous leaders, as well as a recognition of the role that nonhuman natures play in interpellating activists, calling them to defend ecosystems and cultural sites.

Still, the state of Minnesota saw nothing sacred in the site. Day recalled:

> The guy from the Highway Department always says, "But, you know, Native people didn't go there before." And I said, "Well, you know what? It was walled off. The Bureau of Mines owned that property. No one was allowed there." And so, but once we knew about the spring, you know, we'd go. And we still go. And we still make our offerings, and we still get the water for our ceremonies there. You know, for medicine. On September 11, I was at the spring by myself . . . that's where I made my offering for what was happening. You know, for the people.[56]

Solstice was raised as a white American in a conservative Mennonite community in Lancaster, Pennsylvania, but later discovered that he had Native American heritage. He got involved in a variety of social justice campaigns focused on sweatshops and economic justice, much of it directed at Walmart. He appreciates that the traditions he was raised in closely approximated anarchism (though his Mennonite community would probably not use that term):

The mutual aid that was really practical on an everyday basis in that community actually far exceeds a lot of communities that I've been in since then that are very explicitly supposed to be about mutual aid. That's not for lack of trying, that's because of the infrastructure that exists over generations and strong social networks.[57]

In 1998, Solstice received a phone call from an activist colleague who invited him to join the Minnehaha Free State campaign, so he moved to Minneapolis. Like all participants, Solstice had to fulfill multiple duties at any given time. He recalled:

I found myself writing some of the press releases, talking to the media, and training other people to talk to the media . . . anything having to do with communication, whether public or internal, I really found myself doing. But I did direct action too, I did tree sits, I helped build barricades, I dug tunnels, and got arrested I think seven times during the campaign.[58]

Solstice concluded it was cultural, not ecological value, that both the environmental and Indigenous activists were protecting at the Four Oaks and Cold Water Spring:

One of the key values I think was reverence for the sacred. . . . And when I say sacred I don't necessarily mean magical or religious, I mean kind of imbued with meaning, that we were not just thinking mechanically or instrumentally about things like land and things like community and things like sacred sites . . . that trees can have meaning and land has meaning and ceremony has meaning and history in connection with land has meaning, and it's important and it's worth struggling for.[59]

Ian is a veteran animal liberationist who became deeply involved at the Minnehaha Free State campaign.[60] He lived in an on-site encampment for many months and worked tirelessly to bring public attention to their efforts. In *No Compromise*, a magazine primarily dedicated to animal liberation (but also frequently fostering links to social justice movements),[61] he wrote:

The Minnehaha Free State is now the longest-running urban occupation in American history, at over a year, and shows no signs of slowing down. The rerouting of Highway 55 would bulldoze through prairie and parkland, historic and sacred sites, and a 10,00-year-old spring. We will not let this stand, so we are now running two camps on either side of the reroute corridor, a direct action encampment with tree-sits on the north side and a spiritual encampment with tree-sits on the south side.[62]

"Dr. Toxic" was another of those young white activists involved in the Minnehaha Free State campaign, but he brought much more than a love for the land to this struggle. A former army reservist, Christian rock bassist, vegan animal liberationist, and peace activist, he had been active in a University of Minnesota–based group called Student Organization for Animal Rights (SOAR).[63] In the late 1990s, he was arrested for animal liberation activities, including a lockdown at a Neiman Marcus store and an action at the Yerkes Primate Research Center at Emory University.[64] By 1998–1999, he had become a core member of the Minnehaha Free State. Dr. Toxic demonstrated not only in favor of defending the ecologically fragile space but also to show his solidarity with and respect for the Dakota people. He recalled a cutting ritual that members of the Native community initiated, inviting their non-Native allies to join: "There was one ceremony that I was a part of, and that was towards the end. There was a flesh offering. And that was right around the time . . . knowing that we are not going to win this. And there was a flesh-offering ceremony. It was a piece of myself for those four trees."[65]

The stories Solstice, Paul Eaves, Ian, and Dr. Toxic shared with us reveal that the Minnehaha Free State/Four Oaks campaign was made possible not only by a coalition of EF!ers and Native American leaders, but also by others who were active in animal liberation, social justice, and traditional spiritual movements locally and nationally. Four Oaks was a multi-issue campaign with influences from multiple social movements.

Despite voluminous testimony and protests from Indigenous and other communities across the state and region, Minnesota's Department of Transportation (MNDOT) moved ahead.[66] They bulldozed the remaining homes and the activist encampment to proceed with the highway reroute.

At that point, with the "aboveground" protest felled, the ELF stepped in. In its communiqué detailing its damage to construction vehicles, the ELF emphasized the inseparability of eco-defense and solidarity for the Dakota people, insisting that the project be halted to preserve both critical cultural and ecological sites.[67] It was not. MNDOT eventually succeeded in rerouting the highway and removed the sacred four oaks.

The coalition *was* ultimately successful at saving Cold Water Spring from destruction, though. That was only one of many accomplishments. It was the first collaboration between EF! and the AIM and remains one of the longest road occupations in U.S. history. It brought together groups and movements from across numerous cultural and civil society sectors, all embracing various aspects of total liberation and engaging with non-human natures on multiple registers. And it saw the largest police action (at the time) in the state of Minnesota's history: an estimated eight hundred officers were called out in a single day for "Operation Coldsnap" to dislodge and arrest activists.[68] As veteran EF! and Free State activist Ron S. recalled, "The police response was so crazy . . . this massive amount of repression . . . eight hundred cops. I've never seen anything like that. Previously with forest actions I've seen twenty-four cops max, so that shattered any myth of safety that I had."[69] The Minnehaha Free State activists continue to organize today—more than a decade after the four oaks were cut—around earth and animal liberation, Native sovereignty, environmental justice, immigrant rights, prisoner support, LGBTQ politics, worker's rights, antipolice brutality, and anarchist politics.[70]

Defending Life from Biotech

As explored in the anticapitalism section of the previous chapter, genetic engineering (GE) and genetic modification (GM) are changing foods and animal feed, often for the purpose of increasing resistance to herbicides and pesticides, making crops more drought tolerant, or producing higher nutritional content. Genetically modified organisms (GMOs) have had their genetic makeup altered through genetic engineering and are the source of GM/GE foods. GMO production is distinct from traditional techniques through which humans have sought to create desired traits in various crops: GMOs can be made with great precision and in far less time. Their effects, however, can be injurious, and this worries farmers, consumers, and activists, among others. GE crops may produce genetic pollution, create new viruses and bacteria, damage beneficial insects, produce allergens harmful to human health,[71] harm the economic fortunes of farmers around the world,[72] and lead to increased pesticide use with insect resistance. According to at least one prominent study, pollen released from GE corn is lethal to Monarch butterflies.[73] Social movement activists argue agribusinesses are more concerned with profit than with human and ecological health, and governments are too slow to regulate these practices.[74] Radical earth liberation movements point to this rising threat to highlight and challenge capitalist institutions' efforts to profit from controlling food systems and the production of new forms of life.

In the early 2000s, after (according to media reports) a series of meetings to coordinate attacks, the ELF got busy targeting firms, laboratories, and universities where researchers were pursuing genetic engineering and biotechnology projects. On May 21, 2001, an arson at the University of Washington's Center for Urban Horticulture—where GE poplar trees were being grown for the pulp and lumber industries—targeted the office of professor Toby Bradshaw. He had received funding from the timber industry for research on how to accelerate the growth of poplars. The ELF action caused $7 million in damage. [75]

On June 10, 2001, not even three weeks later, the ELF claimed credit for vandalism at the University of Idaho's Biotechnology Building. The ELF cell, calling themselves the Night Action Kids, removed survey stakes at the site and painted slogans including "NO GE!" and "Go Organic" on the building. The communiqué that accompanied this action reflected a sense of solidarity with small farmers:

> Monsanto and other large corporations are patenting seeds and forcing farmers to sign contracts that they will continue buying these GE, and many times pesticide resistant, seeds from the same corporation year after year, effectively taking control over our food sources. . . . The fact is that Biotechnology and Genetic Engineering are scary prospects when placed in the hands of large corporations who care only about profits and not about the health and safety of the people, or the effects they are having on the environment.[76]

Just as animal rights activists have, for more than a century, taken part in "hunt sabs" (actions to sabotage hunting), earth liberation activists launched a series of "crop sabs"—sabotaging genetically engineered crops by pulling them up and destroying them. Ron S. was inspired by others undertaking this practice in other parts of the United States and Europe:

> In other places there were groups like the Bolt Weevils and the Genetic Jokers and they were doing crop sabs, and this was a big influence on me.

We would find sites and destroy crops. There were actions on the West Coast and East Coast. There were crop sabs occurring in England by mainstream groups, but not here, so we took that up. This continued into 2000.[77]

The Bolt Weevils Ron S. mentioned have conducted many crop sabs. In September 1999, they trampled several thousand stalks of GE corn at a seed research facility owned by the multinational Novartis Corporation in Goodhue County, Minnesota.[78] Another band of Bolt Weevils glued and jammed the door locks at the company's corporate offices nearby, "to prevent another day of profiting off the dirty business of genetic engineering," according to the group's communiqué. Reviving the namesake of the Minnesota farmers who toppled lines owned by the Northern States Power company in the 1970s, the Bolt Weevils specifically wanted to take on Novartis—one of the largest "life sciences" conglomerates.[79] Their communiqué read, in part:

> As farmers in the U.S., France, India and elsewhere struggle to maintain a place in the expanding global economy, corporate mergers and acquisitions increase, giving more control over the world's food systems to a handful of huge seed-chemical pharmaceutical conglomerates. The technology of genetic engineering has been developed and marketed to the world by these companies with no regard for the social, ecological or economic consequences of releasing millions of acres of mutated plants into the environment, or the consolidation of seed ownership that has resulted from such a profit-driven science.[80]

This communiqué is an indictment of the social, ecological, and economic harms activists believe GE corporations have wrought, but it continues, sounding less like a chest thumping radical activist manifesto and more like an appeal to cherished midwestern values and traditions:

> Decades of farm policies designed to boost profits for agricultural chemical companies like Monsanto, Dow and Dupont has left the rural farm economy in shambles, with suicide rates among desperate farmers on the rise. Intensive industrial agribusiness has severely degraded, eroded and poisoned the American heartland. . . . This trend spells disaster for the global food supply, from agrarian third world communities to rural America. Family

farms won't survive without a new approach to farm economics and a turn to ecological farming practices.[81]

Activists linked GE/GM to animal liberation as well. One advocate wrote in the *ELF Resistance Journal*:

> When it comes to the creation and modification of animal species used solely to further fraudulent animal experimentation. . . . When it comes to the ownership and exploitation of our genes for the benefit of multinational corporations. . . . When it comes to the existence of food diversity and security as well as the biodiversity this planet . . . GENETIC ENGINEERING MUST BE STOPPED IMMEDIATELY![82]

And, as discussed in chapter 3, anti-capitalist sentiments are strong in these anti-GE/GM campaigns. In a joint ELF/ALF action in January 2002, activists targeted a biotech industrial park under construction in Fairfield, Maine, damaging construction equipment on site:

> Biotechnology is one more tool by the ruling class to control our lives and make more money. Only the rich can produce biotechnology. . . . We enjoy life here and are sick of businessmen coming in and trying to dupe us into trading the good life for wage slavery. People!!! Take action!!! Solidarity to those fighting against the greedy! ELF . . . ALF . . . together with all.[83]

These examples reinforce our assertion that the radical earth and animal liberation movements believe nonhuman natures are endangered because of a system of class, race, and gender politics that benefits an elite minority of humans. *That* is what makes the movements such a threat—it is not that they will necessarily "save" the earth or nonhuman animals, but that they threaten the social order.

SHAC: Anarchism, Anticapitalism, Antispeciesism, and Direct Action

Josh Harper, was one of the SHAC7. As an adolescent, he drifted on the John Day River and listened to pro–animal rights hardcore punk bands from the United Kingdom and United States (including Minor Threat and Craig Rosebraugh's own band, Unamused).[84] He was politicized by the first Iraq War and gravitated toward animal liberation work, including SHAC's action against HLS. He was labeled a terrorist and spent time in prison. Like Harper, fellow SHAC7 defendant Andrew Stepanian developed a love of nonhuman natures during his childhood. He described how his mother would encourage him to paint what he saw in the wilderness:

> At a young age I started to look at, for example, flora in a different way than other kids did. I don't know why, but every time I saw plants with roots and how they would absorb nutrients from the ground, I kinda viewed it as a miraculous thing. And I think that [when people notice] things like that—the small things—then they feel like there's a great mystery and great respect in it, then they're more likely to empathize with the suffering of small creatures or marginalized social groups, and you want to fight for the underdogs because you realize that everybody and everything is important.[85]

Stepanian went on to work with the Nature Conservancy, the New York Public Interest Research Group, and more radical groups such as the Animal Defense League of Rhode Island and Food Not Bombs, a group that provides food to the hungry and problematizes the U.S. government's commitment to military spending over domestic poverty, hunger, health crises, and homelessness.[86] For his work with SHAC, he spent several years in federal prison, including a Communications Management Unit (CMU) dubbed "Guantanamo North."[87]

Stop Huntingdon Animal Cruelty (SHAC) was created in the United Kingdom (then spread to the United States) and used a host of tactics to publicize and challenge Huntingdon Life Sciences' (HLS's) animal testing by going after its finances. In primary targeting, SHAC focused directly on the company's directors and employees. In secondary targeting, activists pressured HLS's business partners to withdraw their services, or cancel contracts, and sell shares. And in tertiary targeting, activists pressured companies working with HLS's business partners to withdraw, too (what I might call "Three Degrees of HLS"). SHAC was wildly successful: more than a hundred firms ceased doing business with HLS. Using secondary and tertiary targeting, tactics developed during the anti-Apartheid movement, animal liberation activists borrowed tried-and-true ideas and methods from past eras. They also demonstrated how anarchist and anticapitalist politics, combined with antispeciesist philosophy, can be applied through direct action.

SHAC USA also posted videotapes of animal cruelty in HLS labs on-line. Public pressure and the loss of HLS's corporate customers led to a plummeting share price, millions of dollars of debt,[88] and being dropped from both the New York and London Stock Exchanges. The consequences of the SHAC campaign were stunning. HLS's share values dropped from 3.55 British pounds ($5.94 U.S.) in 1990 to 1.75 pence (3 cents U.S.) in early 2001.[89] One activist publication gloated about another success: "The current record: five hours. That's how long it took for Mellon Investment Services, Huntingdon's transfer agent, to dump the lab."[90] The list of companies selling shares in HLS as a result of SHAC's work is long and star-studded, including Barclays Global Investors, Barclays PLC, Hartford Investment Management Company, Wells Fargo, Rice Hall James and Associates LLC, and BNY Mellon.[91] The company's largest investor, U.S. investment bank Stephens Inc., gave the company a $15 million loan to keep it afloat, and HLS moved its financial center to the United States. SHAC protests and campaigning continue to this day; weekly actions are directed at the company and its clients around the world.

Like many other radical earth and animal liberation groups, SHAC is anarchist in that it is decentralized, with no official leaders. The "campaign" refers to any action—legal or otherwise—aimed at contributing to the demise of HLS. The organization is, according to activists, merely a news and information service. The activists' decentralization and support of a diversity of tactics enabled the campaign to transcend bickering and divisions.

Camille Hankins is the director of Win Animal Rights (WAR), based in New York, and works as a SHAC activist. At an animal rights conference, she spoke to the way that SHAC blended anarchism with direct action:

> SHAC people rely on the underground liberation forces to do direct actions, with no coordination. So we have no idea who's doing what . . . we put out a target list and things just happen. That's a real distinction from where [for example] Sea Shepherd is controlling their entire campaign. And their campaign has that component of direct action. Our direct action comes from outside sources.[92]

Jake Conroy, another SHAC7 defendant and former prisoner, said it was also hard for the state to figure out who to blame for the group's actions:

The government doesn't understand that things just . . . organically happened like that. We were in this campaign and made our suggestions as to what we thought targets should be . . . and some people agreed to them and some didn't. And the people that didn't, did their own thing. And that was perfectly fine.[93]

"SHACtivism" is now evident around the globe. On a single day in December 2008, there were SHAC demonstrations in Britain, Chile, France, Ireland, the Netherlands, New York, New Zealand, and Sweden targeting companies doing business with HLS. In Gothenburg, Sweden, this meant Bayer and 3M, while in the United Kingdom, demonstrations took place at Bayer, BMS, PDP, Xerox, and Barclays. In New York, the homes of Bayer, BMS, and Novartis staff were picketed, while in Chile a blockade of activists prevented trucks from entering a Bayer facility.[94]

SHAC has empowered a small group of people and individuals in ways that other social movements rarely can. The anarchist collective CrimethInc. wrote:

Whereas an individual might feel insignificant at an antiwar march of thousands, if she was one of a dozen people at a home demonstration that caused an investor to pull out, she could feel that she had personally accomplished something concrete. The SHAC campaign offered the kind of sustained low-intensity conflict through which people can become radicalized and develop a sense of collective power.[95]

Harper agreed. He originally thought the protest targets were powerful "decision makers," while he saw himself as "little, lower-middle-class me, working in a parking garage." His protest targets were "these men whose clothing cost more than I made in a year" who spent time in "country clubs and . . . expensive restaurants . . . behind walls of security guards" and who had secretaries "who go, 'Oh, I'll pass the message on'" when the traditional methods of protest and negotiation are employed. But with the use of high-intensity SHAC campaign tactics, Harper came to believe "my opinions mattered, and that they were going to have to pay attention. That was amazing. And the fact that . . . they had to come to the table, where they had to listen to us and often capitulate to our demands—that was wonderful."[96]

scott crow says he saw SHACtivism as "a beautiful, decentralized campaign . . . and it was super militant. . . . And this campaign was organized by a lot of people who were anarchists." Like Harper, crow felt effective:

> We were making multibillion-dollar companies lose millions of dollars. They can't get toilet paper to wipe their ass with because we're targeting the people who do janitorial supplies. We're going after everybody that's associated with them. There's the primary targets and then there's the tertiary targets. And it was going great, all these companies were dropping.

And in home demonstrations, even when the protest target was initially unconcerned or even out of town, it was often their neighbors who pressured the targets to capitulate or move. crow remembered, "We did home demonstrations at peoples' houses at two in the morning or six in the morning, we made people move out of $1,000,000 mansions, $2,000,000 mansions, they had to get extra security."[97]

Eventually, the level of harassment and intimidation by SHAC activists got out of hand, even for many radicals. In an infamous incident, HLS managing director Brian Cass was physically attacked outside his home in February 2001. In July of that year, a group calling itself the Pirates for Animal Liberation took credit for sinking a yacht owned by a Bank of New York executive, prompting the bank to sever ties with HLS. In the fall of 2003, incendiary devices were planted at the Chiron and Shaklee corporations protesting their relationship to HLS,[98] and in 2005 the ALF firebombed a car belonging to an executive at Vancouver-based brokerage Canaccord Capital, resulting in that firm's announcement that it would drop Phytopharm PLC, a client working with HLS.

Stepanian said:

> That was the part that really annoyed me, as the movement got bigger and bigger, we had no control. And we're not supposed to have control because we're not technically leaders. But you start to see some people with bad temperaments up their tactics . . . [and] all these bad things started happening . . . to where I felt uncomfortable.[99]

In March 2006, the SHAC7 defendants were convicted on charges of violating the Animal Enterprise Protection Act, a controversial law that criminalized activities that reduce profit making at firms that use animals to conduct business. Some were also charged and convicted of interstate stalking and other offenses. The state did not charge them for participating in the threatening acts in which other activists engaged but sought to hold them responsible for such actions. Their prison terms ranged from one to six years. Britain passed the Serious Organized Crime and Police Act, designed to provide protections to animal research firms, and in 2009 and 2010, several SHAC U.K. activists, including founders Heather Nicholson and Greg and Natasha Avery, were sentenced to prison terms of between four and eleven years under the legislation.

SHAC and Ecological Politics

The SHAC campaign might be accused of being yet another single-issue animal liberation effort, but a closer examination reveals that it is a deeply *ecologically* focused project as well. If ecological politics and political ecology are marked by the recognition of the interrelationships and interdependencies among living and inanimate beings, then SHAC is without a doubt an intensely ecological project.[100] Its anarchist mobilizing and organizing were made possible by sharing information and taking action across wide geographic spaces, revealing an ecology of sentiment, belief, knowledge, motivation, and hope. After all, what is a social movement if not a web of beings, passion, and action? Similarly, SHAC's anticapitalist framework reveals the power and presence of ecological politics in the way the activists mapped the ecology of capitalism. As Greg Avery put it: "The campaign has looked at an age-old problem—vivisection—and come up with a novel and devastating way of attacking it. Banks, stockbrokers, shareholders, etc.—the vivisectors all need them, but they don't need the vivisectors."[101] Stepanian picked up the same thread:

> If you look at the SHAC campaign, we looked at the opposition as an organism, and we wanted to cut the life support to the organism, and in this system, the life support of the organism is money flowing in the market. And if you want to cut off any of the fluids that are supporting that market, there are pressure points, whether that be market makers, or people that handle e-commerce, or people that handle logistics of animal imports, etc. So the SHAC campaign worked from that kind of tactical model where it targeted the financial and logistic support of the system in an effort to choke it out.[102]

SHAC understands the ways constituent parts of the capitalist system interrelate, which allows activists to exploit points of vulnerability.[103] The integration of an anticapitalist framework and ecological politics is also present in SHAC's recognition of the links among people, institutions, finances, and the fates of nonhumans in laboratories, and in their demand of acknowledgment and accountability for the consequences of those linkages. The use of primary, secondary, and tertiary targeting illustrates the fragility of this web of connections. This is perhaps the most potent and unsettling aspect of the SHAC campaign: it exposes how people's mundane routines, relationships, careers, and everyday lives are entangled with the suffering of beings they will never meet, who exist in far-off places. SHAC exposed an ecology of power, abuse, death, and profit, and it enforced an ecology of responsibility.

Arguably, reservations about SHAC's tactics are reflective, not of universalist moral principles of nonviolence, but rather of the depths of speciesism. As SHAC activist Kevin Kjonaas puts it:

> If critics of the ALF and SHAC honestly faced the internalized prejudices that they harbor, and imagined that it was white, middle-class kindergartners from Kansas being pumped full of bleach or anally electrocuted, most would be ready to take up arms themselves. It is not children who are suffering and dying by the billions, however, but rather nonhuman animals, and only for that speciesist reason are certain tactics condemned as "terrorist" or taken off the table of discussion.[104]

Ultimately, while Huntingdon Life Sciences survives, it could be argued that SHAC won its fight. First, it crippled the corporation. Second, the fact that its most visible activists were sent to prison and labeled terrorists signaled the state's desperation in the face of a powerful movement. Every activist with whom we spoke agreed SHAC had become a threat in that it was a good example of radical activism meeting its goals. In many ways, the SHAC campaign and other struggles considered here strengthened the movement's cultures of resistance—those shared understandings, ideas, and knowledge that inform and support individual and collective practices of dissent.

The Power of Nonhumans in Social Movements

Throughout this book, nonhumans are considered as, for radical activists, part of the "polity." Recall in chapter 1 how the total liberation frame was described as a movement in which everything is connected: the air we breathe, the land on which we depend, and nonhuman animals are as much a part of the "political" realm as our next-door neighbor. Paul Eaves said that, near the end of the Minnehaha Free State campaign, he could see the writing on the wall: the state would prevail. He wanted to be present on the land to offer support for his nonhuman relations: "It's like hospice service for the land. If a friend is sick, a friend is dying, are you going to leave that friend?" He talked about the way that nonhuman beings communicate not only to him and other humans, but to other more-than-just-humans: "The other thing is, and I've seen biology that supports it, is that the land communicates. . . . I've heard that oaks communicate through their roots . . . so the story of the occupation and the community of the four oaks . . . is not just through the stories we [humans] tell." For Eaves, "the relationship I had with the land . . . continues to this day."[105]

Sociological literature on social movements has overlooked nonhuman natures in motivating activism. More precisely, sociologists have not given enough thought to the ways social movement frames, ideas, values, goals, tactics, and actions result from interactions between human and nonhuman forces. Scholarship from the fields of environmental sociology, political ecology, and ecocriticism, however, reveals humans and other species, ecosystems, and inanimate objects are intimately linked and constantly influence one another.[106] Attention to the ways that social movements articulate and invoke the human/nonhuman nexus allows us to extend the boundaries of environmental sociology and social movement theory by exploring the ways that ecological politics is not just actions to defend nonhuman natures, but a form of collaboration and participation with nonhuman actors as well.

For example, political scientist and environmental studies scholar Steve Vanderheiden describes the targets of radical environmentalists as "inanimate objects (machinery, buildings, fences) that *contribute* to ecological destruction"[107]—suggesting an implicit view that these nonhuman technologies are complicit in ecological violence. Following environmental sociologists and political ecologists, we suggest that such objects—along with nonhuman natures and ecosystems—can also participate in ecological protection and defense. In many ways these radical activists are "called" or "interpellated"[108] by inanimate objects like bulldozers and backhoes, fur farms, laboratories, and buildings to disable and destroy those objects to prevent short-term harm to ecosystems and nonhumans, but also to send a message to other humans who routinely use those implements in destructive ways. The agency of these nonhuman objects, then, lies in their capacity to destroy or to prevent the destruction of life.

The idea that nonhuman entities and objects can be part of the problem contrasts sharply with the dominant cultural framework, of course. For example, the state and capitalist institutions view the protection of private property as one of their core aims, so these nonhuman objects become implicated in the system of domination that earth and animal liberation movements seek to challenge. As one anarchist publication puts it: "To say that it is violent to destroy the machinery of a slaughterhouse or to break windows belonging to a political party that promotes war is to prioritize property over human and animal life . . . [it] subtly validates violence against living creatures by focusing all attention on property rights."[109]

Eating vegan pizza with renowned animal liberation activist Gina Lynn (introduced in chapter 1) and several other activists one evening, we heard someone ask, "How have other animal liberation actions, or just ALF actions—how have those affected you?" Lynn acknowledged that aggressive actions the ALF takes may alienate some people from animal liberation movements, but "It called me." She remembered seeing the news of the 1985 ALF liberation of "Britches," a Macaque monkey born in a breeding colony and subjected to sensory deprivation techniques in what many saw as abusive experimentation at the University of California, Riverside: "When I heard about that, I didn't even know vivisection existed. . . . I remember seeing . . . Britches on the news coming out of that lab. And I was like, '. . . how beautiful that these people are saving these animals.' . . . I think that has everything to do with my involvement."[110] It was not just the animals who called her, but the action, the act of liberation itself.

The animal liberation magazine *Bite Back* featured a "When Animals Bite Back" section in every issue. The section always began with the following statement: "Often our animal rights rhetoric proclaims that we must be the voice for the voiceless. While exploited animals certainly need our intervention and action, they are not always powerless. Our favorite form of 'violence' comes from their own teeth, paws, flippers and girth. To all those tactical fence sitters—try and condemn this!"[111]

The *Earth First! Journal* included a similar segment in one issue:

The animals are angry—and they're fighting back. From China, where six black bears who were kept in cramped, crushing "extraction cages" to have their bile painfully removed via a surgical extraction process, ganged up on their keeper and ate him, to Uganda, where baboons avenged the death of a troop member by ambushing the guilty farmer and tearing out his heart, to the US, where a Siberian tiger leapt from its zoo enclosure, and chased down and killed a visitor seen taunting it, animals are rising up in rebellion against their human oppressors. . . . Animal rights activists can take heart that the victims they seek to liberate are increasingly fighting to liberate themselves. Intensifying the joint liberation struggle can only benefit all species, humans included.[112]

These perspectives might be tasteless, cynical, and vengeful, but they illustrate how activists do not always see themselves solely as protectors of ecosystems and animals, but also as their *collaborators* in a project of joint or total liberation. As Rod Coronado put it: "When we join the centuries-old sacred resistance to the destruction of all life on Earth, we join legions of oppressed, be they human or non-human who have died, willingly and unwillingly, fighting for the very things you and I now believe in and fight for. It is those spirits we fill our hearts with when we stand as they have, against the enemies of life."[113]

We argue that what we are witnessing in earth and animal liberation movements is an opportunity to extend social movement theory into the realm of the nonhuman—specifically the nexus of human/nonhuman interactions. The total liberation framework unveils the presence and power of nonhumans, how their agency and interpellation of human activists are part of social movements. These movements necessarily involve interactions with, constraints, opportunities, resources, and the agency of nonhuman ecosystems, animals, and technologies.

Direct action is a core part of earth and animal liberation movements' tactical and philosophical repertoire and a critical component of the total liberation frame. It is also the most dramatic manifestation of the movement's cultures of resistance. Activists mobilize people, images, symbols, knowledge, and ideas to promote a vision of the world they would like to see and live in. There are tensions, controversies, divisions, and disagreements, but activists agree that the current social order is objectionable and in need of transformative reordering. Whatever tactics they pursue, their work involves an integration of direct action with one or more of the other pillars of total liberation and an engagement between human and nonhuman actors. These radical movements expand their reach and significance beyond traditional ecological politics and beyond the narrow confines of the human.

Learning from the Past

As discussed in chapter 1, a growing number of earth and animal liberation activists pay close attention to previous social movements, particularly as this history can provide methods of confronting state repression—strategies, tactics, and visions of social change. Collectively, the civil rights, Black Power, American Indian, Irish Republican, abolitionist, suffragist, and Industrial Workers of the World movements practiced a spectrum of tactics, including public education, nonviolent civil disobedience, armed resistance, property destruction, industrial sabotage, and public confrontation. SHAC7 defendant Jake Conroy worked diligently to connect animal liberation activists to leaders of the Black Panther Party:

> When we were doing SHAC, we would do these . . . large national demonstrations and conferences, and we'd have speakers come. We'd always try to make a point to have people from other movements. And I would always push for having Black Panthers come speak. . . . So we really felt it was important to try to get all these communities together, at least thinking about, if nothing else, what they could teach us from their own experience.[114]

NAALPO Press Officer and former spokesperson for the Physicians Committee for Responsible Medicine (PCRM) Jerry Vlasak[115] spoke about his historical inspiration:

> We see this as a struggle comparable to other liberation struggles: slavery, Algerian resistance, anti-Apartheid, and the resistance to the wars in Iraq and Afghanistan—all are struggles of oppressed people and nonhumans for freedom. . . . Every successful liberation struggle has always used illegal means. Nelson Mandela was a lawyer who tried to use legal means to fight Apartheid in South Africa, and when it didn't work he broke the law and went to jail. . . . This is a perfectly legitimate form of resistance. When everything else has been tried, then people need to do something else.[116]

scott crow counts, among his influences, the Zapatistas (who provide a challenge and alternative to the neoliberal Mexican state) and the Black Panther Party:

> We weren't trying to gain power, we were just exercising power. . . . You understand all the Zapatista stuff around that, that's where I come from, to lead by asking, to exercise power and to create autonomous spaces. . . . This is one thing I've learned from the Zapatistas, and I also take from the Black Panthers. . . . I want liberation for everybody.[117]

Radical movements of the past, from Europe to Africa, Asia, Latin America, and the United States serve as models for radical earth and animal liberation movements. Those historic movements have been led by Indigenous, ethnic, racial, and religious groups fighting colonization, racism, and patriarchy through direct action, including property destruction and sometimes armed struggle. Watching the earth and animal liberation movements valorize and emulate any (let alone many) of those movements' ideas and actions is a significant concern for the state.

CHAPTER 5

The Green Scare

State Repression of Liberation Movements

Civil disobedience . . . gets things done . . . to those who do take that
road, be willing and prepared to make new friends in jail

> —John Hanna, founder of the Environmental Life Force, author interview

The next thing you know they'll be calling in artists, actors, and anyone
else they can think of to ask of them, "Are you now or have you ever
been a vegetarian?"

> —Bruce Friedrich, in *Terrorists or Freedom Fighters? Reflections on the Liberation
> of Animals,* edited by Steven Best and Anthony Nocella II

If, as chapter 4 concluded, social movements willing to take direct action
and challenge our ideas of what is *possible* in their country's future represent a true threat to the state, the phenomenon is not new. In August
1963, FBI assistant director William Sullivan said of the Rev. Dr. Martin
Luther King Jr.: "We must mark him now . . . as the most dangerous
Negro of the future in this nation from the standpoint of national security." The United States may cherish its status as a "melting pot," but the
state rarely hesitates to slap the hand that attempts to stir it.

State repression is a set of practices that involves coercion or violence
against people who contest existing power arrangements. It is intended
to stop dissent in the present and the future. Sometimes that repression
involves what Jules Boykoff calls "direct violence"—state-sanctioned violent actions intended to stop dissent in its tracks.[1] Other times it involves
what Boykoff calls "suppression," a subtler means of control, involving
raising the costs or minimizing the benefits of dissent through infiltration,
manipulation of media reporting, firings, extraordinary rules and laws,
harassment, propaganda, surveillance, and grand jury interrogations and
indictments—all intended to discourage future activism. For example, in

early February 2009, environmentalist and labor rights organizer Marie Mason was sentenced to twenty-one years and ten months in prison for her role in targeting urban sprawl in the state of Indiana and genetic engineering research at Michigan State University through property destruction. The North American Earth Liberation Front Press Office (NAELFPO) said the sentence was "three years above the average federal sentence for murder."[2] While Boykoff's typology has its value, I group all of these practices together: they are all aimed at neutralizing dissent and undermining social change movements.

Repression is not just about stopping efforts at social change; it is also a *productive* set of practices: it can produce quiescence, fear, compliance, and obedient citizen-subjects, while privileging dominant groups, social relations, and ideas. Time and time again, interviewees for this research told me state repression was meant to instill fear. These activists see three paths open to them: rally support against repression to build community and movement power; scale back activism to "play it safe" and avoid current or future repression; or drop out altogether. Surprisingly, I find that many activists take the first path, but only by working through their fears and drawing on networks of support from their communities of resistance.

Repression is not something that states practice on an occasional basis; it is at the core of what states do and why they exist.[3] Modern nation-states claim a "monopoly on the legitimate use of physical force."[4] They are inherently authoritarian and exclusionary forces, so even though repression against specific causes or threats may rise and fall, repression itself remains a specter, a constant threat of retribution for actions outside the norm. Historically, modern nation-states co-emerged with and made possible the modern categories of race, gender, class, sexuality, citizenship, and species, as well as their bases for inclusion/exclusion, manipulation, and domination. Social movements can learn a lot about addressing repression from this history. Reformist and radical activists often debate whether radical activism or militancy *causes* repression and whether less militant, reformist approaches might then be most effective. I contend that militancy does not cause repression; it just makes that repression more visible and evident.[5] Below, I consider a few examples from social movement history.

Robert F. Williams, author of *Negroes with Guns*, began the militant Black Armed Guard in response to white vigilante violence and segregation in Monroe County, North Carolina, in the 1950s. He was harassed by state authorities and eventually fled to Cuba. If one were to argue that Williams's militancy caused state repression, one would have to confront the fact that white supremacy and racial violence were already the order of the day for African Americans. For its part, the NAACP, seen as more "reasonable" and less militant than the Black Armed Guard, was outlawed in Alabama and nearly banned in several other southern states during the civil rights era.[6]

Similarly, Nelson Mandela's militant arm of the African National Congress—Umkhonto we Sizwe (Spear of the Nation)—represented a more militant approach to racial justice and revealed the lengths to which the Apartheid government would go to maintain its power. White supremacy and racial violence were the norm that led to the emergence of the ANC. So, too, was the Irish Republican Army (IRA) an armed, militant response to centuries of British occupation. One could offer a roughly parallel analysis of the Palestinian resistance to Israeli occupation, the Native American resistance to U.S. occupation, the 1739 Stono Rebellion of slaves in what is now South Carolina, and so on. In other words, rather than causing state repression, militancy was often a response to preexisting repression.[7]

Nationally renowned anarchist Luce Guillén-Givens works through Earth Warriors are OK! (EWOK!)—an animal and earth liberation prisoner support group—and was one of the RNC8 defendants charged with felony conspiracy to commit riot in the furtherance of terrorism and felony to commit damage to property during the 2008 Republican National Convention held in St. Paul, Minnesota. In a presentation she made to a class at the University of Minnesota in 2009, Guillén-Givens said:

State repression is not the exception, it's the rule. Many people mistakenly think that state repression only comes down on people engaged in illegal activity. That's not true. The state will repress movements that have the ability to effect social change and they will do that at all costs.[8]

If the evidence supports this insight—and I believe it does—we must rethink what states and repression are and what social movements can be. From a different perspective, states are institutions that, by definition, practice exclusion, control, and violence (in addition to their other functions), and so state repression is the control and management of our everyday existence and mobility. Social movements—particularly radical movements—can be thought of as efforts aimed not only at stopping objectionable practices or promoting certain worldviews, but also at building community and the capacity for autonomy, self-determination, and mobility.

There are two other concepts I put to work in this chapter. The first is *ecologies of repression*: state and corporate repression have ripple effects beyond immediate targets and work directly and indirectly to apply the principles and practices of repression to nonhuman natures, too. Would-be future activists, supporters, would-be supporters of other social change movements, and the beneficiaries of those movements are all affected. The impacts of repression move through social networks and communities to potentially discourage or encourage future resistance and apply the principles and practices of repression to nonhuman natures through control, manipulation, domination, and attempts to minimize agency. Ecologies of repression are practiced directly through the extractive and predatory practices involved in, for example, agriculture, slaughterhouses, mining, and forestry: nonhumans and ecosystems are prevented from thriving and existing free of institutional violence and control. Ecologies of repression are also practiced indirectly through efforts to prevent or minimize the protection and defense of nonhuman natures by human activists and nonhuman natures.

The second concept extends the idea of state and corporate repression to include entire *cultures of repression*: the discourses, ideas, language, and behaviors—both explicit and implicit—that publics practice wherein resistance movements and dissent are discounted, refused, disallowed, misrecognized, and devalued in the public sphere. Specifically, when radical movements work to articulate a vision and practice of change, there is often an automatic cultural response that the ideas and actions are violent threats that must be contained. Cultures of repression can also involve divisions within movements around ideology, tactics, and strategies, and they are mutually reinforcing with state and corporate repression. They can exert a force on society and movements linked to but partially independent of states and corporations and reveal that there is always a possibility of such phenomena being challenged by a supportive culture of resistance.[9]

Finally, I want to be clear that state repression is more than just a series of acts of brute force. I see it as an *applied science*. It is rooted in a desire to *know* and to develop and deploy knowledge for the advancement of particular interests (in this case, the interest of the state and capital). This knowledge results from the routine, empirical observation, data gathering, experimentation, and analysis that state agencies perform. Studies of institutional repression reveal quite clearly that state and corporate institutions essentially follow these protocols of basic science in order to protect their interests against perceived threats and competitors.[10] In that sense, the science of institutional repression follows the logic of theorist Michel Foucault's idea that knowledge of a population can lead to power and control over that group—surveillance and data gathering on activist organizations are often used to quash or manage political dissent.[11]

For those groups deemed threats to the state, the science of repression can have serious consequences. Consider Foucault's concept of *biopower*, the way that governments exercise power over and manage people and life more generally. Biopower is a set of techniques used for achieving control of bodies and populations, placing an emphasis on the protection of life and health of a population, a citizenry.[12] If you are not a member of that nation-state's citizenry (or not a full citizen), then you are potentially detrimental to the nation's health and security. In the same way that groups like the incarcerated and the undocumented are framed as somehow "less than human" and hold a status "less than citizenship," I argue that state repression and the discourse of "ecoterrorism" works to place earth and animal liberation activists and movements *outside* the realm of citizenship. They are successfully labeled threats to the nation that must be neutralized.

State repression directed at earth and animal liberation movements generally includes surveillance, infiltration, intimidation, and imprisonment—a range of practices that have become known as the Green Scare. Echoing the FBI agent above, in 2005, a prominent federal government official named radical earth and animal liberation movements the number one domestic "terrorist" threat in the United States.[13] While these movements have not, to my knowledge, killed a single person in the United States, they have produced significant economic losses through property damage directed at industries such as forestry, genetic engineering, and animal research. Nonetheless, U.S. federal agencies label the activists "terrorists" and focus on the total liberation framework: two recently declassified FBI reports describe these movements as "anarchist" with an orientation that argues that "animals and humans are inherently the same" and whose participants choose to "engage in direct action instead of legal social protest" by utilizing "economic sabotage" directed at "perceived symbols of capitalism, imperialism, and oppression."[14] If I have not yet convinced the reader of the importance of the total liberation framework, the U.S. government has made the case for me.

Policy and Legislation Directed at "Ecoterrorists" in Historical Perspective

Legislation such as the Animal Enterprise Terrorism Act (AETA) of 2006 declared it "terrorism" to harm the profits of an industry whose products are primarily based on the use of animals. This can include boycotting, picketing, and many other forms of protest that lead to a decline in revenue for industries like furriers, circuses, animal research testing laboratories, and farms. Civil liberties advocates have cried foul at this law as a breach of constitutional rights, but several activists have already been indicted, charged, or imprisoned under the AETA. They join the many other earth and animal liberation activists who have served time in federal penitentiaries and are commonly viewed as political prisoners by movement participants, attorneys, and scholars. Bruce Friedrich of PETA described the AETA

> as basically hate crimes legislation for people who are compassionate toward animals. . . . What this literally means is if you're standing on KFC's property with a sign, and in an act of time-honored tradition of civil disobedience, you refuse to leave when told to leave . . . you can be charged with terrorism. A federal felony for standing with a sign.[15]

This legislation reflects a long legal history in the United States that defines property destruction as "terrorism" and links such acts to persons who are defined as outsiders because of their citizenship from other nations or because of the nature of their political ideas and affiliations. Some scholars argue that that AETA (and its predecessor, the Animal Enterprise Protection Act) and related laws are not actually about the crimes, but about the political stance and thought *behind* the crimes. Numerous laws already address trespassing, harassment, arson, vandalism, and property destruction; the passage of *specific* legislation around "ecoterrorism" reveals the criminalization of political thought.[16] Animal liberation activist-scholar Steven Best remarks: "According to an official

FBI definition 'Eco-terrorism is a crime committed to save nature.' It speaks volumes about capitalist society and its dominionist mindset that actions to 'save nature' are classified as criminal actions while those that destroy nature are sanctified by God and Flag."[17]

The broader discourse of "ecoterrorism" and its application via the USA PATRIOT Act have been devastating to these movements. Why would the state label earth and animal liberation activists "terrorists," and what is the social and political significance of that legal designation?

Repressive Legislation in Early U.S. History

In 1798, the French Revolution had been underway for nearly a decade (even inspiring much of the writing and argument around the United States' own Declaration of Independence). But many in the United States worried that an "alien radicalism" or anarchy stemming out of the upheaval in Europe could be ignited in this country. In this moment of national fear, four pieces of legislation were passed: the Naturalization Act, the Alien Act, the Alien Enemy Act, and the Sedition Act. The Naturalization Act forced immigrants to wait fourteen years, (not five as previously mandated) to apply for citizenship; the Alien Act gave the president the authority to deport any noncitizen judged dangerous to the peace and safety of the United States or as harboring secret plots; and the Sedition Act made it a crime to criticize government officials. The Alien Act was never enforced, the Sedition Act was briefly enforced but (after public protests) allowed to expire after only two years, and the Naturalization Act was repealed after four years. For a moment, it looked like the young country had learned its lesson: that if we fail to respect constitutional freedoms and due process, then all of our liberties are threatened. Unfortunately, the United States passed subsequent Sedition Acts in 1861 (signed by President Lincoln to address the problem of southern secessionists) and in 1918 (to address subversives in the First World War). The 1918 law made it a crime to utter "any disloyal, profane, scurrilous, or abusive language . . . as regards the form of government of the United States, or the Constitution, or the flag."[18] It complemented the 1917 Espionage Act, which prohibited speech intended to result in disloyalty to the military and proscribed any advocacy of resistance to federal law. The Alien Enemy Act, part of the Alien and Sedition Acts, is the only one still on the books. This act authorizes the president (without judicial review) to detain, expel, or restrict the freedoms of anyone whose home country is at war with the United States. This act has been enforced and upheld repeatedly (against Germans and Austro-Hungarians during World War I, against Japanese nationals and Italian and German citizens during World War II, and against Japanese American citizens during and after World War II). The president's authority remained, in some cases, even after hostilities had ceased and peace was declared.[19]

So, while many critics referred to George W. Bush's years in office as an "imperial presidency,"[20] he was, on this point, exercising lawful authority afforded the executive branch of government. What Bush did was declare an amorphous "War on Terror" that painted "global terrorist networks" as armies that were beyond flag and country. In this way, anyone linked to terrorism could be detained or deported as an "enemy alien" or "enemy combatant." Earth and animal liberation activists are, to some extent, a new class of "enemy combatants." In an innovative legal maneuver, these radicals can be considered both "citizens" of terrorist networks (or "nations") and active enemy combatants against the United States. When we talk about globalization, the executive branch's legal reasoning is no artifact. It is a remarkable, but historically consistent, deployment of biopower to exclude dissidents from the realm of citizenship because of their beliefs and affiliations (let alone actions).

Criminalizing Difference

The McCarran-Walter Act (1952) continued the openly racist national origins quotas of the 1924 Johnson-Reed Immigration Act, which favored Northern Europeans over Southern and Eastern Europeans and peoples from Asia and the global South. The McCarran-Walter Act went further to authorize the exclusion or expulsion of noncitizens who advocated Communism, belonged to the Communist Party, or simply believed in prohibited ideas like anarchism.

Much of the law repeated already existing statutes, including the 1903 Anarchist Exclusion Act and the Immigration Acts of 1917 and 1918, both of which included anarchists as undesirables. The 1903 act was officially titled "An Act To regulate the immigration of aliens into the United States" and was passed in the wake of President William McKinley's assassination by Polish anarchist Leo Czolgosz. The 1917 Act was perhaps best known for the construction of the Asiatic Barred Zone, which ensured that persons from across Asia could not be admitted to the United States. It also expanded immigration law to exclude not only foreigners who advocated the overthrow of the U.S. government, but also those who advocated the unlawful destruction of property and were "opposed to organized government"—anarchists and those who believed in anarchism. Along with the 1918 Act, this was the first time federal law was used to codify the principle of guilt by association (it excluded people based on group membership and even on beliefs), and it was specific in listing "sabotage" and damage to property as reasons for deportation. As legal scholar David Cole writes about the development of repressive laws in the early twentieth century: "The culture and the law thus treated dissident citizens as themselves 'alien,' providing the rationale for bridging the citizen-noncitizen divide."[21]

The 1952 law that upheld so much of the earlier legislation also continued the practice of barring gays and lesbians from entering the nation. They were considered "mental defectives" and "sex perverts."[22] Legal scholar Bill Ong Hing connects the dots: it was laws that first targeted immigrants and people of color from Asia that were turned against Communists, anarchists, LGBTQ folks, and other "subversives" in the twentieth century.[23] Seemingly disparate categories (sexuality, political beliefs, immigration status, race, nationality, and political behavior) all converged in this series of laws to exclude and deport foreign nationals in the name of American security. Denied not only citizenship but presence in the United States, these people became, in the eyes of the law and many Americans, less than human.

Repression Evolves

Between 1956 and 1971, FBI director J. Edgar Hoover ran the nation's Counter Intelligence Program (COINTELPRO), designed to "disrupt and destabilize," "cripple," "destroy," or otherwise "neutralize" dissident individuals and political groups in the United States.[24] The bureau pursued these aims through a range of practices, including bogus mail, fabricated evidence, "black propaganda,"[25] infiltration and agents provocateurs, and assassinations targeting the Black Panther Party (BPP), Black Liberation Army (BLA), American Indian Movement (AIM), Puerto Rican independentistas, labor activists, and many others.

In the 1970s, the COINTELPRO was denounced by congressional investigators as "a sophisticated vigilante operation" and was formally shut down. Soon after, the FBI was no longer allowed to launch investigations of domestic political groups without a reasonable indication that they were engaged in criminal activity. Under the George W. Bush presidency, however, these restrictions were overturned. Protests and meetings of law-abiding peace activists and anarchists were once again placed under official surveillance. Several government groups participated as Joint Terrorism Task Forces (JTTFs), comprising teams of local, state, and federal law enforcement officials whose charge was to investigate and prevent terrorism. Antiwar, anarchist, and other leftist groups that earlier were called "radicals," "agitators," and "activists" were relabeled "terrorists" by JTTFs.[26] Groups caught up in such surveillance and repression included activists seeking to demonstrate at the Battle of Seattle in 1999; the 2000, 2004, and 2008 Republican National Conventions; the G20 Group of Nations meetings; the 2012 NATO Summit, and many other global and social justice gatherings.

Make no mistake: U.S. repression is not just the business of conservative administrations. President Bill Clinton (a Democrat) signed the Antiterrorism and Effective Death Penalty Act (AEDPA) of 1996 to alleviate heightened anxieties about immigrants and "terrorist" activities. The act enables the Immigration and Naturalization Services (INS, now Immigration and Customs Enforcement, or ICE) to arrest, detain, and deport noncitizens on the basis of secret evidence if they are deemed national security threats. The AEDPA also removed restrictions on the FBI (it could reopen or expand investigations based on First Amendment–protected activities) and reversed an earlier ban on the "guilt by association" provision from the 1952 McCarran-Walter Act (reviving the practice of denying visas to foreigners based on membership in groups designated as "terrorist" by the secretary of state, even if no evidence existed showing that the individual furthered illegal acts by such groups).[27]

To put these actions in context, AEDPA was passed after events including the 1993 bombing of the World Trade Center in New York City by an Al-Qaeda–affiliated activist; the 1995 bombing of the Alfred P. Murrah Federal Building in Oklahoma City, Oklahoma, by white supremacist Timothy McVeigh; the nearly twenty-year murderous antitechnology campaign by activist Ted Kaczynski (the "Unabomber") that killed three and injured nearly two dozen persons (ending in 1995); and the 1996 Olympic park bombing in Atlanta, Georgia, by Christian anti-abortion activist Eric Rudolph.[28] In the government's eyes these were all acts of terror, but for those who are counting, white men were responsible for three of them while "Islamic extremists" with foreign connections carried out only one attack. However, it was enough to initiate a wholesale intensification of federal legislation aimed at "international terrorism."

Importantly, Kaczynski's Luddite politics were later cited in support of AEDPA legislation against radical environmentalists.[29] Looking beyond "international terrorism" to other kinds of political movements that were causing concern among corporate interests in the United States, industry trade groups then mobilized their powerful lobbying mechanisms to ensure that the kinds of actions taken by the ELF and ALF were *also* applicable under the new terrorism laws. This meant harsher treatment of earth and animal liberation activists and longer prison sentences for crimes like arson and vandalism.

If you ever wondered whether ideas—and revolutionary ideas in particular—matter, the USA PATRIOT Act of 2001 provides some clarity. Pushed through Congress on the heels of the September 11, 2001, attacks against the United States, the PATRIOT Act provides enormous, almost uncountable and unaccountable powers of surveillance to the executive branch (for instance, librarians and bookstores can be compelled to provide lists of materials acquired by patrons). The PATRIOT Act created a new legal category, defining "domestic terrorism" as occurring when a person's activity "appears to be intended to intimidate or coerce a civilian population [or] to influence the policy of government by intimidation or coercion."[30] A few months later, James F. Jarboe, the FBI's Domestic Terrorism section chief, expanded this definition to include "violence . . . committed against persons or property to intimidate or coerce a government, the civilian population, or any segment thereof, in furtherance of political or social objectives."[31] (Keep in mind that the inclusion of property destruction in such definitions is nothing new—it was in the 1917 Immigration Act.) In practice, the AETA and the PATRIOT Act can be used to encompass virtually any form of protest. Moreover, the terrorism sentencing "enhancements" under these laws allow or require judges to give lengthy sentences, sometimes compelling them with mandatory minimum sentencing and sometimes allowing them with open-ended sentencing guidelines. For example, arson directed at an animal research facility previously resulted in a sentence not to exceed twenty years; under the PATRIOT Act, that sentence is "enhanced" to "any term of years or for life."[32]

Years before the PATRIOT Act, the perceived success and radicalization of animal liberationists led powerful groups like the National Association for Biomedical Research to lobby for the Animal Enterprise Protection Act (AEPA) of 1992. This legislation created its own new category of crime called "animal enterprise terrorism" and demanded heavy jail sentences for breaking this law. It applied to any person who travels in "interstate or foreign commerce" and "intentionally causes physical disruption to the functioning of an animal enterprise by intentionally stealing, damaging, or causing the loss of, any property (including animals or records) used by the animal enterprise, and thereby causes economic damage . . . to that enterprise, or conspires to do so." Animal enterprises can include any business or academic institution "that uses animals for food or fiber production, agriculture, research, or testing" such as research facilities, zoos, aquariums, rodeos, and circuses.[33]

A number civil rights and environmental organizations cried foul, reminding elected officials that the time-honored tradition of the boycott is *designed* to produce losses in profits. Under the AEPA, revered historical figures like Martin Luther King Jr., Mahatma Gandhi, Cesar Chavez, and the Sons of Liberty (who led the Boston Tea Party) would be deemed "terrorists" if their actions were directed at animal enterprises. The government essentially sat on its hands, allowing the law to stand, but not enforcing it for six years.

The first use of the AEPA came in 1998, against ALF activists Peter Young and Justin Samuel, who had released thousands of minks from fur farms in the Midwest. The AEPA was then used to target SHAC, the activist network imported from England that nearly brought vivisection and animal testing firm HLS to its knees. Six members of SHAC were jailed on AEPA charges: their website was deemed responsible for motivating others to take illegal actions against HLS. They were not charged with committing any of these acts, just supporting them, which amounted to harassment, intimidation, stalking, and "terrorism." Both SHAC and ALF were successfully prosecuted, but industry and state interests now wanted *more* prosecutorial tools.

"There's been no other movement that has brought as much violence and destruction and vandalism," said FBI deputy assistant director John E. Lewis in 2004. Animal rights and liberation activists clearly had the government's attention. Responding to the spread of "SHACtivism," Congress passed the Animal Enterprise Terrorism Act (AETA) in 2006. A creation of the American Legislative Exchange Council (ALEC), an organization that uses corporate funding to create "model legislation" on issues that promote conservative causes, the AETA makes it a "terrorist" crime to cause any animal enterprise (and its supporting companies, affiliates, and associates) a loss of profit, whether through sabotage or property damage. The American Association of Laboratory Animal Science, the Association of American Universities, the Biotechnology Industry Organization, the Fur Information Council of America, GlaxoSmithKline, and HLS supported the AETA as well.

The AETA contains language that allegedly protects "lawful economic disruption (including a lawful boycott)," but this has been ignored. Activists engaged in peaceful protests, boycotts, leafleting, and media campaigns continue to be targeted. The AETA also increased penalties and the range of activities covered by law, including Internet campaigns and secondary and tertiary targeting (see chapter 4)—allowing prosecutors to go after SHAC for pressuring companies like UPS, FedEx, Marsh Inc., and other major corporations to stop doing business with HLS. It also adds to the list of animal enterprises protected (animal shelters, pet stores, furriers, and breeders) and adds new language, going beyond the AEPA's focus on "physical disruption to the functioning of an animal enterprise" to include "damaging or interfering with the operations of an animal enterprise." Finally, the AETA criminalizes actions that instill a "reasonable fear" in animal enterprise employees or their family members. The AETA effectively brands civil disobedience and a range of other once constitutionally protected acts as "terrorism." Both the AEPA and the AETA have been enforced.

While repression by states is a primary concern, it is often independent of or linked to repression by *corporations* whose CEOs and investors feel threatened by movement actions and ideas. Corporations and governments have found creative and sometimes violent ways to discourage protest movements aimed at environmental and animal liberation. Penelope Canan and George Pring published the first study of strategic lawsuits against public participation—more commonly known as SLAPP suits. Canan and Pring found that there are hundreds, possibly thousands, of such lawsuits annually that are aimed at discouraging people from exercising their right to protest government or corporate practices and that punish those who do so by engendering fear and costly legal defenses for plaintiffs.[34]

Corporations have initiated repression against activists through such lawsuits, but also through surveillance, harassment, death threats, and even murder.[35] In just one example, Beckett Brown International (now S2i)—a security firm organized and managed by former U.S. Secret Service agents—provided "intelligence services" for companies like Dow Chemical, Walmart, Taco Bell, and Sasol. Those services involved spying, surveillance, trespassing, infiltration, and obtaining confidential phone records and other information (for example, donor lists, financial statements, staff social security numbers, and strategy memos) from groups such as Greenpeace.[36] One Greenpeace staff member told me, "We've seen memos from PR consulting firms sent to companies like Clorox and other corporations telling them that if our organization comes after them with a campaign, they can help label us 'ecoterrorists.'"[37] When I asked a Greenpeace forest campaigner if he had ever been called an "ecoterrorist," he said, "Yes. Many times. Industry regularly sends spies to Greenpeace. In fact, we know that many of our interns over the years have been spies for various companies." The Cosmetic, Toiletry and Fragrance Association; Proctor & Gamble; the American Medical Association; and the National Institutes of Health have organized campaigns directed at animal liberation activists, a fact that was made public in confidential memoranda released by People for the Ethical Treatment of Animals (PETA) and In Defense of Animals (IDA).[38] The AMA's "Animal Research Action Plan" contained strategies for dividing "hard core" animal rights activists from more moderate groups and for alienating the former from potentially supportive publics.[39]

Not all members of the U.S. Congress have supported the targeting of earth and animal liberation activists as "ecoterrorists." In fact, then-senator Barack Obama offered his colleagues a particularly eloquent reminder that there are greater threats to people and ecosystems in the United States. At a Senate Environment and Public Works Committee hearing on ecoterrorism in 2005, Obama stated:

> While I want these crimes stopped, I do not want people to think that the threat from these organizations is equivalent to other crimes faced by Americans every day. According to the FBI, there were over 7,400 hate crimes committed in 2003—half of which [were] racially motivated. More directly relevant to this committee, the FBI reports 450 pending environmental crimes cases involving worker endangerment or threats to public health or the environment. So, while I appreciate the Chairman's interest in these fringe groups, I urge the Committee to focus its attention on larger

environmental threats, such as the dangerously high blood lead levels in hundreds of thousands of children. With all due respect, Mr. Chairman, I believe the Committee's time would be better spent learning why [the] EPA has not promulgated regulations to deal with lead paint in remodeled homes. Such an oversight hearing could have a significant impact on improving the lives of children all over the country.[40]

A few short years after this supportive statement, Obama would become president and oversee the targeting of earth and animal liberation activists whose agenda he apparently believed to be far less threatening before he entered the Oval Office.

The so-called Green Scare is said to have begun with the FBI's Operation Backfire in 2004, when the agency merged seven independent investigations focused on ALF and ELF actions in the Pacific Northwest and indicted thirteen people on some sixty-five charges, including arson and the use of destructive devices. Others go back further, locating the Green Scare's beginning with a U.S. Senate hearing on ecoterrorism in 2002. Still other observers believe it began with the FBI's targeting of anarchist groups active in the counterglobalization movement after the 1999 Battle in Seattle when thousands of activists successfully shut down World Trade Organization (WTO) negotiations.[41] Clearly, I locate it in a tradition of repression aimed at subversive thought that goes back to the very founding of the United States. Regardless of its contested origins, the current campaign of state and corporate repression directed at earth and animal liberation movements cannot be grasped without attention to the much longer history of repression of social movements in U.S. and world history.

Grand Juries, Surveillance, and Other Forms of Repression

A grand jury is a legal body empowered to investigate potential crimes and determine whether charges should be brought. Grand juries are supposed to evaluate accusations against persons and determine whether sufficient evidence exists to issue an indictment. A grand jury is also an instrument of law designed to protect citizens from unfounded charges brought by the state. In practice, the grand jury has had a mixed record, because it has evolved into a powerful tool for prosecutorial discretion. According to attorney Brian Glick, author of *War at Home: Covert Action against U.S. Activists*, the grand jury has been used to subvert constitutionally protected rights and to pursue and neutralize social movements. Many activists who refuse to speak to grand juries are jailed on contempt charges (as was Scott DeMuth, mentioned in the introduction), a practice Glick argues has been a hallmark of state repression during upheavals in South Africa and Northern Ireland. Frequently, persons jailed for contempt of court are not the actual defendants in a criminal case—instead, they are suspected of having information about the crime in question. Grand juries in the United States have been used to capture escaped slaves in the 1850s and repress the antiwar, feminist, black liberation, American Indian, and Puerto Rican independence movements in the 1960s, 1970s, and 1980s. Beginning in the late 1980s, federal grand juries were convened to target environmental and animal rights groups in at least a dozen U.S. cities.

Prosecutors frequently use the federal grand jury to intimidate, harass, and undermine social movements without the protection of due process, defense attorneys, or other rights normally afforded to U.S. citizens. In a grand jury process, the person subpoenaed has no right to have an attorney present during questioning. There is often no judge in the room, and the prosecutor is not required to tell the members of the grand jury what the investigation concerns or the reasons for questioning witnesses. Unlike a traditional court of law, the witness has no right to remain silent—the Fifth Amendment to the U.S. Constitution does not apply. Under threat of imprisonment, witnesses are compelled to answer *all* questions, even if they are focused on their personal lives, friends, and family members. In a grand jury proceeding, rumor, hearsay, innuendo, and other unsubstantiated claims can be extracted from witnesses and entered into the record. These are the reasons so many social movement activists despise and refuse to cooperate with grand juries—and why so many of them (including Rik Scarce, Scott DeMuth, Carrie Feldman, and Gina Lynn) end up in jail.

Rik Scarce (also introduced at the start of this book) is a sociologist at Skidmore College and the author of *Eco-warriors: Understanding the Radical Environmental Movement.* He spent several months in jail for refusing to speak to a grand jury about his research on or connections to earth and animal liberation movements:

> If you're sucked into one of these horrible proceedings . . . your attorney looks at you and says, "They can use anything. They can use hearsay. They can use illegally obtained evidence." . . . And then all of the sudden . . . the

prosecutor is saying, "You've been indicted for a crime, based on what the grand jury has said." [And then you say,] "Oh, shit. What do I do now?" . . . It's completely trumped up; it's completely false. This is preposterous. They're tying together a whole bunch of stuff that should never have been tied together.[42]

Scarce spent more than five months in jail for noncooperation. It is often joked that grand juries could indict a ham sandwich.

Enna, who was profiled in the first chapter, is a West Coast animal liberation activist who spent a lot of time on the SHAC campaign. She was summoned to a grand jury to answer questions about certain criminal activities associated with the ALF. She refused to cooperate. The house where she lived with three other animal liberation activists was soon raided: "They took everything that had anything to do with animal rights stuff." She feels they were targeted because they "were pretty unapologetic about the work we were doing, and it was all First Amendment protected activism, so we were outspoken."[43] Lawyers and activists from other social movements advised Enna on how, for example, Puerto Rican independence and Black Panther Party activists have confronted grand jury probes. She remains committed to the cause, but after all she's been through, she has taken a break to think about how best to continue supporting social and ecological justice movements.

Before the SHAC7's Josh Harper was imprisoned, he was the subject of intense surveillance for many months. The state practiced its science of repression: The FBI worked with his mail carrier to record all return addresses on items shipped to his home. The FBI "attempted to get one of my roommates to spy on me, and had successfully convinced a longtime activist and friend of mine to spend three years giving them detailed reports on my day-to-day life." Harper's e-mail and phone conversations were monitored, and his home was burglarized, possibly by the government:

> After all of this time and effort, the government had only one "illegal" action they could pin on me; a speech I had made at the University of Washington. An agent in the audience was wired and had recorded me explaining how to send black sheets of paper to companies supporting Huntingdon Life Sciences. . . . I was arrested on a federal indictment for terrorism charges. My crime? Speaking and writing about my opinions.[44]

Harper continues to support animal liberation work as a public speaker and author. He is also public about his critiques of the movement and how to avoid repeating mistakes the SHAC campaign made.

Gina Lynn was also jailed for refusing to speak to a grand jury (in her case, about ALF actions). I met her at a public event organized in support of DeMuth and Feldman in Minneapolis. She told me that she had gone through great deal of state repression for her animal liberation activities. Her fiancée was a Canadian man "who had spent time in prison for his involvement in actions claimed by the ALF and who, at the time of our relationship, was under investigation for other actions." Lynn and her partner were watched by both the Canadian and U.S. governments: tracking and listening devices were placed in her car and home, their phone calls and e-mails were intercepted, and there was a raid on their home "resulting in the death of one of my dogs." Finally, they were both arrested "and kicked out of one another's countries." The harassment was followed by what she called "smear campaigns by the media and government officials and just about any other way you can imagine having your privacy violated."[45] The ecology and science of repression reveal how no relationship or space is too sacred or too private; if government agents and prosecutors believe penetrating into such spaces might reveal evidence or compel cooperation, then so be it. Lynn continues her animal liberation work.

scott crow, who founded the Common Ground Collective (see chapter 3) is a relentless advocate for social change and has paid for it with years of government repression. crow discussed the FBI's seemingly endless attempts and volumes of documentation meant to discourage his activism:

> They've been trying to get me since 2001, and I say "get me" because they really were trying to get me, like through the IRS and holding grand juries. . . . Brandon Darby, who was the fourth informant in my life— I shared so much information with him, but I didn't tell him anything I wouldn't tell anybody else.

He states that the FBI attempted to entrap him: "They tried to get me and this other woman to burn down this bookstore here in Austin in 2007, and it didn't work. They totally set me up to do it, they were like, 'We'll provide the supplies, here's this place, we can do this,' and I'm like, 'I'm not doing it.'"

crow describes his seven years of constant surveillance:

> I had a trap and trace on my phone, I had pin registers on my computer, I've been under physical surveillance at my house here . . . in Dallas, they have all my bank records, they tried to get me for tax evasion, but luckily I've filed with a CPA since the early '90s. . . . So they've done all these things with all these informants, and with hundreds of thousands of dollars in seven years, and they got nothing. Nothing! Not even a parking ticket.[46]

Like Harper and Lynn, crow has not been dissuaded from his work.

Political Prisoners

Dozens of earth and animal liberation activists have been subpoenaed, indicted, charged, convicted, or imprisoned. Many of the earth and animal liberation activists who have spent time in federal penitentiaries are viewed as political prisoners by movement participants, attorneys, and scholars. Here, I consider a small sample of incarcerated activists, including Kevin Kjonaas, Marie Mason, Jeff "Free" Luers, Carrie Feldman, and Scott DeMuth. Today, only Mason is still serving time, but each of their stories is instructive for anyone seeking to comprehend the power of the state to take away freedom. What I call the science of repression and cultures of repression come into play: states generate and manipulate knowledge about individual activists and movements through careful, empirical observation, experimentation, and data gathering and analysis. They are able to do this when the public is ignorant, acquiescent, or supportive of such efforts within a wider culture of repression. These particular cases offer a range of approaches to politics and issue areas, and characteristics of state repression.

Kevin Kjonaas

In the summer of 2010, I visited Kevin Kjonaas—a SHAC7 defendant—at the Sandstone Federal Correctional Facility in Sandstone, Minnesota. I traveled there with his partner. Kjonaas told me that he found out through a confidant at the prison who works in the main office that he was on "the hotlist, which means a higher level of security—they listen to all my phone calls and read all my mail."[47] I asked him if he would have been informed of the surveillance by the prison staff, and he said "No, I only found out because this guy told me."

When I asked Kjonaas about his willingness to speak out for the cause of animal liberation from behind prison walls, he said: "I'm not sure I trust myself to say things that I really mean from within here because I think I would see things differently the minute I get out, so I've been largely silent over the past few years." His partner told me Kjonaas had written a statement that an artist read over the loudspeaker at a concert, and Kjonaas was punished for the act within the prison walls. (Similarly, Josh Harper got one hundred days in solitary confinement for speaking out from prison.) Kjonaas worked as an active member of the Student Organization for Animal Rights (SOAR), a group at the University of Minnesota in the 1990s. He recalled, "We took over an office in Moos Tower one day" to protest animal research in the building:

> The *Minnesota Daily* [campus newspaper] wrote a lot of stories about me during that time because I was the press officer and spokesman for the ALF.[48] But what's funny about it is that it was an above board internship that was sponsored by the Political Science Department at the University! Every class I was in, people recognized me and the class became a debate session about animal rights issues.

Officials soon targeted Kjonaas. He remembered: "One time when I was sitting in my geology class, FBI agents walked right in during lecture and pointed up at me. So I tried to leave, but two more of them came in through the back of the classroom and gave me a subpoena." He was able to avoid serious jail time until his work as director of SHAC USA got him into trouble.

One morning someone tipped Kjonaas off that federal agents were headed to his home to arrest him. He brushed his teeth, got dressed, and secured his beagle, Willy, to the fence in the backyard just before several agents forced their way into his home wearing all black, one in a balaclava, another brandishing a battering ram, all armed, with guns drawn. The aggression was odd, given the FBI's continuous monitoring of Kjonaas's phone, e-mail, trash, and residence for several months. They knew he was a committed activist whose only weapon was a website. Kjonaas wondered, "What did they think I was gonna do? Attack them with a floppy disk?"[49]

He was convicted of conspiracy to violate the Animal Enterprise Protection Act, conspiracy to stalk, three counts of interstate stalking, and conspiracy to harass using a telecommunications device. These convictions resulted in a six-year sentence, beginning in 2006. He was the last of the SHAC7 to be released from prison, and like his former codefendants, today Kjonaas continues to support the movement through means that are "aboveground."

Marie Mason

A midwestern environmental and social justice activist who has worked as a gardener, Earth First! organizer, musician, writer, and volunteer for a free herbal health care collective, Mason was once known as a mild-mannered mother of two. She was always available to go to rallies and other community events organized for a range of causes. Building on Judi Bari's legacy, Mason worked to engender solidarity between environmentalists and workers as an active member of the International Workers of the World (IWW) and editor of the *Industrial Worker*, the IWW's newspaper. She even recorded a folk album (*Not for Profit*) with Bari's colleague and EF! activist Darryl Cherney.

On December 31, 1999, Mason and her then-husband, Frank Ambrose (a well-known forest defense activist in the Midwest), set fire to the Institute of International Agriculture offices at Michigan State University. The institute—housed in MSU's Agriculture Hall—held records related to re-search on genetically modified, moth-resistant potatoes, funded by USAID and Monsanto. The act was not directed at the GM/GE crops themselves—as seen in crop sabs (see chapter 4)—but at the knowledge production that supports that industry. The fire caused nearly $1 million in damage to the building and equipment, but no injuries or death, in accordance with ELF guidelines. After the action, the ELF released a communiqué:

> The ELF takes credit for a strike on the offices of Catherine Ives, Rm. 324 Agriculture Hall at Michigan State University on Dec. 31, 1999. The offices were doused with gasoline and set afire. This was done in response to the work being done to force developing nations in Asia, Latin America, and Africa to switch from natural crop plants to genetically engineered sweet potatoes, corn, bananas and pineapples. Monsanto and USAID are major funders of the research and promotional work being done through Michigan State University. . . . Cremate Monsanto, Long live the ELF. On to the next G.E. target![50]

Former NAELFPO spokesperson Craig Rosebraugh later wrote: "This was the first time arson had been used to further the cause against genetic engineering in the United States . . . it was the first time the ELF had taken credit for any GE-related action."[51] Daniel Clay, a professor and director of the institute Mason and Ambrose targeted, noted that the attack had a strong effect on his staff. "It really was a shock. . . . It was a very difficult period for all of us. People were frightened and we asked ourselves how close did this come to physically harming someone."[52] Clay viewed his research as supportive of sustainable agriculture, something he thought environmentalists like Mason should embrace.

The day after the MSU arson, Mason and Ambrose set fire to commercial logging equipment at a timber camp in Mesick, Michigan. The ELF claimed responsibility for this action as a protest against deforestation. Mason admitted later that she had also burned boats owned by a mink farmer to protest the fur industry.

Eight years later, authorities apprehended Ambrose. He worked as an informant to ensnare Mason.[53] She faced a life sentence but accepted a plea agreement that stipulated that she had to agree to the "Terrorism Enhancement" designation, which allows judges broad discretion in sentencing. As noted earlier, the twenty-one years and ten months handed down is the longest sentence of any earth or animal liberation activist to date. In her first interview following sentencing, Mason told the *Guardian* of London: "It is obvious the government is trying to send a message—to have a chilling effect, not only on my action, which of course transgressed the laws, but also on 30 years of above-ground actions in the environmental rights spheres."[54] Of Mason's sentence, Heidi Boghosian, director of the National Lawyers Guild, has said: "We are definitely seeing more severe sentences post-9/11, no doubt about it. . . . We have seen a trend of using the terrorist label and federalizing a lot of criminal activities that would have gotten a far less stringent sentence before."[55] Mason's support committee wrote:

The judge has shown that if activists attempt to impede . . . the progress of the marketplace in altering the genetic code of all beings . . . [its] desire to turn all aspects of the natural world into commodities . . . [or its] extraction of natural resources from the land—then they will be treated exactly the same as murderers. Nothing can be more clear about our legal system's priorities.[56]

Mason's attorney John Minock commented that the average sentence for arson in federal court is seven years. Mason's supporters authored an analysis of her motivation:

> Opposition to GMO research is not (just) grounded in a defense of the natural code against human interference; it addresses issues of the influence of capitalism on knowledge, imperialism and democracy. GMO seeds and foods were developed in search of new profits for corporate entities. The scientific establishment is in close alignment with the bureaucratic state, most obviously in State-funded universities like MSU. In these institutions, hard science closely follows the dictates of corporate funding and needs.[57]

Mason's sentencing statement to the court added her own words. She was clear that she and Ambrose targeted a specific faculty member's office because of USAID's and Monsanto's funding of the professor's GMO research. Monsanto's seeds "were being sold to poor farmers overseas; but the plants had been modified not to reproduce seeds, thereby forcing farmers to purchase new seed again every year from Monsanto. This reduced self-sufficiency and depleted seed stock and plant biodiversity." Echoing critiques of GMOs and Monsanto's "terminator seed" (a seed that produces a crop without viable offspring seeds) made by food justice advocates around the globe,[58] Mason stated that contrary to GMO advocates' claims that this technology was "freeing third world nations from poverty . . . GMO crops were being designed so that industrialized countries could maintain economic dominance over the peripheries, a contemporary form of 'imperialism without colonies.'" The end result, Mason argued, is that "collusion between banks, companies and governments was causing starvation, debt and environmental damage through contact with these GMO's. I felt so much grief for this needless suffering, these needless deaths."[59]

Mason said her crimes were "individual acts of conscience," and that the property damage she committed was intended "to protect my community and the Earth, to respond in defense of the living systems of animals, land and water."[60] Mason also expressed regret, rarely seen in the earth and animal liberation movements:

> For more than twenty years, I participated in every legal avenue open to me as a private citizen to educate and persuade government officials and

corporate representatives to reconsider policies. I have also participated in civil disobedience in the style taught by Martin Luther King, Jr. and Mahatma Gandhi, whose non-violent teachings I embraced. Given my commitment to non-violence, it was only under an extreme set of circumstances that I rationalized my actions and put people in danger. I believed that I was taking risks to prevent a greater harm to living beings. I never intended to cause danger of harm to any living thing, and by that standard I failed.[61]

After sentencing, Mason spent time in solitary confinement and was denied vegan food at FCI Waseca, sparking an uproar within the radical environmental community.[62] In August of 2010 she was transferred to FMC Carswell in Forth Worth, Texas. She is allowed limited contact with other people and has periodically been denied access to mail.[63] Mason continues to write poetry, paint, and offer words of inspiration in letters to supporters and activists worldwide.

Jeff "Free" Luers

Quoted in chapters 3 and 4, Jeff "Free" Luers is a celebrated activist who spent nine years in federal prison for an ELF arson action at a car dealership in Oregon. He began his activist work as a teen "motivated by anti-fascist and anti-police brutality campaigns."[64] He worked for the Sierra Club and the California Public Interest Research Group (CALPIRG) but soon gravitated toward more radical methods of social change, joining forest defense campaigns in Oregon. He was idealistic:

> We're talking about creating a world that has true social justice, with equality for all peoples and genders, and is sustainable and free of oppression and tyranny. I think that's a really simplified way of explaining it. I guess that's the ultimate utopian goal.

But Luers also learned how dominant institutions seek to control grassroots movements. He talked about the culture of repression:

> I sadly think that there has been a division created between mainstream grassroots and frontlines activists, and that that division has been perpetuated by the authority figures, by sowing dissent and creating this fictitious "terrorism" label . . . basically, we have . . . mainstream activists now distance themselves from direct action activists because of that "terrorist" label.[65]

When it came to torching a motor vehicle at a car dealership in the Pacific Northwest, Luers stated:

> I look at what we're doing to our planet, and we're in the sixth mass extinction right now. And the cancer rates are rising, and kids are dying of poisoning. And I look at my society and my country, and I see what's wrong. And I felt empowered to act. I felt in a position to act. And I thought that was a necessary step. I thought if communication fails, then you have to resort to something that creates communication. You know, sometimes that's a big, spectacular event that makes everyone stop and pay attention for a moment, and then ask why.[66]

By the time his trial began, Luers was keenly aware of the political value of framing his trial in a way that could spark a public conversation about state repression and ecological sustainability. He recalled how many people—including "moderate liberals"—initially saw him as "some crazy, wing nut, fanatical kid." But when he discussed the politics of species extinction and environmental sustainability in his sentencing statement, and the court referred to him as a "terrorist" and sentenced him to twenty-two years (he ultimately served nine), he said people began asking, "Why's he getting so much time? What's so threatening behind this criminal mischief that he did that deserves this sentence?" He felt "like it gave me a platform that I probably wouldn't have had if they had sentenced me to five years. I would have just simply fallen between the cracks and disappeared. They created what they have with me."[67]

Even before his release from prison, Luers was a frequent contributor to various movement publications and activist media. He considers himself a former political prisoner and is currently working to get that recognition for other earth and animal liberation prisoners through the United Nations:

> And the Eugene [Oregon] human rights commission recognized that my sentence was politically motivated, as did Amnesty International. . . . Someone wanted to send a message to my movement.[68]

The contradiction embodied in an anarchist seeking legitimacy from the UN is palpable, but it is also understandable. Activists believe they can pit certain state-based institutions against others and raise awareness of their cause. Luers's case, like so many others, raised serious questions about the politicization of his crime: if he had committed arson with no connection to ecological politics, his sentence would have been much lighter. Instead, he received a sentence that international human rights advocates have deemed punitive.

Carrie Feldman and Scott DeMuth (the Davenport 2)

On October 13, 2009, the FBI subpoenaed Minneapolis anarchist Carrie Feldman to appear before a federal grand jury in Davenport, Iowa. Although little information was offered at the time, it was soon clear that they were interested in Feldman's knowledge of an unsolved 2004 ALF action at the University of Iowa. One of the most sophisticated and brazen lab raids ever conducted, it remains unsolved today. More than four hundred animals were taken from a highly secure facility, hundreds of thousands of dollars of damage were done, and a new animal research facility was built underground, citing security concerns.[69] The ALF raid was designated a domestic act of terrorism.

Feldman appeared in front of the grand jury but refused to answer any questions. Instead, she read a statement explaining her reasons for noncooperation. She invoked her Fifth Amendment right against self-incrimination (though that is considered invalid in a grand jury investigation) and told the grand jury that she refused to cooperate "based on a sincere belief that to do so would run counter to my deeply held convictions and values." She stated that while grand juries were originally created to prevent arbitrary indictments,

> they are now, and have been for some time, used to investigate and intimidate those who would express dissent. This is only effective when we are complicit, when we are frightened, when we are divided. Today my voice may waver, as I stand alone in this room. But I know I speak with the voice of every one of my friends, loved ones, and comrades when I say this: We will not be intimidated. We will not cooperate. I have nothing more to say to you.[70]

Feldman wrote afterward: "Thanks to everyone for how much support I've gotten already. It means so much to me to know you have my back. . . . And remember—stay safe, stay strong, and fuck grand juries!" In November 2009 the judge placed Feldman—then twenty years old—

under arrest on contempt charges. She spent four months in jail without speaking to authorities.

Around the same time, Feldman's former partner, Scott DeMuth, was subpoenaed for the same investigation. DeMuth also refused to testify and spent five months in federal prison after accepting a plea related to another ALF action. In addition to being active in the Twin Cities anarchist community, DeMuth was a graduate student at the University of Minnesota working in close collaboration with me on research focused on earth and animal liberation movements, so this was a development that was disruptive for both of us on a professional and personal level. Fortunately for me, I was never a target of the investigation, although the FBI requested a meeting with me to divulge information about my research that might be relevant to their investigation of DeMuth. I declined to cooperate and announced my refusal publicly (see preface). DeMuth followed in Feldman's footsteps and refused any cooperation with authorities and paid for it with jail time. I was much more fortunate and never received a subpoena.

An activist group called the Scott and Carrie Support Committee (SCSC) organized immediately after "the Davenport 2" were subpoenaed. SCSC members traveled to every court hearing, organized fundraising events, produced and distributed T-shirts and literature about the case, and publicized the issue through press releases and articles in local and national media and educational events around the nation. Feldman and DeMuth were both active members of SCSC themselves, since there was only a short time when their sentences overlapped. I joined in with various aspects of SCSC work, including traveling to court, attending grand jury resistance rallies, writing updates for the group's website, providing child care, and organizing speakers at public panels with local and nationally renowned activists (including Dhoruba bin Wahad, J. Tony Serra, and Stu Sugarman) to support DeMuth and Feldman's cases.

DeMuth was jailed from February through July 2011. Both he and Carrie Feldman continue to work for various radical movements, including political prisoner support for earth and animal liberation activists and Indigenous decolonization.

Racial Deviants

The earth and animal liberation movements are made up primarily of white, middle-class people, and therefore they are composed of persons who—independent of their politics and actions—hail from privileged groups. However, when one takes into account these activists' politics and actions, the story becomes more complex: that privilege is revealed as contingent. scott crow told me:

> I want collective liberation, and anti-oppression to me is the first step in that it's recognizing the difference between privilege and oppression and recognizing that people like myself have privilege that we receive from being white males from North America, and all the things, achieving middle class, but that it can be *conditional*.[71]

I contend that the language and legal apparatus of "ecoterrorism" momentarily places these activists outside the sphere of citizenship. By treating them as threats to national security and the American way of life, the state enables the neutralization of their movements. I therefore view state and corporate repression of earth and animal liberation movements as an example of the production and repression of *racial deviants*—those whites in the United States who refuse to conform to the nation's cultural, political, and social disciplinary norms. They are deemed "not quite white" in the state's political-legal discourse (here I draw on the work of feminist scholar Anne McClintock).[72]

Racial deviants are whites who choose to deviate from many of the norms of whiteness and are therefore racialized as probationary whites, even if just temporarily. By "norms of whiteness" I mean taking part in a social, cultural, and political system that primarily rewards and benefits people whose racial/ethnic identity is defined as "white" or European American and that extends beyond attitudes to include interests and property relations.[73] This does not mean that these activists are anything other than white outside of this political-legal context. In fact, their white privilege is manifest in many ways, even within the prison system (they are high-profile persons, and other prisoners see that their sentences appear to be much lighter than those of revolutionaries from communities of color and "jihadist" networks).

McClintock notes that, historically, groups included in the category of racial deviants were gays and lesbians, anarchists, feminists, persons with certain diseases such as mental illness, "criminals," sex workers, Jews, and certain immigrants. This phenomenon is observable in many nations, including England (as McClintock demonstrates) and the United States.

For example, historian Mai Ngai writes that the first U.S. immigration laws explicitly defined who was a desirable potential citizen and who would not be welcome. The latter group included "criminals, prostitutes, paupers, the diseased, and anarchists, as well as Chinese laborers."[74] Thus "race" in this sense is less about phenotype or national origins, and much more about politics, social position, and one's relationship to property.

Steven Best sees the political racialization of animal rights activists as linked to a broader wave of "othering" those who speak up even for the basic rights guaranteed in the U.S. Constitution:

> It is time once again to recall the profound saying by Pastor Martin Niemoller about the fate of German citizens during the Nazi genocide. . . . Attacks on foreigners are preludes to attacks on US citizens, which are overtures to assaults on the animal rights and environmental activist communities, which augur the fate of all groups and citizens in the nation. In the world of . . . the FBI, the CIA, and the corporate conglomerates, *we are all becoming aliens*, foreigners . . . by virtue of our very wish to uphold modern liberal values and constitutional rights.[75]

Charles McKenna was the government's lead prosecutor in the SHAC7 case. After successfully jailing those activists, he was promoted to the head of the New Jersey Office of Homeland Security and Preparedness. He had some interesting plans for using new "antiterrorism technology." According to one report, he said: "We are particularly interested in computer profiling, which is much more sophisticated, and quicker, than traditional racial profiling." Regarding the specific targets, McKenna stated: "Jihad, Crips, extreme animal-rights activists, it's all the same: people trying to damage the system. . . . We need every trick in the book to avert disaster."[76]

Journalist Will Potter responded:

> Is it not ironic that nearly every violent act of domestic terrorism has been carried out by a right-wing group or individual (Oklahoma City bombing, abortion doctors murdered, Eric Rudolph's various bombings, etc.), yet Homeland Security still focuses its efforts on activists who have never hurt anyone? And who does McKenna cite as threats? Foreigners, minorities, and people who care about animals.[77]

The label "terrorist" is often deployed as a racialized symbol, in that it targets those who engage in efforts involving challenges to the dominant social order. It is designated for those individuals and groups engaged in antihegemonic politics—that is, they go against the established order, which protects the interests of white supremacy. The "terrorist" label is imposed on those who are deemed different, inferior, savage, brutish, irrational, and uncivilized in the political or ideological sense: all labels associated with traditional racist ideas. Antiterrorism therefore is often a racist political project.

When a colleague of mine, a longtime African American social justice activist, heard about DeMuth's case and his domestic "terrorist" labeling, he responded, "That's how they treat the brothers in the criminal justice system."[78] Courtney Bell, an African American student in my "Race, Class, and the Politics of Nature" course, wrote the following in an essay when I asked the students what role race might play in state prosecution of (white) ELF members: "The irony . . . exists solely because of the fact that the [white] majority is represented by the members of ELF, however because of their acts of 'terrorism' they are treated as minorities are treated regularly."[79]

These movements are a threat because they refuse to treat property as sacrosanct in a capitalist state, when the protection of private property and the system that governs it is at the core of antiterrorism legislation. They are also challenging a core foundation of white supremacy, since in the United States, private property has always upheld the dominant racial system.

As legal scholar Cheryl Harris has argued, whiteness actually functions *like* property in that it can serve as an investment and offers a payoff for those who can claim it.[80] More broadly speaking, property itself is raced in that many people of color have been treated as property (specifically, as the property of white people) and in that people of color could historically see their property destroyed or taken at will by whites, whether through vigilante actions or legal means (the examples are numerous but include forced evictions of Asian Americans from gold claims and Chinatowns throughout the American West, land grabs of entire nations through overseas colonial ventures in places like Hawaii, Guam, and the Philippines, and the mass evictions of people of color during the housing foreclosure crisis of the early twenty-first century). People of color have also been prevented from owning property, for example, through laws that prohibit certain groups from purchasing land (see the Alien Land laws). Finally, and most obviously, the vast majority of property holders—that is, the owners of this nation's wealth, real estate, financial capital, and stocks and bonds—are overwhelmingly white, and their property overwhelmingly serves and protects upper-class, white, male interests.

Anyone who threatens or is seen as a threat to the dominant property relations in this nation is also potentially a threat to white supremacy. Thus when white radical environmental and animal liberation activists destroy property and target this nation's dominant propertied interests (as they most certainly do, given their goals of transforming industrial civilization and hitting powerful corporations in their wallets and bank accounts), they simultaneously deploy white privilege and reject those institutions that support it. And if full citizenship is ultimately predicated on whiteness (and middle-class/affluent status, male identification, and heteronormativity), then these mostly white activists are challenging it. State repression racializes them as "non-white," "other than white," or "not quite white"[81] as they disrupt the traditional relationship between citizenship and whiteness. Of course, it might be argued that these white activists are using their white privilege to confront white supremacy, something that white antiracist activists have done since this nation's beginnings. After all, as I have often said to white students in my classes, "Do not feel guilty about your white privilege; use it to challenge the system and become an ally working in solidarity with groups who do not enjoy such privileges."

Hence, when white earth and animal liberation activists engage in *radical* politics, they are also engaging in a kind of *racial* politics, and they often lose certain privileges when subjected to surveillance, infiltration, intimidation, and imprisonment—a range of practices that have, in this context, become known as the Green Scare. Radical earth and animal liberation activists know they are white-dominated movements, but their repressive treatment reminds them that racial privileges can be revoked.

And truly, there is nothing quite like seeing a white, middle-class activist being treated by the state in ways usually applied to racialized others. Some of these activists have joined the enormous and growing number of people of color, immigrants, and religious minorities languishing in the U.S. prison system. Daniel McGowan has been active in numerous social movement causes. Originally from New York, he has worked for the

Rainforest Action Network, trained with the Ruckus Society, and volunteered for an antidomestic violence advocacy group. He is also an earth liberation activist, volunteered for the *EF! Journal's* political prisoner support page, and worked to support Luers. In June 2007, McGowan was sentenced to seven years (with a terrorism enhancement) in prison for arson and property destruction actions claimed by the ELF in 2001. His case was part of "Operation Backfire."

McGowan spent time in one of the infamous CMUs—a federal Communications Management Unit—"Little Guantanamo" in Marion, Illinois. CMUs are secretive, "self-contained" housing units inside prisons, designed to hold prisoners who "require increased monitoring of communication" in order to "protect the public." The activist attorney Lauren Regan, who represented McGowan, says he was a model prisoner but continued his activism from behind bars, and that is what landed him, in the middle of the night, in the CMU. Regan told me CMU prisoners cannot challenge their transfers and have no right to know why they have been sent there. A CMU is designed, I am told, to "keep terrorists from networking." Regan says for McGowan:

> It is a total media lockdown, and a communications lockdown in general. He gets fifteen minutes of phone calls to his family a week, and only his family. All of his mail, in and out, is scanned and sent to the FBI in Washington, D.C. . . . And normally prisoners get visits and they're contact visits—you know, they sit at tables in a cafeteria. They can hug and say "hi" and whatnot. He only gets one visit a month, and it's through glass on a phone. So no contact visits at all. And his only time outdoors is in a cage that has a basketball hoop in it.[82]

The racial politics of the CMU are instructive. Regan writes in the *EF! Journal*: "[Before McGowan was in the CMU] because the unit only housed brown-skinned people, the feds became concerned they would be sued. So, they kept their eyes peeled for a couple of white guys to add to the mix."[83] Regan continued that, at the time, McGowan was "the only white guy there. Everybody else is Muslim and Middle Eastern. And they're actually talking about shipping some of the Guantanamo detainees into these areas." Since McGowan had no prior convictions, normally he would have been sent to a minimum security facility. Instead, because of the political nature of his crimes and his continued activism from within prison, this "pudgy little smiley . . . friendly, outgoing kid . . . [was sent to] one of the scariest federal prisons in the country."

Regan believes McGowan was punished twice: first, through his imprisonment for his 2001 ELF actions, and second through his transfer to the CMU: "Here's a white kid whose dad is a cop from New York City. Mom was a house maker, you know, [and he] had never spent any time in jail. And now he's there. And why is he there? Because he didn't bow down and shut the hell up when the feds put the clamps on him." Even after being placed in "the black hole," Regan told me that McGowan continued his activism: "We've got a lawsuit . . . to challenge the entire CMU system on behalf of him and the Middle Eastern people that are stuck in there, who have no voice . . . no solidarity."[84]

Regan's analysis points to the reality that prison in general and CMUs in particular are places where disproportionately large populations of people of color are warehoused and contained.[85] And the fact that McGowan is both white and an earth liberation activist suggested to Regan and others that his case was special. The co-location of ELF and "jihadist" prisoners in the same unit speaks volumes about the racialized nature of the "war on terror" and the Green Scare.[86] As total liberation activists, both Regan and her client share a vision of justice that connects McGowan's imprisonment to the injustices visited upon all CMU prisoners: it is a violation of human rights.

Walter Bond is a straight-edge (usually defined as vegan, drug- and alcohol-free, and sexually responsible) animal liberation activist propelled into action after witnessing what he called the "horrors" associated with animal exploitation in general and, in particular, in the two slaughterhouses he helped build when he was nineteen. He was convicted of the "Lone Wolf" arsons claimed by the ALF that burned the Sheepskin Factory in Glendale, Colorado, the Tandy Leather Factory in Salt Lake City, Utah, and the Tiburon Restaurant in Sandy, Utah. The authorities secured help from Bond's own brother, whose monitoring and recording of their conversations led to the conviction. Bond is currently in the CMU in Marion, Illinois, where McGowan and Andy Stepanian also served time. He is due for release in 2021:

> Those of us in the prison system know oppression. We live it everyday, every hour. Authority, slavery and domination are our lot. Any employee, guard, visitor or invisible faceless bureaucrat need only snap their fingers

and we are whisked away to confinement cells smaller than your bathroom. For days, months, or years. In a capitalist system of immense social stratification "prisoner" is the lowest rung in a classist and racist society. . . . Nearly everyone in this system falls into one or more of four categories, those being: 1. Black, 2. Latino, 3. Poor, and 4. Uneducated.[87]

Stepanian, you may recall, is one of the SHAC7. I asked him about his time in prison, specifically since he described himself as a middle-class white American. He spent the first part of his sentence at FCI Butner (in North Carolina), a medium-high security prison he described as having "a lot of racial segregation"—"the Federal Bureau of prisons really condoned that." But Stepanian "refused to sit with the whites because they wore swastikas, and there were a lot of white supremacists. . . . And there was all this nonsense that I wanted nothing to do with." So first he sat alone, then at a mixed-race table. The choice got him into some trouble, but he was able to protect himself by teaching the GED program: "So when all these different groups were able to get their GEDs—including the white supremacists—they all agreed that they gotta keep this white kid around teaching us." Like McGowan, Stepanian also engaged in political work from within the prison:

> Those [GED] classes were really a unifying point that brought them together talking about oppression, talking about segregation and how it hurts all of us in the prisons. . . . So little nuances like that allowed me to wiggle out my own space and be political from within the prison system, and within a year or two I started organizing all these poetry jams and getting people to become involved in books and political stuff, and then eventually I got sent to the Communications Management Unit [CMU].[88]

Stepanian's story speaks to several points. First, the ecologies and science of repression emerge from this discussion as he reminds us that the prison system is a site that is heavily racialized and controlled both by the state and inmates. The prisoners simultaneously self-segregate and are segregated by the state through supporting and condoning those practices. Racial segregation in prison (and outside) reveals the ways the state and capital use the science of repression by continually working to maintain control over potentially rebellious populations. This ecology of repression touches and divides groups that might otherwise revolt separately or jointly. Stepanian also divulges the ways in which he both affirmed and refused his white privilege: he was able to organize a GED class and other projects because of skills he had due to privileges prior to his imprisonment. His whiteness was also destabilized—he became a racial deviant or became *more* of a racial deviant than he had been by simply participating in radical social movements. He rejected the whites-only grouping and other activities (including Odinist—Northern European white supremacist—spiritual ceremonies), and his transfer to a CMU for engaging in antiracist political work inside the prison signaled his probationary "white" status.

People of Color Earth and Animal Liberationists

As I stated earlier, Rod Coronado has been the most visible nonwhite figure in the earth and animal liberation movements, but there are many others. In my view, people of color in these movements are racial deviants, too: they have always existed outside the cultural norms of whiteness that characterize both the United States and the earth and animal liberation movements. Also, as nonwhites who express and articulate a deep compassion for nonhuman animals and natures, they go against the grain of popular wisdom and scholarly research that all too often relies on a "hierarchy of needs" framework that (inaccurately) suggests that these populations are too economically desperate to share concerns outside of a basic survival framework.[89] On this point, Maslow's "hierarchy of needs" has been critiqued for many problematic elements, but its central claim with respect to people of color is belied by the existence of the environmental justice movement globally. So, too, have various religious and political traditions embraced ecological principles (frequently including vegetarianism or veganism) across Asia, Latin America, the Caribbean, Africa, and elsewhere. The racial deviance I attribute to people of color in these movements is a social construction perpetrated both by a white-dominated society and social movement.

In other ways, however, people of color in the earth and animal liberation movements are *not* racial deviants: sometimes they appear to fit the racist mold of the "ecological Indian" or the person of color who is "naturally" closer to nature.[90] In that sense, people of color and Indigenous persons in these movements occupy simultaneous positions as racial deviants and as racially "normative" actors in racist discourses about nature and culture. Coronado embodies these tensions and contradictions.

Introduced more thoroughly elsewhere in this book, Coronado is a Pascua Yaqui Indian activist who spent several years in federal prison for his activism and public statements. He has never been shy about linking his Indigenous heritage with animal and earth liberation. He makes explicit connections between the dispossession of Native peoples by the U.S. federal government and corporations and the harms visited upon nonhuman animals and ecosystems, and he has combined his earth and animal liberation activism with what he views as pro-Indigenous sovereignty and anti-imperialist politics:

> I believe it to be the obligation of the earth warrior never to be ashamed of one's own actions to honor the sacred tradition of indigenous resistance. . . .
> *We are all Subcommandante Marcos, Crazy Horse and the ALF.* . . . This will not be the first time an indigenous person has gone to prison while upholding the obligation to protect our culture, homelands and people, and it most definitely will not be the last.[91]

Coronado is just one of a small number of Indigenous persons and people of color in the earth and animal liberation movements (as opposed to the many thousands in the global environmental justice movement). State repression against communities of color is a constant fact of life, but when one joins these movements, that repression becomes more visible and amplified; racial deviance—by virtue of being nonwhite—is more pronounced because of political work. Thus, in a society marked by white supremacy, people of color embody racial deviance in multiple ways.

What ends up uniting people of color and whites in these movements is that they are both racial deviants in yet another way: they refuse to conform to the expectations and benefits of *human* supremacy. They reject a humanism rooted in speciesism and dominionism—for many, the unexamined and unearned privileges of membership in the human race. And just as the state has treated white activists as probationary whites (and people of color like Coronado as *hyper* racial deviants), they have also made it clear that their humanness is conditional (for people of color, the conditionality of humanness is rarely assumed otherwise). The threat of imprisonment means risking facing some of the horrific treatment that the majority working-class and people of color prison population faces every day. Racial deviance overlaps and diverges among members of these movements, but radicalism unites them in "otherness."

The Trauma of Repression

J. Tony Serra is a legendary civil rights lawyer, activist, and tax resister from San Francisco. He has represented activists from the Black Panther Party, Hells Angels, Earth First!, the Symbionese Liberation Army, and the New World Liberation Front (NWLF). Serra won the Trial Lawyer of the Year award in 2003 (given by the organization Trial Lawyers for Public Justice) for his successful litigation on behalf of EF! activist Judi Bari against the FBI. He opposes all social systems that subjugate poor people and has served time in federal prison for tax resistance. I invited Serra to Minneapolis to speak at a public gathering, and during that visit, he told me about one of the primary goals of state repression: "Well, what I think an express technique of the government is to bring groups of them [activists] to court, because you diffuse your energy and diffuse your resources, because then you're battling in court rather than on the street."[92]

If, as Serra argues, the goals of repression include discouraging activism and neutralizing social change movements, the state and corporations have enjoyed both successes and failures with regard to the earth and animal liberation movements. I was impressed that activists were so willing to discuss the impacts of repression on their personal lives, their activism, and the movement. Much of that conversation centered on the palpable "chilling effect" of repression. Kim McCoy of the SSCS shared: "Everyone is thinking twice right now before doing things because, all of a sudden, we're allowed to be targeted based on our ideological beliefs." Like many attorneys and other activists, McCoy is certain that the AETA is "completely unconstitutional, but [its] very existence definitely puts a chill on people because nobody wants to be associated with the word *terrorism.*" She concluded, "It's definitely a really negative political climate right now for activism in general. And that's troubling."[93]

Many activists shared McCoy's view of increased fear and caution among movement participants. Attorney Regan described the events that happened in the early 2000s when the federal government began conducting grand juries in the Pacific Northwest: "Hundreds and hundreds of people were grand jury subpoenaed . . . to this massive witch hunt because the feds really had no clue how to catch these people." This was, in her recollection, partly a response to the successful shut down of the

1999 WTO meeting in Seattle (the "Battle for Seattle"), when the anarchist movement gained its greatest visibility and notoriety in decades.
"Towns like Eugene became famous after the WTO as being anarchist
hotbeds. You know, our mayor announced that this was the training
ground for anarchists . . . so, the FBI came to Eugene full throttle."
Regan stated that federal agents "began infiltrating aboveground organizations," and "literally, hundreds of innocent people were rounded up
and forced to go to these [grand jury] proceedings." She described the
dilemma they faced: "forced to make a decision . . . to cooperate . . . and
turn their backs on their movements and their ethics and their neighbors
and their friends . . . or . . . stand up to the repression . . . but quite possibly go to jail for as long as six months."[94]

Regan contends that a number of activists were targeted because the
FBI saw them as potentially "weaker"—"people that had mainstream jobs
or had children or had issues that would make them very vulnerable or
susceptible to not wanting to go to jail." In many cases, these people felt
they had no choice but to give the authorities information about friends
and colleagues, dividing much of the community and causing rifts among
previously "tight-knit" activist networks. The ripple effects of the ecology of repression and cultures of repression took hold as activists turned
on (or were turned against) one another. Regan concedes, "in some ways,
the government was effective," because, prior to the onset of grand juries
and infiltrations, "this was a really vibrant, active, effective community."

The impact of state repression is now evident "because those divisions
were forged, you know, cooperators and noncooperators." Another indi-
cator of the fallout of state repression was its discouragement of possible
future activists. Regan said, "You know . . . the feds only have to go and
raid one house, and it can scare hundreds of people into not wanting to
be associated with that person or that movement." She shared the view
of some activists and analysts that social privilege had also worked against
them in the crackdown: "Because especially for a mostly white, somewhat
educated movement like the Northwest environmental movement . . . this
type of government repression and prosecution, you know, hadn't really
occurred to this point."[95]

Josh Harper concurs. About the FBI, he stated flatly:

> The fact of the matter is, is that they're excellent at what they do, you
> know? They're excellent at maintaining the status quo. They're excellent at

beating the crap out of social justice movements, and basically bludgeoning the hope and the fight out of you.[96]

Ben Rosenfeld has served as legal counsel to many high-profile earth liberation activists. He considers the ecologies of repression—the far-reaching negative impacts of the Green Scare—on the future of the movement: "My sense is that there's been an incredible chill in the movement." He no longer sees "a really broad spectrum of people" attending protests like he observed years ago. This used to include people "of all ages, and families with little kids." But, as a result of the "really harsh, nasty response of police at a lot of those protests—I think a lot of people are afraid to show up with their children. And, you know, older folks are afraid to show up." Rosenfeld contends that the unfortunate outcome of this response is that "you don't get that kind of experiential and generational cross-fertilization, which is so important in any social movement."[97]

Ecologies of repression affect bystanders, would-be future activists, and supporters and would-be supporters of other social change movements— even the beneficiaries of those movements (including nonhuman natures). As former ALF political prisoner Peter Young told me, "the real impact of this sort of repression is not just a few activists going to jail."[98] Luckily, the historical, intergenerational, cross-movement collaborations between earth/animal liberation and activists from the 1960s and 1970s revolutionary movements have facilitated stronger efforts to resist the Green Scare (see chapter 6).

J Johnson is a well-known animal liberation activist from Chicago who works with SHAC. He noticed a measurable decline in activism after two particular government victories: "attendance at HLS demos specifically . . . dropped dramatically after the SHAC7 convictions and after the AETA was passed. That was the government's goal."[99] Johnson's own colleagues urged him to tone down his use of language regarding illegal direct action. During his remarks at a demonstration, he spoke about "the legitimacy of underground direct action . . . talking about the ALF and supporting them." Afterward, one of the protest organizers told him, "I agree, but should we be talking about that? Shouldn't we not be saying that type of stuff? I don't want to get in trouble."

"Nothing I was saying was illegal. I read enough that I know the law. There was no imminent threat posed by what I was saying, and it's not illegal to support an illegal organization."[100] Johnson is concerned that despite the legal protections of the First Amendment and case law,

> there is this kind of stigma and fear that comes along with it now, where people aren't really as willing to stand up and say, "Yes, this is illegal, and, yes, I support it." And I feel like . . . that vocal support is necessary for the greater success of tactics like that. [A]ction in a vacuum does not have nearly as much effect as an action that has been championed by a broader social movement, in my opinion.[101]

The "chilling" effect has not only affected material action (such as declining attendance at protest rallies) but also political speech and discourse.

When the AETA was passed, Johnson had hoped that there would be a movement-wide statement: "We are not going to be intimidated. While these laws may now be on the books, that doesn't make them just. . . . [W]e are going to continue fighting for [our just cause] with everything at our disposal." Instead, "what I saw a lot of the time was—both in the grassroots and in the mainstream movement—people . . . being scared to come out . . . [and] speak up in the ways they would have before."

Adding insult to injury, Johnson recalled how the culture of repression took hold within the movement, creating greater divisions between radicals and mainstream activists. He saw people in the mainstream movements "doing everything in their power to distance themselves from anything perceived as controversial" or radical. He pointed to the Humane Society of the United States (HSUS) sending out public notices offering rewards for the capture of persons involved in illegal direct actions: "press releases saying, 'We will offer a reward to whoever catches this person.' You know, thanking the FBI for going after the Animal Liberation Front." Johnson says he is a pragmatist; he understands the HSUS is "a large group. They need to fundraise. They need to put out a certain image." So he does not expect their public support for the ALF, but he still sees it as unacceptable that HSUS would be "actively joined in on . . . the scare tactics and terror-baiting."[102]

Ecologies of repression reach inside and across movements and communities, and they affect individual activists on a personal and emotional level. Enna has a public persona of implacable dedication and strength, but after spending months fighting grand juries and confronting FBI agents, she confided, "I feel like my relationships were taxed."

She had "one or two really close people who were my main emotional support, and I think it was really hard for all of us." The FBI raided her home at dawn, which "was traumatic" and created "a lot of fear" since the agents "held really big guns to our heads and handcuffed us in our house." The aftermath produced a lasting anxiety for her and her housemates, and she recalled that "it was a really scary experience."[103] The psychological stress and pain of dealing with state repression can last a lifetime. A number of activists feel the movement must address this stress more effectively.

Harper described his time in prison as a "monstrous . . . thirty-two-month nightmare." He openly acknowledges being damaged by the experience but is positive about the future: "I feel like there's going to be a time when I'm going to be able to go onward [but] I'm not there yet." The details he shared largely focused on his inability to be present for his family and friends. While he was in prison,

> my girlfriend of six years left me for one of my best friends. My father died. I didn't get to go to my father's funeral. My grandmother died. I didn't get to go to my grandmother's funeral. My sister got sick. My mom ended up having to go and see a neurologist. I couldn't be there to hold her hand . . . And you can't be there to do anything for them. I mean the things that that does to you . . . it's terrible.[104]

Harper is a vocal insider critic of the animal liberation movement. He believes his critiques are aimed at strengthening the movement by addressing some key weaknesses, including the need for activists to be honest about how emotionally trying state repression can be.

Cultivating Cultures of Resistance

Even though most activists interviewed for this book stated that repression was debilitating for movements, they also believed an increased state presence in their communities and networks was evidence that their movement was an effective threat to systems of power. The pushback was strengthening resolve and cultivating a culture of resistance in the midst of a culture of repression.

When I spoke to Justin Goodman, he was research associate supervisor in the Laboratory Investigations Department at PETA. He is an experienced animal rights activist, and during his time as a graduate student at the University of Connecticut, he was instrumental in the campaign to end the use of primate experimentation at the school's Health Center. At PETA, Goodman's focus is on the use of animals in education. Through his efforts, many schools and medical centers across the country have successfully adopted learning methods that do not require the use of animals. He was one of many activists who was upbeat about the implications of state repression:

> More than anything, I think, this is a sign of desperation on the government's part. . . . [I]f we weren't doing a good job, and our message wasn't powerful, then the government and scientists and industry and lobby groups would have no need to try and stifle our ability to get our message out.[105]

NAALPO's Jerry Vlasak put it more succinctly: "The more effective you are, the more you're going to bring down the wrath of the government."[106]

While I think there is sound logic to the argument that government attention shows a measure of movement success, as I stated earlier in this chapter, that reasoning must not overlook the inherently repressive functions of states. That is, radical movements do not necessarily *cause* repression; they tend to render the repressive nature of states more visible and evident. It might be more accurate to say that activist militancy produces a *stronger* expression of state repression. Earth and animal liberation activists' reasoning serves to affirm their choice of politics and tactics, perhaps bolstering their confidence that their work is meaningful and brimming with potential. Since the idea contributes to supporting their culture of resistance, in that sense, there is at least one positive outcome of state repression.

Another refrain I hear among activists is that the new laws that redefine activities that are already illegal as "terrorist" will further radicalize many activists, encouraging them to pursue underground politics. In other words, under such conditions, even aboveground, legal action will become more risky, so committed activists are just as likely to choose a more radical path of action. Regan, the Civil Liberties Defense Center lawyer, says, "in this era . . . what normally would have been a two-year prison stint all of the sudden got elevated to . . . life plus 1,115 years." State institutions might expect such stringent sentencing to discourage activism altogether, but Regan argues that underground activists "already know what they're doing is illegal" and that they would face prison if caught, so "making things that normally would have been a two-year stint into a life sentence just . . . encourages underground activism even more."[107]

NAAALPO's Vlasak talked to me about the AETA4 case in California. A group of animal liberation activists were charged with "animal enterprise terrorism" after writing protest messages in chalk on a sidewalk outside the home of a university vivisectionist. Vlasak said:

> There is a much higher risk of going to protests than doing underground actions now. The chances of doing an underground action and getting caught are almost zero, whereas the AETA4 are facing federal charges and they were doing their protests in broad daylight.[108]

Activists and scholars agree that aboveground protest is no longer necessarily a "retreat" from militant activity; the state often engages in repression regardless of tactical approach. At least if it is underground, you might not get caught.

Another way activists see repression contributing to a positive culture of resistance is bridge building between different social movements targeted by the state. For example, in January 2007, eight former Black Panther Party members were arrested in connection with the 1971 murder of police Sergeant John V. Young at a San Francisco area police station. In response to what they saw as unwarranted harassment of elderly activists—decades after the crime and with little evidence—members of earth and animal liberation networks came out to support the "San Francisco 8." Enna was among them:

> I . . . feel like they spurred this solidarity with other movements. . . . [T]he government harassment . . . built bridges that hadn't really been there before . . . so I feel like that is the major success for me and has changed my life in a really deep and well-rounded sort of way to work with others on issues that are really important to me.[109]

Enna also credits this cross-movement solidarity work with expanding her political vision beyond animal liberation, which is traditionally (and far too often) a single-issue movement: "I do feel like it affected my animal rights activism but broadened the scope of the social work that I'm engaged in. . . . [W]e just have a deeper understanding of all the issues from government harassment, imprisonment, and then also broader social justice."[110] Enna has become an important bridge builder between otherwise disconnected social movements.

"Capitalism teaches us that heroic acts of sabotage against those profiting from the destruction of the natural environment are acts of terrorism," writes Leslie James Pickering. "It teaches us that the systematic destruction of everything that keeps us alive—air, water, and soil—is progress."[111]

Most activists I interviewed accepted that repression is what states *do* when confronted with social change efforts. J Johnson put it this way, "looking at the history of social justice movements, every movement faces repression. And every movement is going to have to go through these sorts of growing pains of dealing with the fact that . . . ideas that go outside of the mainstream are not popular. And they will be fought against."[112]

When I asked about the long-term impact of state repression, a number of activists said they saw the earth and animal liberation movements as the "guinea pig" in a government effort to "test the waters" with respect to how far the state can go toward containing other social movements across the spectrum, including mainstream causes. SHAC7's Jake Conroy adheres to this thesis; repression is an experimental step by the state "to get laws passed and see what they can get away with"—"then they can use that to maybe shut down other movements as well." He states:

> You do it to animal rights activists or environmentalists, and that's perfectly fine because they're crazy or they're weird, and who cares about animals? But, you know, it's just a matter of time before it gets to that level where they're allowed to do that sort of thing [to everyone else]. And we're living in a country that just is so apathetic at this point that they don't really care.[113]

Here Conroy invokes an implication of the radical flank effect (see chapter 1): since the fringe of a social movement may give the core the appearance of being reasonable vis-à-vis the state, it is important to protect the fringe to advance the cause.[114] Conroy's dismay about public apathy reflects how many activists see their work as having little chance of building a mass movement in the short term; mainstream publics simply tend to fear or reject radical politics.

The "guinea pig" thesis has its merit, but it is partially ahistorical since the kind of repression we observe during the Green Scare was arguably "pretested" on movements that predate the earth and animal liberation movements. Claude Marks is a white activist who served time in federal prison for his support of Puerto Rican independence and black liberation movements in the 1960s and 1970s. He currently directs the Freedom Archives, a San Francisco–based organization that collects and makes available to the public audio, video, and other documents chronicling progressive movements in the United States and globally. He and others of his generation of revolutionary movements have reached out to the earth and animal liberation movements, giving advice on numerous occasions. Marks agrees that today's earth and animal liberation activists are only the latest in a long series of state targets. To him, the science of repression (experimentation and learned effects) works together with cultures of repression:

> I think the government has learned from the earlier history of the formal [COINTELPRO] program . . . about how to be impactful. And rather than putting it aside because they arrived at some moral epiphany, the opposite is true. And so, they've worked very carefully to build a level of mass support for an even more vicious and punitive approach to dealing with, or criminalizing, dissent. That's why, today, you've got things like the Animal Enterprise Terrorism Act, or people who are convicted of arson, which is property damage, in a way that exceeds the punishment for activity that harms human life.[115]

Marks urges radicals to pay closer attention to and learn from the history of state repression—particularly those movements led by people of color—so that they can be equipped to confront this social force (much as the state has learned from its past experiences how to best exert repression today). In my conversation Marks reminded me: "There's at least a hundred or so people who are in U.S. prisons because of their involvement with various movements." He mentioned Indigenous activist Leonard Peltier, imprisoned for over thirty years on highly questionable murder charges, as well as members of the Puerto Rican independence movement,

> who remain in prison to this day, who were convicted of seditious conspiracy, which is a political thought crime. The overt act was supporting

Puerto Rican independence. And that is what they were convicted of, and yet they remain in prison.

He mentions the numerous members of the Black Panther Party, targeted by the FBI's COINTELPRO. He states emphatically that these people have "done more than enough time" but remain behind bars "because of what they believe in and the potential of people like that to galvanize resistance to . . . the racist policies of the U.S. . . . It's because of what they think."[116]

Regan offers her own view on why radical movements are important for society:

> We started using that phrase "Green Scare," because clearly, you know, during the "Red Scare," [state repression] wasn't about preventing crime either. It was about an ideology that confronted and challenged the mainstream government and that they [states] were afraid of.[117]

Animal liberation activists and radical environmentalists have common ground with the Black Panthers, Communists, AIM, the Puerto Rican independence movement and others because of their shared state repression, but also because repression frames them as "un-American," as "alien." They have become a *racialized political other*. States and corporations threatened by these movements believe they should be prosecuted and, to whatever extent possible, excluded from the nation (or at least the full rights of citizenship). Thus, we can think of imprisonment of political activists as a form of *social deportation*: they are removed from society while still living under conditions of confinement determined by the nation.[118] Political prisoners are socially and legally defined as "enemy aliens," quasi-foreigners with few if any rights. The specific laws used to label earth and animal liberation activists as "terrorists" stand on a more expansive history of repressive legislation that has been used against many other groups—anyone who dared to think or act in ways that might pose a threat to the social order.

The nation, corporations, and media view such activists as "terrorists" because their *ideas* constitute a threat to the core cultural, legal, political, and economic values embodied in the concept of property; because they threaten the imperative of capitalism and empire to colonize all forms of life (that is what property is, after all);[119] because their rejection of hierarchy threatens a social order rooted in speciesism, white supremacy, classism, and heteropatriarchy; and because, to a large extent, imposing state repression on *any* group of activists sends a strong disciplinary message to the general public (revealing how ecologies of repression function). While I agree with many activists and observers who have argued that the "terrorist" label serves to quell dissent among aboveground activist movements, the more powerful implication is the message sent to the broader public. The stigma of being labeled a "terrorist" might prevent ordinary persons with no political involvement from ever becoming active in social movements in the first place. Repression seeks symbiosis with quiescence.

CHAPTER 6

Resisting the Green Scare

We must remember, the lesson of history teaches us that repression
meant to crush us . . . if we remain united and focused, only serves
to make us stronger and more determined in our dignified fight for
the freedom of earth, animals and those humans who chose to live
in peace.

—Rodney Coronado, *Strong Hearts,* issue 4

After being jailed for arsons in Utah and Colorado, ALF activist Walter
Bond made defiant final statements to the court. In his first hearing in
February 2011, he stated, "In a society that values money over life, I consider it an honor to be a prisoner of war, the war against inter-species
slavery and objectification!"[1] Several months later, he told a Utah judge,
"You can take my freedom, but you can't have my submission,"[2] and he
signed his name "Walter Bond, A.L.F.—P.O.W., A.K.A. Lone Wolf." For
those who support the ALF in particular and animal liberation in general, Bond is now a celebrated political prisoner.

A considerable amount of movement energy is directed at providing
political, legal, financial, material, and emotional support for those earth
and animal liberation activists in prison and for those who are under pressure from the criminal justice system to share information with authorities about movement activities. It is said that "a movement is only as strong
as its prisoner support," and "a movement that doesn't support its prisoners is a sham movement." The *Earth First! Journal* offers free or discounted subscriptions for imprisoned activists and, along with the *ELF
Resistance Journal* and animal liberation publications like *No Compromise*
and *Bite Back,* routinely features stories and updates on prisoners, legal
proceedings, and requests for various forms of support for inmates and
their families. Movement activists host letter-writing events and use these
gatherings to communicate with prisoners, educate the public about

imprisoned activists and the movement's goals, and recruit new participants. Those prisoners fortunate to have their cases highlighted may receive support from around the world.

Prisoner support networks are a response to state repression and the fear it engenders among many activists. While some activists experiencing the full brunt of the science of repression have been devastated by the "chilling effect" associated with the Green Scare, through the groups' efforts, many activists have redoubled their commitment to social change.

The list of prisoners that these movements support includes people who are incarcerated for engaging in activity to support earth and animal liberation in the United States and around the world, but also other revolutionary, anarchist, and social justice organizations and movements such as the Black Panther Party, the Black Liberation Army, MOVE, anti-Nuclear/Peace movements, Puerto Rican Independentistas, the Zapatista National Liberation Army, the American Indian Movement, and Indigenous resistance movements in Latin America and Southeast Asia.[3]

In this branch of their work, activist networks resist state and corporate repression through challenging the discourse of repression and "ecoterrorism," practicing "security culture," providing direct support for prisoners and grand jury resisters, and learning from and building common cause with leaders from other (historic and contemporary) social movements. All of these practices are critical components of the movements' cultures of resistance.

The Power of Language

The most important terrain on which earth and animal liberation activists challenge state repression is the site of discourse around "terror" and "ecoterrorism." As one noted Chicano movement activist stated decades ago, political actors must define themselves or risk being defined by others.[4] Social theorist Antonio Gramsci made the same point: political struggles are also struggles over meaning—both material and discursive.[5] The inseparability of the material and discursive is observable in the lives of earth and animal liberation movement prisoners and those acting and living with the possibility of future internment. Thus, many activists have worked hard to combat and leverage the war of words that accompanies the "war on terror."

Former NAELF Press Office spokesperson Craig Rosebraugh was subpoenaed by the U.S. Congress's House Resources Subcommittee on

Forests and Forest Health to testify at a hearing on "Eco-terrorism and Lawlessness on the National Forests" in February 2002. In a written response to Congressman Scott McInnis (R-Colorado)—the chair of that committee—Rosebraugh questioned the language of "ecoterrorism," asking if what McInnis "meant by ecoterrorism was actually the terror and destruction inflicted on the natural environment by industry."[6] He openly challenged the logic of states calling activists "terrorists" while allowing large corporations to place ecosystems at risk. Rosebraugh refused to cooperate with those leading the hearing. In a press release, he said this was because of the U.S. government's responsibility for "the slaughter of . . . Afghan civilians," as well as "the Sept. 11 attacks due to horrendous US foreign politics of imperialism." He went on to say that, taking into account "these sorts of practices, mixed in with domestic policies of racism, classism, and further imperialism at the expense of life," anyone could see "the truly terrorist reality" of the U.S. state. Rosebraugh concluded, "I could not live with myself if I cooperated with that injustice."[7]

Rosebraugh eventually agreed to appear before the committee, but invoked his Fifth Amendment rights in response to all but a few questions: "in light of the events on September 11, my country has told me that I should not cooperate with terrorists. I therefore am refusing to cooperate with members of Congress who are some of the most extreme terrorists in history."[8]

Rosebraugh and his colleague Leslie James Pickering ran NAELFPO and posted on the organization's website that "real violence" is found where corporations are "clear-cutting forests and destroying ecosystems," where consumers and industry pump pollutants and poisons into the air and water, and in the production and consumption of "commercially-grown, non-organic food." "By labeling the ELF as 'violent,' mainstream society, government, and big business can attempt to forget about the real violence that occurs everyday; *the violence against life*."[9]

Chris Irwin, an EF!er and attorney, agrees that there is a double standard at work: corporations that do extraordinary damage to ecosystems are praised for creating jobs, while environmentalists trying to protect those ecosystems are labeled terrorists. Irwin stated:

> It's ironic that the people blowing up entire mountains point at the people [fighting it] and say, "you're ecoterrorists for daring to protect our watersheds."

We're the new Communists. . . . It's just a historical cycle that they always come up with this term. It's dehumanizing, and that dehumanization makes it easier to justify repression.[10]

Paul Watson, founder of the Sea Shepherd Conservation Society (SSCS), has even replaced the word *terrorist* with a proud label that reflects his commitment to the Earth: "terra-ist."[11]

Animal liberationist J Johnson is an astute observer of the power of public relations and underscored the value of a group of media activists who can communicate the movement's intentions and direct action reports to the public. "I think that's why there has always been an ALF Press Office . . . without that public face . . . and without the sort of greater message . . . the industry is able to just craft those actions [as] terrorism or thuggery . . . [rather than] acts of compassion."[12]

Other activists told me the language of terror was insulting for those targeted by "true terrorism." Ben Rosenfeld said:

I think it cheapens the definition of terrorism and insults the victims of true terror to call . . . arson 'terrorism.' Which it's not. It's arson. Arson is a serious crime. Call it what it is. I don't think anybody's under any delusion that they would not be severely punished for engaging in arson. They just didn't think they would be punished as terrorist.[13]

This invocation of "real terror" is understandable, but problematic. It fundamentally accepts the state's legitimacy in waging war on other movements (particularly those of religious and racial "others") some people view as anti-imperialist.

Activists also frequently compare prison sentences for violent crimes unrelated to political activism versus those crimes associated with earth and animal liberation, so as to emphasize the political nature of the state's response to movement activism. In *Bite Back* magazine, an article read, in part:

A 17 year-old who slashed the face of a 19-year-old to ribbons in Cambridgeshire [U.K.] was jailed for 6 years. A man who raped a woman in our county was jailed for 5 years, and animal rights protestors who conducted a frightening campaign against Huntington Life Sciences and those who had dealings with the company were jailed for up to 11 years.[14]

At a sentencing hearing, Bond stated that one of his "regrets" was "that we live in a day and age where you can rape a child or beat a woman unconscious and receive less prison time than an animal liberation activist that attacked property instead of people."[15]

Great Grey Owl, a veteran environmental and social justice activist, also returned to the theme of state protection of property over people, writing in the *Earth First! Journal*:

> Anyone who significantly defies absolute private property rights or who radically upholds the rights of other species to flourish is a threat to the state. . . . Why else would the Green Scare defendants be threatened with 30 to 1,000 years in prison for mere property destruction when murderers and rapists face average sentences of only eight to 20 years? It helps to keep the real meaning of the Green Scare always clearly in view.[16]

Challenging the language and discourse of "ecoterrorism" on multiple fronts, earth and animal liberation activists have continued pointing out contradictions and seeking support.

Defiance and Resolve

Jason Miller, a former NAALPO Press Officer and Kansas City–based activist, told me federal and local law enforcement officials visited him repeatedly in the wake of his antihunting activism. His response was, "I don't intend to stop doing what I'm doing because of state repression. And we do live in a climate of fear. But we can't let that prevent us from doing what we believe in."[17]

scott crow's experience with FBI surveillance even prompted a front-page story in the *New York Times*.[18] crow told me, "we have to remain resolved in what we're doing" even when activists are jailed or killed:

> It doesn't matter what they do, it doesn't matter how much intelligence they gather on us, it doesn't matter if they have informants, it doesn't matter as long as we do what we do. I just can't emphasize that enough. If you quote me on anything, that is the one thing I want to be quoted on: don't be afraid.[19]

Rachel Bjork, a Seattle-based activist who works with the Northwest Animal Rights Network (NARN) is extraordinarily dedicated: she once rode a bike 3,600 miles to raise awareness of the abusive conditions KFC-bound chickens face in industrial animal processing facilities.[20] About the SHAC7 defendants and AETA legislation, she stated flatly: "The government . . . is trying to scare us. And if people are too scared to do a home demo or chalk, then the government wins." Instead of cowering, after AETA,

> I was like, "I'm gonna go do some home demos." So it made me wanna get out there more, just to kinda, you know, "F you. You can't scare me into not doing stuff." . . . I'll be damned if I'm gonna let somebody scare me into *not* being an activist.[21]

Legions of activists agree. Some work aboveground, while others innovate in autonomous, independent cells (a practice that is standard operating procedure for ALF and ELF activists and limits implication of other activists if one or more is arrested).

Security Culture

"One of the most important things to remember as activists is to keep our mouths shut. Your tongue can literally be a deadly weapon at these times." That is the unvarnished opinion of former ALF prisoner Peter Young. Secrecy, including the autonomous cell structure and other measures, is a critical factor for continuing an effective movement that will not end with one, or even hundreds, of arrests. Activist attorney Lauren Regan said, because of this structure

> [activists] were extremely difficult to catch, and they worked in little tiny cells and they were tight. And there was no breach of security culture amongst them, and they were . . . very careful . . . in committing their crimes to . . . ensure that everybody was safe and nobody would be harmed or injured . . . [or] caught.[22]

It is a security culture that evolves within cultures of resistance.

The Basics

On a cold December day, I met up with Ron "S" at a Minneapolis restaurant. When we met, he was in the middle of a lengthy court battle, facing prison time for federal terrorism charges (he ultimately had strong community support and avoided time behind bars). We ordered pizza and sat far from other patrons. He only allowed me to take notes by hand; I thought to myself, "very smart security culture." Pleased with myself for noticing the gesture, I was nonetheless surprised when Ron "S" asked me what I would do if federal agents subpoenaed me. He knew I was doing research on the same movements our mutual colleague Scott DeMuth has studied, and DeMuth was then in jail for refusing to speak to authorities about an unsolved ALF raid. I quickly regained my composure and told him that I would follow the examples of scholars like DeMuth and Rik Scarce and refuse cooperation, even at the risk of jail time. "If I did anything else, my name would be dirt and I'd have to move to Mars," I told him. I was not about to earn a reputation for violating confidentiality agreements with my study participants—it would ruin my career. Even couched in the language of academic freedom, this was a sufficient statement of appreciation and commitment to the movement. He seemed satisfied with this response, and we began the interview.[23]

Jude Ortiz, a cofounder of Coldsnap Legal Collective (CSLC), has been an anarchist and earth liberation prisoner support activist in the Midwest for many years. CSLC, which offers legal advocacy for activists and groups facing state repression in the Twin Cities, was started in 2008 to prepare activists for the Republican National Convention coming to St. Paul. Ortiz led workshops and training sessions for activists interested in learning about how to pursue their protest work without running afoul of the law, and the CSLC ran a jail support hotline to help activists who have been arrested. Ortiz was also a core member of the Support Committee for DeMuth and Carrie Feldman. He explained that the security culture he helps build is

a way that radical groups stay aware of the state and infiltration and surveillance efforts. This is a way to counter disruptive efforts by the state. It's a way of being aware of those things and being cautious about the way you talk, when, where and with whom you talk. It's very clear why those practices are necessary.[24]

Another group, the Cascadia Forest Alliance (CFA), has a "Disorientation Manual." It says security culture is "a culture where the people

know their rights and, more importantly, assert them." The CFA emphasizes educating people about not partaking in "insecure behavior." They
offer specific guidelines such as "What not to talk about: Your, or someone else's involvement in illegal activities. Your, or someone else's plans for
a future action. Your, or someone else's involvement in an underground
group, or desire to become involved."[25] The CFA goes on to describe a
number of other classic security culture violations, such as lying, gossip-
ing, and bragging about illegal direct actions and individual activists' possible involvement. These behaviors can place individuals, networks, and
entire movements at greater risk of state repression, so activists are urged
to be careful and cognizant to maintain a strong and resilient movement.

There were security culture panels and literature at many activist conferences and gatherings I attended during the course of this research. One
anonymous pamphlet read:

> To be secure, you should think about what you want to keep confidential
> right away and start out with all of the necessary precautions. You should
> use a remote mailbox and have off-site back ups for everything. You should
> use encrypted email and structure your organizations so that there are no
> obvious leaders who can be targeted.[26]

Few activists begin their political lives with a working knowledge of
security culture, but once they are linked into movement networks, this
information is readily available. At many conferences, there are workshops on how to use encryption software—in fact, after the FBI indicated
interest in my research project (and I learned my computer hardware and
any data contained on it were, technically, my employer's property), I
began using encrypted e-mail software and encrypted my computer—or,
rather, I asked activists to show me how to install and use these tools.[27]
Regarding the use of technology for improving security culture, *Bite Back*
magazine wrote glowingly about SHAC's security methods. According
to the article, the FBI seized seven computers from the SHAC campaign
and contracted with a leading technology firm whose employees worked
for months to crack the encryption software codes. They failed. Reportedly, the FBI then subpoenaed executives of the PGP Corporation (the
manufacturer of PGP encryption software) but finally "came to the conclusion that it is beyond their means to break the 'SHAC' computers. The
software can be downloaded at www.pgpi.com."[28]

Noms de Guerre: Security, Funny Names, and Forgiveness

One sometimes humorous aspect of security culture is the use of assumed names. The CFA Disorientation Manual explains how they may sound silly, but the nicknames protect identities: "It is important to respect the names people give themselves. I don't care if someone wants to call themselves Moose crap or Woo Momma. It's not my job to criticize or make fun."[29]

The "fake names" phenomenon is particularly pronounced among earth liberation activists, many of whom call these monikers "forest names." Miss Anne Thropy, Muskrat, Microbe, Nettle, Thrush, Dirt, Critter, Pitch, Tara the Sea Elf, Wolverine, Felonious Skunk, Storm, and Going by Tilts are all respected earth liberation activists. This practice seems less common among animal liberation activists, but ALF activists clearly need anonymity as well. Activists within that movement have frequently adopted pseudonyms for their entire cells: there's the Bee Liberation Front and the Gordon Shumway Brigade (an ALF cell that conducted a mink release in Oregon in 2011 and was apparently named for a character on the 1980s sitcom *Alf*).

During fieldwork at an EF! Round River Rendezvous (RRR), my colleague Hollie Nyseth Brehm witnessed an exchange that spoke to both the importance and lighter side of activist noms de guerre. One activist named Wren was standing in the chow line during lunch and called out to a friend—Lune—who was further down the line and had dropped his hat.[30] After several attempts at yelling "Lune!" Wren was exasperated and finally hollered "Benjamin!" (apparently Lune's birth name). Lune turned, gave Wren a dirty look, and silently picked up his hat.

In a movement that is generally deadly serious, humor ends up being a good tool. During the 2009 EF! Roadshow, activists put on a puppet show to demonstrate key lessons about security culture. The puppet show was called "Danny Don't." The characters included Danny (a fox), Brian Bear, Ben the Snapping Turtle, Rita Raccoon, Olivia Owl, and Peter Pig. Olivia Owl was the "wise" narrator who greeted the eco-warriors and explained that they were taking time off from their busy forest lives to share safety tips with the public. She explained no one should do what Danny Don't does, and that the audience was to yell "Danny Don't" whenever a sign was held up indicating that Danny was about to violate security culture rules. Through laughter and audience participation, the animals explained how their "social norms within a resistance movement need to a be a little different than other people's." They discussed the importance of building trust and being careful of people who are not "really" your friends, and cautioned the audience against falling into federal agents' traps: "If someone you barely know asks you to help them build a bomb, don't do it. Only build a bomb if *you* want to do it!" They said earnestly to never talk to police or FBI ("the police wouldn't be asking questions if they didn't need more information") and cautioned against posting actions or pictures on social media sites. After teaching the audience the mantra "I'm going to remain silent—I'd like to speak to my lawyer," the animals closed by noting that we should also remember that people *do* make honest mistakes and that security culture makes it easy to become paranoid.[31]

At that year's EF Round River Rendezvous (RRR), during a daily morning circle discussion, there was a graphic and humorous collective conversation about latrine usage at the camp that also touched on security culture. Storm Waters told me he had been to more than a dozen of these gatherings. As a meteorologist, he was in charge of giving the daily weather forecast at the "Rondy." On this particular morning, he was also temporarily in charge of offering information about latrines, since the latrine "expert" (the "shitter czar") had not yet arrived. Storm listed all of the camp's latrines, hilariously named in ways that included a nod to solidarity with undocumented immigrant communities and an insult directed at an infamous movement snitch: "We have the 'Shit on the Border Wall' shitter over there and the 'Brandon Darby' [the FBI informant who spied on scott crow and other activists] shitter over there, where you can shit in his wide open mouth."[32] This announcement was received with raucous laughter and applause.

EF!'s approach to security culture is refreshing in its accessibility and comical-but-serious style, which is an EF! movement cultural trademark. This is particularly notable, given how harsh other activist communities can be on this subject. When it comes to police interrogations, *Bite Back* skips the puppets and writes only: "Rule #1: Keep your fucking mouth shut! Rule #2: If you ever think of opening your mouth, refer to Rule #1. . . . Nearly all ALF and ELF arrests have been the result of those who didn't keep their fucking mouths shut."[33]

In its summer 2003 issue, the animal liberation magazine *No Compromise* published a "Snitch Protocol" to formalize the movement's security culture vis-à-vis activists who collaborate with authorities since such behavior can "critically undermine . . . and jeopardize the integrity of our movement." The basic message is that "Activists should never, under any circumstances, provide information or names of other activists to the authorities"; if they do, they will be labeled a "snitch." Snitches "will receive absolutely no support—financial, legal, moral, or otherwise":

> *No Compromise* has no desire to create a movement "witch hunt," . . . [but] In order to reinforce our defenses we must locate, isolate, and dispose of the weak links in the chain. Snitches are the weak links in our movement. . . . There can be no room—no tolerance—for those who pose a direct threat to our movement's vitality and our goal of total and lasting animal liberation.[34]

Great Grey Owl writes about George Orwell's *1984*, in which "the main character sells out his lover and best friend to the Big Brother fascist state." The lesson, she argues, is that cooperation with the state is essentially "a commercial transaction" in which an activist sells their friends and their integrity to a dominant political-economic system. While the authorities pressure people to give information under threats to their personal freedom, "it's not just a personal decision—though it may seem so while you're isolated behind bars." Rather, cooperating with the state

> affects . . . all your fellow activists outside and the fate of our wild plant and animal relations in a tremendous historical ripple effect. . . . Audre Lorde [another author] said, "When I dare to be powerful—to use my strength in the service of my vision, then it becomes less and less important whether I am afraid." Everyone has fears; it's how we deal with them that is crucial.[35]

By referencing the "tremendous historical ripple effect," Owl acknowledges the ecologies of repression—the way repression has consequences for its direct targets and for other activists, entire movement communities, and nonhuman ecosystems. Further, Owl's statement about the power of fear reflects an emerging discussion and effort to grapple with the distress and anxieties of repression in the movement. This seems to reveal evidence of the movement's evolution and embrace of feminist politics and theory, which offer a refreshing counter to the traditionally masculinist orientation to the emotional struggles inherent in social movements. However, Owl's approach is still basically a hard-line stance.

Jeff Hogg's perspective offers a departure from the hard-liner approach. Hogg grew up in the Bay Area. As a result of his exposure to the forest and ocean, and to his mother's antinuclear activism, he came to appreciate and join the movement to defend nonhuman natures. He moved to Eugene, Oregon, where he worked for the *EF! Journal* and was a highly visible supporter of the movement. During the FBI's Operation Backfire in 2005–2006, Hogg was jailed for six months for refusing to speak to a grand jury about the movement and direct actions the FBI was investigating. In an interview later published in the *EF! Journal*, he was asked about another activist who had cooperated with the state. Hogg adopted a nuanced perspective and offered something other than hostility and rejection. He wrote that often, when one looks at the particulars of a case, "cooperator and non-cooperator become less well-defined categories." He feels that the "dogmatic lack of empathy" for "cooperators" is not always helpful or realistic when the person in question is "a close friend" who needs support too. Hogg made a distinction between supporting a person and supporting their actions: "I don't support her actions, but I feel what she did was forgivable. . . . I find it hard not to feel empathy for people being manipulated and pressured by their lawyers, the prosecutors, and their families." He concluded: "I think there has been enough condemnation, and it is time for compassion. . . . In the end, I think compassion is the only radical path."[36]

Limits of Security Culture

A logical outgrowth of the Green Scare, security culture has its own drawbacks. One problem is that if activists adhere strictly to security culture protocols, there may be fewer overall actions and less movement visibility and impact. Stu Sugarman, the eponymous "Ask an EF! Lawyer" columnist, has worked since 1995 to represent (for free) every Oregon civil disobedience activist. During a 2010 visit to Minneapolis to endorse the DeMuth and Feldman support campaigns, Sugarman confirmed:

> I think that there's a lot more security-conscious people. It's stressed not to—if you're going to do anything like that—don't do it with anyone who you don't know very well and haven't known very well for a long time. So [unfortunately] that's going to cut down on the actions that do happen.[37]

Additionally, while security culture may protect activists against unwanted intrusions by government agents and give them a sense of safety, unfortunately it also makes it difficult to attract new recruits to a movement. I witnessed this during a number of gatherings. Even at the rowdy "Rondy," obvious newcomers tended to sit by themselves, unwelcomed and isolated. Calls for greater security culture sometimes encourage activists to work alone, which has its own benefits and drawbacks. Peter Young told me he thinks single-activist actions are extremely effective:

> People don't really think about the power that one person has. We always think of things in terms of groups, and I think that's a great folly because often times one person working alone can actually be more effective. One person . . . can do as much or more damage as a group of people with certain types of actions. And you eliminate the threat of being snitched on.[38]

But Walter Bond's "lone wolf" ALF actions make it clear that a solitary approach to illegal direct action is not foolproof: Bond's own brother "snitched" on him and sent him to prison for years.

"Lone wolf" actions and security culture also impact movement building. crow argues, "Security culture . . . only works if you're working on clandestine action, but it doesn't work for building broader social movements because it isolates us, and I've found it very damaging." He discussed an incident during an event at a radical bookstore where an animal rights activist was speaking about state repression. A friend of crow's "who is not involved in that stuff but is sympathetic wanted to come," and this friend showed up wearing a black leather motorcycle jacket. At one point, the person facilitating the event (which attracted at least fifty people) declared, "And to the cop in the back over there with the black leather motorcycle jacket, we know who you are." The reaction was predictable, crow remembered; "It was awful, and of course that friend of mine never came back to an event ever again, and never went back to that bookstore ever again, so we lost a potential ally."[39]

Security culture has its limits, and many activists are debating and discussing this. But when one steps back to examine the day-to-day work of these movements, something else becomes clear: the topic of underground illegal direct action within ELF and ALF cells is exciting and fascinating, but that type of activism constitutes an exceedingly small percentage of the work that activists do. Its inordinate place in the cultural idea of earth and animal liberation sometimes feeds into a security culture fixation. crow explained:

> I think that 99 percent of the people that I know that engage in stuff don't engage in clandestine activities. . . . [A]nd yet we have this culture of security that we want to reinforce that . . . puts us in a defensive position, and it keeps us separated from those that we could build really good strong relationships with on broader collective liberation fronts.[40]

This problem is particularly personal for crow, since he has worked for years to build multiracial, cross-movement coalitions.

Breakdown

While I have discussed security culture as a response to the Green Scare, some activists believe it was a breakdown of existing security culture practices that contributed to the Green Scare. Karen Coulter, profiled throughout this book, contends that security culture was already common among activist networks prior to the Green Scare: "I mean, it's all just a lot of people not knowing that Jake [Ferguson] was a heroin addict. That didn't help, you know? But [there are] people doing things like [illegal direct action] that ought to know who they're working with."[41]

Jacob Ferguson was an activist who participated in at least a dozen ELF arsons but later became the key FBI informant in Operation Backfire. His deal with the state most likely guaranteed lenience for his illicit drug use and ELF activities in exchange for insider knowledge. Working for the FBI, Ferguson traveled the country to meet with activist colleagues and recorded more than eighty hours of conversations at some forty meetings. He gave authorities information on some twenty-two sabotage actions.[42] His surveillance was the key evidence behind Operation Backfire—the arrest and prosecution of numerous earth and animal liberation activists.

Coulter indicated that she and other activists believe Operation Backfire revealed generational and social class divides within the movement that also undermine security culture. "I know a number of older Earth First!ers who are just appalled by the fact that that [snitching] could even happen" because the movement was originally built on "a lot of loyalty . . . and strong bonds." Her older EF! colleagues believe that "class differences" were at play, "where some people got off easily based on family money, and other people couldn't and were more under pressure in prison."[43] They believe some people snitched because they could not afford legal representation, and others did so because they could access considerable family financial resources to avoid further prosecution.

Other activists concurred, arguing that, historically, white middle-class activists have not had a history of being a part of a culture of resistance. They worry about having a scarlet letter on their future career plans and crumple under pressure. For example, Lacey Phillabaum was a "champion high school debater" who majored in art history at the University of Oregon. She was also a member of the ELF cell that firebombed the University of Washington's Center for Urban Horticulture. When the authorities caught up with her, they soon secured her cooperation. Ron "S," a former friend, still despairs over her decision to turn: "It's easy for someone like Lacey, who has a middle-class background, to rat everyone out and [go] back to her parents."[44] The anarchist collective CrimethInc.'s "Green Scared?" document takes issue with the class divide thesis, however: "We are to take it for granted that arrestees became informants because they were privileged middle class kids; in fact, both the cooperating and non-cooperating defendants are split along class and gender lines."[45] They seem to say, just as there is no one kind of activist, there is no one kind of snitch.

Prisoner Support: "Just Tell Your Friends to Stop Calling"

The first real, personal letter I wrote to an earth/animal liberation prisoner was to Scott DeMuth, my graduate student advisee and colleague at the University of Minnesota. Since that time I have written to others, and it has become an important practice for my intellectual and political development. Soon after I wrote that first letter, I told Ron "S" how surprised and proud I had been to see how calm and confident Scott was during a court appearance, even shackled in chains. Ron responded:

> Scott has it in him, but it's also because he has a strong support community. The Irish Republican Army (IRA) was the same way—over 50 percent of their organizing work went into prisoner support. Scott knows we have his back. Prisoner support is incredibly important. We really need to have each other's back.[46]

I took that advice to heart and joined DeMuth's support group, a committed collective of activists who worked night and day for months to visit him in prison, be present at court appearances, write him letters, send him books, raise funds for his legal defense and commissary, and raise awareness of his case through public events, website postings, and a multicity tour.

The volume of effort dedicated to providing support for prisoners and grand jury resisters is enormous and could be classified as a social movement in and of itself. At the EF! Roadshow in 2009, they put it like this: "We stand up for these political prisoners because, right or wrong, their actions were fueled by an urgency that we also feel."

Prisoners Speak

Rod Coronado's writings from prison have inspired countless activists and would-be activists to support prisoners and the movements for earth and animal liberation. He has never considered himself a "political prisoner," but rather a prisoner of war.[47] From within federal prison, he wrote to his supporters:

> My actions though illegal are simply the price my generation must pay to protect the earth, animals and our own children from those selfish and greedy forces now destroying all that we love and live for. And it is a price I as a citizen of Earth am honored to pay.[48]

Coronado was always conscious of other freedom struggles and writes that he "felt humbled" that his time in prison was so much more tolerable when compared to that of revolutionary activists in other nations. For example, "the ten brave Irish Republican Army Volunteers who starved themselves to death in prison rather than be labeled common criminals" or the "courageous members of the Tupac Amaru Revolutionary Movement" languishing in Peruvian prisons and "eating rats because they dared to be free." He also invoked "my coyote relations at the University of Utah laboratories who are intentionally starved and then forced to eat poisons." Coronado concluded that "nothing I've endured so far has yet to compare with what others in our struggle are forced into."[49]

Jake Conroy spent several years in federal prison for his SHAC-related activism. He told me:

I've always done prisoner support . . . but it's, like, a totally different ballgame to find yourself on the other side of that. . . . I can't even imagine doing the past few years without the support I received. From people putting on benefits to sending me books, sending me letters, pictures, making new friends through correspondences. It was just really, really overwhelming.[50]

As discussed in chapter 5, Conroy, a SHAC7 defendant and activist branded by the state as an animal enterprise "terrorist," became a racial deviant, but his whiteness *inside* the prison was amplified by the privilege and status he enjoyed as a high-profile inmate. He described what it was like to receive "thousands and thousands" of letters:

You can't put a price on your name being called at mail call and having them hand you a letter. Or two letters. Or ten letters. Sometimes I would get up to fifty letters a day when I was at Victorville. . . . And everyone was like, "Who is this little white guy that comes in here? He's some 'domestic terrorist.' And he's running around getting all this mail! Who is this guy?"[51]

During a conference presentation in 2009, Peter Young stated: "I was told by my public defender to expect to serve twelve years in prison. But with the money I received from supporters, I hired a private attorney and got my sentence reduced to two years."[52] The ability to hire a private attorney and get a reduced sentence? That is something a white middle-class social movement can do, and about which radical movements in communities of color can only dream. In that sense, like Conroy and others, Young was a privileged racial deviant—he was denied some of the privileges of his race and class but was afforded others. Young was a high-profile ALF prisoner and received accolades from many corners of the movement:

I had good support—one woman even uprooted her life and moved all the way to Madison, Wisconsin, to do full-time prison support for me. . . . I was in solitary . . . and when I got into the main prison population I got something like forty-five letters and I realized I was not alone in this, and a sense of peace came over me.[53]

Young also enjoyed the benefit of an elevated standing among his fellow prisoners and even his captors: "Your standing in prison is higher if you get a lot of mail. . . . I became known as a guy who had people on the outside thinking he was important." When word got out that the prison was not providing him with vegan meals, "the jailers . . . got a hundred phone calls in two hours demanding that I get vegan food." In a scene right out of a television show, "the jail captain . . . gave me a pen and paper and said, 'Mr. Young, please give me a shopping list and we'll get you what the hell you want. Just tell your friends to stop calling.'"[54]

Lauren Regan was at Peter Young's panel at the Let Live Conference in Portland, and she pointed out: "I didn't hear you mention benefit shows, and that's something we do every week in Eugene. We have punk and rock bands do benefit concerts for prisoners."[55] Young affirmed Regan's comment and expressed appreciation: "The punk and hard core scene covered the bulk of my funding."

One particularly controversial form of support for prisoners is illegal direct action. In a number of cases, movement participants have carried out such actions to support their colleagues and in protest of their detention. Young said:

> When I heard of ALF actions when I was in prison, that was the best form of prisoner support, and I'd give up all the letters and visits for that. When I was in prison, I heard about windows being broken at a fur store and dogs being liberated in Spain—and that was done in support of me, and I see that as the purest form of prisoner support.[56]

A Two-Way Street

Earth and animal liberation prisoner support networks exist worldwide. Increased activist targeting and the intensification of "ecoterrorism" have resulted in more prisoners, and activists believe supporting them will strengthen the movement. The North American Earth Liberation Prisoners Support Network says:

> More and more people are starting to step outside the system of Man-made laws and take "illegal" direct action in defense of the Earth. . . . Our movement will not continue to grow unless we are able to provide this level of support to our comrades who are unfortunate enough to become prisoners of the State.[57]

Twin Cities anarchist and earth/animal liberation prisoner support activist Luce Guillén-Givens, who was mentioned in the previous chapter, offers the following reasoning: "We need radical change. And since state repression will not stop anytime soon, we must prepare for it and provide support for prisoners." Moreover, Guillén-Givens argues that strong prisoner support assures other activists that they, too, will receive such assistance should they need it: "We, as activists, know that we will be supported if we suffer the consequences of state repression and activism."[58]

Tre Arrow, profiled in the first chapter, is famous for occupying the nine-inch-wide ledge of a government building for eleven days to protest a timber sale in the Pacific Northwest. He later ran unsuccessfully for Congress on the Green Party ticket and served a six-year prison sentence for alleged involvement in an ELF arson. *Rolling Stone* magazine called him "America's most wanted eco-terrorist." An author in the *EF! Journal* wrote:

> Tre Arrow must be supported unconditionally. . . . Tre gives every day of his life for the Earth, so I'm calling on everyone to give a day for Tre. Here is my hope: that the actions of Tre Arrow inspire the support of one day of your life, one whole day. If you are a working person, that means you figure a day's wages and send it to Tre's legal defense fund. If you live outside the wage economy, give a full day's work organizing a benefit or spreading the news of Tre's case through every venue you know.[59]

Grand Jury Resisters

Activists who are subpoenaed to appear before federal grand juries and refuse to cooperate fully with those secretive, extra-constitutional bodies occupy a special and complex position within the spectrum of political prisoners. Between the time they are served with a subpoena and the moment they appear in front a grand jury, they are in a liminal state: they are neither entirely free nor entirely not-free. They exist under the enormous shadow of the criminal justice system while building a support network and working to mount a resistance campaign before the date of the grand jury. If they are jailed for their noncooperation, it is usually in a county facility, rarely for more than six months. Nonetheless, grand jury resisters play a crucial role in the movements; since grand juries can be used as instruments of power, movements must mobilize to resist this part of the repressive apparatus, too. Thus, much of the movement's political prisoner support energy has been devoted to grand jury resisters.

Luce Guillén-Givens told a class at the University of Minnesota that grand juries were originally founded to prevent arbitrary prosecutions. They were supposed to consider the evidence put before them—including testimony from various persons summoned—and determine whether anyone should be indicted for a crime (that is, should anyone be charged at all). England eliminated its grand jury system in the early twentieth century, but in the United States, Guillén-Givens said,

> they became a tool of the prosecution, because they circumvent everything you believe you have in terms of rights. You are a witness, not a criminal defendant, so you don't have those rights. It is . . . used to target political activism and people who speak out for their beliefs.[60]

Stu Sugarman adds:

> The U.S. adopted [the grand jury] and put it on steroids. It's a little Inquisition where a person has no rights and is forced to talk with no lawyer, and they can be put in prison for up to eighteen months. It's a horrible form of power. If you are subpoenaed, you have already lost most of your rights.[61]

Rosebraugh spoke on a panel with Sugarman and another activist lawyer, Christine Garcia, at an animal rights conference and stated: "It's a way in U.S. history that the federal government has cracked down on independence movements."[62] NAALPO rep Jerry Vlasak, in the audience, jumped in to say, "Grand juries are a way of getting around a cohesive activist community that doesn't talk."[63]

Rosebraugh went on:

> Throughout history, one of the things that gets people less time is . . . public pressure. Jonathan Paul did an action in Spokane and was serving time in Arizona, and he got less time because of a public campaign. Grand juries get their power from operating in secrecy.[64]

Sugarman, Rosebraugh's attorney, also recalled the power of public support: "Craig's case was great. We postered and made his case public and things melted away. The system is run by cockroaches and they don't like light, so shine light on the process since the grand jury is secretive."[65]

While Sugarman encourages activists to do their work outside the courtroom, inside the legal system there is no substitute for good legal representation. SHAC7 defendant Josh Harper was also a client of Sugarman's. The day he went before the grand jury, Sugarman "prepared several excellent arguments to protect me from having to answer questions concerning other people." On other questions, he answered truthfully, "'I don't recall,' 'Not to the best of my knowledge,' and so forth." At the end of the proceedings, Harper recalls, "the prosecutor, didn't look very happy when I walked out of the room without handcuffs. Sugarman . . . really shut them down." In the end, "the government spent a lot of time and money on this grand jury, and as far as I know, they have nothing to show for it."[66]

Many grand jury resisters are not so lucky. Gina Lynn wrote, "I declined to testify because, as a matter of conscience, I cannot and will not participate in the investigation and potential prosecution of a cause to which I have devoted my life (animal rights)."[67] As for the legitimacy of the grand jury, Lynn said, "It's as if when you walk through the doors of that grand jury room, you cross an international border to a place where the Constitution doesn't exist. I refuse to accept that."[68] This demand for legal rights granted by the state is one of many tensions and contradictions within movements that are also largely anarchist. Sugarman and many other activist attorneys describe themselves as "anarchists" as well, but they recognize that as long as the state exists, movement activists must push for and extract as much from it as possible.

Debating Prisoner Support

Bite Back editor Nick Atwood offered a common view: "Unfortunately, prisoner support is not a national focus of the movement. It's usually a 'support your own people' attitude of various organizations."[69] Vlasak concurs:

> We definitely could do a better job of political support in this movement. If you look at the IRA [Irish Republican Army] in Ireland, they were heroes. Many of them ran for public office from behind bars. They were well known throughout the community. So we have some distance to go on that. Many activists don't know about prisoners or won't support them.[70]

Where prisoner support *is* strong, in many cases ideological rigidity can play an unproductive role. For example, at one time the ALF Prisoner Support Group (U.K.) only recognized a prisoner as an ALF prisoner if that person fulfilled "clause #3—one must be vegan or vegetarian." In response, the North American Earth Liberation Prisoners Support Network writes:

> Drop your lifestyle issues. . . . This archaic clause (written presumably by the people who started the ALF in England) creates a really absurd basis of support. What if a person eats meat but decides that they are going to destroy 12 vivisection labs, liberate 5,000 mink, spike a few timber sales and sab hunts? If they get nicked, who will be life stylist enough to tell them "No, sorry. You are most definitely NOT a member of the ALF and will not receive ALF prisoner support. Please refer to clause 3."[71]

When DeMuth was jailed for refusing to speak to a federal grand jury, I asked the NAALPO to support him by reporting on his case. However, DeMuth never claimed to be an ALF operative and never claimed involvement in the raid; he was simply jailed because the state believed he had information about the movement. Complicating matters (and making it *extremely* unlikely that he was an ALF activist), DeMuth was an avid bow hunter who ate meat regularly: one NAALPO officer pointedly asked me, "Why should I support Scott when he's a hunter? He murders animals."[72] Fortunately, others at NAALPO saw fit to publicize the case, and other key movement groups like the Anarchist Black Cross Federation and EF! added DeMuth to their political prisoner lists.

Prison time also takes an enormous emotional toll on people. SHAC7's Harper says emphatically: "As a movement . . . we really need to be there for people when they come out of prison." When activists come out of prison,

> they might not be who they were. They might not be altogether there. . . . And if we want to get them back on the front lines . . . we're going to have to give them the support they need. And to just talk to somebody as "You're a warrior!" "You're a hero!" "Get back out there!" That's not sufficient.[73]

Just like other prisoners reentering society (or, say, soldiers returning from active duty) require support for successful reintegration, political prisoners need allies even after they come home.

Beyond the Prisoners

To be most impactful, prisoner support must extend to provide sustenance for the prisoners' families, friends, the broader activist community, and potential movement recruits. In these sites, ecologies of repression are intended to produce fear and quiescence. In one form of such help, ALF Prisoners Support Group in the UK states, "we assist prisoners' relatives and friends with travel costs to enable them to visit the prisoner, which can be quite costly as prisoners are often kept hundreds of miles away from their hometowns."[74]

The support is also emotional. Joyanna Sadie Zacher was convicted of two ELF arsons and sentenced to seven years at FCI Dublin (California), while her husband, Nathan "Exile" Block, was imprisoned at FCI Lompoc (California).[75] At a prisoner support event in Minneapolis, Ron "S" spoke glowingly about Sadie and Exile as two earth liberation prisoners who initially faced life plus a thousand years in prison but "never snitched and never backed down. . . . And they are not rock star prisoners, so we should remember them and focus more on people like that." Ron told the group how Sadie's mother had come to a prisoner support event one evening. She arrived unannounced and told the group it was great to know that her daughter had backing, but Ron also noted that it was just as important for Sadie to know that people "had her mom's back—that her mom had a support network too."[76]

J Johnson told me about a friend of his—Jen—who was arrested and jailed on Rikers Island in New York City when she was seventeen. She'd been rounded up at a protest where a building window had been broken. Jen refused to cooperate with the authorities, even when others did, so she received harsher treatment and was imprisoned. Jen's support network had an impact that extended well beyond the prisoner. Johnson told me that one of the most surprising and important outcomes was the "radicalizing effect [of support] on the loved ones of that prisoner." These family members (frequently parents) often "might not be really all that knowledgeable about these issues" or "might not necessarily be activist-minded," but when they learn more about the movement and the issues, and when they witness the way the state treats their loved one, they may become "more interested" and more politically active. Johnson stated, "Jen's mom's a great example. You know she—by the time Jen got out of prison—she was going to protests and was vegan."[77]

Learning from Other Social Movements

In May 2013, the FBI added its first woman to the Most Wanted Terrorists list: Assata Shakur.[78] Shakur was born in Queens, New York, and was first arrested at a protest against what students believed were deficiencies of City College of New York's Black Studies Program. After graduating, she joined the Black Panther Party (BPP) in Harlem and directed one of its free breakfast programs. However, she became disenchanted with the BPP's rampant sexism, its patriarchy, and what she saw as a lack of focus on African American history. She soon joined the Black Liberation Army (BLA), an underground network of militants whose goals included securing freedom and self-determination for African Americans.

The BLA officially embraced socialism, anti-imperialism, antiracism, and antisexism and rejected what they saw as the reformism of the BPP. The BLA took up arms to achieve its goals, and its members are believed to have been responsible for numerous bank robberies, murders, and bombings. The BLA collaborated with groups like the Weather Underground—a white, anti-imperialist radical organization that emerged from Students for a Democratic Society (SDS). Shakur was eventually convicted for killing Werner Foerster, a New Jersey state trooper, during a shootout on May 2, 1973. She was shot twice, and one of her fellow activists (Zayd Shakur) died. The many charges against her included armed robbery, bank robbery, assault and battery, and assault of a police officer acting in the line of duty, assault with intent to kill, murder, and the kidnapping of a Brooklyn heroin dealer.[79]

Shakur was sentenced to life in prison plus thirty-three years, but in 1979 her colleagues from the BLA and the Weather Underground broke her out of jail. She hid out in safe houses until fleeing to Cuba, where she received political asylum in 1984. She has long proclaimed her innocence and accused federal authorities of political persecution.[80]

When the FBI first put Shakur on its Most Wanted Fugitive list decades ago, her supporters produced signs that read "Assata Shakur is Welcome Here" and later adopted the slogan "Hands off Assata." Numerous rap and hip-hop artists have recorded songs praising Shakur. After arriving in Cuba, she famously referred to herself as a "twentieth-century escaped slave." In 2005, the thirty-second anniversary of the New Jersey Turnpike shootings, the FBI classified Shakur as a "domestic terrorist" and increased the award for assistance in her capture to $1 million. Eight years later, the agency elevated her to the Most Wanted Terrorist list and doubled the reward money. A *Washington Times* editorial suggested that the right thing to do would be to confine her to the site in Cuba where scores of other "terrorists" are housed. The editorial read, "There's already a cell waiting at Guantanamo Bay."[81] During her time in exile, Shakur has written several books about political repression and African American history and has worked as an English language editor at Radio Havana Cuba.

Assata Shakur's case illustrates the lengths to which the U.S. government will go to pursue activists in its attempt to neutralize social change movements. It also demonstrates the important cultural and symbolic role played by political prisoners and underscores the critical role of publics and activist communities that provide support for political prisoners and resisters.

I begin this section with Shakur's story, because it is important for earth and animal liberation activists to understand the history and ongoing struggles of freedom movements in communities of color against racism and state/corporate repression. They are inseparable from contemporary repression and the Green Scare. For example, the year the FBI first classified Shakur as a "domestic terrorist" was the same year it launched Operation Backfire against the ALF and ELF. The same agency was using the same language and legal apparatus to go after two seemingly disparate movements at the same time. It was only when a small number of activists across these movements paid attention to these links that these crucial connections were made at the grassroots level.

The San Francisco 8 (SF8)

In chapter 5 I argued that one of the many effects of state repression was to spawn solidarity actions and collaborations between earth/animal liberation movements and radical movements of earlier eras. In that section, I mentioned Enna's realization of the generative potential of cross-movement awareness in relation to the case of the "San Francisco 8."

In January 2007, eight former Black Panther Party members were issued grand jury subpoenas in connection with the 1971 murder of police Sergeant John V. Young at the Ingleside police station in San Francisco. The BPP or BLA was believed responsible, and in 1973, police arrested and charged three men in a New Orleans Police Department station (including Howard Taylor, one of the SF8). During interrogation, officers extracted murder confessions, but only after subjecting the arrestees to several days of sleep deprivation, cattle prods, electric shocks, sensory deprivation, and boiling hot wet blankets used for asphyxiation simulation.[82] In 1975, a judge threw out the charges, citing the use of torture.[83]

The revival of the case twenty-two years later was seen by many as the unwarranted harassment of elderly activists (who at the time included grandfathers and great-grandfathers). It appeared to be a continuation of the FBI's COINTELPRO and an operation that produced "evidence" gleaned from torture. Leaders from the BPP and other left-leaning revolutionary movements led by people of color came out to support the San Francisco 8 (SF8). Activists from earth and animal liberation networks joined in as well; they, too, were under pressure from grand jury subpoenas and sought to build common cause.

In response to the state's campaign against them, the SF8 released a statement in May 2007 that read, in part:

> This case evolves out of a history of political struggle in this country, and it is our duty to fulfill that mission by expressing what happened then, and COINTELPRO's negative impact on today's social movements. Therefore, while we engage in a legal battle in the courtroom, it is imperative we urge our friends and supporters to extend the political front in the various communities. We must reach out to the various street organizations and youth groups, the animal and earth liberation groups, women's rights and LGBT forums, the immigration rights struggles, and the many ethnic communities who are struggling for a better life in this country.[84]

This statement is notable precisely because of its explicit acknowledgment of and solidarity with social movements far outside of the traditional boundaries of Black Power movements. In particular, the SF8's reaching out to earth and animal liberation, LGBT, and women's rights groups challenges the traditional images of the BPP and other black liberation movements as hypermasculinist and ultranationalist.

Veterans of the black freedom struggle and many others worked to publicly support the San Francisco 8. Ashanti Alston is a former Black Panther who has worked in coalition with ALF and ELF groups by providing public support of their movements and offering guidance on responses to state repression. He said of the confluence:

> The FBI and corporations realized that these groups were effective at getting their message out. Just like the Panthers were effective at getting their ideas out. So you [the authorities] have to shut it down because the ideas are threatening and important. The good thing that came out of that was

when our movement around political prisoners starting to interact with animal liberation and earth liberation activists around political prisoners, we started figuring out how to work in solidarity.[85]

Will Potter (author of *Green Is the New Red*) also discusses how the repression of animal and earth liberation movements pushed some to reach out to and learn from other movements:

It's raised a lot of the questions like . . . how to reach out to the broader social justice community. . . . I've seen joint events between animal rights activists and Black Panthers . . . [where] the message is, ". . . we need to learn from the people that have experienced [state repression] first-hand and . . . build those kind of coalitions."[86]

Jeff Luers stated, "I've been giving panels lately with some former political prisoners from the BLA and BPP, and there's this—we're really, really trying hard . . . to start solidifying all our connections. . . . [W]e're going about things from a different angle, but we're all in the same movement."[87]

Lauren Regan (Luers's attorney) recalled the impact of the parallel experiences of the SF8 and the Operation Backfire targets:

We did this incredible solidarity action and campaign of Black Panthers and animal rights in opposition to grand juries. And we did media together and press conferences . . . and I'm sure the feds were probably like, "Oh, shit. What did we just do?" Because, you know, for the first time, we had a very unifying issue, and both movements are pretty solidly on exactly the same page.[88]

Regan's organization, the Civil Liberties Defense Center, supported both the BPP and the animal rights activists. Despite their differences, the groups were able to break bread:

The funniest thing would be we'd go to these meetings, and, you know, you'd have these hardcore vegans and then you'd have, you know, these people eating chicken . . . [at] the other side of the table. And everyone would look beyond their own particular idiosyncrasies, and we were there for a purpose, and you know, what united us made us stronger than what divided us. And that was just such a powerful experience and powerful lesson.[89]

Enna was at the center of this coalitional effort. She was inspired by the strength of the elderly BPP resisters, who, "without talking to each other before hand, each of them chose not to cooperate with the grand jury and each of them was jailed." She thinks of it often: "To this day, it was one of the most important and beautiful things I had witnessed politically. . . . I got to witness their spirit 'Once a Panther, always a Panther' and I knew that if they could resist at this stage of their lives, that I . . . could handle the simple task at hand." She and her fellow activists saw this as an opportunity "to humbly show our support to these extraordinary people who came before us in struggle and who inspired us to fight in the first place."[90]

Enna's experience meeting with Black Panthers and making the analytical and political links between the animal liberation and black liberation movements was facilitated by Claude Marks, highlighted in chapter 5. Marks helped to bring people together for public events to build solidarity and collective power around the SF8 and anti–Green Scare campaigns. Speaking about Marks's role as a bridge builder, Enna told me,

> when I got a grand jury subpoena . . . around the same time the Black Panthers were targeted, we just really came together mostly through Claude. . . . For me Claude was definitely the person who bridged the gap, . . . and [I started] building a greater community around multimovement political prisoner issues. . . . [J]ust meeting him and his community changed my life in a lot of positive ways.[91]

It was through Marks that Luers, too, began making deeper connections between the earth and animal liberation movements and freedom movements in communities of color. Marks told me, "I realized that [Luers] had a very narrow conceptualization of his position as a political prisoner. . . . So I sent him a number of books to read, including Mumia's autobiography." These histories were largely new to Luers, and Marks recalled that it took time for his younger colleague "to engage with issues of race, racism, and colonialism" because initially "he saw his role through this very specific, narrow lens of environmentalism."[92] Eventually Luers embraced a broader approach to political change and has become one of the most vocal and visible advocates of antiracist, cross-movement coalitional work.

The coalition to free the SF8 was given a major boost when leaders like Nobel laureate Archbishop Desmond Tutu, Danny Glover, the Berkeley

City Council, the San Francisco Central Labor Council, and several San Francisco city supervisors signed statements and resolutions in support of dropping the charges. The case began winding down within two years of the arrests. Two of the eight persons charged—Herman Bell and Jalil Muntaqim—were already incarcerated and serving life sentences for other BPP-related activities and murder charges. They pleaded guilty and no contest, respectively, in a deal with authorities who had insufficient evidence to charge the others and allowed Bell and Muntaqim the possibility of parole.[93] The charges for the other defendants were dropped by August 2011.[94] Many activists believe this outcome was the direct result of highly visible and diverse community organizing.[95]

As much as this was a grassroots victory, Marks spoke cautiously about the lessons learned from the SF8 case. He stated, "this is a good example of why COINTELPRO isn't really dead," and asked rhetorically, "what is the political agenda" behind the prosecution of BPP members decades after a case was thrown out of court? To him, it is about the state's view that "organized black people represent a threat to the stability of the United States—which I believe they do." In the 1960s and 1970s, the state decided to neutralize the BPP, and Marks believes it is now attempting to "criminalize the history of the Black Panther Party." The aim was, Marks said, to

> destroy the Panthers *again*, because [from the state's perspective] we certainly don't want people to organize their communities to provide services that the government isn't, and to make people conscious, and to try to keep people out of prison] . . . so that people can somehow create a much more positive life for themselves. I mean, why on earth would we want that to happen?[96]

Sergeant Young's murder was never solved.

Finding Common Cause, Building Strength, and Inspiring Hope

Finding common ground between seemingly disparate movements is not easy. Physical, cultural, economic, racial, and geographic segregation keeps communities divided in the United States, and single-issue politics have strong appeal. Those activists, networks, and movements that *do* reach out are working against a massive tide.

In a sense, social justice and earth/animal liberation activist scott crow had no choice in the matter because he was born into a family that sent him to a school where this kind of solidarity was practiced:

I was actually born and lived in East Dallas [and] . . . I lived in the inner city, and I was one of the only white kids, and I attended a school that was run by members of the Black Panther Party, the Young Lords, and the Young Patriots, which was a white group.[97]

When he was older, crow found it only logical to work for and launch activist groups around multiple issues. They always had an antiracist and anti-oppression ideological core.

Most activists, however, find solidarity work exceedingly challenging, even when they are well intentioned and can imagine the benefits of cross-movement solidarity. PETA's Justin Goodman was very candid about his and PETA's isolation:

I know that most people who are working on social justice issues for women and minorities are probably offended by the suggestion that, you know, the fight for animal liberation is similar to the work they do. I think it's because we haven't approached them in a way that's respectful. But we just haven't done a good job of it, and, you know, I'm not sure why. All I can tell you is that I've never done it.[98]

Writing in Steven Best and Anthony Nocella's *Igniting a Revolution*—a groundbreaking anthology bringing together voices from multiple radical movements—former Black Panther Ashanti Alston declares common cause with earth and animal liberation activists:

Our movements have common ground even when it doesn't seem that way to our constituencies. But I bet you there are others who DO recognize it: the government, the state, the FBI, these racist muthafuckas who know the potential power of alliance and got plenty experience in counter-intelligence operations to throw wrenches into our alliance efforts.[99]

On the difficult subject of the "commonality of oppressions," Alston demonstrates wisdom and diplomacy that has the potential to deepen such alliances. He writes, "Being invited to speak at several Animal-Earth liberation conferences has also taught me a lot. Like about the connection between human AND nonhuman oppression and the LOUD, SCREAMING similarities between the treatment and maintenance of our oppressions."[100]

Writing from prison, earth liberationist Daniel McGowan echoed Alston's words:

> I hope that the environmental and animal liberation movement continues to build bridges and make common cause . . . not out of a self serving "we need your support" mentality but from a place of recognizing the validity of their struggles and realizing that our fate is bound with theirs.[101]

It may seem strange, at this point, to reflect that these movements are predicated on the idea that all oppression is linked, and yet they frequently overlooked that all of the oppressed are linked, too.

I have seen Raphi (the Ukrainian American activist introduced earlier) arrested for protesting the federal government's deportation of thousands of undocumented immigrants through the Immigration Customs and Enforcement (ICE) agency. I have seen him organize a "secret café" fundraiser in his home to support earth and animal liberation prisoners. And I have seen him commit his mental and physical energies into balancing his work as a university scholar and a community activist. He talked with me about the importance of studying history and seeing patterns of state repression—it shows why various seemingly disparate movements must work together. He believes the most important thing is to be aware that state repression "moves across struggles for liberation." He understands how laws are being adapted to new movements:

> You have the connection between the Animal Enterprise Terrorism Act . . . and how similar language was used in the Taft Hartley Act law . . . against labor organizing [that] . . . interfered with the everyday business of corporations. . . . So these laws were already there, and now they are being . . . used for the animal liberation movement.[102]

In winter 2010, I co-organized an event at the University of Minnesota titled "Political Repression and State Violence: From Minneapolis to Palestine." Co-organizers of the event were, at the time, working on two fronts: to build support for Feldman and DeMuth (then facing jail time) and to build support for the Minnesota Break the Bonds movement that works for solidarity and action on behalf of people in the Occupied Palestinian Territories.

The guest speaker was Dhoruba Bin-Wahad, a former U.S. political prisoner, leader of the BPP, and cofounder of the Black Liberation Army (BLA). Bin-Wahad was one of the Panther 21—a group of black liberation activists charged with conspiracy but acquitted in 1971 after what was, at that time, the longest trial in New York City history. Shortly thereafter he was imprisoned for a police shooting. In 1980, the FBI and NYPD were ordered by a court to produce their files revealing that Bin-Wahad was indeed a target of joint covert operations and had been framed in the shooting. Bin-Wahad's conviction was overturned, and he was freed in 1990. He has since successfully sued the FBI and NYPD. He is the coauthor (with Assata Shakur and Mumia Abu-Jamal) *Still Black, Still Strong: Survivors of the War against Black Revolutionaries* and now works to free political prisoners around the world.

When I asked Bin-Wahad how he, a former Black Panther Party member, found common ground with young, white anarchists today, he stated, "Because the anarchists' role in this is that the anarchists bring the heat! They bring on the noise. You see what I'm saying? And without the noise and the heat, all of this other stuff ain't happening."[103] Dramatic social change requires dramatic tactics and strategies, and the anarchist movement today is one of the most visible and radical social forces actively working for change.

As Robin Kelley argues in his book *Freedom Dreams: The Black Radical Imagination*, one of the first and most important steps on the long road to social change is to dream of a different world. That dream fuels hope and ignites future possibilities. J Johnson confesses that "it can be really disheartening to be out on the street feeling like the entire world is kind of against you," and he often asks himself, "How are we ever going to do this?" But then he looks to history, to the abolitionist movement and the civil rights movement, and reminds himself, "Well, they did it." And they did it without consistent public support and in the face of repression. Johnson finds support in knowing that "the past has shown that there can actually be change made even though it seems like no one is on your side."[104]

Cautionary Notes

Perhaps it is because I am an academic, but my conversations with veterans of radical social movements and my readings of their written work all return me to the importance of history. In fact, I believe the history of social change movements cannot be overemphasized. Ignoring it would be to risk overlooking both the mistakes and successes of the past; it would place the very idea of social change at an unnecessary disadvantage. Claude Marks is emphatic on this point, especially when it comes to white earth and animal liberation activists who may think that antiracist and anti-imperialist movements within communities of color are irrelevant to their own movements:

> Let's move this movement forward. But let's not forget where this resistance started, and let's make sure that everybody benefits from it. . . . I'm all for fighting for a better planet, but that better planet sure better not involve a lot of racist institutions. . . . The origins of defense of the planet certainly are not a white, middle-class movement but have to do with . . . the history of resistance against European colonialism and empire-building.[105]

Diana Block has been involved in some of the most important radical movements and organizations of the late twentieth and early twenty-first centuries, including the New York Radical Feminists, the Puerto Rican independence and black liberation movements, the Jericho Movement, and the prison abolition movement. She has worked as the editor of the *Fire Inside*—the newsletter of the California Coalition for Women Prisoners—and was a key supporter of the SF8 defense campaign. She is cautious and critical about the problem of whiteness and social privilege among earth and animal liberation movements: she thinks most ecological movements "have been narrow . . . and not really had a full anti-imperialist analysis." Block is hopeful that this may be shifting, however, and points to McGowan: "[he] has changed and grown in terms of his politics during his time in prison." She goes on:

> As a conscious [white] person, if you are in prison with people of color and Muslims, it has to change you. . . . [But] it's not enough to be linked because of the repression. You have to also then understand that the resistance needs to encompass a complicated and interconnected politics in order for those bonds to really grow and mean something more than just support.[106]

For coalitions to endure, cross-movement alliances born out of a seemingly common experience of repression must be deepened by further analysis and appreciation of peoples' unique histories.

One thing seems certain, and perhaps EF! activist Great Grey Owl said it best: "Our movements for ecological and social justice will all splinter and die without internal and cross-movement solidarity."[107]

Earth and animal liberation movements exert their cultures of resistance by confronting the language of repression and "ecoterrorism"; formalizing and practicing security culture; offering a range of support for prisoners and grand jury resisters; and borrowing from and building bridges with other movements past and present. Not only oppression, but also support, recognition, and respect form powerful links among cultures of resistance and may even create an ecology of resistance.

Piecing It Together

You can stop people, but you can't stop an idea.
    —Craig Rosebraugh, North American ELF press officer,
    author interview

By now, your head is probably full of images: political prisoners languishing in cells, young people lobbing firebombs at labs, elderly Black Panther Party members back in a courtroom, and scholars looking over their shoulders as they conduct research on radical movements. The takeaway, however, is meant to be a wide-ranging story of inequality: some of the many forms it takes, its far-reaching impacts across humans and nonhumans, and creative ways some of us are confronting it.

My work has always centered on the intersection of social inequalities and ecological politics, and my aim here is to deepen our comprehension of inequality by grappling with the often contentious and violent dynamics among and between humans and the more-than-human world. I hope such explorations will help in forming an understanding of *socioecological inequality*: the ways in which humans, nonhumans, and ecosystems intersect to produce hierarchies—privileges and disadvantages—within and across species and space that ultimately place each at great risk.

Socioecological inequality builds upon the concept of environmental injustice (or environmental inequality) by not only highlighting the links between threats to humans and ecosystems but also by interrogating the hierarchical and therefore political relationships that produce harms across each sphere. The concept of socioecological inequality also extends other key traditions in environmental studies in that it does not claim a primary source or origin of our ecological crises, such as capitalism, industrial civilization, racism, patriarchy, androcentrism, or Western culture. There are varied, multiple, and intersecting forms of inequality and hierarchy driving our socioecological crises.

The social movement activists to whom I spoke for this book work, for the most part, to challenge socioecological inequalities through a commitment to *total liberation*. They see an attack upon humans, nonhuman species, or ecosystems as an attack on us all—and an attack worthy of a counterattack. While these movements may be seen as extremist, firmly on the fringe of society, they remind us that when and where inequality exists and intensifies, those of us in the majority risk losing the capacity to shape our own destinies. From outside traditional political institutions, radical activists offer a critical lesson in why we might pay closer attention to inequality in all forms.

The total liberation framework emerged largely as a result of a confluence of three factors, including the intensification of socioecological crises and a perceived need to respond to threats to nonhuman natures, frustration with the relative ineffectiveness of dominant ecological movement tactics, and influences from other social movements.

According to leading scientists, damage to ecosystems over the last fifty years was more severe than during any other period in history. The health of coral reefs, fisheries, oceans, forests, and river systems declined precipitously, while climate change indicators, species extinction, and air and water pollution rose dramatically. Paralleling those trends is the large-scale increase in factory farming and industrialized nonhuman animal production, consumption, and experimentation that results in the slaughter of billions of nonhuman beings each year. These threats to planetary sustainability have been widely reported and have rippled through activist communities. Moreover, they are considered *urgent, violent* threats that must be met with urgent, direct action.

The palpable frustration among radical activists with the political orientation, values, and tactics of mainstream ecological movements is most visibly punctuated when activists reject mainstream avenues in favor of total liberation. Across each of the four pillars of total liberation we see the division between mainstream and radical activism.[1] Data from the earlier discussion of anti-oppression politics (see chapter 2) are partly rooted in the experiences of many radical activists who perceive some campaigns, tactics, language, and behavior by mainstream activists as racially offensive and culturally insensitive. One of the most important approaches to movement building, they believe, should involve developing anti-oppression principles and practices within their ranks. The gulf between mainstream and radical activists with respect to state and market-centered politics and strategies is also a primary site of contention, where anarchism, anti-capitalism, and direct action politics converge. Animal liberation activist-scholar Steven Best writes that as mainstream animal welfare activists

> lounge around swank hotels preaching to the choir in endless conferences and Ego Fests, the enemy is growing in number and strength. . . . Main-stream ideologues are under the spell of Gandhi, King, and "legalism," the system-created ideology that urges dissenters to seek change only in and through non-violence and the pre-approved legislative channels of the state. As the opiate of the masses, legalism disempowers resistance movements and leaves corporations and governments to monopolize power.[2]

Earth First! was founded in direct response to radical environmentalists' perception of ready compromise and timidity in the face of state and corporate power. Today, the rejection of the mainstream strongly shapes the direction of radical ecological movements.

Finally, many activists in radical ecological movements draw inspiration from the civil rights, Black Power, American Indian, Irish Republican, abolitionist, Luddite, anti-Apartheid, women's suffrage, and Industrial Workers of the World movements of the nineteenth and twentieth centuries. They respect and learn from those movements' commitment to anti-oppression philosophies and illegal direct action tactics. Solidarity work, information exchange, and other collaborations between earth/animal liberation activists and social justice movements (particularly with members of movements that have also experienced the brunt of the FBI's COINTELPRO) suggest an infinite range of possibilities for the evolution of social change efforts.

These three social forces gave rise to—and continually shape—total liberation and its emphasis on anti-oppression, anarchism, anticapitalism, and direct action.

The Role of Nonhumans in Social Movements

Sociological literature on social movements largely overlooks nonhuman natures in motivating the emergence, growth, and sustainability of social movements. I address this deficiency by drawing from environmental sociology, political ecology, and ecocriticism. For example, Paul Robbins charts the way lawns shape, manipulate, and produce *subjects*—homeowners who care for, worry, and fret about the look, feel, and health of the turf around their houses.³ "Lawn people" use fertilizers and large volumes of water, and they weed and mow with religious fervor. Robbins demonstrates the relations of mutual production by showing how this simple act of landscaping results in both the creation of the *lawn* and the *lawn person*. The "call" or "interpellation" felt by the homeowner who guiltily sees their lawn looking scruffy and spends the weekend cleaning it up is similar to the call that environmentalists and animal rights activists "hear" from nonhuman natures; it is just that their call pushes them to defend ecosystems and nonhuman animals. This refusal of the nature/culture divide that has historically characterized many Western intellectual traditions is the bedrock of these interdisciplinary fields that are shaping environmental scholarship.

Robbins's work comes out of an emerging tradition known as *political ecology*, a body of scholarship perhaps best known for developing the concept of "socionatures"—the idea that human and nonhuman spaces, cities, and environments are inseparable and involved in co-production.⁴ This work builds on and connects to a broader tradition from environmental history that recognizes the ways in which nonhuman and human forces intersect, interact, and affect each other over time, with major consequences—leading, for example, to the rise of European states and colonization⁵ and the impacts of viruses and diseases on the course of human civilization.⁶ Just as Charles Darwin described how it was worms that produced vegetable mold that enriched the topsoil that ultimately made human agriculture possible,⁷ scientists have recently determined that human bodies are made up of 90 percent microbial matter—even *we*, in our corporeal finest, are only 10 percent "human."⁸

Nonhuman natures, then, exert major influences on both "anti-environmental" practices like fossil fuel production and "pro-environmental" practices like social movements promoting sustainability and animal rights. Political theorist Jane Bennett offers a relevant perspective connecting human and nonhuman agents in a framework of politics and action by presenting a "vital materialist" theory of politics and democracy that places the interactions among human and nonhuman agents at the center. She writes:

> If human culture is inextricably enmeshed with vibrant, nonhuman agencies, and if human intentionality can be agentic only if accompanied by a vast entourage of nonhumans, then it seems that the appropriate unit of

analysis for democratic theory is neither the individual human nor an exclusively human collective but the (ontologically heterogeneous) "public" coalescing around a problem.[9]

Bennett draws from Bruno Latour and his rejection of the culture/nature divide and its relevance for a new kind of politics. Latour preferred the concepts of "collective" and "parliament of things," by which he meant an ecology of human and nonhuman elements that might cohere into some sort of polity.[10] Latour's "parliament" closely parallels what Joanna Macy and other deep ecologists have called the Council of All Beings—a ritual in which humans attempt to set aside their human identities so as to listen to and speak for nonhumans, to envision and enact a sustainable future.[11] Bennett's goal is "to devise new procedures, technologies, and regimes of perception that enable us to consult nonhumans more closely, or to listen and respond more carefully to their outbreaks, objections, testimonies, and propositions . . . profoundly important to the health of the political ecologies to which we belong."[12]

In this book, I have presented just one framework for how human activists and nonhuman agents interact to produce social and socioecological change. In my view, the total liberation frame is an example of vital materialism, a nascent attempt at imagining a "parliament of things." These ideas allow us to extend the boundaries of environmental sociology and social movement theory by exploring the ways that nonhuman actors also define and redefine ecological politics.

State Repression versus Community Building

Much of the material in the preceding chapters is devoted to examining the character and consequences of state repression and responses by activist communities. I describe state repression as a *scientific* endeavor because it is often a methodical, empirical, observation-driven project that follows the basic form of the scientific method (via spying and "treatment effects" like infiltration), but also in the sense that dominant modes of science tend to serve entrenched societal institutional interests through what some scholars call "production science."[13] That is, whether in the laboratory or among FBI agents, dominant forms of scientific pursuit tend to reflect the interests of the state and capital over the public interest. Not incidentally, these frequently favor ecologically unsustainable policies.[14]

The science of repression is intended to discourage and contain revolts and other forms of dissent, but it is also aimed at producing quiescence, obedience, and conformity. I describe the far-reaching impacts of this process as an *ecology of repression*. It impacts its direct targets, to be sure, but also impacts would-be activists and the sustainability and well-being of would-be beneficiaries (including nonhumans) of such movements. These ripple effects are often devastating to social movements, but they can also fuel further resistance and resolve to continue the work of social change among activist networks. In that respect, one of the unintended consequences of ecologies of repression is the enhancement of cultures of resistance.

Ultimately, resisting state repression requires—and is itself a form of—community building. Twin Cities activist Luce Guillén-Givens states, "the strongest response to state repression is to build strong communities."[15] In my conversation with journalist and activist Will Potter, he stated that the activist community can respond to repression in one of two ways: they can "look at it and be very overwhelmed and depressed and frustrated by it because it seems like this stuff just keeps going and going every generation," or, more productively, they can

> look at it and say, "we can start piecing together how this is all working. We can build relationships with these amazing activists and learn from what they've done, and build stronger communities to resist it." So I think there's a lot of fear, but there's also a lot of positive work being done now as well that probably wouldn't have been happening if it weren't for all the bad things going on.[16]

Members of the CrimethInc. anarchist collective concur: "Healthy relationships are the backbone of such communities, not to mention secure direct action organizing. The stronger the ties that bind an individual to a community, the less likely it is he or she will inform against it." Speaking to the particular problems that the largely white earth and animal liberation movements have faced, CrimethInc. contends that "North American radicals from predominantly white demographics have always faced a difficult challenge in this regard, as most of the participants are involved in defiance of their families and social circles rather than because of them."[17]

One small but pervasive community building practice in earth and animal liberation activist networks is the vegan potluck. I have been to several. We met to share and eat food, deepen relationships, and sometimes raise funds and provide other forms of support for ecoprisoners. In an amusing image, FBI agents reportedly try to infiltrate these get-togethers (I wonder what they bring to the potluck?).[18] More broadly, earth and animal liberation activists work to build community with other social movements, as we saw in previous chapters.

Contradictions and Limitations

One conundrum is the fact that while these movements are anarchist in orientation, many of them still regularly engage the state through protesting repression, the courts, FBI actions, and legislation and sometimes promoting new legislation. For example, the Federal Prison Work Incentive Act, also known as the "Good Time" Bill, is congressional legislation that, if passed, would reduce a prisoner's sentence for good conduct. Many ecoprisoner support groups sought to build grassroots support for this legislation, wanting to see their colleagues free sooner even while acknowledging the contradiction this effort embodies.[19] Moreover, many of the most ardent anarchists in these movements are *attorneys*, people whose livelihood is based on a daily engagement with the most feared and despised arms of the state and its repressive apparatus—the court system, police, and grand juries. Other committed anarchists work long hours on efforts to resist state repression and support ecoprisoners; they learn the law, pore over endless court documents, and often attend hearings in support of their colleagues caught up in the legal system.

Total liberation also offers a real sign of hope and possibility for linking key concepts from many movements and pushing them forward intellectually and politically, but it is burdened by the legacies of racism, classism, and heteropatriarchy. In confronting the socially constructed hierarchies and divisions between human and nonhumans, activists run up against the historically entrenched subject of the association of non-Europeans, women, the working classes, and queer folk with a "state of nature," as highlighted in the writings of philosophers like Hobbes, Pufendorf, Locke, and Rousseau.[20] That is, every step toward fighting speciesism and anthropocentrism is also a step that comes dangerously close to what philosopher David Theo Goldberg calls "naturalism"—those theories of humanity that place non-Europeans and women in an inherent state of inferiority because of their supposed subhuman (read "animal" or "natural") qualities. Yes, some activists are aware that this is a problem, and some are aware that being the subject of government repression also strips away some of their privileges. But this is a formidable, if not intractable, challenge for the foreseeable future.

Most earth and animal liberation activists are white, middle class, and heterosexual and seek to work as allies with vulnerable human populations, but many seem to circumvent rather than acknowledge the issue of "naturalism." They earnestly emphasize that the association and kinship with nonhuman nature must be applied to *all* humans as one of many interdependent species, while conveniently glossing over the deep histories of differentiation and oppression *within* the human community.

Another way of putting this is that radical activists are attempting to challenge socially constructed hierarchies with the goal of liberating all. The problem is that *some* of these barriers were actually already flattened and broken down via centuries of European and Euro-American racism, a class system, and heteropatriarchy that placed people of color, women, working-class persons, and LGBTQ folk on a single plane. As part of a unified project of *dominating* all, these groups were associated with nonhuman animals and a state of nature. That co-location is a root of environmental racism: people of color are generally associated with nonhuman nature (in this view, impure and socially contaminated spaces), so ecological violations against them are normal and appropriate. The dilemma, then, is that earth and animal liberation activists are trying to confront those divides in a way that might ignore the long-standing legacies of earlier efforts to do so (albeit for different reasons), which was central to the development of European modernity. These groups then run the risk of reintroducing or reproducing the foundational problems of racism, class domination, heteropatriarchy, and anthropocentrism that gave rise to the current day socioecological crises.

What this project is also about is *borders*, those borders between humans, species, and ecosystems, and how people try to challenge and negotiate them. But challenging these borders and arguing for equality is not the same as collapsing them entirely and arguing for sameness. If activists do this—and they do sometimes—it violently erases uniqueness, varied experiences, histories, and biographies. Feminist theorist Chandra Mohanty sees the challenge as the need to work across difference, to recognize the ways that we are all differently implicated in structures of power and oppression in order to build communities of resistance and achieve "unity without uniformity."[21] For total liberation activists, the "we" in that process must include all beings and ecosystems.

A related limitation is that these movements are dominated by white middle-class heterosexuals in a capitalist-state society. They wish to build a world that is antiracist, antisexist, antihomophobic, antispeciesist, anarchist, and anticapitalist. That is hard anywhere, but especially challenging in the United States—a nation founded and maintained on principles and practices that are the antithesis of these perspectives. These activists are, relatively speaking, from privileged backgrounds and, through the quest for total liberation, wish to abolish virtually all forms of hierarchy and privilege known to society. As much as total liberation may be an admirable vision of change, there is something troubling, and yet very powerful, about it being led by those who enjoy considerable privileges. Refusing to accept society as is and all the privileges available to them speaks to a different commitment and a unique perspective on its own.

As I have argued, these activists are racial deviants in that they refuse to conform to the nation's cultural, political, and social disciplinary norms. They become "not-quite-white" in the state's politico-legal discourse. Particularly white, middle-class, male activists are also racial deviants because they refuse to conform to the expectations and benefits of *human* supremacy. That is, they reject a humanism rooted in speciesism and domination of nonhuman natures that are, for many of us, the unexamined and unearned privileges of membership in the human race. Just as the state has treated white activists as probationary whites, their very *humanity* is conditional.

For example, in 2008, Canadian police arrested Sea Shepherd's Swedish first officer, Peter Hammarstedt, and captain, Alex Cornelissen, because in Canada it is illegal to witness or document the slaughter of the seals. The activists were interrogated for four and a half hours, but they said absolutely nothing, refusing to even acknowledge the police in the room. The video clip from the interrogation of Peter Hammarstedt, "Nobody talks, everybody walks," reveals a Royal Canadian Mounted Police officer comparing the Sea Shepherd activist to the prototypical Arab terrorist figure, "that Palestinian . . . with that huge backpack full of nails, walking into a mall and detonating explosives," and wonders whether they were "planning a 9/11 or something here."[22]

Thus, being an animal liberationist sometimes places white activists into a social category generally thought to be reserved for radicalized people of color. This reinforces the fact that race need not be linked to color, phenotype, culture, or nation; it is a socially constructed category that can stand in as a way of thinking, as a way of life, and for one's politics. Thus, race is a political category: "white" activists are free to embrace or reject whiteness, thus destabilizing the relationships between race and politics. As Tim Wise writes, "as whites, we may be *in* this skin, but we do not have to be *of* it."[23] Similarly, legal scholars Lani Guinier and Gerald Torres locate the sites of many social injustices in communities of color but do not confine the struggle against these forces to these spaces and bodies. They argue that "political race" is not just what you do; it is also what is done to you by elites. Thus state repression can racialize radicals as an "other" while ironically reinforcing their social privileges associated with whiteness, middle-class status, and heteronormativity by spurring public backlash. The outcry around the Green Scare, the high visibility of vegans in prison, the elevated status of many of ecoprisoners within prisons, and their relatively short sentences when compared to participants in revolutionary movements among people of color all reflect white privilege.

While there is much that may be liberatory with regard to the total liberation frame, there is also much that is undeniably and distinctly white about it. Not only white but, more to the point, imperial. Consider the arrogance of claiming to know what *every being on Earth needs* to enjoy a fulfilling existence. Then consider that the total liberation project aims to impose that model on every single being on Earth! As well meaning as total liberation may be, it unintentionally embraces imperialist values and modernist notions of a universal truth—that a free future will be pure and devoid of complexities. In fact, many activists have fashioned the struggle for earth and animal liberation as "the ultimate freedom movement" or the "final frontier" of social change—presumably, this means either all other freedom struggles have been won, or nonhuman animals and ecosystems are the "most oppressed" among us.[24]

There are obviously problems with this purity of purpose and vision of these radical movements as the "final frontier." First, the very principles of anti-oppression and ecofeminism assume an inseparable link between all forms of domination; no one form can be challenged without simultaneously challenging the others. But also, this perspective problematically views social change as a linear process that follows traditional Western evolutionary models of literary narrative and history.[25] Social change occurs in fits and starts, and movements experience as many or more "reversals" and setbacks as they do "progress." The struggle for environmental sustainability and animal liberation is centuries old, having existed at least as long as freedom movements focused on humans, and none of these struggles is done.[26] Social change is messy, and that notion should be both humbling and emboldening: there is a great deal of work to be done, so there must be many forms of activism and many types of activists.

Total Liberation and Environmental Justice

As a scholar and activist who has spent many years working in the field of environmental justice (EJ) studies and in the EJ movement, I hold dear the hope that advocates of earth and animal liberation and advocates of EJ will recognize and build upon the many generative links and possibilities between them. The EJ movement is largely composed of people from communities of color, Indigenous communities, and the working class. They are focused on combating environmental inequality, racism, and injustice—the disproportionate burden of environmental harm facing these populations. For the EJ movement, the battle for global sustainability cannot be won without addressing the ecological violence imposed on vulnerable human populations. Thus, social justice (that is, justice for humans) is inseparable from environmental protection.

While much of the material in the preceding chapters details the ways that earth and animal liberation movements exert energy making links to social justice causes, in this section I demonstrate that many ideas at the root of EJ movements are consonant with total liberation. In fact, the ideas that radical animal and earth liberation activists express in their public and internal movement conversations are almost entirely reflective of concepts contained at the heart of the Principles of Environmental Justice—a sort of founding document of the U.S. EJ movement.[27]

Activist delegates to the First National People of Color Environmental Leadership Summit adopted the Principles in 1991. The Preamble reads, in part,

WE, THE PEOPLE OF COLOR, gathered together at this multinational People of Color Environmental Leadership Summit, to begin to build a national and international movement of all peoples of color to fight the destruction and taking of our lands and communities, do hereby re-establish our spiritual interdependence to the sacredness of our Mother Earth.

Principle 1 affirms "the *interdependence of all species*," while principle 5 supports "the fundamental right to political, economic, cultural, and environmental self-determination of all peoples." The delegates to that meeting—commonly referred to as the first Environmental Justice Summit—set forth their opposition to racism and ecological destruction, recognized the inherent and cultural worth of nonhuman natures, and explicitly acknowledged the inseparability of humans and the more than human world.

As if existing in a parallel universe with the ELF and ALF guidelines, principle 2 reads: "Environmental Justice demands that public policy be based on mutual respect and justice for all peoples, free from any form of discrimination or bias," and principle 3 states: "Environmental Justice mandates the right to ethical, balanced and responsible uses of land and renewable resources in the interest of a sustainable planet *for humans and other living things*." Principle 15 "opposes military occupation, repression and exploitation of lands, peoples and cultures, *and other life forms*." The EJ movement embraces ethical relations between and among all beings, both human and nonhuman—a cornerstone of total liberation.

Thus the EJ and earth/animal liberation movements may oppose myriad forms of hierarchy, inequality, and domination for different reasons and with different emphases, but their focus on such similar practices suggests possibilities for cross-movement conversation, analysis, and collaborative action. The EJ movement's support of human rights, civil rights, and the sacredness of nonhuman nature reflects these values. Both movements also view human society as the source or point of origin for the harm visited upon vulnerable bodies and spaces—to varying degrees, they adhere to a biocentric orientation.

Like all movements, the EJ movement in the United States has significant limitations that make it challenging to imagine bridge building with earth and animal liberation activists. While EJ activists and leaders have repeatedly demonstrated a willingness to challenge state and corporate policy making, the movement is ultimately rooted in a reformist model of social change. EJ activists largely accept the fundamental legitimacy and existence of state and corporate institutions, including the legal system.[28] If, as Goldberg argues, states are inherently racist and exclusionary social forces,[29] then antiracist social movements should not expect such institutions to be capable of securing a world in which racial justice prevails. Yet, EJ movements implicitly support that view as they work to introduce (or undo) legislation and state and corporate policies and pursue claims through the courts. In that way, the EJ movement's strategic orientation more closely mirrors the mainstream ecological movements' approach to change.

Critical race theorists and legal scholars Lani Guinier and Gerald Torres's book *The Miner's Canary* makes two key arguments of use here. The first is that the experiences of those of us who are marginalized by virtue of being people of color in a racist society are an early warning system for those who ignore racism. Racism certainly offers advantages to certain individuals and groups, but Guinier and Torres contend that, ultimately, it harms us all: economically, politically, socially, culturally, and psychologically. The second argument comes in response to the first: to address the collectively destructive effects of racism and white supremacy, we must enlist the support of a diverse cross section of humanity to embrace social justice in all forms. This "political race" project is a model of coalition building across groups of people that begins with attention to race, then extends to class, gender, and other social categories, but never loses sight of race and the role of antiracist theory and politics.[30] Race is a central organizing principle and anchor around which people of color and white allies can mobilize. Whites and others who enjoy privileges will have to consciously reject those social systems and practices that support their gains, and all participants will have to expand their conception of social justice to include multiple categories beyond race.

Melding Guinier and Torres's concept with insights from critical animal studies, ecofeminism, critical environmental justice studies, and critical race theory, I offer four related observations. First, while human privilege has produced seemingly infinite benefits for a single species on Earth, it has led to catastrophic impacts on nonhuman species and ecosystems. Second, as a direct and indirect result of the exercise of human privilege, humans suffer and will continue to suffer from the effects of their harm to ecosystems and nonhuman animals.[31]

Third, ecological justice is one method of addressing these crises. By the term *ecological justice*, I mean to suggest a more respectful and egalitarian relationship of human beings to one another and to the broader nonhuman world, combining the core ideas of total liberation and EJ.[32] This model of politics begins with humans taking responsibility for practicing transformative socioecological political work and extends to understanding inequalities within and across species and space to imagine and struggle for a more democratic world. Nonhuman species and ecosystems may not engage in politics the way humans tend to, but they can and do exert influence in many ways.[33] Ecological justice destabilizes the notion of the human as a biological category at the apex of a human/nature hierarchy and, instead, embraces it as a political category that engages with the broader ecological community.[34] This model of politics rejects the state as an arbiter of justice and inclusion. The state has managed, included, excluded, homogenized, and controlled humans and nonhuman natures for the benefit of a small elite. That should be reason enough to embrace an anarchist approach to social change.

A final observation is that we might expand Guinier and Torres's notion of the miner's canary to include humans, nonhuman species, and ecosystems. In a sense, I extend that metaphor to include the miner, the canary, the mine, and the ecosystem in which all are situated. They are partners in a collaborative effort for mutual sustenance. In my view, this is one vision for freedom movements struggling for total liberation and ecological justice.

Notes

Preface

1. See Best and Nocella 2004, 2006; Jasper and Nelkin 1992; Scarce 2006.

2. Lofland et al. 2005.

3. Scarce 2006, 260.

4. Eyerman and Jamison 1991, 55.

5. Marx and Engels 1998, 39.

6. Condon 2009.

7. Scott DeMuth statement regarding his grand jury resistance, December 7, 2009.

8. Brady 2013.

9. For more on this particular case, see Scarce 2005.

10. Nocella, Best, and McLaren 2010.

Introduction

1. See Eyerman and Jamison 1991; Kelley 2003.

2. ELF communiqué, July 27, 2001, emphasis added.

3. I include animal rights movements under the banner of *ecological* politics because these activists are focused on the relationship of human beings to the broader nonhuman world; see White 2003.

4. Robbins 2007.

5. An infamous example of this comes from chief economist of the World Bank Lawrence Summers, who wrote a memo that laid out the economic calculus of global environmental racism. It included the statement: "The 'costs' of pollution can only be relative to the 'value' of life, and if we put aside 'moral reasons' and 'social concerns,' how can we avoid concluding that Northern lives are 'worth' hundreds of times more than Southern lives? This is simply the result we get if we apply the test of the market and value lives by what they can be sold

for; if we value people, that is, by what they can demand in wages." (Lawrence Summers, internal memo, World Bank, December 12, 1991).

6. Geronimus et al. 1996; Krieger and Sidney 1996.

7. Adamson, Evans, and Stein 2002; Bullard and Wright 2012.

8. I am grateful to Dylan Rodriguez for this point.

9. Gaard 2004, 36.

10. Androcentrism refers to any idea, belief, behavior, social system, etc., that is centered on men. Jim Mason defines dominionism as "the view that human beings have a God-given power or right to use and control the living world for their exclusive benefit" (Mason 2006, 180). Mason sees dominionism as the root of all socioecological crises. In other words, it is like speciesism writ large so as to include all of nonhuman natures.

11. McCully 2001.

12. See Gedicks 1993, 2001; Pellow and Park 2002; World Bank 2005.

13. See Lerner 2006; Shearer 2011; Widener 2011.

14. See Cole and Foster 2000.

15. See Schlosser 2005; Torres 2007.

16. Gramsci 1971.

17. In June of 1990, Secretary of Health and Human Services Louis W. Sullivan referred to animal rights activists who raid research laboratories as "terrorists." He was not the first nor the last government official to do so.

18. Commoner 1971, 176.

19. Nonhuman nature certainly has agency in this matter (Bennett 2009; Braun and Whatmore 2010; Goldman and Schurman 2000).

20. McClintock 1995.

21. Ibid., 43.

22. Ngai 2004, 76.

23. Ibid., 18.

24. See, for example, Boykoff 2007; Davenport 2000.

25. Catton and Dunlap 1980; Dunlap and Van Liere 1978; Milbrath 1984.

26. For an excellent critique, see Humphrey, Lewis, and Buttel 2002.

27. Park and Pellow 2011; A. Smith 2005.

28. Gaard 1993, 1; see also Y. King 1989.

29. Gaard 1993; see also Warren 1994,1.

30. Warren 1997a, 4.

31. MacGregor 2006, 19.

32. Gaard 1993; Mellor 1992; Seager 1994; Sturgeon 1997a.

33. Mies and Bennholdt-Thomsen 1999.

34. Sturgeon 1997a, 1997b; D. Taylor 1997.

35. Mack-Canty 2004; Plumwood 1993; A. Smith 2005; Warren 1990.

36. See Gaard 1993, 6.

37. Bookchin 2005.

38. Bookchin 2004; Garland 2006.

39. See MacGregor 2006; Mellor 1992.

40. Birkeland 1993.

41. MacGregor 2006.

42. Plumwood 1994, 68.

43. O'Connor 1994; Faber 1998; Foster 1999; and Schnaiberg and Gould 2000.

44. Downey and Strife 2010.

45. Boyce 1994, 2008.

46. D. Taylor 2000, 551.

47. Benford 2005; Cole and Foster 2001.

48. Crenshaw 1994.

49. McClintock 1995.

50. For exceptions, see Lahar 1991; Mack-Canty 2004.

51. See Collins 2000; Haraway 1991; Santa Anna 2002; Stein 2004.

1. Never Apologize for Your Rage

1. My interview sample comes from the United States, although these movements are active in other countries. U.S. radical ecological movements are influenced by and connected to related groups in other countries as well, but the U.S. "branches" of these movements are the biggest and most impactful and have triggered the most severe state repression. The connections and relationships between movements in different countries would be a fruitful avenue for future research.

2. Gina Lynn, author interview, December 7, 2009.

3. Ibid.

4. Kim Marks, author interview, July 2010.

5. Ibid.

6. Enna, author interview, June 2011.

7. Ibid.

8. Chris Irwin, author interview, fall 2009.

9. Ibid.

10. Storm, author interview, July 2009.

11. Josh Harper, author interview, fall 2009.

12. Shell Oil is vilified by many human rights and environmental justice activists for its considerable investments in Nigerian oil fields at the time that nation's military government executed poet and environmental justice leader Ken Saro-Wiwa and several other Indigenous activists for advocating environmental justice in the region of Ogoniland (Fischman 2006).

13. Tre Arrow, author interview, March 26, 2011.

14. USPIRG is a progressive advocacy organization founded by consumer advocate Ralph Nader.

15. United Nations 2005.

16. Foster, Clark, and York 2010, 14.

17. Bennett 2009.

18. Faber 1998, 4. It is ironic that capitalism itself (a system premised on the primacy of private property) causes property damage through climate change and more direct forms of displacement, dispossession, eviction, and home demolition that often occasion industrial operations around the planet.

19. Alexander 2010; Faber 1998, 38–39.

20. See Steingraber 1997.

21. Faber 2008.

22. Best and Nocella 2006, 10.

23. See Francione and Gardner 2010; Manes 1990; T. Regan 2006; Scarce 2006; Jasper and Nelkin 1991; Singer 1975.

24. For example, I served on the Board of Directors of Citizens for a Better Environment, a Chicago-based organization with a history of doing outstanding work with a dedicated staff. Unfortunately, a new executive director came on board in the late 1990s and was paid a salary that far exceeded the compensation of any previous director. The first thing he told us was that he wanted to work *with* businesses and corporations, not against them, and that he did "not believe in protest and unfurling banners off of buildings." I immediately resigned, and within two years the organization went out of existence.

25. Mainstream environmental groups in Canada are generally no different, with an emphasis on a strict "environmentalist" frame that ignores social and environmental justice (Haluza-DeLay and Fernhout 2011).

26. It *is* effective at keeping some mainstream organizations in business and restricting the definition of the movement's goals.

27. Best 2009; Faber 1998.

28. Wolkie, qtd. in Best and Nocella 2004, 38.

29. FAQs about the ELF, qtd. in Pickering 2007, 56.

30. Best 2009.

31. Singer 1975, 231.

32. Torres 2007, 101.

33. Whole Foods gradually drove out employees at its store in Madison, Wisconsin, who had organized workers into a union (Nathans 2003). The following year, with a new set of workers, a vote to recertify the union failed.

34. Humane Society Legislative Fund mailing.

35. See Alexander 2010.

36. Arpaio is an internationally recognized figure within the immigration control movement for supporting the most stringent U.S.–Mexico border control policies, publicly parading detained undocumented immigrants in shackles, and enthusiastically embracing racial profiling of Latinos in Arizona (Associated Press 2008).

37. McGillivary 2008.

38. World Wire 2008b.
39. Featherstone 2005.
40. World Wire 2008a.
41. Associated Press 2012.
42. Hari 2010.
43. Sierra Club 2009.
44. Jaynes 2009.
45. Faber 1998, 112.
46. Manes 1990, 17.
47. Ibid., 18. Letter dated November 11, 1986.
48. Best 2009.
49. For an example of how this dynamic played out during the civil rights movement see Haines 1984.
50. Scarce 2006, 6–7.
51. Brower 2006, 11.
52. jones 2004, 151–52.
53. Qtd. in Pickering 2007, 58.
54. Qtd. in Pickering 2007, 57.
55. Jack Conroy, author interview, June 2010.
56. Darius Fullmer (of the SHAC7) speaking at the 2009 Animal Rights Conference (ARC), Los Angeles, California.
57. "MOVE's Work," On a MOVE: Website of the MOVE Organization, http://www.onamove.com.
58. Ibid.
59. One example is the banning of books and critical educational programs like Mexican American studies and ethnic studies, as happened in the school district of Tucson, Arizona, in 2012.
60. Eaton 1888, 22.
61. Jasper and Nelkin 1991.
62. At a meeting of people supporting LGBTQ rights and marriage equality in Minneapolis in 2011, I was struck by how many participants were AR activists who saw animal liberation and gay liberation as linked because they viewed ending all forms of oppression as their goal. In fact, the meeting was organized by two prominent AR activists who are themselves a gay couple, one of whom spent time in prison for his involvement in the SHAC campaign.
63. Singer 1975, 234.
64. Kheel 2006, 309.
65. In addition to founding the ASPCA in 1866, Bergh helped found the New York Society for the Prevention of Cruelty to Children in 1875. The Cruelty to Children Act of 1883 was the first legislation of its kind in the United States and was made possible largely by the work of the American Humane Association, an organization that formed in 1877 (Renzetti and Edleson 2008).

66. Singer 1975, 253.

67. Ibid., ix.

68. T. Regan 2004.

69. Gottlieb 1994; Jacoby 2003.

70. Gottlieb 1994.

71. Manes 1990,14.

72. *Earth First! Journal* 3, Litha (June 21, 1983): 9.

73. Scarce 2006, 67.

74. Guha 1989.

75. Heynen, Kaika, and Swyngedouw 2006.

76. Meyler 2003, 60–82.

77. Bell 2003.

78. Karen Coulter, author interview, October 3, 2009. In an *EF! Journal* article responding to his critics, Foreman stated clearly that the movement needed more diversity, but he felt that it was becoming an obsession that was preventing people from taking action (see Foreman 1989, 20).

79. Bowling 1998, 4.

80. Tree spiking was viewed as controversial in large part because it could lead to injury or death for timber workers. Denouncing tree spiking was one of Judi Bari's many efforts to build bridges between environmentalists and labor organizers (see chapter 4).

81. Vidal 2006.

82. Well-known supporters or members of various SSCS advisory boards include Martin Sheen, Sean Penn, Bob Barker, Daryl Hannah, the Red Hot Chili Peppers, Alex Pacheco (of PETA), Dave Foreman (of Earth First!), and Tom Regan.

83. Federal Bureau of Investigation, congressional testimony, February 12, 2002. The Institute for Cetacean Research in Japan has also called the Sea Shepherds a terrorist group.

84. Park and Pellow 2011.

85. The ALF made the U.S. domestic terrorism list in 1987 with a lab raid at the University of California (see U.S. FBI 1989).

86. Best and Nocella 2004, 25.

87. Ibid.

88. "The ALF Credo," Animal Liberation Front.com, http://www.animal liberationfront.com/ALFront/alf_credo.htm.

89. Anonymous ALF communiqué, n.d.

90. Molland 2006.

91. See Pring and Canan 1996. This was to become a classic example of a SLAPP suit—a strategic lawsuit against public participation. SLAPPs are lawsuits that organizations bring against people not for the purpose of actually reaping damages but rather to silence and intimidate them and others like them

who may choose to exercise their legally protected rights to free expression. I should also note that the McLibel Two—Helen Steel and David Morris—were members of a group called London Greenpeace but were not affiliated with Greenpeace International because they saw that organization as too mainstream and reformist. SLAPPs and the McLibel case are also key moments in this history because they underscore the power and prevalence of *corporate* repression, while far too many scholars fixate only on state repression (see Davenport 2000).

92. Beltane is a Celtic word that roughly corresponds with the month of May. The *Earth First! Journal* uses Celtic and pagan months to designate publication dates.

93. Qtd. in Rosebraugh 2004a, 20.

94. These claims are made in the following source: "Interview with ELF Founder, John Hanna," September 5, 2001, http://www.originalelf.com/interview_with_elf_founder.html.

95. John Hanna, author interview, November 2009.

96. Ibid.

97. Pickering 2007, 116.

98. "Frequently Asked Questions about the Earth Liberation Front," Animal Liberation Front, 2001, http://www.animalliberationfront.com/ALFront/ELF/elf_faq.pdf. Emphasis in original.

99. Tara the Sea Elf 1996.

100. Jarboe 2002. Presumably Jarboe was referring to joint ELF/ALF actions in Britain, since the ELF's first known U.S. action was in 1996.

101. Rosebraugh 2004a: 33.

102. For example, see "Interview with Craig Rosebraugh," *No Compromise*, no. 16 (Summer 2000): 3. *No Compromise* is an animal liberation magazine that regularly featured interviews with and stories about earth liberation activists. Rosebraugh was a spokesperson for the North American Earth Liberation Front Press Office and an outspoken advocate for that movement, and he faced continuous surveillance and questioning from the FBI and Congress for his work. See also Jeff "Free" Luers, "Some Words on Prisoner Support," *No Compromise*, no. 23 (Spring 2004): 12. This is an article by well-known radical environmentalist and former ecopolitical prisoner Jeff "Free" Luers. The article appeared in *No Compromise*, which billed itself as "The Militant, Direct Action Publication of Grassroots Animal Liberationists & their Supporters." See also "Prisoner Listings," *No Compromise*, no. 24 (Summer 2004): 22. This issue, like others, featured "animal liberation" and "eco-defense" prisoners from the United States and around the world, including a listing for Matius Nasira, who was a target of state authorities for "taking part in a road block to prevent illegal logging" in Papua New Guinea (he was later shot dead by authorities at a protest), and Tre Arrow, who was targeted for "involvement in an arson of logging trucks and of vehicles owned by a sand & gravel company."

103. For example, one contributor to the *EF! Journal* writes, "I agree with many others who feel the two movements are so closely related that they are, in essence, the same movement. Earth liberation, by its very nature, cannot exclude animal liberation concerns. The truly informed animal advocates understand advocating for animals requires advocating for the Earth" (Jaynes 2009). In a typical listing of political prisoners, the *EF! Journal* features a range of people under the categories of "animal liberation," "ecodefense," "Indigenous Resistance," and "MOVE." Under the "animal liberation" category, one can find Kevin Kjonaas, who served several years in federal prison "for conspiracy charges stemming from his work with SHAC," and Jordan Halliday, who was "held in contempt for resisting a grand jury investigation into Utah mink liberations." Under the "MOVE" category, one will find several of the MOVE 9, "members of an eco-revolutionary group [who] were framed for the murder of a cop," while under "Indigenous Resistance," Leonard Peltier is listed as serving "life in prison after being framed for the deaths of two FBI agents killed during the 1975 Pine Ridge siege" (see *EF! Journal* 2009, 27–28). In that same edition of the *EF! Journal* there is an article on the successes of the Stop Huntingdon Animal Cruelty (SHAC) campaign directed at the product testing corporation Huntingdon Life Science (HLS) (see Trill 2009, 28).

104. Jasper and Nelkin 1991.

105. In one instance, in March 2000, two activists with the animal advocacy group Compassion Over Killing (COK) scaled the MCI Center in Washington, D.C., where the Ringling Bros. and Barnum & Bailey Circus was presenting a show, and unfurled a fifty-foot banner that read "Ringling Kills Animals." They were protesting allegations that Ringling Bros. animals have been physically and psychologically abused, as documented in the company's many noncompliances with the Animal Welfare Act issued by the USDA, among other violations (Shapiro 2000). The activists were arrested, but charges were dropped.

106. Anonymous Earth First! activist, author interview, fall 2009.

107. Kim McCoy, interview by Hollie Nyseth Brehm of the author's research team, October 2009.

108. Ben Rosenfeld, interview by Brehm, November 30, 2009.

109. Irwin, author interview, fall 2009.

2. Justice for the Earth and All Its Animals

1. See Panagioti 2006
2. Anonymous Earth First! activist, author interview, July 2009.
3. Author's field notes, June 2009.
4. Park and Pellow 2011.
5. Storm, author interview, July 23, 2009.
6. Ibid.
7. Jade, conversation with the author, spring 2010.

8. This particular panelist works for a group called the Animals Asia Foundation.

9. Personal e-mail communication from a colleague, spring 2009.

10. Claude Marks, author interview, February 25, 2010

11. Molland 2006, 56.

12. Qtd. in Pickering 2007, 46.

13. Petermann 1999, 3.

14. Qtd. in Gil 2002, 35.

15. Rosebraugh 2002.

16. Storm, author interview, July 23, 2009.

17. Qtd. in Pickering 2007, 44–45.

18. Nik Hensey, interview by Brehm, summer 2009.

19. Paul Shapiro, interview by Brehm, June 13, 2010.

20. Norm Phelps, author interview, June 30, 2010.

21. Unnamed activist on "Applying Direct Action" panel at the annual Animal Rights Conference, n.d.

22. The Food Empowerment Project website, "Food Is Power," http://www.foodispower.org.

23. Lauren Ornelas, author interview, July 8, 2009.

24. Peter Young, author interview, July 13, 2009.

25. Singer 1975, 7.

26. Veda Stram, author interview, July 14, 2009.

27. Shapiro, interview by Brehm, June 13, 2010.

28. Josh Harper, author interview, November 9, 2009.

29. Katie, author interview, June 7, 2010.

30. Wolfe 2010.

31. Coronado 1999.

32. Seager 1994; A. Smith 2005.

33. pattrice jones, presentation at "Their Lives, Our Voices" conference, University of Minnesota, June 13, 2009.

34. John Hanna, author interview, November 2009.

35. Ibid.

36. Kim McCoy, interview by Brehm, October 2009.

37. Hensey, interview by Brehm, June 2009.

38. Storm, author interview, July 2009.

39. "Trenches Spotlight: Boston Animal Defense League," *No Compromise*, no. 29 (Winter/Spring 2006): 31.

40. Radical environmentalists have had much more success and achieved greater depth with these efforts than have AR movements, but there is significant evidence that this is changing. For example, while we do not see the language of total liberation in animal rights publications or within the discourse or documents produced by most AR groups, we do see support for these ideas

among the more recently formed groups. Thus, there are anti-oppression panels at various animal rights conferences and gatherings, and the North American Animal Liberation Press Office's communiqués regularly articulate the discourse of total liberation.

41. *Earth First! Journal* Editorial Collective 2007.

42. Cascadia Forest Alliance, Anti-Oppression Policy, n.d..

43. *Earth First! Journal* 2003, 12. The Fall Creek Tree Village was one of the most famous of its kind. It was an extraordinary network of traverses, platforms, and other structures constructed by tree sitters protecting the site from timber companies in the Willamette National Forest between 1998 and 2003.

44. jones 2005.

45. Nicoal Sheen, "In Defense of Total Liberation: A Response to Animal Liberation Canada/USA's Racialized Rhetoric," North American Animal Liberation Press Office press release, December 4, 2011.

46. Ibid.

47. *Earth First! Journal* Editorial Collective 2013.

48. "What Is White Supremacy?" is an essay written by the renowned Chicana activist-scholar Elizabeth "Betita" Martinez (Martinez 1998).

49. Brehm field notes. June 2009.

50. People of Color Caucus 2008.

51. The Indigenous Environmental Network is a Native-led organization that advocates for economic and environmental justice in Indigenous communities throughout the Western Hemisphere in particular and also globally. The Common Ground Collective was founded in the wake of Hurricane Katrina as a grassroots social service and social justice organization that provided crucial resources in the absence of a dedicated government presence in poor neighborhoods and communities of color in the region.

52. "What is an ally?," document made available during the Earth First! Roadshow, spring 2009.

53. Panagioti, interview by the author and Brehm, spring 2009. For more on the Umoja Village, see Rameau 2008.

54. Panagioti, interview. No More Deaths is an Arizona-based group that advocates for humanitarian intervention to prevent death and suffering among migrants crossing the U.S.–Mexico border and provides assistance to persons deported back to Mexico. The organization was founded by a group of interfaith community leaders in Arizona—a state with some of the harshest anti-immigrant policies in the United States.

55. Irwin 2002.

56. Chris Irwin, author interview, October and November 2009.

57. Qtd. in Pickering 2007, 16.

58. jones ran the Eastern Shore Sanctuary and Education Center in rural Maryland for many years, waking up at the crack of dawn each day to feed the chickens.

59. Longshanks 2003.

60. Qtd. in Pickering 2007, 14.

61. Meyler 2003.

62. Ibid., 163–64.

63. Author's field notes from Earth First! Round River Rendezvous, June 2009. The term *settler* is used to describe non-Indigenous populations who occupy Indigenous land as part of settler-colonial states such as the United States, Canada, Australia, New Zealand, and Israel. The Unsettling Minnesota collective edited and released a sourcebook as a guide for decolonization and for building principled alliances between settlers and Natives (Unsettling Minnesota 2009).

64. Fully aware of these difficulties associated with solidarity work, Global Response was an NGO (and project of the organization Cultural Survival) that worked on human rights and environmental justice campaigns for Indigenous peoples *only* when invited by those communities to do so (see http://www.culturalsurvival.org).

65. The fact that a number of tribal governments in the United States have invited or accepted nuclear waste materials inside their borders is just one example of this kind of dynamic (LaDuke 2008).

66. Marx 1976, 637–38.

67. Marx 1974, 328; emphasis in original.

68. For an excellent review and critique of this matter, see Goldman and Schurman 2000.

69. Foster 1999, 381.

70. Schlosberg 2007.

71. Boggs 2001, 326.

72. Torres 2007, 80–81, emphasis in original; see also Mason 2005.

73. North American Animal Liberation Press Office (NAALPO), *NAALPO Newsletter* 4, no. 1 (January 2008).

74. Anonymous activist, author interview, summer 2009.

75. Anonymous activist, author interview, summer 2009.

76. *Earth First! Journal* Editorial Collective 2002, 13.

77. Foreman 1987.

78. jones 2004, 142.

79. Pickering 2007, 2.

80. Hensey, interview by Brehm, summer 2009.

81. Wemoonsarmy, untitled and undated zine. Wemoonsarmy is an anarcha-feminist collective dedicated to envisioning and realizing a radical restructuring of society's gender and sexual dynamics.

82. Cascadia Forest Alliance 2003.

83. pattrice jones, author interview, July 9, 2010.

84. Rena, author interview, July 30 2009.

85. Because We Must Mission Statement, http://www.becausewemust.org.

86. Rylee, "Writer Introduction: Meet Rylee," posted October 22, 2011, http://www.becausewemust.org.

87. Jeff, posted October 17, 2011, http://www.becausewemust.org.

88. For an excellent study of how activist groups in the United Kingdom have approached the politics of intersectionality and total liberation see Plows, Wall, and Doherty 2004.

89. Jeff "Free" Luers, interview by Brehm, March 7, 2010.

90. Josh Harper, author interview, November 9, 2009.

91. Ben Rosenfeld, interview by Brehm, October 3, 2009.

92. Rosenfeld 2010.

93. Irwin 2007.

94. Seego, interview by the author and Brehm, July 2009.

95. Colt, author interview, October 3, 2009. There is an increasing number of portrayals (both comical and serious) of this kind of gender and sexual politics in popular culture, including the television shows *The L Word* and *Portlandia*. Even the *New York Times* printed an article on the growing use of PGPs—preferred gender pronouns—among gender/sexuality conscious young people in the United States (Conlin 2011). The seriousness with which a growing number of people take PGPs is supported by evidence that language reflects and shapes power relations, which is also much of the basis of poststructuralist and feminist theory.

96. Dara, author interview, fall 2009.

97. While activists embracing total liberation bring a host of views to this question, I should be clear about where I stand. The discussions and debates about animal rights often get mired in unproductive and poorly thought-out comparisons between the oppression of nonhumans to humans—particularly women, Jewish victims of the Nazi Holocaust, and people of color. I do not subscribe to the notion that oppression of one kind is the same or even remotely equivalent to another kind. I cannot claim to know what one species or population experiences, and I would never draw an equivalence between or among such phenomena. What I *do* conclude, however, as a sociologist, is that the ideological justifications among humans in support of racism, classism, patriarchy, heterosexuality, nativism, and speciesism operate using a similar logic. That is, while the above are distinct practices that create and legitimate hierarchies across social categories of difference (and certainly the categories themselves are not equivalent and are unique), they all are supported by the idea that one group is superior to another and therefore deserving of superior consideration, treatment, and life chances. This logic of domination and hierarchy is defined and deployed *differently* across each of these social categories, so that it appears in distinct forms and variations, but it is nonetheless an ideology that supports unearned privileges and advantages for some through the oppression of others.

That point should be obvious but, sadly, requires emphasis because it is often lost or rarely if ever stated in these debates. Rather than wading into the frequently convoluted logic of social ecology or ecofeminism, or comparing oppression across populations, this argument simply focuses on the *human* ideology of hierarchy itself.

98. Ornelas 2009.

3. Anarchism and Anticapitalism

1. For example, Roderick Ferguson (2004), David Theo Goldberg (2002), Mick Smith (2011), and Bob Torres (2007).

2. See Pickering 2011.

3. Ron S., author interview, December 10, 2009.

4. Panagioti, author interview, May 18, 2009. Many regular contributors to the *EF! Journal* reflect this point of view. For example, one contributor writes: "In the past decade, an anarchistic worldview has had a growth spurt within EF!. Certain elements of anarchy have, of course, been there all along, but most would agree that a shift of some sort appears to be occurring" (Earth First! Organizers' Conference 2006).

5. Many observers believe the 1999 Battle in Seattle between left-leaning social movements and the World Trade Organization was the first major visible sign of the resurgence of anarchist movements in recent U.S. history (Amster et al. 2009; crow 2011).

6. Scarce 2006, 89.

7. See Amster et al. 2009, 3; crow 2011; Scott 2009.

8. Weber et al. 2004.

9. John Curl's *For All the People* details the long history of movements that might be called anarchist in the United States (Curl 2012).

10. Coulter 2007, 27.

11. Ibid.

12. Nedelsky 1990.

13. Qtd in Coulter 2007, 16. Original is Woodcock 1956, 58.

14. Pateman 1988.

15. Luibheid 2002, ix.

16. Hing 2004, 83.

17. Luibheid 2002, x.

18. Mills 1999; Goldberg 2002.

19. Ramnath 2011. Anarchist People of Color (APOC) "is an anti-authoritarian group created to address issues of race, anti-authoritarianism, and people of color struggle politics within the context of anarchism, and to create/increase political safe spaces for people of color" (http://www.anarchistpeopleof color.tumblr.com).

20. Kant 1970, 74; qtd. in Goldberg 2002, 48.

21. Ibid.

22. Ngai 2004.

23. Gualtieri 2009.

24. Best and Nocella 2004, 2006; jones 2004; Mason 2005, 2006; Torres 2007.

25. M. Smith 2011, 66.

26. Gaard 1993,1; see also Warren 1994, 1; Gaard 2004.

27. M. Smith 2011.

28. Ibid., xii.

29. I write this with the important clarification that a number of radical Indigenous studies and African American studies scholars and activists conclude that sovereignty within their communities is a necessary condition of survival (see, for example, LaDuke 2008; Waziyatawin 2008; see also Alston 2008). I believe one can organize for sovereignty without also equating that principle with state formation.

30. M. Smith 2011, xviii.

31. Torres 2007, 12.

32. Bennett 2009; Latour 1999. Latour's concept of a "parliament of things" has echoes of what Joanna Macy and other ecologists have called the Council of All Beings—ritual in which humans convene and attempt to set aside their human identities and speak for nonhumans; see Seed et al. 2007. The idea of speaking for others is, of course, problematic.

33. The black flag is a traditional symbol of anarchist movements, intended to signal a refusal of nation states and, as the opposite of the white flag of surrender, a stance of defiance.

34. Chris Irwin, author interview, October 29 and November 5, 2009.

35. See Curl 2012; Hartmann 2010.

36. FAQs about the ELF, http://earth-liberation-front.com/; qtd. in Pickering 2007, 59.

37. North American Animal Liberation Press Office, *NAALPO Newsletter* 3 (October 2009): 3. The names Jentsch and Ringach refer to Professors David Jentsch and Dario Ringach of UCLA. Both faculty members have come under fire from animal liberationists for their work on animal experimentation.

38. Josh Harper, author interview, November 9, 2009.

39. Stu Sugarman, author interview, March 24, 2009.

40. scott crow, author interview, January 1, 2011.

41. Dinerstein 2003; Krausch 2012.

42. Curl 2012, 6.

43. Tocqueville 2010.

44. Polletta 2002, 6; see also Breines 1989.

45. Boggs 2001, 22.

46. Irwin, author interview, October 29 and November 5, 2009. See Kropotkin 2008.

47. jones 2004, 143–44.

48. crow, author interview, January 1, 2011.

49. Cascadia Forest Alliance 2003.

50. Ibid.

51. Irwin, author interview, October 29 and November 5, 2009.

52. Cascadia Forest Alliance 2003.

53. crow, author interview, January 1, 2011.

54. Amster et al. 2009; Graeber 2004.

55. crow, author interview, January 1, 2011.

56. SHAC activist, author interview, winter 2011.

57. Rosebraugh 2002.

58. Schuster 2005.

59. NAALPO, *NAALPO Newsletter* 3, no. 2 (April 2007).

60. Claude Marks, author interview, February 25, 2010.

61. Civil Liberties Defense Center, Eugene, Oregon, http://CLDC.org/about, 2013.

62. Lauren Regan, author interview, April 2, 2009.

63. Alston 2008.

64. Ashanti Alston, author interview, April 6, 2010.

65. Bennett 2009; Latour 1999.

66. Foster 2000.

67. Ibid.

68. Torres 2007, 11.

69. Foster, Clark, and York 2010.

70. Ibid., 47.

71. Ibid., 207.

72. O'Connor 1994.

73. Merchant 2005, 8–9. Merchant defines capitalism's first contradiction as the tension between the economic forces of production and local environmental conditions.

74. Schnaiberg 1980; Schnaiberg and Gould 2000; Gould, Pellow, and Schnaiberg 2008.

75. Foster, Clark, and York 2010, 211.

76. Gibson-Graham 2006. "There is no alternative," or TINA, was a slogan that conservative British prime minister Margaret Thatcher often invoked in an attempt to garner support for her administration's harsh application of "free market" policies.

77. Ferguson 2004, 15–17, 39; Lowe 1997, 28.

78. Lowe 1997, 25.

79. Robbins 2007.

80. There is a great deal of overlap on this topic between the total liberation frame and the works of Marxist environmental sociologists (see Foster 1999, 2000; O'Connor 1994; Schnaiberg and Gould 2000; Torres 2007).

81. Hooks and Smith 2004.

82. Plenary session, Animal Rights Conference, speaker unknown, July 2009, Los Angeles.

83. Nik Hensey, interview by Brehm, fall 2009.

84. Field notes are by Brehm. Kay informed the group that she found much of this material in Jerry Mander's book *In the Absence of the Sacred*, in which there is a section titled "11 Rules of Corporate Behavior" (Mander 1999). This perspective is also prominent in Max Weber's theory of bureaucracy (Weber 1978) and in Joel Bakan's *The Corporation* (Bakan 2005).

85. *Earth First! Journal* 2002a, 21.

86. Raphi, author interview, May 21, 2009.

87. Jeff Luers, interview by Brehm, spring 2010.

88. Krill 1999, 25.

89. Stop Huntingdon Animal Cruelty, http://SHAC.net, 2011.

90. ELF, "ELF and ALF Claim Joint Credit for Economic Sabotage at McDonald's Corporate Offices on Long Island, N.Y.," *ELF Resistance Journal* no. 4 (2000).

91. NAALPO, *NAALPO Newsletter* 2 (2009): 11–13.

92. Many mainstream animal advocates and environmentalists share this general view without subscribing to anticapitalist and anarchist politics and while condemning aggressive forms of direct action.

93. NAALPO, *NAALPO Newsletter* 4, no. 1 (January 2008): 10.

94. John Hanna, author interview, November 2009.

95. Schurman and Munro 2010.

96. Rosebraugh n.d., 10.

97. NAALPO, *NAALPO Newsletter* 4, no. 1 (January 2008): 10.

98. Bari, qtd. in Scarce 2006, 94. Original quote is from an interview with Rik Scarce.

99. Coronado 1994. This is from *Strong Hearts* 1, a classic series of hand-made zines Coronado wrote and produced during the mid-1990s while serving time in federal prison for acts committed on behalf of the ALF. The content of *Strong Hearts* focused on Coronado's life and actions taken in support of animal and earth liberation.

100. Coronado 2004/2005.

101. See, for example, Reinsborough 2003, 33-34.

102. The G8 is the name given to a group of eight of the world's largest national economies whose representatives meet regularly to discuss and some-times coordinate responses to global economic and financial trends.

103. *Earth First! Journal* 2004, 48. The authors are members of a committee empowered by the 2004 Earth First! Organizers' Conference.

104. Anonymous communiqué, "1000+ Mink Liberated from Gifford, Washington Ranch This Morning," posted on NAALPO website, October 12, 2011.

105. NAALPO, *NAALPO Newsletter* 4, no. 1 (January 2008): 11.

106. Hartmann 2010.

107. Coulter has worked on these campaigns in, among other places, Oregon, Washington State, Nevada, and New England. She has worked for EF!, Greenpeace, American Friends Service Committee, and many other groups.

108. Karen Coulter, author interview, October 3, 2009. Coulter also cofounded the End Corporate Dominance group, which sponsored a series of annual conferences in Portland during the late 1990s and early 2000s, during the height of the anti/alter/counter globalization (or global justice) movement.

109. From a workshop led by Coulter at the TWAC camp (June 2009). Field notes are by Brehm.

110. April, correspondence with Brehm, fall 2009.

111. Ibid.

112. See Jensen 2006a, 2006b; Zerzan 1999, 2005.

113. Screening of *END-CIV*, Walker Community Church, Minneapolis, June 6, 2011. See Kolodny 2007 for a discussion of the "ecological Indian."

114. "Strategies For Defending Mother Earth & Resisting Ecocide," public meeting to organize an underground movement, Minneapolis, July 25, 2011.

115. *Earth First! Journal* Collective 2013.

116. Seager 1994; Torres 2007.

117. Pickering 2007, 103, emphasis added.

118. NAALPO, *NAALPO Newsletter* 5, no. 1 (January 2009): 2, emphasis added.

4. Direct Action

This chapter was coauthored with Hollie Nyseth Brehm.

1. Peter Young, author interview, July 13, 2009.

2. Robbins 2007.

3. In her work on ecofeminist politics, Noel Sturgeon emphasizes that ecofeminist social movements engage in their own theorizing and link their work to previous and other ongoing social movements, what she calls "direct theory" (1997a, 5).

4. *Earth First! Journal* 2002b, 22–23.

5. Bell et al. 2002. The authors are members of the SmartMeme Project and led a three-day, six-session workshop at the 2002 Earth First! Round River Rendezvous in Washington State.

6. *Earth First! Journal* 1999, 2.

7. Bearfoot 1994, 21.

8. Jeffrey "Free" Luers, interview by Hollie Nyseth Brehm, June 30, 2010.

9. Jake Conroy, author interview, June 10, 2010.

10. Ibid.

11. Plenary session, Animal Rights Conference, speaker unknown, July 2009, Los Angeles.

12. See ELF, "What Is the Earth Liberation Front?" *ELF Resistance Journal*, no. 4 (2000). See also "The ALF Credo," n.d., http://www.animalliberation front.com/ALFront/alf_credo.htm.

13. Bell et al. 2002.

14. Manes 1990, 175.

15. This statement was posted on the *Earth First! Journal* website, http://earthfirstjournal.org.

16. Dennis Davey, author interview, July 1, 2009.

17. Murphy-Ellis 2011.

18. Peter Young, Let Live Conference, June 27, 2009, Portland, Oregon.

19. Kim McCoy, interview by Brehm, October 2009.

20. Tree spiking involves hammering metal or ceramic spikes into a tree. EF! veteran and movement historian Andy Caffrey told us that Judi Bari's renunciation of tree spiking on behalf of EF! made little sense to him since EF! had no formal administrative structure or membership. He stated, "We disagreed with the moratorium and felt that EF! couldn't formally renounce tree-spiking because there is no membership to EF!" (Andy Caffrey, author interview, July 1, 2009).

21. Qtd. in Pickering 2007, 35.

22. See, for example, Steven Best's 2007 review of animal welfarist Norm Phelps's book *The Longest Struggle*, in which Phelps demonstrates little patience for militant direct action. See also Kjonaas 2004. See also an ELF article that excoriates mainstream environmentalists for their rejection of the ELF. The article states, "There is no tolerable excuse for an individual or organization that claims to be a part of the movement to protect all life on the planet to come out publicly against the actions of the ELF" (*ELF Resistance Journal*, no. 5).

23. Cecil-Cockwell 2008. This article is available at http://lesliejamespick ering.com/epocharticle.pdf. For Cecil-Cockwell's interview with John Hanna, March 25, 2008, see http://old-elf.tripod.com/questions.html.

24. Karen Coulter, author interview, October 3, 2009.

25. Jake, "Thoughts on Diversity of Tactics," Because We Must, http://www .becausewemust.org, 2012.

26. Coronado 2000.

27. Magdalinious 2009, 18.

28. Pickering 2002.

29. Polletta 2002, 6; see also Breines 1989.

30. *Earth First! Journal* 2003b.

31. Chris Irwin, author interview, October 29, 2009.

32. ELF communiqué, March 5, 2001.

33. See Cisneros 2007; Colliver 1999; McVeigh 2007; Smithers and Ramesh 2008. Members of the group Global Exchange protested the opening of an Old Navy store in San Francisco in 1999 by undressing and shouting in the nude, "We'd rather wear nothing than wear Old Navy!" (Colliver 1999).

34. Greenhouse 2000.

35. ELF communiqué, April 2, 2001.

36. Author's field notes at the Earth First! Roadshow, May 2009, Walker Church, Minneapolis.

37. Ibid.

38. Ecofeminist Front 2003.

39. Triple C 2007.

40. Author's interview with EF! veterans, July 1, 2009, Earth First! Round River Rendezvous, Umpqua National Forest, Oregon. Doug and Dennis were the only names offered.

41. "'Trans' and Womyn's Action Camp," *Earth First! Journal* 29, Beltane (May–June 2009): 18.

42. Lewddite Uprising 2011.

43. Kheel 2006, 307.

44. Joshua Harper, author interview, November 9, 2009.

45. This figure comes from a government official's testimony (Jarboe 2002).

46. Coronado 1995. The professor whose research laboratory was targeted—Dr. Richard Aulerich—at that time was the recipient of the second highest number of Mink Farmers Research Foundation grants and had ongoing government contracts to study the effects of PCBs and other toxins on mink, with his own published work revealing the details of violent deaths these animals suffered as a result of these experiments (Kuipers 2009,189; "Michigan State: Animal Rights Raiders Destroy Years of Work," *New York Times*, March 8, 1992).

47. Coronado 1995.

48. Ibid.

49. Ibid.

50. Earth First! 2000.

51. Sharon Day, interview by the author and Scott DeMuth of the author's research team, November 6, 2009.

52. Ibid.

53. Ibid.

54. Paul Eaves, interview with the author and DeMuth, October 27, 2010.

55. Ibid.

56. Day, interview with the author and DeMuth. November 6, 2009.

57. Solstice, interview with the author and DeMuth, November 5, 2010.

58. Ibid.

59. Ibid.

60. In July 1998, Ian, active with the New Jersey Animal Defense League, was involved in a lockdown and antifur protest that shut down Macy's Herald Square in New York City—known as the world's largest store. He and others connected a U-lock to their necks and to a pole holding up the store awning, and dropped a banner to send a message to onlookers about Macy's making a

profit from the slaughter of nonhuman animals for fur. An animal rights publication reported on the event and stated, "Due to all of the chaos that ensued, the store evacuated its customers and closed its doors. ADL rejoiced, 'We shut down the world's largest store!'" (see *Do Not Consider Yourself Free*, no. 3 [newsletter of the New York City chapter of the Animal Defense League]).

61. *No Compromise* is not in print form anymore, but this magazine was produced by activists in the late 1990s as a means of building and supporting a grassroots movement, and it supported the ALF and other groups taking direct action.

62. Ian 1999.

63. SOAR was founded by Freeman Wicklund during the summer of 1993. Wicklund was also a founder of the Animal Liberation League, a founder and editor of the animal liberation magazine *No Compromise*, and, on occasion, a spokesperson for the ALF.

64. The action at Yerkes was part of the Primate Freedom Tour—a summer-long series of animal liberation protests in 1999 against vivisection and animal experimentation at universities and federally funded facilities. For a critique of the Yerkes Primate Research Center, see the video "Release & Restitution," http://releasechimps.org/support/item/neavs-release-restitution-video, produced by Project R&R (Release and Restitution for Chimpanzees in U.S. Laboratories). While animal liberationists' concerns were for the health and well-being of the primates at Yerkes, the government was also concerned about the safety of Yerkes human staff. In the fall of 1997, a worker at the Yerkes Regional Primate Research Center (PRC) Field Station in Lawrenceville, Georgia, died after contracting an illness from exposure to a Rhesus Macaque monkey. The worker was splashed in the eye with body fluid from a monkey during a "group capture" and was subsequently infected with B virus (Cercopithecine herpesvirus 1 or Herpesvirus simian), which is endemic in the macaque species. The worker died on December 10, 1997 (Keifer and Deitchman 1998).

65. Dr. Toxic, author interview, December 15, 2010.

66. John Anfinson (a Minnesota government official), author interview, May 24, 2010. Anfinson told me that he disputes the claim that the Four Oaks site is of historical significance and therefore sacred in that sense. Rather, he believes the sacred designation occurred in the late 1990s when Native and non-Native activists wanted to save the area: "Because if one person says its sacred, but especially if they're American Indian, and then others latch on, and new-agers part of this movement, Earth First!ers and others, just latched on like crazy to this place. And it is a place of spiritual significance to many different people right now—I don't question that in the least. [But] it's a post-1997 story."

67. ELF communiqué, March 24, 2000.

68. On the morning of Sunday, December 20, 1998, at 4 a.m., "Operation Coldsnap," the largest police action in the history of the state of Minnesota, was

carried out by the Minneapolis Police Department, the Hennepin County Sheriff's Department, and the Minnesota State Patrol. An estimated eight hundred law enforcement officers arrested thirty-six people at the Minnehaha Free State encampment, many of whom were—according to activists—brutalized by police. Police dismantled an Indigenous M'dewin sweat lodge, razed tipis, and broke and burned items sacred to the Dakota people such as drums and personal property. Police barred media from the site and smashed cameras owned by observers who tried to document the action (see Losure 2002).

69. Ron S., author interview, December 10, 2009.

70. The Cold Snap Legal Collective emerged from this episode. They are a group that offers legal support for the radical activist community in the Twin Cities. Their website states: "By taking the name of this massive abuse of police power, we're sending the message that never again will we be taken off guard. With every action and demonstration, we're going to become more organized, more educated, more empowered. And we'll never stop fighting for our rights!" (http://coldsnaplegal.wordpress.com, 2013).

71. One study found the presence of allergens in transgenic soybeans, which could pose a risk to human health upon consumption (Nordlee et al. 1996). There are also concerns that GE products will contribute to the rapid pace at which antibiotics are becoming less effective in medicines (Dawkins 1999).

72. Monsanto's infamous "terminator" gene has been widely criticized because it prevents crops from naturally producing new seeds that farmers could replant at little cost, as they have done for generations; instead it produces a sterile crop and forces farmers to continually purchase new seeds from Monsanto each season (Hayes 1999). The *Multinational Monitor* reported that the Thai government overturned the prime minister's decision to allow the planting of crops containing GMOs in part because of the fear that organic farmers' livelihoods would be undermined by the contamination of their crops by neighboring farms using GMOs (*Multinational Monitor* 2004).

73. Losey, Rayor, and Carter 1999.

74. See Schurman and Munro 2010.

75. Bernton and Clarridge 2006. Apparently, Bradshaw's office sustained only minimal damage, while the offices of other professors who were not targets were hit hardest. According to the University of Washington, this included damage to research on wetlands restoration and endangered stickweed plants (ibid.).

76. ELF communiqué, 2001, qtd. in Rosebraugh 2004a: 205–6.

77. Ron S., author interview, December 10, 2009.

78. Novartis later merged with Zeneca to create Syngenta, a multibillion-dollar Swiss corporation that markets seeds and pesticides.

79. The original Bolt Weevils were a group of Minnesota farmers who, in the 1970s, engaged in illegal sabotage and direct action to seek to prevent and disrupt efforts by power companies to run power lines from a North Dakota

generating station into the Twin Cities. The controversy stemmed from the decision to route the power lines through lands owned by small farmers, while leaving large industrial farms out of harm's way. Small farmers toppled numerous power lines, pulled up survey stakes, blocked roads, and publicly encouraged other forms of sabotage. Eventually, the Minnesota Supreme Court ruled against them (Budd 2013).

80. Bolt Weevils communiqué, September 13, 1999 (qtd. in *ELF Resistance Journal,* no. 2 (1999): 12.

81. Ibid.

82. "Anti-Genetix Direct Actions Sprout in the U.S.," *ELF Resistance Journal,* no. 2 (1999): 6.

83. Qtd. in Rosebraugh 2004a: 259–60.

84. Harper, author interview, November 9, 2009.

85. Andrew Stepanian, author interview, June 5, 2010.

86. See Food Not Bombs, http://foodnotbombs.net. Food Not Bombs has been ensnared in a number of infamous cases where government officials have described its members as terrorists and have harassed them when they feed free vegan meals to homeless persons. FNB has no official leaders and has many "chapters" or "franchises" across the United States that operate autonomously from each other. This is an anarchist model of movement building that groups such as Critical Mass and Earth First! have employed as well.

87. Johnson and Williams 2011. The two main prison units referred to as "Guantanamo North" are at the federal correctional facilities in Terre Haute, Indiana, and Marion, Illinois. These Communications Management Units house radicalized prisoners who are majority U.S. citizens, largely Muslim, and considered by many to be political prisoners.

88. In a 2008 animal rights publication, the author claimed that HLS had $100 million in debt at that time ("What Are the Huntingdon Life Sciences?" *Bite Back,* no. 13 [Summer 2008]: 7).

89. Alleyne 2001.

90. "Update: Dismantling Huntingdon Life Sciences," *No Compromise,* no. 23 (Spring 2004): 14.

91. Trill 2009, 27.

92. Camille Hankins, Animal Rights Conference, Los Angeles, 2009.

93. Conroy, author interview, June 10, 2010.

94. "Pick Your Own Day! Monday 29th December 2008," *SHAC Newsletter* (Kent, U.K.), no. 51 (Spring 2009): 8.

95. CrimethInc. Ex-Workers' Collective, "The SHAC Model: A Critical Assessment," n.d., http://www.crimethinc.com/texts/rollingthunder.shac.php.

96. Harper, author interview, November 9, 2009.

97. scott crow, author interview, January 1, 2011.

98. See Lambert 2004. The group that took credit for the use of incendiary devices was the Revolutionary Cells—Animal Liberation Brigade, which

apparently took this action after Chiron refused to sell its HLS stock. This was an elevation of tactics in the United States (while similar actions have long occurred in the U.K. animal liberation movement), making many activists uncomfortable and worried about increased state repression. The RC-ALB also took the unusual step of acknowledging the fact that it was upping the tactical ante and, in its communiqué regarding this action, issued its own set of guidelines, which are essentially identical to the ALF's and ELF's with the notable exception of the allowance of explicitly violent actions. One of the guidelines read "Respect a diversity of tactics, whether they be non-violent or not" (Lambert 2004). Some have argued that the emergence of the Revolutionary Cells and other SHAC-related groups that had no code of nonviolence was perhaps a predictable outcome of the SHAC's anarchist structure.

99. Stepanian, author interview, June 5, 2010.

100. One may be reminded of two great American social movement leaders, John Muir and Martin Luther King, who demonstrated a penetrating understanding of ecology and its implications. Muir famously wrote in 1911: "When we try to pick out anything by itself, we find it hitched to everything else in the Universe" (Muir 1988, 110). In his extraordinary "Letter from a Birmingham Jail," Dr. King wrote: "Injustice anywhere is a threat to justice everywhere. We are caught in an inescapable network of mutuality, tied in a single garment of destiny. Whatever affects one directly, affects all indirectly" (M. King 1963).

101. "Interview with SHAC UK's Greg Avery," *No Compromise*, no. 19 (Fall 2002): 3.

102. Stepanian, author interview, June 5, 2010.

103. As CrimethInc.'s analysis of the SHAC campaign stated: "The SHAC campaign set about depriving HLS of its support structure. Just as a living organism depends on an entire ecosystem for the resources and relationships it needs to survive, a corporation cannot function without investors and business partners. In this regard, more so than any standard boycott, property destruction, or publicity campaign, SHAC confronted HLS on the terms most threatening to a corporation" (CrimethInc., "SHAC Model").

104. Kjonaas 2004, 270. While pacifism in the U.S. political context is frequently defined as making peace through nonviolent resistance at all cost, Gandhi fundamentally believed in the role of self-defense in the face of immediate violence. Radical activists have extended this logic to support defending beings who are unable to defend themselves (Rosebraugh 2004b; see also Churchill 2007).

105. Paul Eaves, interview with the author and DeMuth, October 27, 2010.

106. Adamson 2001; Adamson and Ruffin 2013; Goldman and Schurman 2000; Heynen, Kaika, and Swyngedouw 2006; Humphrey, Lewis, and Buttel 2002.

107. Vanderheiden 2005, 427.

108. Robbins 2007.

109. CrimethInc. Ex-Workers Collective, *A Civilian's Guide to Direct Action*, 4. This document was available at several movement events we attended and is available for free download on many websites. CrimethInc. is a decentralized anarchist collective of autonomous cells that emerged in the mid-1990s, initially via the hardcore zine *Inside Front*, and began operating as a collective in 1996. Since that time, it has published many other documents and books, and its members have been involved with various national and international anticapitalist movements and the anarcho-punk art and music scene.

110. Gina Lynn, author interview, December 7, 2009.

111. "When Animals Bite Back," *Bite Back*, no. 12 (September–March 2007/ 2008): 32. Nicholas Atwood distributed *Bite Back*, an animal rights magazine, though his website and set up a Florida company, Bite Back Inc. The name is believed to relate to "Operation Bite Back," a 1990s arson campaign aimed at the U.S. fur industry.

112. MacDougal 2009, 25. A popular postcard that Earth First! mails to its supporters is of a photo taken by the National Park Service of giant sequoia tree that apparently fell on and crushed a jeep. The post card is titled "Nature bites back," and the message includes the statement "No one was injured, but the vehicle was completely destroyed."

113. Coronado 2004/2005, 8.

114. Conroy, author interview, June 10, 2010.

115. Not surprisingly, the Physicians Committee for Responsible Medicine has distanced itself from Vlasak, particularly given his public statements endorsing physical violence against vivisectors (Doward and Townsend 2004). PCRM opposes animal experimentation on scientific grounds.

116. Jerry Vlasak, author interview, July 24, 2009. See also Atwood 1999 for an animal liberationist's glowing review of Nelson Mandela's autobiography *Long Walk to Freedom*: "Mandela eventually recognized that legal methods of protest were failing the ANC, and, that by themselves, the tactics of Gandhi and King would never overcome Apartheid in South Africa. . . . 'In the end,' Mandela continues, 'we had no alternative to armed and violent resistance.'" We should note that while Vlasak and others are press officers of NAALPO, there is debate and disagreement about whether they should see themselves as representing the animal liberation movement versus simply reporting news. This issue came up in response to Vlasak's public statements that appear to support armed struggle. *No Compromise* magazine reminded readers that the ALF has a strict code of nonviolence and rejected the idea that NAALPO spokespersons "are actually representative of our entire movement." *No Compromise* printed a response by Vlasak, which included his view that "violence has been a necessary component of every serious liberation struggle. . . . The Press Office wishes to be clear on this matter: we support all liberationists" ("Getting P.O.'D: Taking a

Critical Look at the North American Animal Liberation Press Office," *No Compromise*, no. 29 [Winter/Spring 2006]: 18–19).

117. crow, author interview, January 1, 2011.

5. The Green Scare

1. Boykoff 2007.

2. NAELFPO, "Earth Liberation Front Press Office Calls Environmentalist's 22 Year Prison Sentence 'Cruel and Unusual Punishment,'" press release, February 5, 2009.

3. As one CrimethInc. pamphlet states, "Repression will exist as long as there are states and people who oppose them" (CrimethInc. n.d.).

4. Weber et al. 2004.

5. For an excellent discussion of this debate see Guillén-Givens, Mullett, and Small 2013.

6. Williams was himself the president of the Monroe County, North Carolina, chapter of the NAACP until the national leadership suspended him for disagreements over nonviolent tactics.

7. Former Sojourner Truth Organization militant Ken Lawrence wrote in a pamphlet titled *The New State Repression* (2006) that since the state today views popular resistance not as a series of sporadic occurrences but rather as a permanent insurgency, the response is to develop a "strategy of *permanent repression* as the full-time task of the security forces. This difference has been elaborated theoretically largely as a consequence of the Indochina war, which gave this strategy its name: *counter-insurgency.*"

8. Luce Guillén-Givens, presentation in class on social change, University of Minnesota, Minneapolis, November 2009.

9. By "cultures of resistance" I mean those shared understandings, ideas, and knowledge that inform and support individual and collective practices of resistance.

10. Boykoff 2007; Churchill and Vanderwall 2001; Rodriguez 2006.

11. Foucault 1995.

12. Foucault 1990.

13. Schuster 2005.

14. U.S., FBI, 2011a, 2011b.

15. Bruce Friedrich, author interview, June 9, 2009.

16. Torres 2007, 75.

17. Best 2004, 309.

18. Sedition Act of 1918, Public Law No. 150, 40 Statute 553 (repealed in 1921); qtd in Cole 2003,112.

19. Cole 2003, 92–93.

20. Schlesinger 2004.

21. Cole 2003, 115.

22. Hing 2004: 83.

23. Ibid., 92.

24. Churchill and Vanderwall 2001.

25. Black propaganda is false information that appears to come from one side in a conflict but is actually from another entity.

26. See Meeropol 2005, 21.

27. The ban on "guilt by association" was put into place with the 1990 Immigration and Nationality Act.

28. This is a list of only the most visible attacks that garnered sensationalist media attention and fails to include the numerous attacks against family planning and abortion clinic workers and against persons targeted by Islamic-identified activists supporting various causes.

29. Arnold 2010.

30. Qtd. in Best 2004, 308.

31. Jarboe 2002.

32. Best 2004, 308.

33. Animal Enterprise Protection Act, Public Law 102-346, passed August 26, 1992 by the 102nd U.S. Congress.

34. Pring and Canan 1996.

35. The stories of Chico Mendes and Karen Silkwood are classic examples. For more on Mendes, see Revkin (2004), and for Silkwood's story, see Rashke and Bronfenbrenner (2000). Corporations have also targeted scholars doing research that may threaten their reputation and profits, even when strong evidence of ecological harm associated with their products exists. This sums up the relationship between Syngenta Corporation and UC Berkeley Professor Tyrone Hayes (Aviv 2014).

36. Ridgeway 2008. The operation against Greenpeace is believed to have lasted from 1998 to 2000. Greenpeace later sued a number of companies for these actions. In a statement that anticipates current concerns about the Green Scare, Manes wrote: "The rise of private security forces funded by corporations and directed at lawful environmental organizations is an ominous development in the history of the environmental movement and our political system. . . . Surveillance of groups that oppose a corporation's policies cannot help but have a chilling effect on public participation in the democratic process" (1990, 199). Greenpeace has also been the subject of numerous FBI investigations (see U.S. Department of Justice 2010) and U.S. government harassment, including a politically motivated IRS audit in the early 2000s. Also, for a story about how electronics industries monitor activist groups such as Friends of the Earth and Greenpeace that urge them to implement green practices, see Danielle Knight, "Sony Monitoring Environmental Activists," InterPress Service, September 22, 2000. In July 1985, French intelligence services, intent on preventing Greenpeace from interfering with France's nuclear testing on the Pacific island of Moruroa,

blew up the iconic Greenpeace ship, *Rainbow Warrior*, in Auckland harbor. The blast sank the ship, killing Fernando Pereira, a Greenpeace photographer who was on board. On a personal note, my grandfather was a security guard at the Auckland harbor and just happened to be off duty the evening the ship was blown up.

37. Greenpeace staff member, conversation with author, June 2010.

38. Scarce 2006, 133.

39. Ibid.

40. Obama 2005.

41. See crow 2011. FBI director Louis Freeh stated during public testimony: "Anarchists and extremist socialist groups—many of which, such as the Workers' World Party, Reclaim the Streets, and Carnival Against Capitalism—have an international presence and, at times, also represent a potential threat in the United States. For example, anarchists, operating individually and in groups, caused much of the damage during the 1999 World Trade Organization ministerial meeting in Seattle" (qtd. in Hoffman 2001).

42. Rik Scarce, author interview, June 7, 2010.

43. Enna, author interview, June 10, 2011.

44. Harper 2004, 23.

45. "Gina Lynn: Just Say NO to Grand Juries," *No Compromise*, no. 25 (Fall 2004); 8–10.

46. scott crow, author interview, January 1, 2011.

47. Kevin Kjonaas, conversation with author, summer 2010.

48. See Thomas 2002.

49. Maag 2006.

50. ELF communiqué concerning December 31, 1999, action.

51. Rosebraugh 2004a: 99.

52. Goldenberg 2009.

53. The case broke in 2007 when Ambrose, after he and Mason had split up, was cleaning out his home and left incriminating materials such as fuses, explosives, maps, and gas masks in a dumpster. Someone discovered these items and contacted authorities. Ambrose agreed to wear a wire and gave Mason a bugged cell phone that the FBI used to monitor her conversations. Ambrose also gathered information on a number of other activists during that time. In return, he received a reduced sentence of nine years and a top spot in the growing gallery of reviled snitches who cooperate with authorities against the movement. This was a particularly painful blow to the movement because Ambrose was previously viewed as a reliable and well-respected activist who worked for many progressive and radical organizations over the years (see Bloomington Defense Committee n.d.).

54. Goldenberg 2009.

55. Ibid.

56. "Support Marie Mason" flyer, n.d.

57. Friends of Marie Mason, "Support Marie Mason, Fight the Green Scare," 2009.

58. Shiva 2013.

59. Marie Mason's sentencing statement to the court, Western District of Michigan, Lansing, February 5, 2009.

60. Ibid.

61. Ibid.

62. In a February 2010 e-mail message from her support committee, Marie Mason was described as being denied access to vegan food (see "Write the Warden for Marie Mason!," February 3, 2010, e-mail sent out on *freemarie@riseup. net* listserv). There are many other instances when animal and earth liberation prisoners who are vegan are denied meals in accordance with their diets. Often supporters will quickly organize a phone call-in campaign to pressure prison authorities to comply with the prisoner's request. I participated in one such call-in, and by the time I phoned the prison, the person receiving the call was quite exasperated and informed me with audible frustration that prison officials had addressed the problem and that we should stop calling.

63. Potter 2011b. Another political prisoner served time at FCI Carswell—Helen Woodson, the antinuclear/peace activist who became famous for trespassing at a Missouri missile silo and symbolically "beat swords into plowshares" by bringing a jackhammer and sledgehammer to the site (see Potter 2011a).

64. Jeff "Free" Luers, interview by Brehm, Spring 2010.

65. Ibid.

66. Ibid.

67. Ibid.

68. Ibid.

69. McGlynn 2010.

70. Carrie Feldman, statement to the grand jury, Davenport, Iowa, October 2009.

71. crow, author interview, January 1, 2011.

72. McClintock 1995.

73. See Harris 1993; Lipsitz 2006.

74. Ngai 2004,18.

75. Best 2004, 335.

76. Potter 2010. The McKenna quote comes from Judy Peet, "NJIT Homeland Security Center Studies Groundbreaking Anti-terrorism Technology," NJ.com, June 13, 2010, http://www.nj.com/news/index.ssf/2010/06/njit_sci entists_homeland_secur.html.

77. Potter 2010.

78. "Warren," conversation with author, December 6, 2009.

79. Courtney Bell, essay for the course "Race, Class, and the Politics of Nature," December 2009.

80. Harris 1993.

81. Gualtieri 2009; Roediger 2006.

82. Lauren Regan, author interview, April 2, 2009.

83. L. Regan 2009.

84. Regan, author interview, April 2, 2009. On March 30, 2010, on behalf of Daniel McGowan and several other plaintiffs, the Center for Constitutional Rights and the Civil Liberties Defense Center sued the Bureau of Prisons, challenging the policies and conditions at two CMUs, as well as challenging the establishment of CMUs. A court dismissed the suit on July 15, 2013 (Tim Phillips, "Former Inmate Daniel McGowan's Claims against the Bureau of Prisons Dismissed," Activist Defense, July 15, 2013, http://activistdefense.wordpress.com).

85. Alexander 2010; Rodriguez 2006.

86. An article in an undated *ELF Resistance Journal* puts it this way: "Think of what goes through your mind when you hear the term terrorist. Usually it relates somehow to racist beliefs and stereotypes about Arabs, about airline hijackings, violence, and about how terrorists need to be caught and/or killed to be kept away from society. So when the federal government and the mainstream press immediately label actions of the ELF as eco-terrorism all this can do is create a negative stereotype in the minds of the public" ("Someone Remind Me Again Please . . . What Are We Fighting For?," *ELF Resistance Journal* 2, no. 1 [n.d.]).

87. Walter Bond, "Political Prison," posted on NAALPO, March 10, 2013.

88. Andy Stepanian, author interview, June 5, 2010.

89. See Mohai 1990 for a critique of this idea.

90. See Adamson and Slovic 2009; Kolodny 2007.

91. Coronado 1995; emphasis added.

92. J. Tony Serra, author interview, October 9, 2010.

93. Kim McCoy, interview by Brehm, October 2009.

94. Regan, author interview, April 2, 2009.

95. Ibid.

96. Josh Harper, author interview, November 9, 2009.

97. Ben Rosenfeld, interview by Brehm, November 30, 2009.

98. Peter Young, author interview, July 13, 2009.

99. J Johnson, author interview, December 11, 2009.

100. Johnson is referring to the landmark First Amendment ruling in the *Brandenburg v. Ohio* (1969) case, which began when a leader of the KKK was convicted under the state of Ohio's criminal syndicalism laws after making a fiery speech at a rally. Ohio's law made it a crime to advocate crime, violence, sabotage, or terrorism in order to achieve a political objective. The Supreme

Court declared Ohio's law unconstitutional because it failed to draw a distinction between the teaching or advocacy of extremist political doctrines and whether that advocacy would incite imminent lawless action, thus setting a more protective standard for political speech. Specifically, the Supreme Court ruled that the government cannot punish inflammatory speech unless that speech is directed at inciting and is likely to incite imminent lawless action. Ohio's statute essentially banned the mere advocacy of violence or other illegal activities.

101. Johnson, author interview, December 11, 2009.

102. Ibid.

103. Enna, author interview, June 10, 2011.

104. Harper, author interview, November 9, 2009.

105. Justin Goodman, author interview, December 1, 2009.

106. Jerry Vlasak, author interview, July 24, 2009.

107. Regan, author interview, April 2, 2009.

108. Vlasak, author interview, July 24, 2009.

109. Enna, author interview, June 10, 2011.

110. Ibid.

111. Pickering 2007,66.

112. Johnson, author interview, December 11, 2009.

113. Jake Conroy, author interview, June 10, 2010.

114. See chapter 1 for more on this. See also Haines 1984.

115. Claude Marks, author interview, February 25, 2010.

116. Ibid.

117. Regan, author interview, April 2, 2009.

118. This is what CIA "black sites" and other spaces of extra juridical control like Guantanamo Bay are. They are paradoxically and deliberately beyond the nation-state's laws but fully under the control of that nation-state.

119. Political prisoner Marie Mason's support committee makes the same argument about why she was sentenced to twenty-two years for arson at a GMO research facility and for damage to a piece of logging equipment ("Support Marie Mason" flyer n.d.).

6. Resisting the Green Scare

1. Walter Bond, final statement to the court, Denver, Colorado, February 11, 2011.

2. Walter Bond, final statement to the court in Utah, October 3, 2011.

3. See, for example, ELF, "Move 9 Release Update: Debbie, Janine, Janet for the Move 9," *ELF Resistance Journal*, no. 2 (n.d.).

4. This statement has been attributed to Chicano activist-scholar Ernesto Vigil.

5. Gramsci 1971.

6. Rosebraugh 2002. Scott McInnis was a member of the controversial American Legislative Exchange Council, was the U.S. House of Representatives majority leader, and served as chairman of the Agriculture and Natural Resources Committee.

7. Ibid.

8. Ibid.

9. Qtd. in Pickering 2007, 62, "FAQs about the ELF," emphasis added.

10. Chris Irwin, author interview, October 29 and November 5, 2009.

11. See Scarce 2006,113. PETA founder Ingrid Newkirk has also invoked this language.

12. J Johnson, author interview, December 11, 2009.

13. Ben Rosenfeld, interview by Hollie Nyseth Brehm, November 30, 2009.

14. "It All Adds Up," *Bite Back*, no. 14 (Winter 2009): 5.

15. Walter Bond, final statement to the court, posted on NAALPO, October 13, 2011.

16. Great Grey Owl 2006.

17. Jason Miller, author interview, November 24, 2009.

18. Moynihan and Shane 2011.

19. scott crow, author interview, January 1, 2011.

20. See Dawdy 2006; Shukovsky 2004.

21. Rachel Bjork, author interview, July 30, 2009.

22. Lauren Regan, author interview, April 2, 2009.

23. From field notes and author interview with Ron "S," December 10, 2009.

24. Jude Ortiz, presentation, University of Minnesota, November 2009.

25. Cascadia Forest Alliance 2003.

26. Anonymous pamphlet on security culture, distributed at Let Live conference, June 2009.

27. A chief counsel at my university stated this during a meeting of a regular university committee. I was not present, but a colleague of mine sent me the minutes from that meeting.

28. "SHAC and a Security Culture," *Bite Back*, no. 8 (n.d.): 24. PGP stands for "pretty good privacy."

29. Cascadia Forest Alliance 2003, 23.

30. These are not their real activist names.

31. Field notes from the author and Brehm, June 2009.

32. Author's field notes from the 2009 Earth First! Round River Rendezvous.

33. "Handling Police Interrogations," *Bite Back*, no. 8 (n.d.).

34. "No Compromise Special: Snitch Protocol," *No Compromise*, no. 21 (Summer 2003): 3.

35. Great Grey Owl 2006.

36. Gangi 2007. It is reasonable to assume that the person to whom Jeff Hogg is referring is his former girlfriend, Lacey Phillabaum, who cooperated with authorities to avoid a possible thirty-year-plus sentence (Bernton and Clarridge 2006).

37. Stu Sugarman, author interview, March 24, 2009.

38. Peter Young, author interview, July 13, 2009.

39. crow, author interview, January 1, 2011.

40. Ibid.

41. Karen Coulter, author interview, October 3, 2009.

42. See Grigoriadis 2006; Williams, Munger, and Messersmith-Glavin 2013.

43. Coulter, author interview, October 3, 2009.

44. Ron "S," author interview, December 10, 2009; see also Bernton and Clarridge 2006.

45. CrimethInc. n.d.

46. Ron "S," author interview, December 10, 2009.

47. Coronado 1994.

48. Coronado 1999.

49. Ibid.

50. Jake Conroy, author interview, June 10, 2010.

51. Ibid.

52. Peter Young, panel presentation at the Let Live Conference, Portland State University, Portland, Oregon, June 2009.

53. Ibid.

54. Ibid.

55. Lauren Regan, comments at the Let Live Conference, Portland State University, June 2009.

56. Young, panel presentation at the Let Live Conference. When Rod Coronado was imprisoned as a result of the FBI's Operation Backfire, the ALF responded with a series of fur farm liberations throughout the midwestern United States, dedicating them to him. On New Year's Eve 2000, the ELF set fire to four unsold and nearly completed luxury homes on Long Island. According to the ELF communiqué, this action was a protest against sprawl that threatens farmland and forests on Long Island and benefits wealthy elite homeowners, and was a solidarity statement for several prisoners. The communiqué reads: "This action was done in solidarity with Josh Harper, Craig Rosebraugh, Jeffrey 'Free' Luers and Craig 'Critter' Marshall, Andrew Stepanian, Jeremy Parkin, and the countless other known and unknown activists who suffer persecution, interrogation, police brutality, crappy jail conditions, yet stand strong" (*ELF Resistance Journal*, no. 5).

57. North American Earth Liberation Prisoners Support Network, "Why Prisoner Support?," October 14, 2002, http://portland.indymedia.org/en/2002/10/26644.shtml.

58. Luce Guillén-Givens, presentation at the University of Minnesota, November 2009.

59. Ream 2004, 11.

60. Guillén-Givens, presentation at the University of Minnesota.

61. Stu Sugarman, presentation at Let Live Conference, Portland State University, Portland, Oregon, June 27, 2009.

62. Craig Rosebraugh, presentation at Let Live Conference, Portland State University, Portland, Oregon, June 27, 2009.

63. Jerry Vlasak, comment at Stu Sugarman, Craig Rosebraugh, and Christine Garcia's panel on grand juries, Let Live Conference, Portland State University, Portland, Oregon, June 2009.

64. Rosebraugh, comment at ibid. In November 2007, animal liberation activist Jonathan Paul pleaded guilty to one count of conspiracy and one count of arson for his role in the 1997 fire at the Cavel West horsemeat slaughterhouse in Redmond, Oregon, which destroyed the plant and led to its permanent closure. Even though no one was injured in the fire, federal prosecutors described it as a "classic case of terrorism." Paul was arrested as part of the FBI's 2005 Operation Backfire. He began serving a fifty-one-month sentence at FCI Phoenix in October 2007.

65. Sugarman, comment at ibid.

66. Josh Harper n.d.

67. Lynn 2004.

68. Ibid.

69. Nick Atwood, presentation at the Let Live Conference, Portland State University, Portland, Oregon, June 2009.

70. Jerry Vlasak, author interview, July 24, 2009.

71. North American Earth Liberation Prisoners Support Network, "Why Prisoner Support?"

72. Communication with unnamed NAALPO press officer, November 30, 2009.

73. Harper, author interview, November 9, 2009.

74. ALF Prisoners Support Group, U.K., July 2013, http://www.alfsg.org .uk/prisoner_support.html.

75. Zacher and Block's time in prison was made more trying when, in 2012, a judge ceased allowing them to correspond with each other as a result of his determination that Zacher was "unrepentant" for her crimes. Activists believe that decision was made because of a publicly released letter Zacher wrote in which she stated: "There have been some dark days in here, when the rage of being imprisoned boils over into tears of frustration—but never regret, *not ever*. Even knowing this would be the price to pay—seven years of my life here, I still would not change my actions in any way" (qtd. in Pickering 2012). The letter was made public when former ELF press officer Leslie James Pickering read it

at an event at Burning Books in Buffalo, New York, and shortly afterward the judge made the ruling.

76. Ron "S," comments on prisoner support, Walker Church, Minneapolis, fall 2009.

77. Johnson, author interview, December 11, 2009.

78. Democracy Now, "Former Black Panther Assata Shakur Added to FBI's Most Wanted Terrorists List," May 2, 2013. This announcement occurred barely two weeks after the Boston Marathon bombings, which embarrassed law enforcement officials who let one of the suspects slip through their hands years earlier.

79. See National Lawyers Guild 2013. It is fascinating to compare and contrast the BLA's kidnapping and disciplining of a heroin dealer in the African American community with the ELF/ALF's apparently willful turning a blind eye to FBI informant Jacob Ferguson's heroin addiction, which contributed to the success of the FBI's Operation Backfire. Dhoruba Bin-Wahad was a BLA leader and colleague of Shakur's who spoke plainly about this dynamic in a 1995 radio interview: "The police used the drug dealers as their network against the black underground. They would tell them, 'look, you're not dealing any drugs here unless you give us what we want.' So they would use their network of drug dealers and informants in order to get information on the Black Liberation Army. . . . We, the Black Liberation Army, the underground in the black community, had a policy of anti-heroin interdiction. . . . So we would try to identify where they hung out, where their processing places were, and we would knock them off. The most heinous drug dealers, of course, we would have to try to make an example out of. I can't go into that" (Bin-Wahad 1995).

80. Shakur 2001.

81. "Assata Shakur, Terrorist," editorial, *Washington Times*, May 10, 2013.

82. Terrall 2009.

83. Committee for the Defense of Human Rights, "The Victory Celebration Was Great!," Free the San Francisco Eight!, July 2013, http://www.freethesf8.org/.

84. San Francisco 8, "Joint statement against Torture, COINTELPRO," May 20, 2007. This statement was e-mailed by the NYC Jericho prisoner support group and signed by BPP/BLA prisoner Jalil Muntaqim, who remains incarcerated at the time of this writing.

85. Ashanti Alston, author interview, April 6, 2010.

86. Will Potter, author interview, April 2, 2009.

87. Jeff Luers, interview by Brehm, June 30, 2010.

88. Regan, author interview, April 2, 2009.

89. Ibid.

90. Enna, speech at a cross-movement solidarity gathering in Portland, Oregon, n.d.

91. Enna, author interview, June 10, 2011.

92. Claude Marks, author interview, February 25, 2010.

93. Herman Bell and Jalil Muntaqim are considered political prisoners who occupy a venerable status within the black liberation movement.

94. Coleman 2009.

95. Committee for the Defense of Human Rights, "Victory Celebration."

96. Claude Marks, author interview, February 25, 2010.

97. crow, author interview, January 1, 2011. The Young Lords was a Puerto Rican movement organization that fought for social justice and self-determination in a number of U.S. cities in the 1960s and 1970s. The Young Patriots was a radical organization run by white activists that grew out of SDS and started in Chicago, with an initial focus on supporting white migrants from Appalachia and later extended to collaborations with the BPP and the Young Lords to fight racism, police brutality, and housing discrimination.

98. Justin Goodman, author interview, December 1, 2009.

99. Alston 2006, 225.

100. Ibid., 228.

101. Daniel McGowan, *Bite Back,* no. 12, n.d.

102. Raphi, author interview, May 21, 2009. The Taft-Hartley Act of 1947 (formally known as the Labor Management Relations Act) severely restricted the power of labor unions to strike and forced them to exclude members of Communist organizations from their leadership. It was a deliberate effort by Congress to roll back key gains made in the wake of the 1935 National Labor Relations Act (also known as the Wagner Act) and to curb the power of unions that were engaged in numerous strikes at the time. The act was supported by the National Association of Manufacturers and was called the "slave labor" bill by many labor leaders.

103. Dhoruba Bin-Wahad, author interview, March 2, 2010.

104. Johnson, author interview, December 11, 2009.

105. Marks, author interview, February 25, 2010.

106. Diana Block, author interview, June 13, 2011.

107. Great Grey Owl 2006.

Conclusion

1. It is also critical to note that the process goes beyond a "mainstream/radical" binary in that, even within radical groups, splinters have occurred around total liberation politics. For example, Earth First! saw significant changes and disagreements between members during the early 1990s. For an excellent study on the consequences associated with differences between mainstream and radical movement groups, see Haines 1984.

2. Best 2009.

3. Robbins 2007.

4. Swyngedouw and Heynen 2003.

5. Crosby 2004; Diamond 1999.

6. McNeill 1977.

7. Darwin 1881.

8. Wenner 2007.

9. Bennett 2009, 108.

10. Latour 1993, 1999.

11. Seed et al. 2007.

12. Bennett 2009, 108.

13. Gould 2012; Gould, Pellow, and Schnaiberg 2008.

14. Beck 1995.

15. Luce Guillén-Givens, presentation at the University of Minnesota, November 2009.

16. Will Potter, author interview, April 2, 2009.

17. CrimethInc. Ex-Workers' Collective n.d.

18. Potter 2008.

19. At the time of this writing, the act has not passed.

20. See Goldberg 2002.

21. Mohanty 2004. I am indebted to Madison Van Oort, Jessie Pintor, Anna Popkova, Stephen Suh, Rachel Hardeman, Diana Muradova, and Kai Bosworth for their invaluable discussions of Mohanty's work in my class on social theory.

22. Sea Shepherd Conservation Society, "Nobody Talks, Everybody Walks," April 13, 2008, video clip available at http://www.youtube.com/v/-4PPjladbsg& color1=0xb1b1b1&color2=0xcfcfcf&hl=en&feature=player_embedded&fs=1.

23. Wise 2008.

24. This quote comes from British ALF press officer Robin Webb (qtd. in Best and Nocella 2004, 11). Similarly, animal liberation activists Jason and Jennifer Black write: "Animal liberation is the next logical development in moral evolution. Animal liberation builds on the most progressive ethical and political advances human beings have made in the last 200 years and carries them to their logical conclusions" (Black and Black 2004,14).

25. See Lowe 1997.

26. Phelps 2007.

27. The Principles of Environmental Justice, 1991, http://www.ejnet.org/ej/principles.html.

28. Benford 2005.

29. Goldberg 2002.

30. Guinier and Torres 2000.

31. Beck 1995.

32. White 2008.

33. Braun and Whatmore 2010.

34. Schlosberg 2007.

Bibliography

Abbey, Edward. 1975. *The Monkey Wrench Gang*. New York: HarperCollins.

Adamson, Joni. 2001. *American Indian Literature, Environmental Justice, and Ecocriticism: The Middle Place*. Tucson: University of Arizona Press.

Adamson, Joni, and Kimberly N. Ruffin, eds. 2013. *American Studies, Ecocriticism, and Citizenship: Thinking and Acting in the Local and Global Commons*. New York: Routledge.

Adamson, Joni, Mei Mei Evans, and Rachel Stein, eds. 2002. *The Environmental Justice Reader: Politics, Poetics, and Pedagogy*. Tucson: University of Arizona Press.

Adamson, Joni, and Scott Slovic. 2009. "Guest Editors' Introduction: The Shoulders We Stand On: An Introduction to Ethnicity and Ecocriticism." *MELUS* 34, no. 2 (Summer): 5–24.

Alexander, Michelle. 2010. *The New Jim Crow: Mass Incarceration in the Age of Colorblindness*. New York: New Press.

Alleyne, Richard. 2001. "Terror Tactics That Brought a Company to Its Knees." *Telegraph* (London), January 19.

Alston, Ashanti. 2006. "Mojo Workin'!" In Best and Nocella, *Igniting a Revolution: Voices in Defense of the Earth*, 224–31.

———. 2008. "Interview with Ashanti Alston, Anarchist People of Color (APOC)." *NAALPO Newsletter* 4, no. 3 (July).

Amster, Randall, Abraham DeLeon, Luis A. Fernandez, Anthony J. Nocella II, and Deric Shannon, eds. 2009. *Contemporary Anarchist Studies: An Introductory Anthology of Anarchy in the Academy*. New York: Routledge.

Arnold, Ron. 2010. *EcoTerror: The Violent Agenda to Save Nature: The World of the Unabomber*. Bellevue, Wash.: Merril Press.

Associated Press. 2008. "Latino Caucus Backing Mayor's Call for Federal Probe of Arpaio." April 18.

———. 2012. "Peru: Mine Protest Resumes." January 2.

Atwood, Nicolas. 1999. "Book Review: Long Walk to Freedom." *No Compro-mise*, no. 14 (Fall 1999): 27.

Aviv, Rachel. 2014. "A Valuable Reputation." *New Yorker*, February 10.

Bakan, Joel. 2005. *The Corporation: The Pathological Pursuit of Profit and Power*. New York: Free Press.

Bearfoot. 1994. [No title] *Earth First! Journal*, Lughnasadh (July–August): 21.

Beck, Ulrich. 1995. *Ecological Enlightenment: Essays on the Politics of the Risk Society*. Atlantic Highlands, N.J.: Humanities Press.

Bell, James. 2003. "Hayduke, Ecofeminism and Monkeywrenching." *Earth First! Journal* 23, Mabon (September–October): 8–9.

Bell, James, John, J. Cookson, Ilyse Hogue, and Patrick Reinsborough. 2002. "Direct Action at the Points of Assumption." *Earth First! Journal* 22, Samhain (November): 4–7.

Benford, Robert. 2005. "The Half-Life of the Environmental Justice Frame: Innovation, Diffusion, and Stagnation." In *Power, Justice and the Environment: A Critical Appraisal of the Environmental Justice Movement*, edited by D. N. Pellow and R. J. Brulle, 33–53. Cambridge, Mass.: MIT Press.

Bennett, Jane. 2009. *Vibrant Matter: A Political Ecology of Things*. Durham, N.C.: Duke University Press.

Bernton, Hal, and Christine Clarridge. 2006. "Earth Liberation Front Members Plead Guilty in 2001 Firebombing." *Seattle Times,* October 5.

Best, Steven. 2004. "It's War! The Escalating Battle between Activists and the Corporate-State Complex." In Best and Nocella, *Terrorists or Freedom Fighters?*, 300–339.

———. 2007. Review of *The Longest Struggle: Animal Advocacy from Pythagoras to PETA*, by Norm Phelps. *North American Animal Liberation Press Office Newsletter* 3, no. 4 (October).

———. 2009. "The Iron Cage of Movement Bureaucracy." July 28. Repub-lished on NAALPO website.

Best, Steven, and Anthony Nocella II, eds. 2004. *Terrorists or Freedom Fighters? Reflections on the Liberation of Animals*. New York: Lantern Books.

———, eds. 2006. *Igniting a Revolution: Voices in Defense of the Earth*. Oakland, Calif.: AK Press.

Bin-Wahad, Dhoruba. 1995. "Interview with Bill Weinberg." http://www.redrat .net/years/01/11apr/dhoruba_interview.htm.

Bin-Wahad, Dhoruba, Assata Shakur, and Mumia Abu-Jamal. 1993. *Still Strong, Still Black: Survivors of the War against Black Revolutionaries*. Edited by Jim Fletcher, Tanaquil Jones, and Sylvère Lotringer. New York: Semiotext(e).

Birkeland, Janis. 1993. Ecofeminism: Linking Theory and Practice." In *Eco-feminism: Women, Animals, and Nature*, edited by Greta Gaard. Philadelphia: Temple University Press.

Black, Jason, and Jennifer Black. 2004. "The Rhetorical 'Terrorist': Implications of the USA Patriot Act on Animal Liberation." In Best and Nocella, *Terrorists or Freedom Fighters?*, 288-99.

Block, Diana. 2009. *Arm the Spirit: A Woman's Journey Underground and Back.* Oakland, Calif.: AK Press.

Bloomington Defense Committee. N.d. "The FBI's Current Campaign against Activism in Indiana: The Case of Frank Ambrose," *ELF Resistance Journal,* no. 5.

Boggs, Carl. 2001. *The End of Politics: Corporate Power and the Decline of the Public Sphere.* New York: Guilford Press.

Bond, Walter. 2011. "Final Statement to the Court in Utah." Posted on NAALPO, October 13.

Bookchin, Murray. 2004. *Post-Scarcity Anarchism.* Oakland, Calif.: AK Press.

———. 2005. *The Ecology of Freedom: The Emergence and Dissolution of Hierarchy.* Oakland, Calif.: AK Press.

Bowling, John. 1998. "Protecting the Earth: An Interview with John Trudell." *Earth First! Journal* 18, Beltane (May–June): 4.

Boyce, James K. 1994. "Inequality as a Cause of Environmental Degradation." *Ecological Economics* 11 (December): 169–78.

———. 2008. "Is Inequality Bad for the Environment?" *Research in Social Problems and Public Policy* 15: 267–88.

Boykoff, Jules. 2007. *Beyond Bullets: The Suppression of Dissent in the United States.* Oakland, Calif.: AK Press.

Brady, Tim. 2013. "Patriotism and the Professor." *Minnesota* (University of Minnesota Alumni Association magazine), Summer, 27–32.

Braun, Bruce. 2002. *The Intemperate Rainforest: Nature, Culture, and Power on Canada's West Coast.* Minneapolis: University of Minnesota Press.

Braun, Bruce, and Sarah J. Whatmore, eds. 2010. *Political Matter: Technoscience, Democracy, and Public Life.* Minneapolis: University of Minnesota Press.

Breines, Wini. 1989. *Community and Organization in the New Left, 1962–1968: The Great Refusal.* New Brunswick, N.J.: Rutgers University Press.

Broughton, Zoe. 2001. "Seeing Is Believing: Cruelty to Dogs at Huntingdon Life Sciences." *Ecologist* 31, no. 2: 31–33.

Brower, David. 2006. Foreword to *Eco-Warriors: Understanding the Radical Environmental Movement,* by Rik Scarce. Walnut Creek, Calif.: Left Coast Press.

Budd, Alex. 2013. "Time Is Short: The Bolt Weevils and the Simplicity of Sabotage." Deep Green Resistance News Service. February 20.

Bullard, Robert D., and Beverly Wright. 2012. *The Wrong Complexion for Protection: How the Government Response to Disaster Endangers African American Communities.* New York: New York University Press.

Carson, Rachel. 1962. *Silent Spring.* Boston: Houghton Mifflin.

Cascadia Forest Alliance. 2003. *Disorientation Manual.* Portland, Ore.

Castree, Noel, and Bruce Braun. 1998. "The Construction of Nature and the Nature of Construction: Analytical and Political Tools for Building Survivable Futures." In *Remaking Reality: Nature at the Millennium*, edited by Bruce Braun and Noel Castree, 3–42. New York: Routledge.

Catton, William, and Riley Dunlap. 1980. "A New Ecological Paradigm for Post-exuberant Sociology." *American Behavioral Scientist* 24, no. 1 (September/October): 15–48.

Cecil-Cockwell, Malcolm. 2008. "The Earth Liberation Front: Sabotaging a Way of Life." *Epoch Journal*. Annapolis, Md. Available at http://lesliejames pickering.com/epocharticle.pdf.

Churchill, Ward. 2007. *Pacifism as Pathology: Reflections on the Role of Armed Struggle in North America*. Oakland, Calif.: AK Press.

Churchill, Ward, and Jim Vanderwall. 2001. *Agents of Repression: The FBI's Secret Wars against the Black Panther Party and the American Indian Movement*. New York: South End Press.

Cisneros, Noel. 2007. "Gap Sweatshop Videos Cause Uproar." ABC News. November 1. http://abclocal.go.com/kgo/story?section=news/business&id= 5732845.

Cole, David. 2003. *Enemy Aliens: Double Standards and Constitutional Freedoms in the War on Terrorism*. New York: New Press.

Cole, David, and James X. Dempsey. 2006. *Terror and the Constitution: Sacrificing Civil Liberties in the Name of National Security*. 3rd ed. New York: New Press.

Cole, Luke, and Sheila Foster. 2001. *From the Ground Up: Environmental Racism and the Rise of the Environmental Justice Movement*. New York: New York University Press.

Coleman, Andre. 2009. "A San Francisco Treat." *Pasadena Weekly*, July 16.

Collins, Patricia Hill. 2000. *Black Feminist Thought: Knowledge, Consciousness, and the Politics of Empowerment*. 2nd ed. New York: Routledge.

Colliver, Victoria. 1999. "Old Navy S.F. Store Opens to a Protest." *San Francisco Examiner*, October 21.

Commoner, Barry. 1971. *The Closing Circle: Nature, Man, and Technology*. New York: Alfred A. Knopf.

Condon, Scott. 2009. "Minnesota Animal Terrorism Suspect Says He's No Threat." Associated Press. December 3.

Conlin, Jennifer. 2011. "The Freedom to Choose Your Pronoun." *New York Times*, September 30.

Contention Builder. 1997. "Military Assault on Animals." Vol. 1. San Diego.

Coronado, Rodney. 1994. *Strong Hearts*, no. 1. Zine produced in prison.

———. 1995. "Spread Your Love through Action." *Militant Vegan*, no. 8 (March): 10–11.

————. 1999. [No title] *Journal of Grassroots Direct Action*, no. 1 (Summer).

————. 2000. "Reject Corrupt Government." *No Compromise*, no. 15 (Spring): 3, 14.

————. 2004/2005. "Fighting Back: Crimes of Resistance." *No Compromise*, no. 26 (Winter): 3, 8.

Coronil, Fernando. 1997. *The Magical State: Nature, Money, and Modernity in Venezuela*. Chicago: University of Chicago Press.

Coulter, Karen. 2007. *The Rule of Property*. Lanham, Md.: Apex Press.

Crenshaw, Kimberle. 1994. "Mapping the Margins: Intersectionality, Identity Politics, and Violence against Women of Color. In *The Public Nature of Private Violence: The Discovery of Domestic Abuse*, edited by Martha Albertson Fineman and Roxanne Mykitiuk, 93–118. New York: Routledge.

CrimethInc. Ex-Workers' Collective. N.d. "Green Scared? Preliminary Lessons of the Green Scare." Compiled and presented by the Civil Liberties Defense Center, Eugene, Ore.

Crosby, Alfred. 2004. *Ecological Imperialism: The Biological Expansion of Europe, 900–1900*. 2nd. ed. Cambridge: Cambridge University Press.

crow, scott. 2011. *Black Flags and Wind Mills: Hope, Anarchy, and the Common Ground Collective*. Oakland, Calif.: PM Press.

Curl, John. 2012. *For All the People: Uncovering the Hidden History of Cooperation, Cooperative Movements, and Communalism in America*. 2nd ed. Oakland, Calif.: PM Press.

Darwin, Charles. 1881. *The Formation of Vegetable Mould, through the Action of Worms, with Observations on Their Habits*. London: John Murray.

Davenport, Christian, ed. 2000. *Paths to State Repression: Human Rights Violations and Contentious Politics*. Lanham, Md.: Rowman & Littlefield.

Dawdy, Philip. 2006. "Two Sides of Beef." *Seattle Weekly*, October 9.

Dawkins, Kristin. 1999. "Unsafe in Any Seed: U.S. Obstructionism Defeats Adoption of an International Biotechnology Safety Agreement." *Multinational Monitor* 20, no. 3 (March).

Devall, William, and George Sessions. 1985. *Deep Ecology: Living as if Nature Mattered*. Salt Lake City: Gibbs M. Smith.

Diamond, Jared. 1999. *Guns, Germs, and Steel: The Fates of Human Societies*. New York: W. W. Norton.

Dinerstein, Ana C. 2003. "¡Que Se Vayan Todos! Popular Insurrection and the Asambleas Barriales in Argentina." *Bulletin of Latin American Research* 22, no. 2: 187–200.

Dorling, Daniel. 2011. *Injustice: Why Social Inequality Persists*. Bristol: Policy Press.

Doward, Jamie, and Mark Townsend. 2004. "Beauty and the Beasts." *Observer* (London), July 31.

Downey, Liam, and Susan Strife. 2010. "Inequality, Democracy, and Environment." *Organization & Environment* 23, no. 2: 155–88.

Dunlap, Riley, Frederick Buttel, Peter Dickens, and August Gijswijt, eds. 2002. *Sociological Theory and the Environment: Classical Foundations, Contemporary Insights*. Lanham, Md.: Rowman & Littlefield.

Dunlap, Riley, and K. D. Van Liere. 1978. "The 'New Environmental Paradigm.'" *Journal of Environmental Education* 9, no. 4: 10–19.

Earth First! 2000. "Road Occupations and Free States." *Direct Action Manual: Uncompromising Nonviolent Resistance in Defense of Mother Earth!* 2nd ed., 161. Tucson: DAM Collective.

Earth First! Journal. 1983. "Wilderness Preserve System." *Earth First! Journal* 3, Litha (June 21): 9.

———. 1999. "Suppression of Truth." *Earth First! Journal* 29, Mabon (September–October): 2.

———. 2002a. "Capitalist Society Sucks." *Earth First! Journal* 22, Samhain (November–December): 21.

———. 2002b. "For a Better World We All." *Earth First! Journal* 22, Samhain (November–December): 22–23.

———. 2003a. "CFD and Fall Creek Part Ways." *Earth First! Journal* 23, Mabon (2003): 12.

———. 2003b. "Massasauga EF! Confronts Water Tyrants." *Earth First! Journal* 23, Mabon (September–October): 27.

———. 2004. "Global Days of Action against Ecocide & Empire." *Earth First! Journal* 24, Beltane (May–June): 48.

———. 2009. "Prisoners in the Struggle, Support Them!" *Earth First! Journal* 29, Lughnasadh (July–August): 27–28.

Earth First! Journal Editorial Collective. 2002. "Round River Rendezvous 2002." *Earth First! Journal* 22, Lughnasadh (August–September): 12–13.

———. 2007. "EF! Anti-Oppression Policy." *Earth First! Journal* 27, Mabon (September–October): 13.

———. 2013. "Deep Green Transphobia." *Earth First! Journal* 33, Beltane (May 15).

Earth First! Organizers' Conference Organizing Committee. "International Earth First! Organizers' Conference and Winter Rendezvous." *Earth First! Journal* 26, Brigid (January–February): 41.

Eaton, Leonard. 1888. Statement to the American Humane Association, 12th Annual Report. Annual Meeting of the AHA, October 17–19. Published in 1889, Eagle Book Company.

Ecofeminist Front. 2003. "Moving beyond a History of Corsets and Clearcuts: Womyn's Occupation at Straw Devil Timber Sale." *Earth First! Journal* 23, Mabon (October): 12.

Eyerman, Ron, and Andrew Jamison. 1991. *Social Movements: A Cognitive Approach*. University Park: Pennsylvania State University Press.

Faber, Daniel. 1998. *The Struggle for Ecological Democracy: Environmental Justice Movements in the United States.* New York: Guilford Press.

———. 2008. *Capitalizing on Environmental Justice: The Polluter-Industrial Complex in the Age of Globalization.* Lanham, Md.: Rowman & Littlefield.

Featherstone, Liza. 2005. "Wal-Mart: Rise of the Goliath." *Multinational Monitor* 26, no. 1 (January/February).

Ferguson, Roderick. 2004. *Aberrations in Black.* Minneapolis: University of Minnesota Press.

Fischmann, Benjamin. 2006. "Binding Corporations to Human Rights Norms through Public Law Settlement." *New York University Law Review* 81, no. 4: 1433–68.

Fischer, Dana. 2006. "Bringing the Material Back In: Understanding the U.S. Position on Climate Change." *Sociological Forum* 21, no. 3 (September): 467–94.

Foreman, Dave. 1987. "Deep Ecology: Vision, Passion, Courage." *Earth First! Journal* 27, Eostar (March 20).

———. 1989. "Some Thoughts on True Believers, Intolerance, Diversity, and Ed Abbey." *Earth First! Journal* 9, Beltane (May): 20.

Foster, John Bellamy. 1999. "Marx's Theory of Metabolic Rift: Classical Foundations for Environmental Sociology." *American Journal of Sociology* 105, no. 2: 366–405.

———. 2000. *Marx's Ecology: Materialism and Nature.* New York: Monthly Review Press.

Foster, John Bellamy, Brett Clark, and Richard York. 2010. *The Ecological Rift: Capitalism's War on the Earth.* New York: Monthly Review Press.

Foucault, Michel. 1995. *Discipline and Punish: The Birth of the Prison.* Translated by Alan Sheridan. New York: Vintage.

———. 1990. *The History of Sexuality: An Introduction.* Translated by Robert Hurley. Vol. 1. New York: Vintage.

Francione, Gary, and Robert Gardner. 2010. *The Animal Rights Debate: Abolition or Regulation?* New York: Columbia University Press.

Freudenburg, William, Scott Frickel, and Robert Gramling. 1995. "Beyond the Society/Nature Divide: Learning to Think about a Mountain." *Sociological Forum* 10, no. 3: 361–92.

Gaard, Greta. 1993. "Living Interconnections with Animals and Nature." In *Ecofeminism: Women, Animals, and Nature,* edited by Greta Gaard, 1–12. Philadelphia: Temple University Press.

———. 2004. "Toward a Queer Ecofeminism." In *New Perspectives on Environmental Justice: Gender, Sexuality, and Activism,* edited by Rachel Stein, 21–44. New Brunswick, N.J.: Rutgers University Press.

Gangi, Marlena. 2007. "Some Sort of Anti-Snitch: An Interview with Green Scare Grand Jury Resister Jeff Hoff." *Earth First! Journal* 27, Eostar (March–April): 40–41.

Garland, Davey. 2006. "To Cast a Giant Shadow: Revolutionary Ecology and Its Practical Implementation through the Earth Liberation Front." In Best and Nocella, *Igniting a Revolution*, 59–70.

Gastone, Max. 2005. "The Rise and Rise of the Anti-Vivisectionists." *Earth First! Journal* 25, Samhain/Yule (November–December): 28–29.

Gedicks, Al. 1993. *The New Resource Wars: Native and Environmental Struggles against Multinational Corporations*. New York: South End Press.

———. 2001. *Resource Rebels: Native Challenges to Mining and Oil Corporations*. New York: South End Press.

Geronimus, Arline T., et al. 1996. "Excess Mortality among Blacks and Whites in the United States." *New England Journal of Medicine* 335, no. 21 (November 21) 1552–58.

Gibson-Graham, J. K. 2006. *A Postcapitalist Politics*. Minneapolis: University of Minnesota Press.

Gil, Steve. "A Century of Inspiration: The Legacy of Mardy Murie, A Legacy of Love." *Earth First! Journal* 22, Lughnasadh (August–September 2002): 35.

Glick, Brian. 1999. *War at Home: Covert Action against U.S. Activists*. New York: South End Press.

Goldberg, David Theo. 2002. *The Racial State*. Malden, Mass.: Blackwell.

Goldenberg, Suzanne. 2009. "Activist or Terrorist? Mild-Mannered Eco-militant Serving 22 Years for Arson." *Guardian* (Manchester), March 24.

Goldman, Michael, and Rachel Schurman. 2000. "Closing the 'Great Divide': New Social Theory on Society and Nature." *Annual Review of Sociology* 26:563–84.

Gottlieb, Robert. 1994. *Forcing the Spring: The Transformation of the American Environmental Movement*. Washington, D.C.: Island Press.

Gould, Kenneth A. 2012. "Unsustainable Science in the Treadmill of Production." Paper presented at the Annual Meetings of the American Sociological Association, Denver, August 17–20.

Gould, Kenneth A., David N. Pellow, and Allan Schnaiberg. 2008. *The Treadmill of Production: Injustice and Unsustainability in the Global Economy*. Boulder, Colo.: Paradigm.

Graeber, David. 2004. *Fragments of an Anarchist Anthropology*. Chicago: Prickly Paradigm Press.

Gramsci, Antonio. 1971. *Selections from the Prison Notebooks of Antonio Gramsci*. Edited and translated by Quintin Hoare and Geoffrey Nowell Smith. New York: International.

Great Grey Owl. 2006. "The Political Becomes Personal." *Earth First! Journal* 26, Samhain/Yule (November–December): 24–26.

Greenhouse, Steven. 2000. Nike's Chief Cancels a Gift over Monitor of Sweatshops. *New York Times*, April 25.

Grigoriadis, Vanessa. 2006. "The Rise and Fall of the Eco-Radical Underground." *Rolling Stone*, August 10.

Gualtieri, Sarah M. A. 2009. *Between Arab and White: Race and Ethnicity in the Early Syrian American Diaspora.* Berkeley: University of California Press.

Guha, Ramachandra. 1989. "Radical American Environmentalism and Wilderness Preservation: A Third World Critique." *Environmental Ethics* 11, no. 1: 71–83.

Guillén-Givens, Luce, Layne Mullett, and Sarah Small. 2013. "From Repression to Resistance: Notes on Combating Counterinsurgency." *Life during War: Resisting Counterinsurgency*, edited by Kristian Williams, Will Munger, and Lara Messersmith-Glavin, 383–418. Oakland, Calif.: AK Press.

Guinier, Lani, and Gerald Torres. 2003. *The Miner's Canary: Enlisting Race, Resisting Power, Transforming Democracy.* Cambridge, Mass.: Harvard University Press.

Haines, Herbert. 1984. "Black Radicalization and Funding Civil Rights, 1957–1970." *Social Problems* 32, no. 1 (October): 31–43.

Haluza-DeLay, Randolph, and Heather Fernhout. 2011. "Sustainability and Social Inclusion? Examining the Frames of Canadian English-Speaking Environmental Movement Organizations." *Local Environment* 16, no. 7: 727–45.

Hamilton, Mike. 2001. "Sweetener Slaughter: 12,800 Animals Die for No-Calorie Pills." *Sunday Mirror* (London), August 5.

Haraway, Donna J. 1991. *Simians, Cyborgs, and Women: The Reinvention of Nature.* New York: Routledge.

Hari, Johann. 2010. "The Wrong Kind of Green." *Nation.* March 4.

Harper, Josh. 2004. "The SHAC 7." *Bite Back*, no. 8: 23.

———. N.d. "Portland Grand Jury Harassment Ends for Now." *ELF Resistance Journal*, no. 5.

Harris, Cheryl. 1993. "Whiteness as Property." *Harvard Law Review* 106, no. 8: 1707–91.

Hartmann, Thom. 2010. *Unequal Protection: How Corporations Became "People"—and How You Can Fight Back.* 2nd ed. San Francisco: Berrett-Koehler.

Harvey, David. 1996. *Justice, Nature, and the Geography of Difference.* Malden, Mass.: Blackwell.

Hayes, Erin. 1999. "Seeds of Controversy." ABC News. http://abcnews.go.com, August 2.

Heynen, Nik, Maria Kaika, and Erik Swyngedouw, eds. 2006. *In the Nature of Cities: Urban Political Ecology and the Politics of Urban Metabolism.* New York: Routledge.

Hing, Bill Ong. 2004. *Defining America through Immigration Policy.* Philadelphia: Temple University Press.

Hoffman, Hank. 2001. "To The Extreme: FBI Testimony Provokes Fear of New CoIntelPro." *In These Times*, October 1.

Hooks, Gregory, and Chad L. Smith. 2004. "The Treadmill of Destruction: National Sacrifice Areas and Native Americans." *American Sociological Review* 69, no. 4: 558–76.

Horsman, Reginald. 1981. *Race and Manifest Destiny: The Origins of American Racial Anglo-Saxonism*. Cambridge, Mass.: Harvard University Press.

Humphrey, Craig, Tammy Lewis, and Frederick Buttel. 2002. *Environment, Energy, and Society: A New Synthesis*. Belmont, Calif.: Wadsworth.

Ian. 1999. "Minnehaha Free State Campaign Continues." *No Compromise*, no. 14 (Fall): 7.

Irwin, Chris. 2002. "Kicking the KKK out of Katuah." *Earth First! Journal* 22, Beltane (May–June): 17.

———. 2007. "Where Have All the Rednecks Gone? Transsexuals and the Death of the Earth First! *Counterpunch*, October 17.

Jacoby, Karl. 2003. *Crimes against Nature: Squatters, Poachers, Thieves, and the Hidden History of American Conservation*. Berkeley: University of California Press.

Jarboe, James F. 2002. "The Threat of Eco-terrorism." Testimony before the House Resources Committee, Subcommittee on Forests and Forest Health. February 12. http://www.fbi.gov/news/testimony/the-threat-of-eco-terrorism.

Jasper, James, and Dorothy Nelkin. 1991. *The Animal Rights Crusade: The Growth of a Moral Protest*. New York: Free Press.

Jaynes, Mike. 2009. "Animal Defense and Earth Defense: Compassionate Bed-fellows." *Earth First! Journal* 29, Eostar: 20–21.

Jensen, Derrick. 2006a. *Endgame*. Vol. 1: *The Problem of Civilization*. New York: Seven Stories Press.

———. 2006b. *Endgame*. Vol. 2: *Resistance.* New York: Seven Stories Press.

Johnson, Carrie, and Margot Williams. 2011. "'Guantanamo North': Inside Secretive U.S. Prisons." National Public Radio. March 3.

jones, pattrice. 2004. "Mothers with Monkeywrenches: Feminist Imperatives and the ALF." In Best and Nocella, *Terrorists or Freedom Fighters?*, 137–56.

———. 2005. "Violation & Liberation: Grassroots Animal Rights Activists Take on Sexual Assault." *Earth First! Journal* 25, Mabon (September– October): 22–25.

Kant, Immanuel. 1970. *Kant's Political Writings*. Edited and with an introduction by Hans Reiss. Translated by H. B. Nisbet. Cambridge: Cambridge University Press.

Keifer, Max, and Scott Deitchman 1998. Technical Assistance Report 98–0061–2687, Yerkes Primate Center. April. Washington, D.C.: National Institute for Occupational Safety and Health.

Kelley, Robyn. 2003. *Freedom Dreams: The Black Radical Imagination*. Boston: Beacon Press.

Kheel, Marti. 2006. "Direct Action and the Heroic Ideal: An Ecofeminist Critique." In Best and Nocella, *Igniting a Revolution*, 306–18.

King, Martin Luther. 1963. "Letter from a Birmingham Jail." Open letter. April 16.

King, Ynestra. 1989. "The Ecology of Feminism and the Feminism of Ecology." In *Healing the Wounds: The Promise of Ecofeminism,* edited by Judith Plant, 328–38. Philadelphia: New Society.

Kjonaas, Kevin. 2004. "Bricks and Bullhorns." In Best and Nocella, *Terrorists or Freedom Fighters?,* 263–71.

Kolata, Gina. 1998. "New Jersey Lab Is Fined over Care of Animals." *New York Times,* April 16.

Kolodny, Annette. 2007. "Rethinking the 'Ecological Indian': A Penobscot Precursor." *ISLE: Interdisciplinary Studies in Literature and Environment* 14, no. 1 (Winter): 1–23.

Kolowich, Steve. 2010. "Virtual Sit-in." *Inside Higher Ed,* April 9.

Krausch, Meghan. 2012. "From Marginalization to Utopianism in Post-2001 Buenos Aires." Latin American Studies Association Congress, panel session, San Francisco, May 23–26.

Krieger, Nancy, and Stephen Sidney. 1996. "Racial Discrimination and Blood Pressure: The CARDIA Study of Young Black and White Adults." *American Journal of Public Health* 86, no. 10 (October): 1370–78.

Krill, Jen. 2009. "Intercom Wrenching." *Earth First! Journal* 25, Mabon (September–October).

Kropotkin, Petr. 2008. *Mutual Aid: A Factor of Evolution.* Hong Kong: Forgotten Books.

Kuipers, Dean. 2009. *Operation Bite Back: Rod Coronado's War to Save American Wilderness.* New York: Bloomsbury.

LaDuke, Winona. 2008. *All Our Relations: Native Struggles for Land and Life.* New York: South End Press.

Lahar, Stephanie. 1991. "Ecofeminist Theory and Grassroots Politics." *Hypatia* 6, no. 1 (Spring): 28–45.

Lambert, Jenny. 2004. "Revolutionary Cells' Animal Liberation Brigade Targets HLS Clients." *No Compromise,* no. 23 (Spring): 18.

Latour, Bruno. 1993. *We Have Never Been Modern.* Cambridge, Mass.: Harvard University Press.

———. 1999. *Pandora's Hope: Essays on the Reality of Science Studies.* Cambridge, Mass.: Harvard University Press.

Lawrence, Ken. 2006. *The New State Repression.* Rept., Portland, Ore.: Tarantula.

Leopold, Aldo. 1949. *A Sand County Almanac.* New York: Oxford University Press.

Lerner, Steve. 2006. *Diamond: A Struggle for Environmental Justice in Louisiana's Chemical Corridor.* Cambridge, Mass.: MIT Press.

Lewddite Uprising. 2011. "TWAC 2011 Report Back." *Earth First! Journal* 31 Mabone (September–October): 42.

Lipsitz, George. 2006. *The Possessive Investment in Whiteness: How White People Profit from Identity Politics.* Philadelphia: Temple University Press.

Lofland, John, David A. Snow, Leon Anderson, and Lyn H. Lofland. 2005. *Analyzing Social Settings: A Guide to Qualitative Observation and Analysis*. 4th ed. Belmont, Calif.: Wadsworth/Thomson Learning.

Longshanks, Strider. 2003. "Wilding the Revolution." *Earth First! Journal* 23, Mabon (September–October): 6–7.

Losey, John E., Linda S. Rayor, Maureen E. Carter. 1999. "Transgenic Pollen Harms Monarch Larvae." *Nature* 399 (May): 214.

Losure, Maria. 2002. *Our Way or the Highway: Inside the Minnehaha Free State*. Minneapolis: University of Minnesota Press.

Lowe, Lisa. 1997. *Immigrant Acts: On Asian American Cultural Politics*. Durham, N.C.: Duke University Press.

Luibheid, Eithne. 2002. *Entry Denied: Controlling Sexuality at the Border*. Minneapolis: University of Minnesota Press.

Lush, Tamara. 2007. "FTAA Settlement Reached." *Miami New Times*, October 4.

Lynn, Gina. 2004. "Gina Lynn: Just Say NO to Grand Juries." *No Compromise*, no. 25 (Fall): 8–10.

Maag, Chris. 2006. "America's #1 Threat (and His Little Dog, Too)." *Mother Jones*, January/February, 19.

MacDougal, Kent. 2009. "Vengeful Animals Are Getting Even." *Earth First! Journal* 29, Brigid (January–February): 25.

MacGregor, Sherilyn. 2006. *Beyond Mothering Earth: Ecological Citizenship and the Politics of Care*. Vancouver: UBC Press.

Mack-Canty, Colleen. 2004. "Third-Wave Feminism and the Need to Reweave the Nature/Culture Duality." *NWSA Journal* 16, no. 3 (Autumn): 154–79.

Magdalinious. 2009. "Direct Action?" *Earth First! Journal* 29, Eostar (March–April): 18.

Mander, Jerry. 1999. *In the Absence of the Sacred: The Failure of Technology & the Survival of the Indian Nations*. Gloucester, Mass.: Peter Smith.

Manes, Christopher. 1990. *Green Rage: Radical Environmentalism and the Unmaking of Civilization*. Boston: Little, Brown.

Marshall, Robert. 1930. "The Problem of Wilderness." *Scientific Monthly* 30 (February): 141–48.

Martinez, Elizabeth. 1998. "What Is White Supremacy?" Definition from the Challenging White Supremacy Workshops Conference. San Francisco.

Marx, Karl. 1974. *Early Writings*. New York: Vintage.

———. 1976. *Capital*. Vol. 1. New York: Vintage.

Marx, Karl, and Friedrich Engels. 1998. *The German Ideology, including Theses on Feuerbach*. Amherst, N.Y.: Prometheus Books.

Mason, Jim. 2005. *An Unnatural Order: Roots of Our Destruction of Nature*. New York: Lantern Books.

———. 2006. "The Animal Question." In Best and Nocella, *Igniting a Revolution*, 180–85.

McClintock, Anne. 1995. *Imperial Leather: Race, Gender, and Sexuality in the Colonial Contest.* New York: Routledge.

McCully, Patrick. 2001. *Silenced Rivers: The Ecology and Politics of Large Dams.* London: Zed Books.

McGillivary, Brian. 2008. "Entire Board of Sierra Club Chapter Resigns." *Traverse City (Mich.) Record Eagle,* July 12.

McGlynn, Ann. 2010. "Animal Rights Activist Released from Custody." *Sioux City (Iowa) Journal,* March 18.

McNeill, William. 1977. *Plagues and People.* New York: Anchor Books.

McVeigh, Karen. 2007. "Third Death in a Year in Indian Factory That Supplies Gap." *Guardian* (Manchester), October 14.

Meeropol, Rachel, ed. 2005. *America's Disappeared: Secret Imprisonment, Detainees, and the "War on Terror."* New York: Seven Stories Press.

Mellor, Mary. 1992. *Breaking the Boundaries: Towards a Feminist Green Socialism.* London: Virago Press.

Merchant, Carolyn. 1980. *The Death of Nature: Women, Ecology, and the Scientific Revolution.* New York: HarperCollins.

———. 2005. *Radical Ecology: The Search for a Livable World.* 2nd ed. New York: Routledge.

Meyler, Deanna. 2003. "Understanding Diversity in the Radical Environmental Movement." Ph.D. diss., University of Nebraska–Lincoln.

Mies, Maria, and Vandana Shiva. 1993. *Ecofeminism.* London: Zed Books.

Mies, Maria, and Veronika Bennholdt-Thomsen. 1999. *The Subsistence Perspective: Beyond the Globalized Economy.* London: Zed Books.

Milbrath, Lester. 1984. *Environmentalists: Vanguard for a New Society.* Albany: State University of New York Press.

Mills, Charles W. 1999. *The Racial Contract.* Ithaca, N.Y.: Cornell University Press.

Mohai, Paul. 1990. "Black Environmentalism." *Social Science Quarterly* 71, no. 4: 744–65.

Mohanty, Chandra Talpade. 2004. *Feminism without Borders: Decolonizing Theory, Practicing Solidarity.* Durham, N.C.: Duke University Press.

Molland, Noel. 2006. "A Spark That Ignited a Flame: The Evolution of the Earth Liberation Front." In Best and Nocella, *Igniting a Revolution,* 47–58.

Moynihan, Colin, and Scott Shane. 2011. "For Anarchist, Details of Life as F.B.I. Target." *New York Times,* May 28.

Muir, John. 1907. "The Tuolumne Yosemite in Danger." *Outlook* 87, no. 9: 486–89.

———. 1988. *My First Summer in the Sierra.* San Francisco: Sierra Club Books. First published 1911 by Houghton Mifflin.

Murphy, Raymond. 1995. "Sociology As If Nature Did Not Matter: An Ecological Critique." *British Journal of Sociology* 46, no. 4 (December): 688–707.

Murphy-Ellis, Emma. 2011. "My Name Is Emma Murphy-Ellis and I Support Sabotage." *Earth First! Journal* 31, Beltane (May–June): 40–41.

Multinational Monitor. 2004. "Thailand Stays Biotech Free." *Multinational Monitor* 25, no. 9 (September 1).

Naess, Arne. 1973. "The Shallow and the Deep, Long-Range Ecology Movement." *Inquiry* 16:95–100.

Nathans, Aaron. 2003. "Love the Worker, Not the Union, A Store Says as Some Organize." *New York Times*, May 24.

National Lawyers Guild. 2013. "National Lawyers Guild Urges FBI to Respect Political Asylum Status of Assata Shakur." http://www.nlg.org.

Nedelsky, Jennifer. 1990. *Private Property and the Limits of American Constitutionalism: The Madisonian Framework and Its Legacy.* Chicago: University of Chicago Press.

Ngai, Mai. 2004. *Impossible Subjects: Illegal Aliens and the Making of Modern America.* Princeton, N.J.: Princeton University Press.

Nixon, Ron. 2013. "U.S. Postal Service Logging All Mail for Law Enforcement." *New York Times*, July 3.

Nocella, Anthony J., II, Steven Best, and Peter McLaren, eds. 2010. *Academic Repression: Reflections from the Academic Industrial Complex.* Oakland, Calif.: AK Press.

Nordlee, Julie, Steve Taylor, Jeffrey Townsend, Laurie Thomas, and Robert Bush. 1996. "Identification of a Brazil-Nut Allergen in Transgenic Soybeans." *New England Journal of Medicine* 334, no. 11 (March 14): 688–92.

Obama, Barack. 2005. "Statement of Senator Barack Obama." U.S. Senate Committee on Environment and Public Works. Oversight Hearing on Eco-terrorism, Specifically Examining the Earth Liberation Front ("ELF") and the Animal Liberation Front ("ALF"). May 18.

O'Connor, James. 1994. "Is Sustainable Capitalism Possible?" In *Is Capitalism Sustainable? Political Economy and the Politics of Ecology*, edited by Martin O'Connor, 152–75. New York: Guilford Press.

Omi, Michael, and Howard Winant. 1994. *Racial Formation in the United States: From the 1960s to the 1990s.* New York: Routledge.

Ornelas, Lauren. 2009. "Engaging Ethnic Minorities." Presentation at Animal Rights Conference. Los Angeles.

Panagioti. 2006. "Down with Borders, Up with Spring!" *Earth First! Journal* 26, Lughnasadh (July–August): 8–11.

Park, Lisa Sun-Hee, and David Naguib Pellow. 2011. *The Slums of Aspen: The War on Immigrants in America's Eden.* New York: New York University Press.

Pateman, Carol. 1988. *The Sexual Contract.* Palo Alto, Calif.: Stanford University Press.

Patterson, Charles. 2002. *Eternal Treblinka: Our Treatment of Animals and the Holocaust.* New York: Lantern Books.

Pellow, David Naguib, and Lisa Sun-Hee Park. 2002. *The Silicon Valley of Dreams: Environmental Injustice, Immigrant Workers, and the High-Tech Global Economy*. New York: New York University Press.

Peluso, Nancy. 1992. *Rich Forests, Poor People: Resource Control and Resistance in Java*. Berkeley: University of California Press.

People of Color Caucus. 2008. "We See Color and It Fucking Matters." *Earth First! Journal* 28, Beltane (May–June): 11.

Petermann, Anne. "Tales of a Recovering Misanthrope." *Earth First! Journal* 29, Litha (June–July 1999): 3.

Phelps, Norm. 2007. *The Longest Struggle: Animal Advocacy from Pythagoras to PETA*. New York: Lantern Books.

Pickering, Leslie James. 2002. "Burn, Baby, Burn: The ELF: Terrorists or Defenders of the Planet?" Interview with Guerrilla News Network. Spring.

———. 2007. *The Earth Liberation Front: 1997–2002*. Minneapolis: Arissa Media Group.

———, ed. 2011. *Conspiracy to Riot in Furtherance of Terrorism: The Collective Autobiography of the RNC 8*. Minneapolis: Arissa Media Group.

———. 2012. "Earth Liberation Political Prisoners Sadie and Exile Punished for Being 'Unrepentant.'" *Earth First! Newswire*, March 28.

Plows, Alexandra, Derek Wall, and Brian Doherty. 2004. "Covert Repertoires: Ecotage in the U.K." *Social Movement Studies* 3, no. 2 (October): 199–221.

Plumwood, Val. 1993. *Feminism and the Mastery of Nature*. New York: Routledge.

———. 1994. "The Ecopolitics Debate and the Politics of Nature." In *Ecological Feminism*, edited by Karen J. Warren. New York: Routledge.

Polletta, Francesca. 2002. *Freedom Is an Endless Meeting: Democracy in American Social Movements*. Chicago: University of Chicago Press.

Potter, Will. 2008. "FBI Looking for Informants to Infiltrate Vegan Potlucks." Green Is the New Red, May 15. http://www.greenisthenewred.com/blog/.

———. 2010. "'Jihad, Crips, Extreme Animal-Rights Activists, It's All the Same,' Says Homeland Security Official." Green Is the New Red, June 15. http://www.greenisthenewred.com/blog/.

———. 2011a. *Green Is the New Red: An Insider's Account of a Social Movement under Siege*. San Francisco: City Lights.

———. 2011b. "Marie Mason Is Being Denied Visitors and Mail in a Special Prison Unit." Green Is the New Red, March 16. http://www.greenisthenew red.com/blog/.

Pring, George W., and Penelope Canan. 1996. *SLAPPs: Getting Sued for Speaking Out*. Philadelphia: Temple University Press.

Rameau, Max. 2008. *Take Back the Land: Land, Gentrification and the Umoja Village Shantytown*. Miami: Nia Interactive Press.

Ramnath, Maia. 2011. *Decolonizing Anarchism*. Oakland, Calif.: AK Press.

Rashke, Richard L., and Kate Bronfenbrenner. 2000. *The Killing of Karen Silkwood: The Story behind the Kerr-McGee Plutonium Case*. 2nd ed. Ithaca, N.Y.: ILR Press.

Ream, Tim. 2004. "FBI's Most Wanted Arrested in Canada." *Earth First! Journal* 24, Beltane (May–June): 11.

Reed, T. V. 2005. *The Art of Protest: Culture and Activism from the Civil Rights Movement to the Streets of Seattle*. Minneapolis: University of Minnesota Press.

Regan, Lauren. 2009. "Silencing the Sentenced: Daniel McGowan and Little Guantanamo." *Earth First! Journal* 29, Beltane (May–June): 24.

Regan, Tom. 2004. *The Case for Animal Rights*. Berkeley: University of California Press.

———. 2006. *Defending Animal Rights*. Urbana: University of Illinois Press.

Reinsborough, Patrick. 2003. "Busting Up Biotech." *Earth First! Journal* 23, Mabon (September–October): 33-34.

Release and Restitution for Chimpanzees in U.S. Laboratories (Project R&R). N.d. "Yerkes National Primate Research Center." http://www.releasechimps.org/research/facility/yerkes-national#.

Renzetti, Claire M., and Jeffrey Edleson. 2008. *Encyclopedia of Interpersonal Violence*. Vol. 1. Thousand Oaks, Calif.: Sage.

Revkin, Andrew. 2004. *The Burning Season: The Murder of Chico Mendes and the Fight for the Amazon Rainforest*. Washington, D.C.: Island Press.

Ridgeway, James. 2008. "Black Ops, Green Groups." *Mother Jones*, April 11.

Robbins, Paul. 2007. *Lawn People: How Grasses, Weeds, and Chemicals Make Us Who We Are*. Philadelphia: Temple University Press.

Robnett, Belinda. 2000. *How Long? How Long? African-American Women in the Struggle for Civil Rights*. New York: Oxford University Press.

Rodriguez, Dylan. 2006. *Forced Passages: Imprisoned Radical Intellectuals and the U.S. Prison Regime*. Minneapolis: University of Minnesota Press.

Roediger, David. 2006. *Working toward Whiteness: How America's Immigrants Became White: The Strange Journey from Ellis Island to the Suburbs*. New York: Basic Books.

Rosebraugh, Craig. 2002. "Testimony Submitted to the U.S. House Subcommittee on Forests and Forest Health Hearing on 'Ecoterrorism.'" Washington, D.C., February 12.

———. 2004a. *Burning Rage of a Dying Planet: Speaking for the Earth Liberation Front*. New York: Lantern Books.

———. 2004b. *The Logic of Political Violence: Lessons in Reform and Revolution*. Minneapolis: Arissa Media Group.

———. N.d. "Ideological Ranting from Rosebraugh," *ELF Resistance Journal*, no. 2:10.

Rosenfeld, Ben. 2010. "Team STUFITT." *Earth First! Journal* 30, Beltane (May–June): 5.

Santa Anna, Otto. 2002. *Brown Tide Rising: Metaphors of Latinos in Contemporary American Public Discourse*. Austin: University of Texas Press.

Scarce, Rik. 2005. *Contempt of Court: A Scholar's Battle for Free Speech from Behind Bars*. Lanham, Md.: AltaMira Press.

———. 2006. *Eco-Warriors: Understanding the Radical Environmental Movement*. Walnut Creek, Calif.: Left Coast Press.

Schlesinger, Arthur M., Jr. 2004. *The Imperial Presidency*. New York: Mariner Press.

Schlosberg, David. 2007. *Defining Environmental Justice: Theories, Movements, and Nature*. New York: Oxford University Press.

Schlosser, Eric. 2005. *Fast Food Nation: The Dark Side of the All-American Meal*. New York: Harper Perennial.

Schnaiberg, Allan. 1980. *The Environment: From Surplus to Scarcity*. New York: Oxford University Press.

Schnaiberg, Allan, and Kenneth Alan Gould. 2000. *Environment and Society: The Enduring Conflict*. Caldwell, N.J.: Blackburn Press.

Schurman, Rachel, and William Munro. 2010. *Fighting for the Future of Food: Activists versus Agribusiness in the Struggle over Biotechnology*. Minneapolis: University of Minnesota Press.

Schuster, Henry. 2005. "Domestic Terror: Who's Most Dangerous?" CNN.com., August 24. http://www.cnn.com/2005/US/08/24/schuster.column/index.html.

Scott, James. 2009. *The Art of Not-Being Governed: An Anarchist History of Upland Southeast Asia*. New Haven, Conn.: Yale University Press.

Seager, Joni. 1994. *Earth Follies: Coming to Feminist Terms with the Global Environmental Crisis*. New York: Routledge.

Seed, John, Joanna Macy, Pat Fleming, and Arne Naess. 2007. *Thinking Like a Mountain: Towards a Council of All Beings*. Gabriola Island, B.C.: New Catalyst Books.

Seshadri, Kalpana Rahita. 2012. *HumAnimal: Race, Law, Language*. Minneapolis: University of Minnesota Press.

Shakur, Assata. 2001. *Assata: An Autobiography*. Chicago: Lawrence Hill Books.

Shapiro, Paul. 2000. "Anti-Ringling Campaign Hits Another Landmark." *No Compromise*, no. 16 (Summer): 6.

———. 2007. "Arizona Makes History for Farm Animals." *Satya*, April/May. http://www.satyamag.com/apr07/shapiro.html.

Shearer, Christine. 2011. *Kivalina: A Climate Change Story*. Chicago: Haymarket Books.

Shiva, Vandana. 2013. "Seeds of Suicide." *Asian Age* (Delhi), April 4.

Shukovsky, Paul. 2004. "Pro-animal Activist Accused of Terrorism." *Seattle Post-Intelligencer*, May 26.

Sierra Club. 2009. "Yep. We're Too White." *Sierra Club Insider*, July 28.

Singer, Peter. 1975. *Animal Liberation: A New Ethics for Our Treatment of Animals*. New York: Avon Books.

Smith, Andrea. 2005. *Conquest: Sexual Violence and American Indian Genocide*. New York: South End Press.

Smith, Mick. 2011. *Against Ecological Sovereignty: Ethics, Biopolitics, and Saving the Natural World*. Minneapolis: University of Minnesota Press.

Smithers, Rebecca, and Randeep Ramesh. 2008. "Charity Planning Banana Republic Protest over Employees' Plight." *Guardian* (Manchester), March 19.

Stein, Rachel, ed. 2004. *New Perspectives on Environmental Justice: Gender, Sexuality, and Activism*. New Brunswick, N.J.: Rutgers University Press.

Steingraber, Sandra. 1997. *Living Downstream: An Ecologist Looks at Cancer and the Environment*. Boston: Addison-Wesley.

Sturgeon, Noel. 1997a. *Ecofeminist Natures: Race, Gender, Feminist Theory, and Political Action*. New York: Routledge.

———. 1997b. "The Nature of Race: Discourses of Racial Difference in Ecofeminism." In Warren, *Ecofeminism*, 260–78.

Swyngedouw, Erik, and Nikolas C. Heynen. 2003. "Urban Political Ecology, Justice, and the Politics of Scale." *Antipode* 35, no. 5 (November): 898–918.

Tara the Sea Elf. 1996. "The Earth Liberation Front." *Earth First! Journal* 16, Lughnasadh (September 21): 18.

Taylor, Bron Raymond, ed. 1995. *Ecological Resistance Movements: The Global Emergence of Radical and Popular Environmentalism*. Albany: State University of New York Press.

Taylor, Dorceta. 1997. "Women of Color, Environmental Justice, and Ecofeminism." In Warren, *Ecofeminism*, 38–70.

———. 2000. "The Rise of the Environmental Justice Paradigm: Injustice Framing and the Social Construction of Environmental Discourses." *American Behavioral Scientist* 43, no 4 (January): 508–80.

Terrall, Ben. 2009. "The Trial of the San Francisco 8." *San Francisco Bay Guardian*, May 4.

Thomas, Dylan. 2002. "Animal Rights Advocates and University Researchers Clash." *Minnesota Daily* (Minneapolis), November 11.

Tocqueville, Alexis de. 2010. *Democracy in America*. New York: Signet Classics.

Torres, Bob. 2007. *Making a Killing: The Political Economy of Animal Rights*. Oakland, Calif.: AK Press.

Trill, Still. "SHAC Is Winning." *Earth First! Journal* 29, Lughnasadh (July–August 2009): 27.

Triple C. 2007. "EF! Trans and Wimmin's Action Camp." *Earth First! Journal* 27, Mabon (October): 9.

Tuttle, William. 2009. "History and Evolution of the Animal Rights Movement." Presentation at the Animal Rights Conference. Los Angeles, July.

United Nations. 2005. *Ecosystems and Human Well-Being*. Report of the Conceptual Framework Working Group of the Millennium Ecosystem Assessment. Washington, D.C.: Island Press and United Nations.

United States, Department of Justice, Federal Bureau of Investigation. 1989. *Terrorism in the United States*. Washington, D.C.

———. 2011a. *Anarchist Extremism Overview*. Washington, D.C.: FBI, Domestic Terrorism Operations Unit.

———. 2011b. *Animal Rights/Environmental Extremism*. Washington, D.C.: FBI, Counterterrorism Division.

United States, Department of Justice, Office of the Inspector General, Oversight and Review Division. 2010. *A Review of the FBI's Investigations of Certain Domestic Advocacy Groups*. Washington, D.C.

Unsettling Minnesota, comp. 2009. *Reflections and Resources for Deconstructing Colonial Mentality: A Sourcebook Compiled by the Unsettling Minnesota Collective*. Minneapolis. September.

Vanderheiden, Steve. 2005. "Eco-terrorism or Justified Resistance? Radical Environmentalism and the "War on Terror."" *Politics & Society* 33, no. 3 (September): 425–47.

Vidal, John. 2006. "Greenpeace Fights Sea Battle with Rival Anti-whaling Ship." *Guardian* (Manchester), January 2.

Warren, Karen J. 1990. "The Power and the Promise of Ecological Feminism." *Environmental Ethics* 12, no. 2 (Summer): 125–46.

———. 1994. Introduction to *Ecological Feminism*, edited by Karen J. Warren. New York: Routledge.

———, ed. 1997a. *Ecofeminism: Women, Culture, Nature*. Bloomington: Indiana University Press.

———. 1997b. "Taking Empirical Data Seriously: An Ecofeminist Philosophical Perspective." In Warren, *Ecofeminism*, 3–20.

Watts, Michael. 1998. "Nature as Artifice and Artifact. In *Remaking Reality: Nature at the Millennium*, edited by Bruce Braun and Noel Castree, 243–68. New York: Routledge.

Waziyatawin. 2008. *What Does Justice Look Like? The Struggle for Liberation in Dakota Homeland*. St. Paul: Living Justice Press.

Weber, Max. 1978. *Economy and Society: An Outline of Interpretive Sociology*. Edited by Guenther Roth and Claus Wittich. 4th ed. Berkeley: University of California Press.

Weber, Max, David S. Owen, Tracy B. Strong, and Rodney Livingstone. 2004. *The Vocation Lectures: Science as a Vocation, Politics as a Vocation*. Cambridge, Mass.: Hackett.

Wenner, Melinda. 2007. "Humans Carry More Bacterial Cells Than Human Ones." *Scientific American*, November 30.

White, Rob. 2003. "Environmental Issues and the Criminological Imagination." *Theoretical Criminology* 7, no. 4 (November): 483–506.

————. 2008. *Crimes against Nature: Environmental Criminology and Ecological Justice.* Cullompton, U.K.: Willan.

Widener, Patricia. 2011. *Oil Injustice: Resisting and Conceding a Pipeline in Ecuador.* Lanham, Md.: Rowman & Littlefield.

Widick, Richard. 2009. *Trouble in the Forest: California's Redwood Timber Wars.* Minneapolis: University of Minnesota Press.

Williams, Kristian, Will Munger, and Lara Messersmith-Glavin, eds. 2013. *Life during War: Resisting Counterinsurgency.* Oakland, Calif.: AK Press.

Wise, Tim. 2008. *Speaking Treason Fluently: Anti-Racist Reflections from an Angry White Male.* Berkeley, Calif.: Soft Skull Press.

Wolfe, Cary. 2010. *What Is Posthumanism?* Minneapolis: University of Minnesota Press.

Wolverine. 2000. "Where to Next? A Post-WTO Analysis." *Earth First! Journal* 20, Brigid (February 1): 3.

Woodcock, George. 1956. *Pierre Joseph Proudhon: A Biography.* London: Routledge & Paul.

World Bank. 2005. *Extractive Industries and Sustainable Development: An Evaluation of World Bank Group Experience.* Washington D.C.: World Bank, IFC, MIGA.

World Wire. 2008a. "Newmont Selected to Partner with Wal-Mart and Conservation International in Responsible Mine-to-Market Jewelry Initiative." Denver, July 16.

————. 2008b. "Environmental Defense Fund Partners with Wal-Mart to Cut Global Shopping Bag Waste." New York, September 25.

Zerzan, John. 1999. *Elements of Refusal.* 2nd ed. Columbia, Mo.: C.A.L. Press.

————, ed. 2005. *Against Civilization: Readings and Reflections.* Los Angeles: Feral House Books.

Index

Abbey, Edward, 49; "Immigration and Liberal Taboos," 62; *The Monkey Wrench Gang,* 46–47, 131–32

abolitionist movement, 34, 40, 43, 45–46, 242. *See also* antiracist movements; black liberation movements; civil rights movement; slavery and slaves

Abu-Jamal, Mumia, 238; *Still Black, Still Strong,* 242

academic freedom. *See* universities, academic freedom in

activism and activists: aboveground, 205, 209, 216; anarchist, 106–9, 231; decline in, 201–2; labeled as terrorists, 156, 187, 192, 209, 260n17, 287n86; lacking protection of citizenship, 12, 167, 168, 170–71, 190, 208; music's influence on, 28, 88, 94, 150, 228; nonhumans' interpellations to, 157–58; pseudonyms used by, 219–22; radical, 204–5, 246, 250, 252; targeting of, xvi, 228; white, middle-class, 89, 190, 225, 227, 250, 252, 253. *See also* prisoners;

racial deviants; *and individual activists*

Addams, Jane, 46

AEDPA. *See* Antiterrorism and Effective Death Penalty Act (AEDPA) of 1996

AEPA. *See* Animal Enterprise Protection Act (AEPA) of 1992

AETA. *See* Animal Enterprise Terrorism Act (AETA) of 2006

Africa, John, 40

African National Congress (ANC), 165, 282–83n117

Agee, James, "A Mother's Tale," 24–25

agriculture, 117, 121. *See also* crop sabs; farms, factory; genetically engineered (GE)/genetically modified (GM) foods

AIM. *See* American Indian Movement (AIM)

ALEC. *See* American Legislative Exchange Council (ALEC)

ALF. *See* Animal Liberation Front (ALF)

Alien Act of 1790, 169

Alien Enemy Act of 1798, 169–70

Primate Freedom Tour, 278n64
primitivism, 16, 121–22, 123
Principles of Environmental Justice
    (EJ movement), 255–56
Pring, George W., 175
prisoners: from animal/earth
    liberation movements, 56, 168,
    181–90, 211, 228, 265n102,
    286n62; arson sentences, 173, 214,
    291n64; eco-defense, 56, 265n102;
    political, 181–90, 207–8, 238,
    266n103; racial variations in
    sentencing and treatment, 13,
    190–91, 195, 197, 199, 227–28;
    severity of sentences, 13, 173, 195,
    214–15, 227, 288n119
prisoner support campaigns, 56,
    211–12, 225–33, 235, 244, 251,
    286n62
privilege: humans', 72–73; male, 42,
    46, 48, 73, 96, 260n10; oppression
    and, 83, 190, 270–71n97; social,
    5, 200–201; social justice politics
    and, 78–83
privilege, white, 12–14, 38, 73, 197,
    201, 250, 257; in environmental
    movements, 37, 46, 57, 89–90, 99,
    190–91, 193–94, 227–28, 252–53.
    See also racial deviants
probationary whites, 12–13, 190–91,
    197, 199, 253
production: capitalist, 84, 111;
    industrial, 31, 42, 108, 113–15,
    117, 121; treadmill of, 112–13
production science, 249
Program on Corporations, Law, and
    Democracy (POCLAD), 120
progressive, use of term, 57–58
property: capitalism's damage of,
    262n18; monopolies over, 111;
    people of color treated as, 192–93;
    private, 95–96, 103, 118, 124,

158, 262n18; state protection of,
    169, 206, 215. See also arson
    actions
property, destruction of, 131–34;
    ELF actions, 146–47; protecting
    nonhuman natures through, 51,
    158, 193; terrorism label attached
    to, 107, 167, 168, 171, 173, 175,
    206. See also arson actions; monkey
    wrenching; sabotage; tree spiking
Proudhon, Pierre-Joseph, 95
Publishers' Paper Company
    (Oregon), ELF action against, 54
Puerto Rican independence move-
    ment, 179, 207–8, 293n97

race: immigration laws' definitions of,
    191; politics of, 18, 193–94, 254,
    257; promoting justice for, 28, 165
racial deviants, 12–14, 190–99, 227,
    253. See also privilege, white
racism, 76, 122, 165; in animal
    liberation movements, 64–66, 71,
    90–91; in EF!, 48, 49, 62–64, 78;
    environmental, 252, 259–60n5;
    legacies of, 251–52; opposition to,
    213, 235; state-sponsored, 97, 208,
    257. See also white supremacy
radical flank effect, 38, 206–7
radical movements and radicals,
    23–59; anarchist, 101, 208; animal
    liberation, 41–46, 140, 254;
    anti-imperialism in, 119–20;
    building community through, 166;
    culture work in, 128; direct action
    tactics, 5, 20–21, 29, 247;
    disagreements in, 293n1; earth and
    animal liberation convergences,
    25–26, 56–59; ecological, 82,
    88–92; emerging, 46–51; environ-
    mental, 12–14, 32, 46; external
    motivators, 30–38; gender and

community building *vs.*, 249–51;
consequences of, 166, 229; of
ecoterrorists, 107, 167, 168–77,
190, 228; guinea pig thesis, 206–7;
ideas and discourses on, 10,
264–65n91; of liberation movements, 12–13, 24, 25, 94–95,
107–8, 190; militancy as response
to, 164–65; Pellow's experience
with, xv–xx; of people of color,
197–99, 235, 243; racial deviants
labeled by, 12–14, 190–99, 227,
253; of radical ecological movements, 261 n1; resistance to, 40,
203–9, 212, 250, 280–81n98;
security culture and, 135, 217,
218; of social movements, 164–66;
solidarity spawned by, 235, 250;
trauma of, 199–203, 221–22. *See
also* cultures, security; grand juries;
prisoners, political; surveillance,
state; U.S. Federal Bureau of
Investigation (FBI)
Steel, Helen, 264–65n91
Stepanian, Andrew, 151, 154, 155,
196–97
Stone, Lucy, 43
Stop Huntingdon Animal Cruelty
(SHAC), 45, 53, 127, 218; AEPA/
AETA used against, 174–75;
anarchist orientation, 151, 152,
154, 280–81n98; HLS campaign,
39, 106–7, 115–16, 129–30,
150–56, 266n103, 281n103
Stop Huntingdon Animal Cruelty
imprisoned activists (SHAC7),
179–80, 181, 183, 191, 196,
201–2, 216, 227
Stram, Veda, 69–70
Straw Devil Timber Sale, 138
Student Organization for Animal
Rights (SOAR), 182, 278n63

Students for a Democratic Society
(SDS), 102, 234, 293n97
Sturgeon, Noel, 275n3
S2i. *See* Beckett, Brown International
(S2i)
suffragette movement, 39
Sugarman, Stu, 100–101, 189, 222,
230
Sullivan, Louis W., 260n17
Sullivan, William, 163
Summers, Lawrence, 259–60n5
surveillance, state, 167, 172, 173,
179–81, 215, 249, 284–85n36.
See also cultures, security; state
repression
sustainability, xv–xvi, 15, 88, 248,
255; for nonhuman natures, 248,
249, 250
Syngenta AG, 279n78, 284n35

Taft Hartley Act of 1947, 241,
293n102
Take Back the Land movement, 80
Tara the Sea Elf, 55
targeting. *See* primary targeting;
secondary targeting; tertiary
targeting
Taylor, Dorceta, 17–28
Taylor, Howard, 235
terrorism and terrorists: activists
labeled as, 187, 192, 209; under
animal enterprise act, 174, 175,
205, 227; connotations of,
287n86; discourses around,
212–15; as incentive for radicalization, 204–5; property destruction
labeled as, 107, 167, 168, 171,
173, 175, 206. *See also* animal
liberation movements, labeled as
terrorists; domestic terrorism and
terrorists; ecoterrorism and
ecoterrorists

DAVID NAGUIB PELLOW is Don Martindale Professor of Sociology at the University of Minnesota. He is the author of *Resisting Global Toxics: Transnational Movements for Environmental Justice* and *Garbage Wars: The Struggle for Environmental Justice in Chicago.* He is the coauthor, with Lisa Sun-Hee Park, of *The Slums of Aspen: Immigrants vs. The Environment in America's Eden* and *The Silicon Valley of Dreams: Environmental Injustice, Immigrant Workers, and the High-Tech Global Economy.* He has served on the board of directors for the Center for Urban Transformation, Greenpeace USA, and International Rivers.